Head First **Python**

> Wouldn't it be dreamy if there were a Python book that didn't make you wish you were anywhere other than stuck in front of your computer writing code? I guess it's just a fantasy...

Paul Barry

O'REILLY®

Beijing • Cambridge • Farnham • Köln • Sebastopol • Tokyo

"*Head First Python* is a great introduction to not just the Python language, but Python as it's used in the real world. The book goes beyond the syntax to teach you how to create applications for Android phones, Google's App Engine, and more."

— **David Griffiths, author and Agile coach**

"Where other books start with theory and progress to examples, *Head First Python* jumps right in with code and explains the theory as you read along. This is a much more effective learning environment, because it engages the reader to *do* from the very beginning. It was also just a joy to read. It was fun without being flippant and informative without being condescending. The breadth of examples and explanation covered the majority of what you'll use in your job every day. I'll recommend this book to anyone starting out on Python."

— **Jeremy Jones, coauthor of *Python for Unix and Linux System Administration***

"*Head First Python* is a terrific book for getting a grounding in a language that is increasing in relevance day by day."

— **Phil Hartley, University of Advancing Technology**

Praise for other *Head First* books

"Kathy and Bert's *Head First Java* transforms the printed page into the closest thing to a GUI you've ever seen. In a wry, hip manner, the authors make learning Java an engaging 'what're they gonna do next?' experience."

— **Warren Keuffel,** *Software Development Magazine*

"Beyond the engaging style that drags you forward from know-nothing into exalted Java warrior status, *Head First Java* covers a huge amount of practical matters that other texts leave as the dreaded 'exercise for the reader....' It's clever, wry, hip and practical—there aren't a lot of textbooks that can make that claim and live up to it while also teaching you about object serialization and network launch protocols."

— **Dr. Dan Russell, Director of User Sciences and Experience Research IBM Almaden Research Center (and teaches Artificial Intelligence at Stanford University)**

"It's fast, irreverent, fun, and engaging. Be careful—you might actually learn something!"

— **Ken Arnold, former Senior Engineer at Sun Microsystems Coauthor (with James Gosling, creator of Java),** *The Java Programming Language*

"I feel like a thousand pounds of books have just been lifted off of my head."

— **Ward Cunningham, inventor of the Wiki and founder of the Hillside Group**

"Just the right tone for the geeked-out, casual-cool guru coder in all of us. The right reference for practical development strategies—gets my brain going without having to slog through a bunch of tired, stale professor-speak."

— **Travis Kalanick, founder of Scour and Red Swoosh Member of the MIT TR100**

"There are books you buy, books you keep, books you keep on your desk, and thanks to O'Reilly and the Head First crew, there is the penultimate category, Head First books. They're the ones that are dog-eared, mangled, and carried everywhere. *Head First SQL* is at the top of my stack. Heck, even the PDF I have for review is tattered and torn."

— **Bill Sawyer, ATG Curriculum Manager, Oracle**

"This book's admirable clarity, humor and substantial doses of clever make it the sort of book that helps even non-programmers think well about problem-solving."

— **Cory Doctorow, co-editor of Boing Boing Author,** *Down and Out in the Magic Kingdom* **and** *Someone Comes to Town, Someone Leaves Town*

"I received the book yesterday and started to read it…and I couldn't stop. This is definitely très 'cool.' It is fun, but they cover a lot of ground and they are right to the point. I'm really impressed."

— **Erich Gamma, IBM Distinguished Engineer, and coauthor of *Design Patterns***

"One of the funniest and smartest books on software design I've ever read."

— **Aaron LaBerge, VP Technology, ESPN.com**

"What used to be a long trial and error learning process has now been reduced neatly into an engaging paperback."

— **Mike Davidson, CEO, Newsvine, Inc.**

"Elegant design is at the core of every chapter here, each concept conveyed with equal doses of pragmatism and wit."

— **Ken Goldstein, Executive Vice President, Disney Online**

"I ♥ *Head First HTML with CSS & XHTML*—it teaches you everything you need to learn in a 'fun-coated' format."

— **Sally Applin, UI Designer and Artist**

"Usually when reading through a book or article on design patterns, I'd have to occasionally stick myself in the eye with something just to make sure I was paying attention. Not with this book. Odd as it may sound, this book makes learning about design patterns fun.

"While other books on design patterns are saying 'Bueller…Bueller…Bueller…' this book is on the float belting out 'Shake it up, baby!'"

— **Eric Wuehler**

"I literally love this book. In fact, I kissed this book in front of my wife."

— **Satish Kumar**

Other related books from O'Reilly

Learning Python

Programming Python

Python in a Nutshell

Python Cookbook

Python for Unix and Linux System Administration

Other books in O'Reilly's *Head First* series

Head First Algebra

Head First Ajax

Head First C#, Second Edition

Head First Design Patterns

Head First EJB

Head First Excel

Head First 2D Geometry

Head First HTML with CSS & XHTML

Head First iPhone Development

Head First Java

Head First JavaScript

Head First Object-Oriented Analysis & Design (OOA&D)

Head First PHP & MySQL

Head First Physics

Head First PMP, Second Edition

Head First Programming

Head First Rails

Head First Servlets & JSP, Second Edition

Head First Software Development

Head First SQL

Head First Statistics

Head First Web Design

Head First WordPress

Head First Python

by Paul Barry

Published by O'Reilly Media, Inc., 1005 Gravenstein Highway North, Sebastopol, CA 95472.

O'Reilly Media books may be purchased for educational, business, or sales promotional use. Online editions are also available for most titles (*http://my.safaribooksonline.com*). For more information, contact our corporate/institutional sales department: (800) 998-9938 or *corporate@oreilly.com*.

Series Creators:	Kathy Sierra, Bert Bates
Editor:	Brian Sawyer
Cover Designer:	Karen Montgomery
Production Editor:	Rachel Monaghan
Proofreader:	Nancy Reinhardt
Indexer:	Angela Howard
Page Viewers:	Deirdre, Joseph, Aaron, and Aideen

Deirdre

Aideen

Joseph

Aaron

Printing History:

November 2010: First Edition.

No athletes were pushed too hard in the making of this book.

 This book uses RepKover™, a durable and flexible lay-flat binding.

ISBN: 978-1-449-38267-4

[M]

I dedicate this book to all those generous people in the Python community who have helped to make this great little language the *first-rate* programming technology it is.

And to those that made learning Python and its technologies just complex enough that people need a book like this to learn it.

Author of Head First Python

Paul →

Paul Barry recently worked out that he has been programming for close to a quarter century, a fact that came as a bit of a shock. In that time, Paul has programmed in lots of different programming languages, lived and worked in two countries on two continents, got married, had three kids (well…his wife Deirdre actually *had them*, but Paul was there), completed a B.Sc. and M.Sc. in Computing, written or cowritten three other books, as well as a bunch of technical articles for *Linux Journal* (where he's a Contributing Editor).

When Paul first saw *Head First HTML with CSS & XHTML,* he loved it so much he knew immediately that the Head First approach would be a great way to teach programming. He was only too delighted then, together with David Griffiths, to create *Head First Programming* in an attempt to prove his hunch correct.

Paul's day job is working as a lecturer at The Institute of Technology, Carlow, in Ireland. As part of the Department of Computing and Networking, Paul gets to spend his day exploring, learning, and teaching programming technologies to his students, including Python.

Paul recently completed a post-graduate certificate in Learning and Teaching and was more than a bit relieved to discover that most of what he does conforms to current third-level best practice.

Table of Contents (Summary)

Table of Contents (the real thing)

Intro

Your brain on Python. Here you are trying to learn something, while here your brain is doing you a favor by making sure the learning doesn't stick. Your brain's thinking, "Better leave room for more important things, like which wild animals to avoid and whether naked snowboarding is a bad idea." So how do you trick your brain into thinking that your life depends on knowing Python?

meet python

Everyone loves lists

1

You're asking one question: "What makes Python different?"

The short answer is: *lots of things*. The longer answers starts by stating that there's lots that's familiar, too. Python is a lot like any other *general-purpose* programming language, with **statements**, **expressions**, **operators**, **functions**, **modules**, **methods**, and **classes**. All the *usual stuff*, really. And then there's the other stuff Python provides that makes the programmer's life—*your* life—that little bit easier. You'll start your tour of Python by learning about **lists**. But, before getting to that, there's another important question that needs answering…

The Holy Grail, 1975, Terry Jones & Terry Gilliam, 91 mins

Graham Chapman

Michael Palin, John Cleese, Terry Gilliam, Eric Idle & Terry Jones

sharing your code

Modules of functions

Reusable code is great, but a shareable module is better.

By sharing your code as a Python module, you open up your code to the entire Python community…and it's always good to share, isn't it? In this chapter, you'll learn how to create, install, and distribute your own shareable modules. You'll then load your module onto Python's software sharing site on the Web, so that *everyone* can benefit from your work. Along the way, you'll pick up a few new tricks relating to Python's functions, too.

nester

```
├── nester.py
└── setup.py
```

files and exceptions

Dealing with errors

3

It's simply not enough to process your list data in your code.

You need to be able to get your data *into* your programs with ease, too. It's no surprise then that Python makes reading data from **files** easy. Which is great, until you consider what can go *wrong* when interacting with data *external* to your programs… and there are lots of things waiting to trip you up! When bad stuff happens, you need a strategy for getting out of trouble, and one such strategy is to deal with any exceptional situations using Python's **exception handling** mechanism showcased in this chapter.

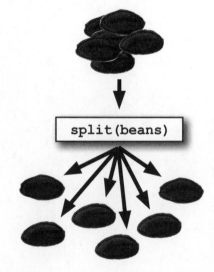

split(beans)

persistence

Saving data to files

4

It is truly great to be able to process your file-based data.

But what happens to your data when you're done? Of course, it's best to save your data to a disk file, which allows you to use it again at some later date and time. Taking your memory-based data and storing it to disk is what **persistence** is all about. Python supports all the usual tools for writing to files and also provides some cool facilities for *efficiently* storing Python data.

```
['Is this the right room for an
argument?', "No you haven't!",
'When?', "No you didn't!", "You
didn't!", 'You did not!', 'Ah!
(taking out his wallet and paying)
Just the five minutes.', 'You most
certainly did not!', "Oh no you
didn't!", "Oh no you didn't!", "Oh
look, this isn't an argument!",
"No it isn't!", "It's just
contradiction!", 'It IS!', 'You
just contradicted me!', 'You DID!',
'You did just then!', '(exasperated)
Oh, this is futile!!', 'Yes it
is!']
```

5

comprehending data

Work that data!

Data comes in all shapes and sizes, formats and encodings.

To work effectively with your data, you often have to manipulate and transform it into a common format to allow for efficient processing, sorting, and storage. In this chapter, you'll explore Python goodies that help you work your data up into a sweat, allowing you to achieve data-munging greatness.

This chapter's guaranteed to give you a workout!

6

custom data objects
Bundling code with data

It's important to match your data structure choice to your data.

And that choice can make a big difference to the complexity of your code. In Python, although really useful, lists and sets aren't the only game in town. The Python **dictionary** lets you organize your data for speedy lookup by *associating your data with names*, not numbers. And when Python's built-in data structures don't quite cut it, the Python **class** statement lets you define your own. This chapter shows you how.

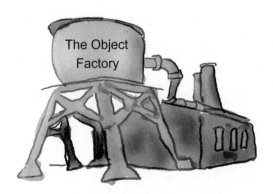
The Object Factory

web development
Putting it all together

Sooner or later, you'll want to share your app with lots of people.

You have many options for doing this. Pop your code on PyPI, send out lots of emails, put your code on a CD or USB, or simply install your app manually on the computers of those people who need it. Sounds like a lot of work…not to mention boring. Also, what happens when you produce the next best version of your code? What happens then? How do you manage the update? Let's face it: it's such a pain that you'll think up really creative excuses not to. Luckily, you don't have to do any of this: just create a webapp instead. And, as this chapter demonstrates, using Python for web development is a breeze.

mobile app development

Small devices

Putting your data on the Web opens up all types of possibilities.

Not only can anyone from anywhere interact with your webapp, but they are increasingly doing so from a collection of diverse computing devices: PCs, laptops, tablets, palmtops, and even mobile phones. And it's not just humans interacting with your webapp that you have to support and worry about: *bots* are small programs that can automate web interactions and typically want your data, not your human-friendly HTML. In this chapter, you exploit Python on Coach Kelly's mobile phone to write an app that interacts with your webapp's data.

8

9

manage your data
Handling input

The Web and your phone are not just great ways to display data.
They are also great tools to for accepting input from your users. Of course, once your
webapp accepts data, it needs to put it somewhere, and the choices you make when
deciding what and where this "somewhere" is are often the difference between a webapp
that's easy to grow and extend and one that isn't. In this chapter, you'll extend your
webapp to accept data from the Web (via a browser or from an Android phone), as well
as look at and enhance your back-end data-management services.

scaling your webapp

Getting real

10

The Web is a great place to host your app…until things get real.

Sooner or later, you'll hit the jackpot and your webapp will be *wildly successful*. When that happens, your webapp goes from a handful of hits a day to thousands, possibly ten of thousands, *or even more*. Will you be ready? Will your web server handle the **load**? How will you know? What will it **cost**? *Who will pay?* Can your data model scale to millions upon millions of data items without *slowing to a crawl*? Getting a webapp up and running is easy with Python and now, thanks to Google App Engine, **scaling** a Python webapp is achievable, too.

dealing with complexity

Data wrangling

It's great when you can apply Python to a specific domain area.

11

Whether it's *web development*, *database management*, or *mobile apps*, Python helps you **get the job done** by *not* getting in the way of you coding your solution. And then there's the other types of problems: the ones you can't categorize or attach to a domain. Problems that are in themselves so *unique* you have to look at them in a different, highly specific way. Creating **bespoke** software solutions to these type of problems is an area where Python *excels*. In this, your final chapter, you'll *stretch* your Python skills to the limit and solve problems along the way.

File   Edit   View   Insert   Format   Form   Tools   Help

Formula: V02

	A	B	C	D	E	F	G	H	I
1	V02	84.8	82.9	81.1	79.3	77.5	75.8	74.2	72.5
2	2mi	8:00	8:10	8:21	8:33	8:44	8:56	9:08	9:20
3	5k	12:49	13:06	13:24	13:42	14:00	14:19	14:38	14:58
4	5mi	21:19	21:48	22:17	22:47	23:18	23:50	24:22	24:55
5	10k	26:54	27:30	28:08	28:45	29:24	30:04	30:45	31:26
6	15k	41:31	42:27	43:24	44:23	45:23	46:24	47:27	48:31
7	10mi	44:46	45:46	46:48	47:51	48:56	50:02	51:09	52:18
8	20k	56:29	57:45	59:03	1:00:23	1:01:45	1:03:08	1:04:33	1:06:00
9	13.1mi	59:49	1:01:09	1:02:32	1:03:56	1:05:23	1:06:51	1:08:21	1:09:53
10	25k	1:11:43	1:13:20	1:14:59	1:16:40	1:18:24	1:20:10	1:21:58	1:23:49
11	30k	1:27:10	1:19:08	1:31:08	1:33:11	1:35:17	1:37:26	1:39:37	1:41:52
12	Marathon	2:05:34	2:08:24	2:11:17	2:14:15	2:17:16	2:20:21	2:23:31	2:26:44

leftovers

The Top Ten Things (we didn't cover)

You've come a long way.

But learning about Python is an activity that never stops. The more Python you code, the more you'll need to learn new ways to do certain things. You'll need to master new tools and new techniques, too. There's just not enough room in this book to show you everything you might possibly need to know about Python. So, here's our list of the top ten things we didn't cover that you might want to learn more about next.

Intro

In this section, we answer the burning question:
"So why DID they put that in a Python book?"

Who is this book for?

If you can answer "yes" to all of these:

1 Do you already know how to program in another programming language?

2 Do you wish you had the know-how to program Python, add it to your list of tools, and make it do new things?

3 Do you prefer actually doing things and applying the stuff you learn over listening to someone in a lecture rattle on for hours on end?

this book is for you.

Who should probably back away from this book?

If you can answer "yes" to any of these:

1 Do you already know most of what you need to know to program with Python?

2 Are you looking for a reference book to Python, one that covers all the details in excruciating detail?

3 Would you rather have your toenails pulled out by 15 screaming monkeys than learn something new? Do you believe a Python book should cover *everything* and if it bores the reader to tears in the process then so much the better?

this book is **not** for you.

[Note from marketing: this book
is for anyone with a credit card...
we'll accept a check, too.]

We know what you're thinking

"How can *this* be a serious Python book?"

"What's with all the graphics?"

"Can I actually *learn* it this way?"

We know what your *brain* is thinking

Your brain craves novelty. It's always searching, scanning, *waiting* for something unusual. It was built that way, and it helps you stay alive.

So what does your brain do with all the routine, ordinary, normal things you encounter? Everything it *can* to stop them from interfering with the brain's *real* job—recording things that *matter*. It doesn't bother saving the boring things; they never make it past the "this is obviously not important" filter.

How does your brain *know* what's important? Suppose you're out for a day hike and a tiger jumps in front of you, what happens inside your head and body?

Neurons fire. Emotions crank up. *Chemicals surge.*

And that's how your brain knows…

This must be important! Don't forget it!

But imagine you're at home, or in a library. It's a safe, warm, tiger-free zone. You're studying. Getting ready for an exam. Or trying to learn some tough technical topic your boss thinks will take a week, ten days at the most.

Just one problem. Your brain's trying to do you a big favor. It's trying to make sure that this *obviously* non-important content doesn't clutter up scarce resources. Resources that are better spent storing the really *big* things. Like tigers. Like the danger of fire. Like how you should never have posted those "party" photos on your Facebook page. And there's no simple way to tell your brain, "Hey brain, thank you very much, but no matter how dull this book is, and how little I'm registering on the emotional Richter scale right now, I really *do* want you to keep this stuff around."

Your brain thinks THIS is important.

Great. Only 450 more dull, dry, boring pages.

Your brain thinks THIS isn't worth saving.

We think of a "Head First" reader as a learner.

So what does it take to *learn* something? First, you have to *get* it, then make sure you don't *forget* it. It's not about pushing facts into your head. Based on the latest research in cognitive science, neurobiology, and educational psychology, *learning* takes a lot more than text on a page. We know what turns your brain on.

Some of the Head First learning principles:

Make it visual. Images are far more memorable than words alone, and make learning much more effective (up to 89% improvement in recall and transfer studies). It also makes things more understandable. **Put the words within or near the graphics** they relate to, rather than on the bottom or on another page, and learners will be up to *twice* as likely to solve problems related to the content.

Use a conversational and personalized style. In recent studies, students performed up to 40% better on post-learning tests if the content spoke directly to the reader, using a first-person, conversational style rather than taking a formal tone. Tell stories instead of lecturing. Use casual language. Don't take yourself too seriously. Which would *you* pay more attention to: a stimulating dinner party companion or a lecture?

Get the learner to think more deeply. In other words, unless you actively flex your neurons, nothing much happens in your head. A reader has to be motivated, engaged, curious, and inspired to solve problems, draw conclusions, and generate new knowledge. And for that, you need challenges, exercises, and thought-provoking questions, and activities that involve both sides of the brain and multiple senses.

Get—and keep—the reader's attention. We've all had the "I really want to learn this but I can't stay awake past page one" experience. Your brain pays attention to things that are out of the ordinary, interesting, strange, eye-catching, unexpected. Learning a new, tough, technical topic doesn't have to be boring. Your brain will learn much more quickly if it's not.

Touch their emotions. We now know that your ability to remember something is largely dependent on its emotional content. You remember what you care about. You remember when you *feel* something. No, we're not talking heart-wrenching stories about a boy and his dog. We're talking emotions like surprise, curiosity, fun, "what the…?" , and the feeling of "I Rule!" that comes when you solve a puzzle, learn something everybody else thinks is hard, or realize you know something that "I'm more technical than thou" Bob from engineering *doesn't*.

Metacognition: thinking about thinking

If you really want to learn, and you want to learn more quickly and more deeply, pay attention to how you pay attention. Think about how you think. Learn how you learn.

I wonder how I can trick my brain into remembering this stuff...

Most of us did not take courses on metacognition or learning theory when we were growing up. We were *expected* to learn, but rarely *taught* to learn.

But we assume that if you're holding this book, you really want to learn how to design user-friendly websites. And you probably don't want to spend a lot of time. If you want to use what you read in this book, you need to *remember* what you read. And for that, you've got to *understand* it. To get the most from this book, or *any* book or learning experience, take responsibility for your brain. Your brain on *this* content.

The trick is to get your brain to see the new material you're learning as Really Important. Crucial to your well-being. As important as a tiger. Otherwise, you're in for a constant battle, with your brain doing its best to keep the new content from sticking.

So just how *DO* you get your brain to treat programming like it was a hungry tiger?

There's the slow, tedious way, or the faster, more effective way. The slow way is about sheer repetition. You obviously know that you *are* able to learn and remember even the dullest of topics if you keep pounding the same thing into your brain. With enough repetition, your brain says, "This doesn't *feel* important to him, but he keeps looking at the same thing *over* and *over* and *over*, so I suppose it must be."

The faster way is to do **anything that increases brain activity,** especially different *types* of brain activity. The things on the previous page are a big part of the solution, and they're all things that have been proven to help your brain work in your favor. For example, studies show that putting words *within* the pictures they describe (as opposed to somewhere else in the page, like a caption or in the body text) causes your brain to try to makes sense of how the words and picture relate, and this causes more neurons to fire. More neurons firing = more chances for your brain to *get* that this is something worth paying attention to, and possibly recording.

A conversational style helps because people tend to pay more attention when they perceive that they're in a conversation, since they're expected to follow along and hold up their end. The amazing thing is, your brain doesn't necessarily *care* that the "conversation" is between you and a book! On the other hand, if the writing style is formal and dry, your brain perceives it the same way you experience being lectured to while sitting in a roomful of passive attendees. No need to stay awake.

But pictures and conversational style are just the beginning...

Here's what WE did:

We used **pictures**, because your brain is tuned for visuals, not text. As far as your brain's concerned, a picture really *is* worth a thousand words. And when text and pictures work together, we embedded the text *in* the pictures because your brain works more effectively when the text is *within* the thing the text refers to, as opposed to in a caption or buried in the text somewhere.

We used **redundancy**, saying the same thing in *different* ways and with different media types, and *multiple senses*, to increase the chance that the content gets coded into more than one area of your brain.

We used concepts and pictures in **unexpected** ways because your brain is tuned for novelty, and we used pictures and ideas with at least *some **emotional** content*, because your brain is tuned to pay attention to the biochemistry of emotions. That which causes you to *feel* something is more likely to be remembered, even if that feeling is nothing more than a little **humor**, **surprise**, or **interest.**

We used a personalized, **conversational style**, because your brain is tuned to pay more attention when it believes you're in a conversation than if it thinks you're passively listening to a presentation. Your brain does this even when you're *reading*.

We included more than 80 **activities**, because your brain is tuned to learn and remember more when you **do** things than when you *read* about things. And we made the exercises challenging-yet-do-able, because that's what most people prefer.

We used **multiple learning styles**, because *you* might prefer step-by-step procedures, while someone else wants to understand the big picture first, and someone else just wants to see an example. But regardless of your own learning preference, *everyone* benefits from seeing the same content represented in multiple ways.

We include content for **both sides of your brain**, because the more of your brain you engage, the more likely you are to learn and remember, and the longer you can stay focused. Since working one side of the brain often means giving the other side a chance to rest, you can be more productive at learning for a longer period of time.

And we included **stories** and exercises that present **more than one point of view,** because your brain is tuned to learn more deeply when it's forced to make evaluations and judgments.

We included **challenges**, with exercises, and by asking **questions** that don't always have a straight answer, because your brain is tuned to learn and remember when it has to *work* at something. Think about it—you can't get your *body* in shape just by *watching* people at the gym. But we did our best to make sure that when you're working hard, it's on the *right* things. That **you're not spending one extra dendrite** processing a hard-to-understand example, or parsing difficult, jargon-laden, or overly terse text.

We used **people**. In stories, examples, pictures, etc., because, well, because *you're* a person. And your brain pays more attention to *people* than it does to *things*.

Here's what YOU can do to bend your brain into submission

So, we did our part. The rest is up to you. These tips are a starting point; listen to your brain and figure out what works for you and what doesn't. Try new things.

Cut this out and stick it on your refrigerator.

---

1 **Slow down. The more you understand, the less you have to memorize.**

Don't just *read*. Stop and think. When the book asks you a question, don't just skip to the answer. Imagine that someone really *is* asking the question. The more deeply you force your brain to think, the better chance you have of learning and remembering.

2 **Do the exercises. Write your own notes.**

We put them in, but if we did them for you, that would be like having someone else do your workouts for you. And don't just *look* at the exercises. **Use a pencil.** There's plenty of evidence that physical activity *while* learning can increase the learning.

3 **Read the "There are No Dumb Questions."**

That means all of them. They're not optional sidebars, *they're part of the core content!* Don't skip them.

4 **Make this the last thing you read before bed. Or at least the last challenging thing.**

Part of the learning (especially the transfer to long-term memory) happens *after* you put the book down. Your brain needs time on its own, to do more processing. If you put in something new during that processing time, some of what you just learned will be lost.

5 **Talk about it. Out loud.**

Speaking activates a different part of the brain. If you're trying to understand something, or increase your chance of remembering it later, say it out loud. Better still, try to explain it out loud to someone else. You'll learn more quickly, and you might uncover ideas you hadn't known were there when you were reading about it.

6 **Drink water. Lots of it.**

Your brain works best in a nice bath of fluid. Dehydration (which can happen before you ever feel thirsty) decreases cognitive function.

7 **Listen to your brain.**

Pay attention to whether your brain is getting overloaded. If you find yourself starting to skim the surface or forget what you just read, it's time for a break. Once you go past a certain point, you won't learn faster by trying to shove more in, and you might even hurt the process.

8 **Feel something.**

Your brain needs to know that this *matters*. Get involved with the stories. Make up your own captions for the photos. Groaning over a bad joke is *still* better than feeling nothing at all.

9 **Write a lot of code!**

There's only one way to learn to program: **writing a lot of code**. And that's what you're going to do throughout this book. Coding is a skill, and the only way to get good at it is to practice. We're going to give you a lot of practice: every chapter has exercises that pose a problem for you to solve. Don't just skip over them—a lot of the learning happens when you solve the exercises. We included a solution to each exercise—don't be afraid to **peek at the solution** if you get stuck! (It's easy to get snagged on something small.) But try to solve the problem before you look at the solution. And definitely get it working before you move on to the next part of the book.

Read Me

This is a learning experience, not a reference book. We deliberately stripped out everything that might get in the way of learning whatever it is we're working on at that point in the book. And the first time through, you need to begin at the beginning, because the book makes assumptions about what you've already seen and learned.

This book is designed to get you up to speed with Python as quickly as possible.

As you need to know stuff, we teach it. So you won't find long lists of technical material, no tables of Python's operators, not its operator precedence rules. We don't cover *everything*, but we've worked really hard to cover the essential material as well as we can, so that you can get Python into your brain *quickly* and have it stay there. The only assumption we make is that you already know how to program in some other programming language.

This book targets Python 3

We use Release 3 of the Python programming language in this book, and we cover how to get and install Python 3 in the first chapter. That said, we don't completely ignore Release 2, as you'll discover in Chapters 8 through 11. But trust us, by then you'll be so happy using Python, you won't notice that the technologies you're programming are running Python 2.

We put Python to work for you right away.

We get you doing useful stuff in Chapter 1 and build from there. There's no hanging around, because we want you to be *productive* with Python right away.

The activities are NOT optional.

The exercises and activities are not add-ons; they're part of the core content of the book. Some of them are to help with memory, some are for understanding, and some will help you apply what you've learned. ***Don't skip the exercises.***

The redundancy is intentional and important.

One distinct difference in a Head First book is that we want you to *really* get it. And we want you to finish the book remembering what you've learned. Most reference books don't have retention and recall as a goal, but this book is about *learning*, so you'll see some of the same concepts come up more than once.

The examples are as lean as possible.

Our readers tell us that it's frustrating to wade through 200 lines of an example looking for the two lines they need to understand. Most examples in this book are shown within the smallest possible context, so that the part you're trying to learn is clear and simple. Don't expect all of the examples to be robust, or even complete—they are written specifically for learning, and aren't always fully functional.

We've placed a lot of the code examples on the Web so you can copy and paste them as needed. You'll find them at two locations:

http://www.headfirstlabs.com/books/hfpython/

http://python.itcarlow.ie

The Brain Power exercises don't have answers.

For some of them, there is no right answer, and for others, part of the learning experience of the Brain Power activities is for you to decide if and when your answers are right. In some of the Brain Power exercises, you will find hints to point you in the right direction.

The technical review team

David Griffiths

Phil Hartley

Jeremy Jones

Technical Reviewers:

David Griffiths is the author of *Head First Rails* and the coauthor of *Head First Programming*. He began programming at age 12, when he saw a documentary on the work of Seymour Papert. At age 15, he wrote an implementation of Papert's computer language LOGO. After studying Pure Mathematics at University, he began writing code for computers and magazine articles for humans. He's worked as an agile coach, a developer, and a garage attendant, but not in that order. He can write code in over 10 languages and prose in just one, and when not writing, coding, or coaching, he spends much of his spare time traveling with his lovely wife—and fellow *Head First* author—Dawn.

Phil Hartley has a degree in Computer Science from Edinburgh, Scotland. Having spent more than 30 years in the IT industry with specific expertise in OOP, he is now teaching full time at the University of Advancing Technology in Tempe, AZ. In his spare time, Phil is a raving NFL fanatic

Jeremy Jones is coauthor of *Python for Unix and Linux System Administration*. He has been actively using Python since 2001. He has been a developer, system administrator, quality assurance engineer, and tech support analyst. They all have their rewards and challenges, but his most challenging and rewarding job has been husband and father.

_____

Acknowledgments

My editor:

Brian Sawyer was *Head First Python*'s editor. When not editing books, Brian likes to run marathons in his spare time. This turns out to be the perfect training for working on another book with me (our second together). O'Reilly and Head First are lucky to have someone of Brian's caliber working to make this and other books the best they can be.

Brian Sawyer

The O'Reilly team:

Karen Shaner provided administrative support and very capably coordinated the techical review process, responding quickly to my many queries and requests for help. There's also the back-room gang to thank—the O'Reilly Production Team—who guided this book through its final stages and turned my InDesign files into the beautiful thing you're holding in your hands right now (or maybe you're on an iPad, Android tablet, or reading on your PC—that's cool, too).

And thanks to the other Head First authors who, via Twitter, offered cheers, suggestions, and encouragement throughout the entire writing process. You might not think 140 characters make a big difference, but they really do.

I am also grateful to **Bert Bates** who, together with **Kathy Sierra**, created this series of books with their wonderful *Head First Java*. At the start of this book, **Bert** took the time to set the tone with a marathon 90-minute phone call, which stretched my thinking on what I wanted to do to the limit and pushed me to write a better book. Now, some nine months after the phone call, I'm pretty sure I've recovered from the mind-bending **Bert** put me through.

Friends and colleagues:

My thanks again to **Nigel Whyte**, Head of Department, Computing and Networking at The Institute of Technology, Carlow, for supporting my involvement in yet another book (especially so soon after the last one).

My students (those enrolled on 3rd Year Games Development and 4th Year Software Engineering) have been exposed to this material in various forms over the last 18 months. Their positive reaction to Python and the approach I take with my classes helped inform the structure and eventual content of this book. (And yes, folks, some of this is on your final).

Family:

My family, **Deirdre**, **Joseph**, **Aaron,** and **Aideen** had to, once more, bear the grunts and groans, huffs and puffs, and more than a few roars on more than one occasion (although, to be honest, not as often they did with *Head First Programming*). After the last book, I promised I wouldn't start another one "for a while." It turned out "a while" was no more than a few weeks, and I'll be forever grateful that they didn't gang up and throw me out of the house for breaking my promise. Without their support, and especially the ongoing love and support of my wife, Deirdre, this book would not have seen the light of day.

The without-whom list:

My technical review team did an excellent job of keeping me straight and making sure what I covered was spot on. They confirmed when my material was working, challenged me when it wasn't and not only pointed out when stuff was wrong, but provided suggestions on how to fix it. This is especially true of **David Griffiths**, my co-conspirator on *Head First Programming*, whose technical review comments went above and beyond the call of duty. **David's** name might not be on the cover of this book, but a lot of his ideas and suggestions grace its pages, and I was thrilled and will forever remain grateful that he approached his role as tech reviewer on *Head First Python* with such gusto.

Safari® Books Online

 Safari Books Online is an on-demand digital library that lets you easily search over 7,500 technology and creative reference books and videos to find the answers you need quickly.

With a subscription, you can read any page and watch any video from our library online. Read books on your cell phone and mobile devices. Access new titles before they are available for print, and get exclusive access to manuscripts in development and post feedback for the authors. Copy and paste code samples, organize your favorites, download chapters, bookmark key sections, create notes, print out pages, and benefit from tons of other time-saving features.

O'Reilly Media has uploaded this book to the Safari Books Online service. To have full digital access to this book and others on similar topics from O'Reilly and other publishers, sign up for free at *http://my.safaribooksonline.com/?portal=oreilly*.

1 meet python

Everyone loves lists

Yes, yes...we have lots of Pythons in stock... I'll just make a quick list.

You're asking one question: "What makes Python different?"

The short answer is: *lots of things*. The longer answers starts by stating that there's lots that's familiar, too. Python is a lot like any other *general-purpose* programming language, with **statements**, **expressions**, **operators**, **functions**, **modules**, **methods**, and **classes**. All the *usual stuff*, really. And then there's the other stuff Python provides that makes the programmer's life—*your* life—that little bit easier. You'll start your tour of Python by learning about **lists**. But, before getting to that, there's another important question that needs answering…

What's to like about Python?

Lots. Rather than tell you, this book's goal is to *show* you the greatness that is Python.

Yeah... I need something that I can deploy on PCs, Macs, handhelds, phones, the Web, on big servers and small clients...and it has to let me build GUIs quickly and painlessly... OK, yes, yeah, I'm listening... What?!? You're kidding! Python can do all that?

Before diving head first into Python, let's get a bit of housekeeping out of the way.

To work with and execute the Python code in this book, you need a copy of the **Python 3 interpreter** on your computer. Like a lot of things to do with Python, it's not difficult to install the interpreter. Assuming, of course, it's not already there...

Install Python 3

Before you *write* and *run* Python code, you need to make sure the Python interpreter is *on* your computer. In this book, you'll start out with Release 3 of Python, the very latest (and best) version of the language.

A release of Python might already be on your computer. Mac OS X comes with Python 2 preinstalled, as do most versions of Linux (which can also ship with Release 3). Windows, in contrast, doesn't include any release of Python. Let's check your computer for Python 3. Open up a command-line prompt and, if you are using Mac OS X or Linux, type:

$$\texttt{python3 -V}$$

That's an UPPERCASE "V", by the way.

On Windows, use this command:

$$\texttt{c:\textbackslash Python31\textbackslash python.exe -V}$$

Do this!

If Python 3 is missing from your computer, download a copy for your favorite OS from the ***www.python.org*** website.

Using the UPPERCASE "V" results in the Python version appearing on screen.

Without the UPPERCASE "V", you are taken into the Python interpreter.

Use the quit() command to exit the interpreter and return to your OS prompt.

```
File Edit Window Help WhichPython?
$ python3 -V
Python 3.1.2
$
$ python3
Python 3.1.2 (r312:79360M, Mar 24 2010, 01:33:18)
[GCC 4.0.1 (Apple Inc. build 5493)] on darwin
Type "help", "copyright", "credits" or "license" for more info.
>>>
>>> quit()
$
```

When you install Python 3, you also get **IDLE**, Python's simple—yet surprisingly *useful*— integrated development environment. IDLE includes a color syntax-highlighting editor, a debugger, the Python Shell, and a complete copy of Python 3's online documentation set.

Let's take a quick look at IDLE.

Use IDLE to help learn Python

IDLE lets you *write* code in its full-featured code editor as well as *experiment* with code at the **Python Shell**. You'll use the code editor later in this book but, when learning Python, IDLE's shell really rocks, because it lets you try out new Python code *as you go*.

When you first start IDLE, you are presented with the "triple chevron" prompt (**>>>**) at which you enter code. The shell takes your code statement and *immediately* executes it for you, displaying any results produced on screen.

IDLE knows all about Python syntax and offers "completion hints" that pop up when you use a **built-in function** like print(). Python programmers generally refer to built-in functions as **BIFs**. The print() BIF displays messages to *standard output* (usually the screen).

Unlike other C-based languages, which use { and } to delimit blocks, Python uses indentation instead.

Enter your code at the >>> prompt.

See results immediately.

```
Python Shell

Python 3.1.2 (r312:79360M, Mar 24 2010, 01:33:18)
[GCC 4.0.1 (Apple Inc. build 5493)] on darwin
Type "copyright", "credits" or "license()" for more information.
>>>
>>> print("You can experiment with code within IDLE's shell. Cool, eh?")
You can experiment with code within IDLE's shell. Cool, eh?
>>> if 43 > 42:
        print("Don't panic!")


Don't panic!
>>> |

                                                    Ln: 12 Col: 4
```

IDLE uses colored syntax to highlight your code. By default, built-in functions are purple, strings are green, and language keywords (like if) are orange. Any results produced are in blue. If you hate these color choices, don't worry; you can easily change them by adjusting IDLE's preferences.

IDLE also knows all about Python's indentation syntax, which requires code blocks be **indented**. When you start with Python, this can be hard to get used to, but IDLE keeps you straight by automatically indenting as needed.

IDLE knows Python's syntax and helps you conform to the Python indentation rules.

Work effectively with IDLE

IDLE has lots of features, but you need to know about only a few of them to get going.

TAB completion

Start to type in some code, and then press the **TAB** key. IDLE will offer suggestions to help you complete your statement.

This is how IDLE looks on my computer. It might look a little different on yours, but not by much. (And, yes, it's meant to look this ugly.)

Type "pr" and then TAB at the >>> prompt to see IDLE's list of command completion suggestions.

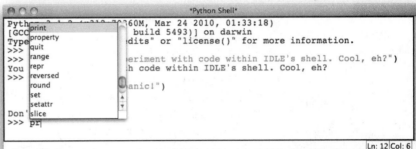

Recall code statements

Press **Alt-P** to recall the *previous* code statement entered into IDLE or press **Alt-N** to move to the *next* code statement (assuming there is one). Both key combinations can be used to cycle rapidly through all of the code you've entered into IDLE, re-executing any code statements as needed.

Alt-P for Previous

Alt-N for Next

Unless you're on a Mac, in which case it's Ctrl-P and Ctrl-N.

Edit recalled code

Once you recall your code statement, you can *edit* it and move around the statement using the arrow keys. It's possible to edit any statement that you've previously entered, even code statements that span multiple lines.

Adjust IDLE's preferences

IDLE's preferences dialog lets you adjust its default behavior to your tastes. There are four tabs of settings to tweak. You can control font and tab behavior, the colors used to syntax highlight, the behavior of certain key-combinations, and IDLE's start-up settings. So, if shocking pink strings is really your thing, IDLE gives you the power to change how your code looks on screen.

Tweak IDLE to your heart's content.

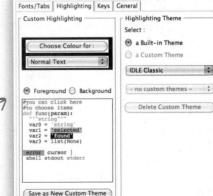

Deal with complex data

Any program of any worth that you create has to work with **data**. Sometimes, the data is simple and straightforward—*easy to work with*. Other times, the data you have to work with is *complex* in its structure and meaning, forcing you to work hard to make sense of it all, let alone write code to process it.

To tame complexity, you can often arrange your data as a **list**: there's the list of customers, your friend's list, the shopping list, and your to-do list (to name a few). Arranging data in lists is so common that Python makes it easy for you to create and process lists in code.

Let's look at some complex data before learning how to create and process list data with Python.

On first glance, this collection of data does indeed look quite complex. However, the data appears to conform to some sort of structure: there's a line for a list of basic movie facts, then another line for the lead actor(s), followed by a third line listing the movie's supporting actors.

This looks like a structure you can work with...

Create simple Python lists

Let's start with the following simple list of movie titles and work up from there:

The Holy Grail

The Life of Brian

The Meaning of Life ← A short list of some Monty Python movies

Here's the same list written in a way that Python understands:

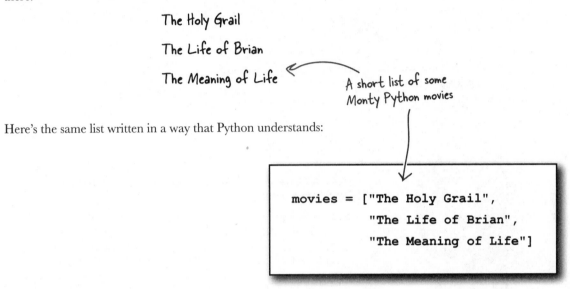

```
movies = ["The Holy Grail",
          "The Life of Brian",
          "The Meaning of Life"]
```

To turn the human-friendly list into a Python-friendly one, follow this four-step process:

1. **Convert** each of the names into strings by surrounding the data with quotes.

2. **Separate** each of the list items from the next with a comma.

3. **Surround** the list of items with opening and closing square brackets.

4. **Assign** the list to an identifier (movies in the preceding code) using the assignment operator (=).

It's perfectly OK to put your list creation code *all on one line*, assuming, of course, that you have room:

```
movies = ["The Holy Grail", "The Life of Brian", "The Meaning of Life"]
```

This works, too.

Hang on a second! Aren't you forgetting something? Don't you need to declare type information for your list?

No, because Python's variable identifiers don't have a type.

Many other programming languages insist that every identifier used in code has type information declared for it. Not so with Python: identifiers are simply names that refer to a data object *of some type*.

Think of Python's list as a **high-level collection**. The type of the data items is not important to the list. It's OK to state that your `movies` list is a "collection of strings," but Python *doesn't* need to be told this. All Python needs to know is that you need a list, you've given it a name, and the list has some data items in it.

Lists are like arrays

When you create a list in Python, the interpreter creates an array-like data structure in memory to hold your data, with your data items stacked from the bottom up. Like array technology in other programming languages, the first slot in the stack is numbered 0, the second is numbered 1, the third is numbered 2, and so on:

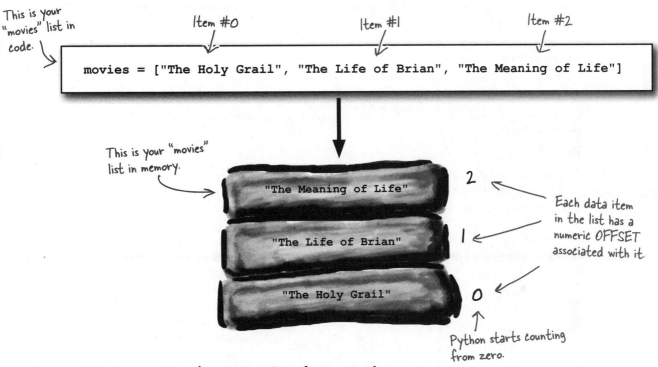

This is your "movies" list in code.

Item #0   Item #1   Item #2

movies = ["The Holy Grail", "The Life of Brian", "The Meaning of Life"]

This is your "movies" list in memory.

"The Meaning of Life"   2

"The Life of Brian"   1

"The Holy Grail"   0

Each data item in the list has a numeric OFFSET associated with it.

Python starts counting from zero.

Access list data using the square bracket notation

As with arrays, you can access the data item in a list slot using the *standard square bracket offset notation*:

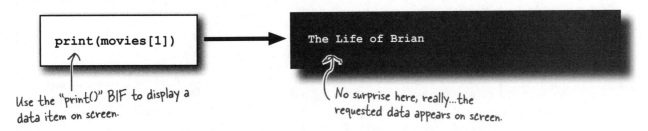

```
print(movies[1])
```

The Life of Brian

Use the "print()" BIF to display a data item on screen.

No surprise here, really...the requested data appears on screen.

Let's use IDLE to learn a bit about how lists work.

An IDLE Session

Lists in Python might look like arrays, but they are much more than that: they are full-blown Python *collection objects*. This means that lists come with ready-to-use functionality in the form of **list methods**.

Let's get to know some of Python's list methods. Open up IDLE and follow along with the code entered at the **>>>** prompt. You should see exactly the same output as shown here.

Start by defining a list of names, which you then display on screen using the `print()` BIF. Then, use the `len()` BIF to work out how many data items are in the list, before accessing and displaying the value of the second data item:

```
>>> cast = ["Cleese", 'Palin', 'Jones', "Idle"]
>>> print(cast)
['Cleese', 'Palin', 'Jones', 'Idle']
>>> print(len(cast))
4
>>> print(cast[1])
Palin
```

It's OK to invoke a BIF on the results of another BIF.

With your list created, you can use list methods to add a single data item to the end of your list (using the `append()` method), remove data from the end of your list (with the `pop()` method), and add a collection of data items to the end of your list (thanks to the `extend()` method):

```
>>> cast.append("Gilliam")
>>> print(cast)
['Cleese', 'Palin', 'Jones', 'Idle', 'Gilliam']
>>> cast.pop()
'Gilliam'
>>> print(cast)
['Cleese', 'Palin', 'Jones', 'Idle']
>>> cast.extend(["Gilliam", "Chapman"])
>>> print(cast)
['Cleese', 'Palin', 'Jones', 'Idle', 'Gilliam', 'Chapman']
```

Methods are invoked using the common "." dot notation.

It's another list: items separated by commas, surrounded by square brackets.

Finally, find and remove a *specific* data item from your list (with the `remove()` method) and then add a data item before a *specific* slot location (using the `insert()` method):

```
>>> cast.remove("Chapman")
>>> print(cast)
['Cleese', 'Palin', 'Jones', 'Idle', 'Gilliam']
>>> cast.insert(0, "Chapman")
>>> print(cast)
['Chapman', 'Cleese', 'Palin', 'Jones', 'Idle', 'Gilliam']
```

After all that, we end up with the cast of Monty Python's Flying Circus!

Add more data to your list

With your list of movie names created, now you need to add more of the movie buff's complex data to it. You have a choice here:

I think I'll use the appropriate list methods to add the extra data I need.

With something this small, I'm gonna simply re-create my list from scratch.

Either strategy works. Which works best for *you* depends on what you are trying to do. Let's recall what the movie buff's data looks like:

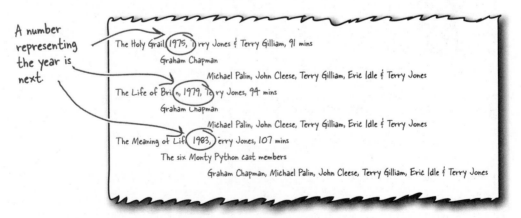

A number representing the year is next.

The Holy Grail, 1975, Terry Jones & Terry Gilliam, 91 mins
    Graham Chapman
            Michael Palin, John Cleese, Terry Gilliam, Eric Idle & Terry Jones
The Life of Brian, 1979, Terry Jones, 94 mins
    Graham Chapman
            Michael Palin, John Cleese, Terry Gilliam, Eric Idle & Terry Jones
The Meaning of Life, 1983, Terry Jones, 107 mins
        The six Monty Python cast members
            Graham Chapman, Michael Palin, John Cleese, Terry Gilliam, Eric Idle & Terry Jones

The next piece of data you need to add to your list is a **number** (which represents the year the movie was released), and it must be inserted *after* each movie name. Let's do that and see what happens.

What?!? There's no way you can mix data of different types in lists, is there? Surely this is madness?

No, not madness, just the way Python works.

Python lists can contain data of **mixed type**. It's perfectly OK to mix strings with numbers within the *same* Python list. In fact, you can mix more than just strings and numbers; you can store data of *any type* in a single list, if you like.

Recall that a Python list is a high-level collection, designed from the get-go to store a collection of "related things." What *type* those things have is of little interest to the list, because the list exists merely to provide the mechanism to store data in list form.

So, if you really need to store data of mixed type in a list, Python won't stop you.

Exercise

Let's take a bit of time to try to work out which strategy to use when adding data to your list *in this case.*

Given the following list-creation code:

```
movies = ["The Holy Grail", "The Life of Brian", "The Meaning of Life"]
```

1 Work out the Python code required to insert the numeric year data into the preceding list, changing the list so that it ends up looking like this:

```
["The Holy Grail", 1975, "The Life of Brian", 1979, "The Meaning of Life", 1983]
```

Write your
insertion ⟶
code here.

....

....

....

....

....

....

....

....

2 Now write the Python code required to re-create the list with the data you need all in one go:

Write your
re-creation ⟶
code here.

....

....

....

....

In this case, which of these two methods do you think is best? (Circle your choice).

1   or   **2**

Exercise Solution

Let's take a bit of time to try and work out which strategy to use when adding data to your list *in this case.*

Given the following list-creation code:

```
movies = ["The Holy Grail", "The Life of Brian", "The Meaning of Life"]
```

1 You were to work out the Python code required to insert the numeric year data into the preceding list:

Insert the first year BEFORE the second list item.

`movies.insert(1, 1975)`

Insert the second year BEFORE the fourth list item. → `movies.insert(3, 1979)` ←

Did you get the math right? After the first insertion, the list grows, so you have to take that into consideration when working out where to do the second insert.

`movies.append(1983)`

Then append the last year to the end of the list.

2 You were also to write the Python code required to recreate the list with the data you need all in one go:

```
movies = ["The Holy Grail", 1975,
          "The Life of Brian", 1979,
          "The Meaning of Life", 1983]
```

Assign all your data to the "movies" identifier. What was previously there is replaced.

In this case, which of these two methods do you think is best? (You were to circle your choice.)

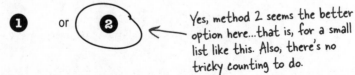

1 or **2**

Yes, method 2 seems the better option here...that is, for a small list like this. Also, there's no tricky counting to do.

Work with your list data

You often need to *iterate* over your list and perform some action on each item as you go along. Of course, it is always possible to do something like this, which works but *does not scale*:

Define a list and populate its items with the names of two movies.

```
fav_movies = ["The Holy Grail", "The Life of Brian"]

print(fav_movies[0])
print(fav_movies[1])
```

This is the list-processing code.

Display the value of each individual list item on the screen.

This code works as expected, making the data from the list appear on screen. However, if the code is later amended to add *another* favorite movie to the list, the list-processing code stops working as expected, *because the list-processing code does not mention the third item.*

Big deal: all you need to do is add another `print()` statement, right?

Yes, adding one extra `print()` statement works for one extra movie, but what if you need to add another hundred favorite movies? The *scale* of the problem defeats you, because adding all those extra `print()` statements becomes such a chore that you would rather find an excuse not to have to do.

It's time to iterate

Processing every list item is such a common requirement that Python makes it especially convenient, with the built-in **for** loop. Consider this code, which is a rewrite of the previous code to use a **for** loop:

Define a list and populate it just as you did before.

Use "for" to iterate over the list, displaying the value of each individual item on screen as you go.

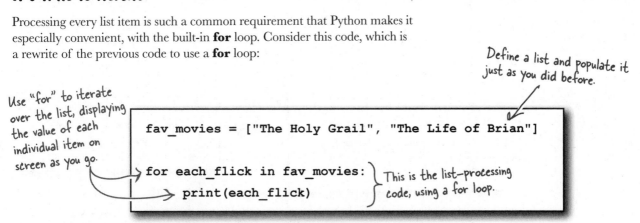

```
fav_movies = ["The Holy Grail", "The Life of Brian"]

for each_flick in fav_movies:
    print(each_flick)
```

This is the list-processing code, using a for loop.

Using a for loop scales and works with any size list.

For loops work with lists of any size

Python's **for** loop exists to process lists and other *iterations* in Python. Lists are the most common iterated data structure in Python, and when you need to iterate a list, it's best to use **for**:

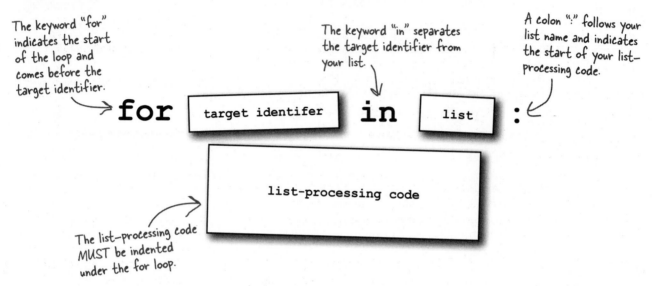

The keyword "for" indicates the start of the loop and comes before the target identifier.

The keyword "in" separates the target identifier from your list.

A colon ":" follows your list name and indicates the start of your list-processing code.

for   target identifer   in   list   :

list-processing code

The list-processing code MUST be indented under the for loop.

The *list-processing code* is referred to by Python programmers as the **suite**.

The **target identifier** is like any other name in your code. As your list is iterated over, the target identifier is assigned *each* of the data values in your list, in turn. This means that each time the loop code executes, the target identifier refers to a *different* data value. The loop keeps iterating until it exhausts all of your list's data, no matter how big or small your list is.

An alternative to using **for** is to code the iteration with a **while** loop. Consider these two snippets of Python code, which perform the *same action*:

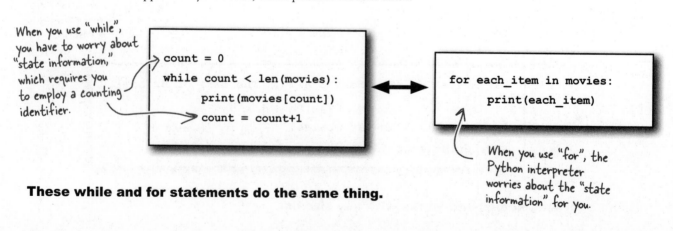

When you use "while", you have to worry about "state information," which requires you to employ a counting identifier.

```
count = 0
while count < len(movies):
    print(movies[count])
    count = count+1
```

```
for each_item in movies:
    print(each_item)
```

When you use "for", the Python interpreter worries about the "state information" for you.

These while and for statements do the same thing.

Q: So...when iterating over a list, I should always use for instead of while?

A: Yes, unless you have a really good reason to use (or need the extra control of) a **while** loop. The **for** loop takes care of working from the start of your list and continuing to the end. It's next to impossible to get stung by an off-by-one error when you use **for**. This is not the case with **while**.

Q: So, lists aren't really like arrays then, because they do so much more?

A: Well...they are in that you can access individual data items in your list with the standard square bracket notation, but—as you've seen—Python's lists can do so much more. At Head First Labs, we like to think of lists as "arrays on steroids."

Q: And they work this way only in Python 3, right?

A: No. There are certain enhancements to lists that were added in Python 3, but release 2 of Python has lists, too. All of what you've learned about lists so far will work with lists in Releases 2 and 3 of Python.

Q: Why are we using Python 3? What's wrong with Python 2, anyway? Lots of programmers seem to be using it.

A: Lots of programmers are using Python 2, but the future of Python development lies with Release 3. Of course, moving the entire Python community to Python 3 won't happen overnight, so there's an awful lot of projects that will continue to run on Release 2 for the foreseeable future. Despite 2's dominance *at the moment*, at Head First Labs we think the new bits in 3 are well worth the added investment in learning about them now. Don't worry: if you know 2, Python 3 is easy.

Q: Seeing as Python's lists shrink and grow as needed, they must not support bounds-checking, right?

A: Well, lists are *dynamic*, in that they shrink and grow, but they are *not magic*, in that they cannot access a data item that does not exist. If you try to access a nonexistent data item, Python responds with an `IndexError`, which means "out of bounds."

Q: What's with all the strange references to Monty Python?

A: Ah, you spotted that, eh? It turns out that the creator of Python, *Guido van Rossum*, was reading the scripts of the Monty Python TV shows while designing his new programming language. When Guido needed a name for his new language, he chose "Python" as a bit of a joke (or so the legend goes).

Q: Do I need to know Monty Python in order to understand the examples?

A: No, but as they say in the official Python documentation: "it helps if you do." But don't worry: you'll survive, even if you've never heard of *Monty Python*.

Q: I notice that some of your strings are surrounded with double quotes and others with single quotes. What's the difference?

A: There isn't any. Python lets you use either to create a string. The only rule is that if you start a string with one of the quotes, then you have to end it with the same quote; you can't mix'n'match. As you may have seen, IDLE uses single quotes when displaying strings within the shell.

Q: What if I need to embed a double quote in a string?

A: You have two choices: either escape the double quote like this: `\"`, or surround your string with single quotes.

Q: Can I use any characters to name my identifiers?

A: No. Like most other programming languages, Python has some rules that must be adhered to when creating names. Names can start with a letter character or an underscore, then include any number of letter characters, numbers, and/or underscores in the rest of the name. Strange characters (such as `%$£`) are not allowed and you'll obviously want to use names that have meaning *within the context of your code*. Names like `members`, `the_time`, and `people` are much better than `m`, `t`, and `p`, aren't they?

Q: Yes, good naming practice is always important. But what about case sensitivity?

A: Yes, Python is the "sensitive type," in that Python code *is* case sensitive. This means that `msg` and `MSG` are two different names, so be careful. Python (and IDLE) will help with the problems that can occur as a result of this. For instance, you can use an identifier in your code only if it has been given a value; unassigned identifiers cause a runtime error. This means that if you type `mgs` when you meant `msg`, you'll find out pretty quickly when Python complains about your code having a *NameError*.

Store lists within lists

As you've seen, lists can hold data of mixed type. But it gets even better than that: lists can hold collections of anything, *including other lists*. Simply **embed** the *inner* list within the *enclosing* list as needed.

Looking closely at the movie buff's data, it is possible to determine a structure which looks much like a list of lists:

> There's only one lead actor listed here, but there could be more.

> There's a list of movie facts...

> ...which itself contains a list of lead actors...

> ...which itself contains a list of supporting actors.

The Holy Grail, 1975, Terry Jones & Terry Gilliam, 91 mins

Graham Chapman

Michael Palin, John Cleese, Terry Gilliam, Eric Idle & Terry Jones

In Python, you can turn this real list of data into code with little or no effort. All you need to remember is that every list is a collection of items separated from each other with commas and surrounded with square brackets. And, of course, any list item can itself be another list:

> The start of the first, outer list

```
movies = [
    "The Holy Grail", 1975, "Terry Jones & Terry Gilliam", 91,
    ["Graham Chapman",
        ["Michael Palin", "John Cleese", "Terry Gilliam", "Eric Idle", "Terry Jones"]]]
```

> The end of all the lists is here.

> The start of the second, inner list: "movies[4]"

> The start of the third, inner inner list: "movies[4][1]"

> This looks a little weird...until you remember that there are three opening square brackets, so there must also be three closing ones.

So, a list within a list is possible, as is a list within a list within a list (as this example code demonstrates). In fact, it's possible to nest lists within lists to most any level with Python. And you can *manipulate* every list with its own list methods and *access it* with the square bracket notation:

```
print(movies[4][1][3])
```

Eric Idle

> A list within a list within a list

> Eric is this deeply nested, so he can't possibly be idle. ☺

An IDLE Session

Creating a list that contains another list is straightforward. But what happens when you try to process a list that contains another list (or lists) using the **for** loop from earlier in this chapter?

Let's use IDLE to work out what happens. Begin by creating the list of the movie data for "The Holy Grail" in memory, display it on screen, and then process the list with your **for** loop:

```
>>> movies = ["The Holy Grail", 1975, "Terry Jones & Terry Gilliam", 91,
                ["Graham Chapman", ["Michael Palin", "John Cleese",
                    "Terry Gilliam", "Eric Idle", "Terry Jones"]]]
>>> print(movies)
['The Holy Grail', 1975, 'Terry Jones & Terry Gilliam', 91, ['Graham Chapman', ['Michael Palin',
'John Cleese', 'Terry Gilliam', 'Eric Idle', 'Terry Jones']]]
>>> for each_item in movies:
        print(each_item)


The Holy Grail
1975
Terry Jones & Terry Gilliam
91
['Graham Chapman', ['Michael Palin', 'John Cleese', 'Terry Gilliam', 'Eric Idle', 'Terry Jones']]
```

The list within a list within a list has been created in memory.

The "for" loop prints each item of the outer loop ONLY.

The inner list within the inner list is printed "as-is."

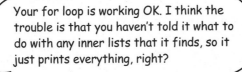

> Your for loop is working OK. I think the trouble is that you haven't told it what to do with any inner lists that it finds, so it just prints everything, right?

Yes, that's correct: the loop code isn't complete.

At the moment, the code within the loop simply prints each list item, and when it finds a list at a slot, it simply displays the entire list on screen. After all, the inner list is just another list item as far as the outer enclosing list is concerned. What's we need here is some mechanism to spot that an item in a list is in fact *another* list and take the appropriate action.

That sounds a little tricky. But can Python help?

Check a list for a list

Each time you process an item in your list, you need to check to see if the item is another list. If the item is a list, you need to process the **nested list** *before* processing the next item in your outer list. Deciding *what to do when* in Python follows the familiar **if**... **else**... pattern:

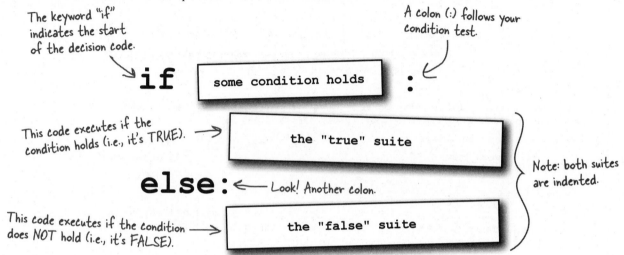

The keyword "if" indicates the start of the decision code.

A colon (:) follows your condition test.

if `some condition holds` :

This code executes if the condition holds (i.e., it's TRUE). → the "true" suite

Note: both suites are indented.

else: ← Look! Another colon.

This code executes if the condition does NOT hold (i.e., it's FALSE). → the "false" suite

No surprises here, as the **if** statement in Python works pretty much as expected. But what *condition* do you need to check? You need a way to determine if the item currently being processed is a list. Luckily, Python ships with a BIF that can help here: `isinstance()`.

What's cool about the `isinstance()` BIF is that it lets you check if a *specific* identifier holds data of a *specific* type:

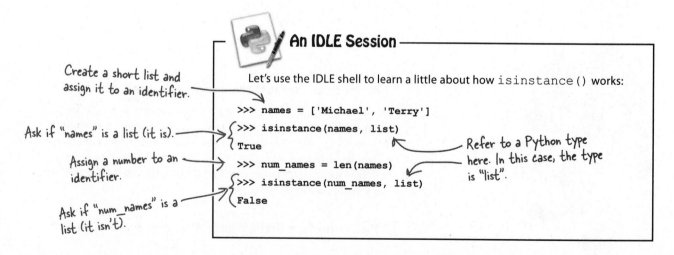

An IDLE Session

Let's use the IDLE shell to learn a little about how `isinstance()` works:

Create a short list and assign it to an identifier.

```
>>> names = ['Michael', 'Terry']
>>> isinstance(names, list)
True
>>> num_names = len(names)
>>> isinstance(num_names, list)
False
```

Ask if "names" is a list (it is).

Assign a number to an identifier.

Ask if "num_names" is a list (it isn't).

Refer to a Python type here. In this case, the type is "list".

Exercise

Here's a copy of the current list-processing code. Your task is to rewrite this code using an **if** statement and the `isinstance()` BIF to process a list that displays another list.

```
for each_item in movies:
        print(each_item)
```

Write your
new code →
here.

....

....

....

....

....

....

....

....

....

....

there are no
Dumb Questions

Q: Are there many of these BIFs in Python?

A: Yes. At the last count, there were over 70 BIFs in Python 3.

Q: Over 70! How am I to remember that many, let alone find out what they all are?

A: You don't have to worry about remembering. Let Python do it for you.

Q: How?

A: At the Python or IDLE shell, type `dir(__builtins__)` to see a list of the built-in stuff that comes with Python (that's two leading and trailing underscore characters, by the way). The shell spits out a big list. Try it. All those lowercase words are BIFs. To find out what any BIF does—like `input()`, for example—type `help(input)` at the shell for a description of the BIFs function.

Q: Why so many BIFs?

A: Why not? Because Python comes with lots of built-in functionality, it can mean less code for you to write. This Python philosophy is known as "batteries included": there's enough included with Python to let you do most things well, without having to rely on code from third parties to get going. As well as lots of BIFs, you'll find that Python's standard library is rich and packed with features waiting to be exploited by you.

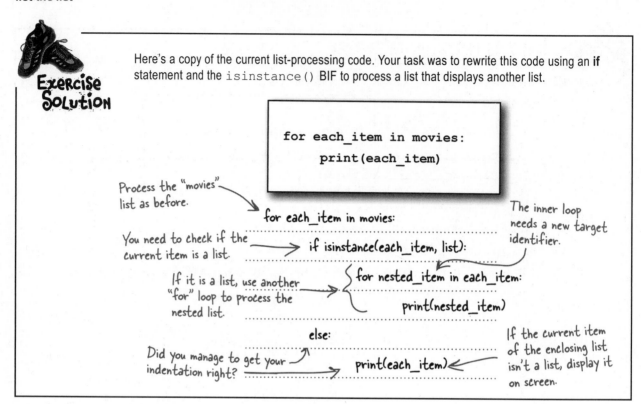

Here's a copy of the current list-processing code. Your task was to rewrite this code using an **if** statement and the `isinstance()` BIF to process a list that displays another list.

```
for each_item in movies:
    print(each_item)
```

Process the "movies" list as before.

for each_item in movies:

You need to check if the current item is a list.

if isinstance(each_item, list):

The inner loop needs a new target identifier.

If it is a list, use another "for" loop to process the nested list.

for nested_item in each_item:

print(nested_item)

else:

Did you manage to get your indentation right?

print(each_item)

If the current item of the enclosing list isn't a list, display it on screen.

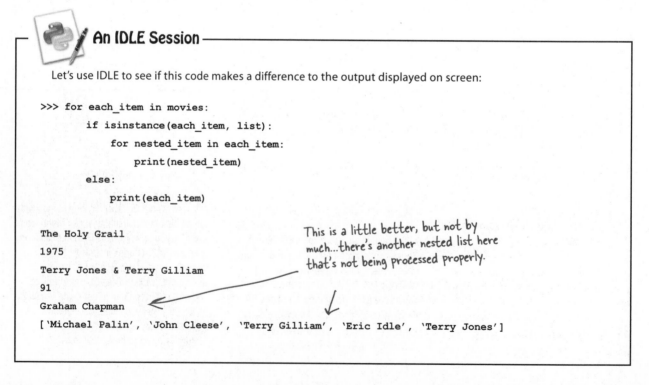

An IDLE Session

Let's use IDLE to see if this code makes a difference to the output displayed on screen:

```
>>> for each_item in movies:
        if isinstance(each_item, list):
            for nested_item in each_item:
                print(nested_item)
        else:
            print(each_item)


The Holy Grail
1975
Terry Jones & Terry Gilliam
91
Graham Chapman
['Michael Palin', 'John Cleese', 'Terry Gilliam', 'Eric Idle', 'Terry Jones']
```

This is a little better, but not by much...there's another nested list here that's not being processed properly.

Complex data is hard to process

The movie buff's data is *complex*. Let's take another look at a subset of the
data and your Python code that processes it.

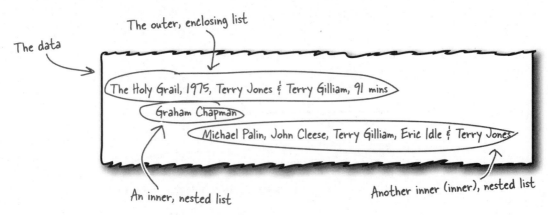

The data

The outer, enclosing list

```
The Holy Grail, 1975, Terry Jones & Terry Gilliam, 91 mins
    Graham Chapman
        Michael Palin, John Cleese, Terry Gilliam, Eric Idle & Terry Jones
```

An inner, nested list

Another inner (inner), nested list

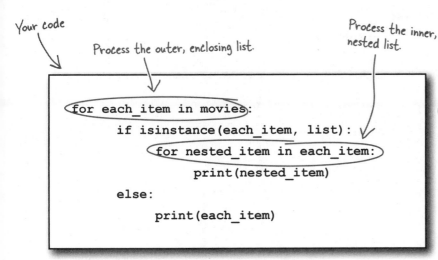

Your code

Process the outer, enclosing list.

Process the inner, nested list.

```python
for each_item in movies:
    if isinstance(each_item, list):
        for nested_item in each_item:
            print(nested_item)
    else:
        print(each_item)
```

Yeah.. that's almost
working...it's just a
pity about that list of
supporting actors...

⚛ BRAIN POWER

Can you spot the problem with your Python
code as it is currently written? What do you
think needs to happen to your code to allow it to
process the movie buff's data correctly?

Handle many levels of nested lists

The data and your code are not in sync.

The movie buff's data is a list that contains a nested list that itself contains a nested list. The trouble is that your code knows only how to process a list nested inside an enclosing list.

The solution, of course, is to *add more code to handle the additionally nested list.* By looking at the existing code, it's easy to spot the code you need to repeat:

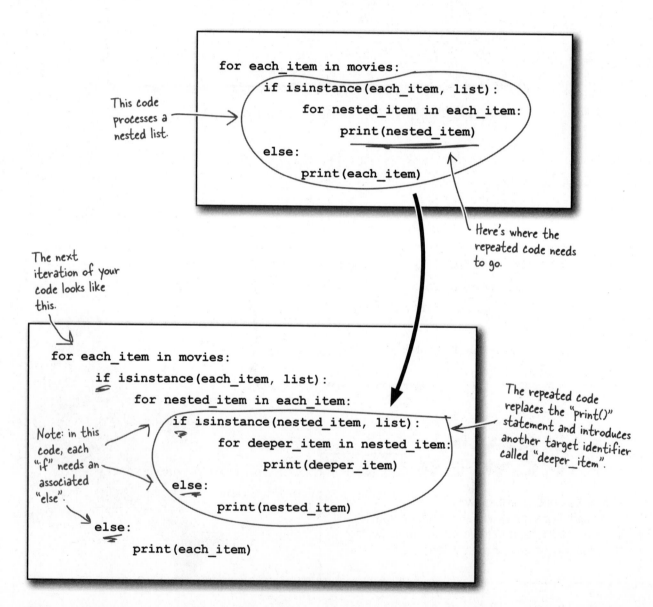

This code processes a nested list.

Here's where the repeated code needs to go.

The next iteration of your code looks like this.

```
for each_item in movies:
    if isinstance(each_item, list):
        for nested_item in each_item:
            if isinstance(nested_item, list):
                for deeper_item in nested_item:
                    print(deeper_item)
            else:
                print(nested_item)
    else:
        print(each_item)
```

Note: in this code, each "if" needs an associated "else".

The repeated code replaces the "print()" statement and introduces another target identifier called "deeper_item".

 **An IDLE Session**

Let's use IDLE once more to test this latest iteration of your code:

```
>>> for each_item in movies:
        if isinstance(each_item, list):
            for nested_item in each_item:
                if isinstance(nested_item, list):
                    for deeper_item in nested_item:
                        print(deeper_item)
                else:
                    print(nested_item)
        else:
            print(each_item)


The Holy Grail
1975
Terry Jones & Terry Gilliam
91
Graham Chapman
Michael Palin
John Cleese
Terry Gilliam
Eric Idle
Terry Jones
```

Process a deeply nested list inside a nested list inside an enclosing list.

It works! This time, you see all of your list data on screen.

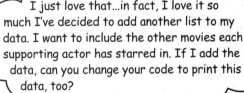

I just love that...in fact, I love it so much I've decided to add another list to my data. I want to include the other movies each supporting actor has starred in. If I add the data, can you change your code to print this data, too?

That's more list data and more Python code.

The data has to be embedded as *another* nested list within the already deeply nested list of supporting actors. That's possible to do, even though it makes your head hurt just to think about a list of lists of lists of lists! Amending your code is just a matter of adding another **for** loop and an **if** statement.

That doesn't sound like too much trouble, does it?

I think I'd rather have a root canal than change that code again.

Adding another nested loop is a huge pain.

Your data is getting more complex (that mind-bending list of lists of lists of lists) and, as a consequence, your code is getting overly complex, too (that brain-exploding **for** loop inside a **for** loop inside a **for** loop). And overly complex code is rarely a good thing…

Wouldn't it be dreamy if there were an efficient way to process lists, preferably using a technique that resulted in less code, not more? But I know it's just a fantasy...

Don't repeat code; create a function

Take a look at the code that you've created so far, which (in an effort to save *you* from having *your* brain explode) has already been amended to process *yet another* nested list. Notice anything?

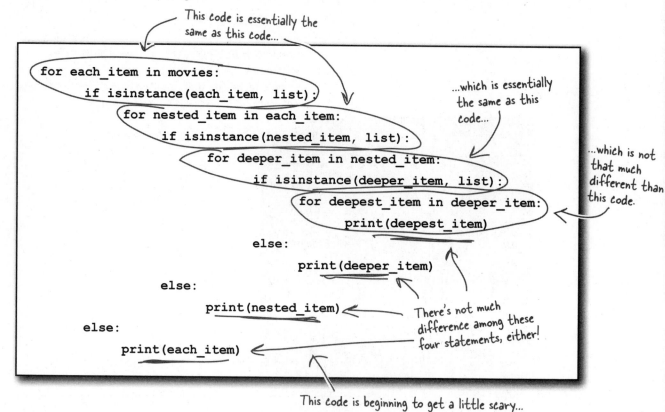

This code is essentially the same as this code...

```
for each_item in movies:
    if isinstance(each_item, list):
        for nested_item in each_item:
            if isinstance(nested_item, list):
                for deeper_item in nested_item:
                    if isinstance(deeper_item, list):
                        for deepest_item in deeper_item:
                            print(deepest_item)
                    else:
                        print(deeper_item)
            else:
                print(nested_item)
    else:
        print(each_item)
```

...which is essentially the same as this code...

...which is not that much different than this code.

There's not much difference among these four statements, either!

This code is beginning to get a little scary...

Your code now contains a lot of *repeated code*. It's also a mess to look at, even though it works with the movie buff's amended data. All that nesting of **for** loops is hard to read, and it's even harder to ensure that the **else** suites are associated with the correct **if** statement.

There has to be a better way...but what to do?

When code repeats in this way, most programmers look for a way to take the general pattern of the code and turn it into a **reusable function**. And Python programmers think this way, too. Creating a reusable function lets you invoke the function as needed, as opposed to cutting and pasting existing code.

So, let's turn the repeating code into a function.

Create a function in Python

A function in Python is a *named suite of code*, which can also take an **optional** list of arguments if required.

You define a Python function using the **def** statement, providing a name for your function and specifying either an empty or populated argument list within parentheses. The standard form looks something like this:

The keyword "def" introduces the name of the function.

Argument lists are optional, but the parentheses are NOT.

A colon (:) follows the closing parenthesis and indicates the start of your functions code suite.

```
def    function name    (    argument(s)    ) :
```

```
function code suite
```

The function's code MUST be indented under the def statement.

What does your function need to do?

Your function needs to take a list and process each item in the list. If it finds a nested list within the first list, the function needs to **repeat**. It can do this by *invoking itself* on the nested list. In other words, the function needs to **recur**—that is, *invoke itself* from within the funtion code suite.

Sharpen your pencil

Let's call the function that you'll create `print_lol()`. It takes one argument: a list to display on screen. Grab your pencil and complete the code below to provide the required functionality:

```
def print_lol(the_list):

    for ..................................................................

        if .................................................................

            ..............................................................

        else:

            ..............................................................
```

Sharpen your pencil
Solution

You were to call the function that you'll create `print_lol()`. It takes one argument: a list to display on screen. You were to grab your pencil and complete the code to provide the required functionality:

```
def print_lol(the_list):
```

Process the provided list with a "for" loop. → `for` **each_item in the_list:**

If the item being processed is itself a list, invoke the function.

     `if` **isinstance(each_item, list):** ←

        print_lol(each_item) ←

     `else:`

        print(each_item) ← *If the item being processed ISN'T a list, display the item on screen.*

An IDLE Session

Let's use IDLE one final time to test your new function. Will it work as well as your earlier code?

```
>>> def print_lol(the_list):
        for each_item in the_list:
            if isinstance(each_item, list):
                print_lol(each_item)
            else:
                print(each_item)
```
← *Define the function.*

```
>>> print_lol(movies)
```
← *Invoke the function.*

```
The Holy Grail
1975
Terry Jones & Terry Gilliam
91
Graham Chapman
Michael Palin
John Cleese
Terry Gilliam
Eric Idle
Terry Jones
```
← *It works, too! The recusrive function produces EXACTLY the same results as the earlier code.*

Recursion to the rescue!

The use of a *recursive function* has allowed you to **reduce** 14 lines of messy, hard-to-understand, brain-hurting code into a *six-line function*. Unlike the earlier code that needs to be amended to support additional nested lists (should the movie buff require them), the recursive function *does not need to change* to process any depth of nested lists properly.

Python 3 defaults its *recursion limit* to 1,000, which is a lot of lists of lists of lists of lists...and this limit can be changed should you ever need even more depth than that.

Ah, yes, that's terrific! I can now relax, knowing that your code can process my movie data. I really should've done this years ago...

What a great start!

By taking advantage of functions and recursion, you've solved the code complexity problems that had crept into your earlier list-processing code.

By creating `print_lol()`, you've produced a reusable chunk of code that can be put to use in many places in your (and others) programs.

You're well on your way to putting Python to work!

Your Python Toolbox

You've got Chapter 1 under your belt and you've added some key Python goodies to your toolbox.

BULLET POINTS

- Run Python 3 from the command line or from within IDLE.

- Identifiers are names that refer to data objects. The identifiers have no "type," but the data objects that they refer to *do*.

- `print()` BIF displays a message on screen.

- A **list** is a collection of data, separated by commas and surrounded by square brackets.

- Lists are like arrays on steroids.

- Lists can be used with BIFs, but also support a bunch of list methods.

- Lists can hold any data, and the data can be of mixed type. Lists can also hold other lists.

- Lists shrink and grow as needed. All of the memory used by your data is managed by Python for you.

- Python uses indentation to group statements together.

- `len()` BIF provides a length of some data object or count the number of items in a collection, such as a list.

- The **for** loop lets you iterate a list and is often more convenient to use that an equivalent **while** loop.

- The **if**... **else**... statement lets you make decisions in your code.

- `isinstance()` BIF checks whether an identifier refers to a data object of some specified type.

- Use **def** to define a custom function.

Python Lingo

- "BIF" – a built-in function.

- "Suite" – a block of Python code, which is indented to indicate grouping.

- "Batteries included" – a way of referring to the fact that Python comes with most everything you'll need to get going quickly and productively.

IDLE Notes

- The IDLE shell lets you experiment with your code as you write it.

- Adjust IDLE's preferences to suit the way you work.

- Remember: when working with the shell, use Alt-P for Previous and use Alt-N for Next (but use Ctrl if you're on a Mac).

2 sharing your code

Modules of functions

I'd love to share...but how am I supposed to function without a module?

Reusable code is great, but a shareable module is better.

By sharing your code as a Python module, you open up your code to the entire Python community…and it's always good to share, isn't it? In this chapter, you'll learn how to create, install, and distribute your own shareable modules. You'll then load your module onto Python's software sharing site on the Web, so that *everyone* can benefit from your work. Along the way, you'll pick up a few new tricks relating to Python's functions, too.

It's too good not to share

You've been showing your function to other programmers, and they like what they see.

You should make your function shareable, so that everyone can use it.

Yes, a function this good should be shared with the world.

Python provides a set of technologies that make this easy for you, which includes *modules* and *the distribution utilities*:

- **Modules let you organize your code for optimal sharing.**

- **The distribution utilities let you share your modules with the world.**

Let's turn your function into a module, then use the distribution utilities to share your module with the wider Python programming community.

Turn your function into a module

A **module** is simply a text file that contains Python code. The main requirement is that the name of the file needs to end in .py: the Python extension. To turn your function into a module, save your code into an appropriately named file:

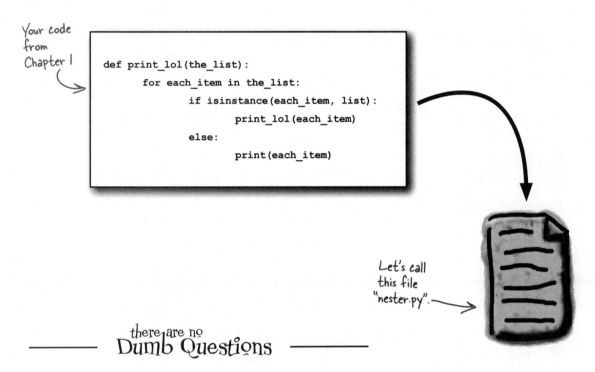

Your code from Chapter 1

```
def print_lol(the_list):
    for each_item in the_list:
        if isinstance(each_item, list):
            print_lol(each_item)
        else:
            print(each_item)
```

Let's call this file "nester.py".

there are no
Dumb Questions

Q: What's the best Python editor?

A: The answer to that question really depends on who you ask. However, you can, of course, use *any* text editor to create and save your function's code in a text file. Something as simple as NotePad on Windows works fine for this, as does a full-featured editor such as TextMate on Mac OS X. And there's also full-fledged IDEs such as Eclipse on Linux, as well as the classic vi and emacs editors. And, as you already know, Python comes with IDLE, which also includes a built-in code editor. It might not be as capable as those other "real" editors, but IDLE is installed with Python and is essentially guaranteed to be available. For lots of jobs, IDLE's edit window is all the editor you'll ever need when working with your Python code. Of course, there are other IDEs for Python, too. Check out WingIDE for one that specifically targets Python developers.

Do this!

Go ahead and create a text file called nester.py that contains your function code from the end of Chapter 1.

Modules are everywhere

As might be expected, you'll find Python modules in lots of places.

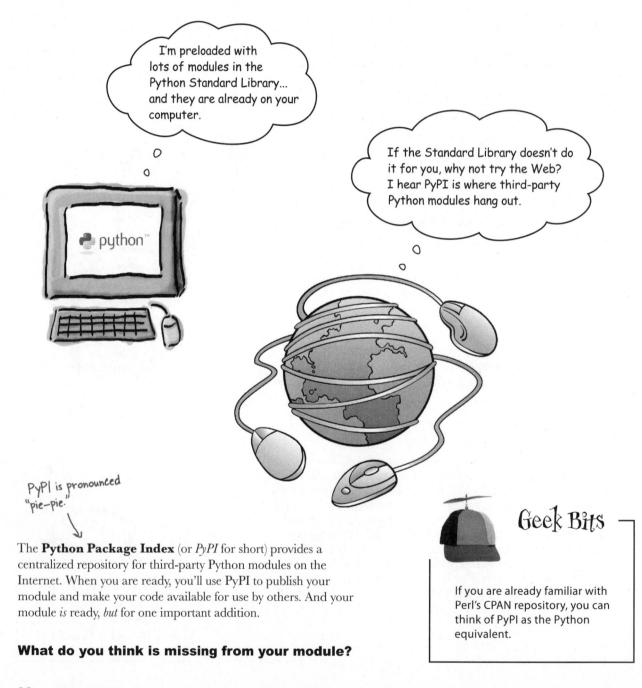

I'm preloaded with lots of modules in the Python Standard Library... and they are already on your computer.

If the Standard Library doesn't do it for you, why not try the Web? I hear PyPI is where third-party Python modules hang out.

PyPI is pronounced "pie-pie."

The **Python Package Index** (or *PyPI* for short) provides a centralized repository for third-party Python modules on the Internet. When you are ready, you'll use PyPI to publish your module and make your code available for use by others. And your module *is* ready, *but* for one important addition.

What do you think is missing from your module?

Geek Bits

If you are already familiar with Perl's CPAN repository, you can think of PyPI as the Python equivalent.

Comment your code

It's always a good idea to include comments with your code. As your plan to share your module with the world, well-written comments help to document your work.

In Python, a common commenting technique is to use a **triple quote** for multiple-line comments. When you use a triple quote without assigning it to a variable, everything *between* the triple quotes is considered a comment:

> Hello! I'm a big string who just happens to be a Python comment, too. Nice, eh?

Start with a triple quote...

```
"""This is the standard way to
   include a multiple-line comment in
   your code."""
```

...and end with a triple quote.

Sharpen your pencil

Here is your module code (which is saved in the file `nester.py`). In the spaces provided, use your pencil to compose two comments: the first to describe the module and the second to describe the function.

Put your module comment here.

....
....
....

```
def print_lol(the_list):
```

Add a comment for your function here.

....
....
....

```
    for each_item in the_list:
        if isinstance(each_item, list)
            print_lol(each_item)
        else:
            print(each_item)
```

Sharpen your pencil
Solution

Here is your module code (which is saved in the file `nester.py`). In the spaces provided, you were asked to use your pencil to compose two comments: the first to describe the module and the second to describe the function.

"""This is the "nester.py" module, and it provides one function called print_lol() which prints lists that may or may not include nested lists."""

Did you remember to include the triple quotes?

```python
def print_lol(the_list):
```

"""This function takes a positional argument called "the_list", which is any Python list (of, possibly, nested lists). Each data item in the provided list is (recursively) printed to the screen on its own line."""

```python
    for each_item in the_list:
        if isinstance(each_item, list):
            print_lol(each_item)
        else:
            print(each_item)
```

There are no changes to the actual code here; you're just adding some comments.

---

there are no
Dumb Questions

Q: How do I know where the Python modules are on my computer?

A: Ask IDLE. Type `import sys; sys.path` (all on one line) into the IDLE prompt to see the list of locations that your Python interpreter searches for modules.

Q: Hang on a second. I can use ";" to put more than one line of code on the same line in my Python programs?

A: Yes, you can. However, I don't recommend that you do so. Better to give each Python statement its own line; it makes your code much easier for you (and others) to read.

Q: Does it matter where I put my `nester.py` module?

A: For now, no. Just be sure to put it somewhere where you can find it later. In a while, you'll install your module into your local copy of Python, so that the interpreter can find it without you having to remember when you actually put it.

Q: So comments are like a funny-looking string surrounded by quotes?

A: Yes. When a triple-quoted string is not assigned to a variable, it's treated like a comment. The comments in your code are surrounded by three double quotes, but you could have used single quotes, too.

Q: Is there any other way to add a comment to Python code?

A: Yes. If you put a "#" symbol anywhere on a line, everything from that point to the end of the current line is a comment (unless the "#" appears within a triple quote, in which case it's part of *that* comment). A lot of Python programmers use the "#" symbol to quickly switch on and off a single line of code when testing new functionality.

An IDLE Session

Now that you've added your comments and created a module, let's test that your code is still working properly. Rather than typing your function's code into IDLE's prompt, bring the `nester.py` file into IDLE's edit window, and then press F5 to run the module's code:

Note that the comments are color coded.

```
nester.py – /Users/barryp/HeadFirstPython/chapter2/nester.py
"""This is the "nester.py" module and it provides one function called print_lol()
    which prints lists that may or may not include nested lists."""

def print_lol(the_list):
    """This function takes one positional argument called "the_list", which
        is any Python list (of - possibly - nested lists). Each data item in the
        provided list is (recursively) printed to the screen on it's own line."""

    for each_item in the_list:
        if isinstance(each_item, list):
            print_lol(each_item)
        else:
            print(each_item)
```
Ln: 15 Col: 0

Nothing appears to happen, other than the Python shell "restarting" and an empty prompt appearing:

```
>>> =============================== RESTART ================================
>>>
>>>
```

What's happened is that the Python interpreter has reset and the code in your module has executed. The code defines the function but, other than that, does little else. The interpreter is patiently waiting for you to do something with your newly defined function, so let's create a list of lists and invoke the function on it:

```
>>> movies = [
    "The Holy Grail", 1975, "Terry Jones & Terry Gilliam", 91,
        ["Graham Chapman",
            ["Michael Palin", "John Cleese", "Terry Gilliam", "Eric Idle", "Terry Jones"]]]
```
Define the list of movies facts from Chapter 1.

```
>>> print_lol(movies)
```
Invoke the function on the list.
```
The Holy Grail
1975
Terry Jones & Terry Gilliam
91
Graham Chapman
Michael Palin
John Cleese
Terry Gilliam
Eric Idle
Terry Jones
```
Cool. Your code continues to function as expected. The data in the list of lists is displayed on screen.

Prepare your distribution

In order to share your newly created module, you need to prepare a **distribution**. This is the Python name given to the collection of files that together allow you to build, package, and distribute your module.

Once a distribution exists, you can install your module into your local copy of Python, as well as upload your module to PyPI to share with the world. Follow along with the process described on these two pages to create a distribution for your module.

Do this!

Follow along with each of the steps described on these pages. By the time you reach the end, your module will have transformed into a Python distribution.

1 **Begin by creating a folder for your module.**
With the folder created, copy your `nester.py` module file into the folder. To keep things simple, let's call the folder `nester`:

The "nester.py" module file.

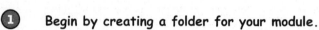

The newly created "nester" folder (or directory).

nester

2 **Create a file called "setup.py" in your new folder.**
This file contains metadata about your distribution. Edit this file by adding the following code:

Import the "setup" function from Python's distribution utilities.

These are the setup function's argument names.

Associate your module's metadata with the setup function's arguments.

These are the values Head First Labs use with their modules; your metadata will be different.

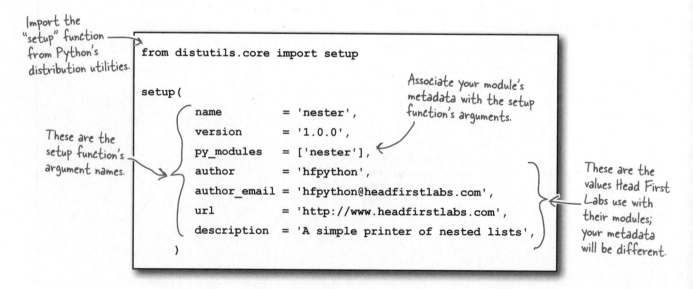

```python
from distutils.core import setup

setup(
        name         = 'nester',
        version      = '1.0.0',
        py_modules   = ['nester'],
        author       = 'hfpython',
        author_email = 'hfpython@headfirstlabs.com',
        url          = 'http://www.headfirstlabs.com',
        description  = 'A simple printer of nested lists',
    )
```

Build your distribution

You now have a folder with two files in it: your module's code in `nester.py` and metadata about your module in `setup.py`. Now, it's time to build your distribution.

Note: if you are using Windows, replace "python3" in these commands with "c:\Python31\python.exe".

3 **Build a distribution file.**

The distribution utilities include all of the smarts required to build a distribution. Open a terminal window within your `nester` folder and type a single command: `python3 setup.py sdist`.

Enter the command at the prompt.

```
File Edit Window Help Build
$ python3 setup.py sdist
running sdist
running check
warning: sdist: manifest template 'MANIFEST.in' does not exist

warning: sdist: standard file not found: should have README

writing manifest file 'MANIFEST'
creating nester-1.0.0
making hard links in nester-1.0.0...
hard linking nester.py -> nester-1.0.0
hard linking setup.py -> nester-1.0.0
creating dist
Creating tar archive
removing 'nester-1.0.0' (and everything under it)
$
```

A collection of status messages appears on screen, confirming the creation of your distribution.

4 **Install your distribution into your local copy of Python.**

Staying in the terminal, type this command: `sudo python3 setup.py install`.

```
File Edit Window Help Install
$ python3 setup.py install
running install
running build
running build_py
creating build
creating build/lib
copying nester.py -> build/lib
running install_lib
copying build/lib/nester.py -> /Library/Frameworks/Python.
framework/Versions/3.1/lib/python3.1/site-packages
byte-compiling /Library/Frameworks/Python.framework/Versions/3.1/
lib/python3.1/site-packages/nester.py to nester.pyc
running install_egg_info
Writing /Library/Frameworks/Python.framework/Versions/3.1/lib/
python3.1/site-packages/nester-1.0.0-py3.1.egg-info
```

Another bunch of status messages appear on screen, confirming the installation of your distribution.

Your distribution is ready.

A quick review of your distribution

Thanks to Python's distribution utilities, your module has been *transformed* into a distribution and *installed* into your local copy of Python.

You started with a single function, which you entered into a file called `nester.py`, creating a module. You then created a folder called `nester` to house your module. The addition of a file called `setup.py` to your folder allowed you to build and install your distribution, which has resulted in a number of additional files and two new folders appearing within your `nester` folder. These files and folders are all created for you by the distribution utilities.

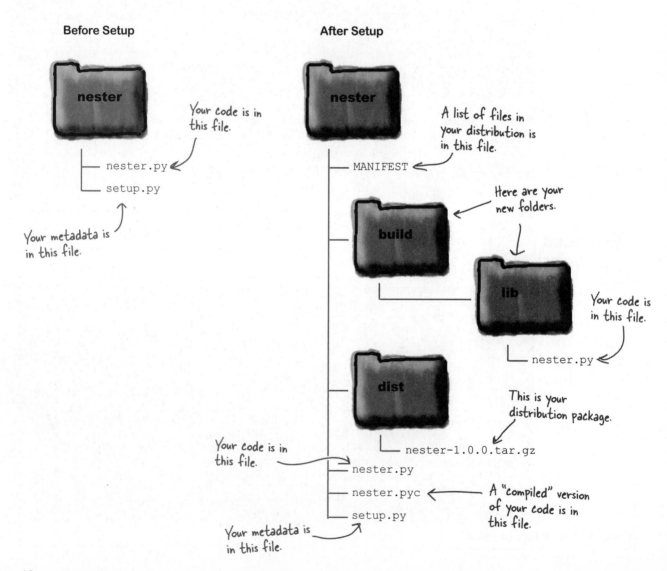

Before Setup

nester

├── nester.py   *Your code is in this file.*
└── setup.py

Your metadata is in this file.

After Setup

nester

├── MANIFEST   *A list of files in your distribution is in this file.*

build   *Here are your new folders.*

lib   *Your code is in this file.*

└── nester.py

dist   *This is your distribution package.*

└── nester-1.0.0.tar.gz

├── nester.py   *Your code is in this file.*
├── nester.pyc   *A "compiled" version of your code is in this file.*
└── setup.py   *Your metadata is in this file.*

Import a module to use it

Now that your module is built, packaged as a distribution, and installed, let's see what's involved in using it. To use a module, simply import it into your programs or import it into the IDLE shell:

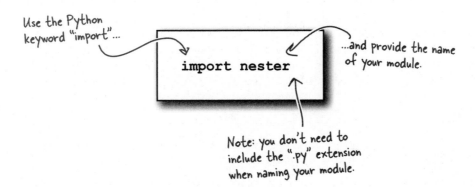

Use the Python keyword "import"...

```
import nester
```

...and provide the name of your module.

Note: you don't need to include the ".py" extension when naming your module.

The import statement tells Python to include the nester.py module in your program. From that point on, you can use the module's functions as if they were entered directly into your program, right? Well...that's what you might expect. Let's check out the validity of your assumption.

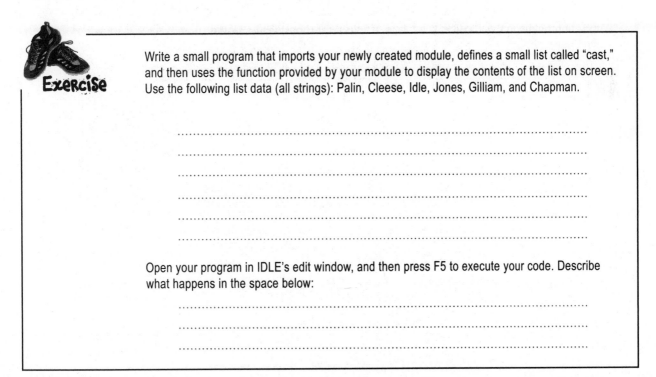

Exercise

Write a small program that imports your newly created module, defines a small list called "cast," and then uses the function provided by your module to display the contents of the list on screen. Use the following list data (all strings): Palin, Cleese, Idle, Jones, Gilliam, and Chapman.

....
....
....
....
....
....

Open your program in IDLE's edit window, and then press F5 to execute your code. Describe what happens in the space below:

....
....
....

Exercise Solution

You were to write a small program that imports your newly created module, defines a small list called "cast," and then uses the function provided by your module to display the contents of the list on screen. You were to use the following list data (all strings): Palin, Cleese, Idle, Jones, Gilliam, and Chapman.

It's a simple three-line program. There's nothing too difficult here.

```
import nester

cast = ['Palin', 'Cleese', 'Idle', 'Jones', 'Gilliam', 'Chapman']
print_lol(cast)
```

Open your program in IDLE's edit window, and then press F5 to execute your code. Describe what happens in the space below:

But it didn't work! ⟶ IDLE gives an error, and the program does not run!

An IDLE Session

With your program in the IDLE edit window, pressing F5 (or choosing Run Module from the Run menu) does indeed cause problems:

```
try_nester.py – /Users/barryp/HeadFirstPython/chapter2/try_nester.py

import nester

cast = ['Palin', 'Cleese', 'Idle', 'Jones', 'Gilliam', 'Chapman']
print_lol(cast)

                                                            Ln: 6 Col: 0
```

Your program does not appear to have executed and an error message is reported:

```
>>> ============================== RESTART ==============================
>>>
Traceback (most recent call last):
  File "/Users/barryp/HeadFirstPython/chapter2/try_nester.py", line 4, in <module>
    print_lol(cast)
NameError: name 'print_lol' is not defined
>>>
```

With your program in IDLE, pressing F5 causes a NameError...it looks like your function can't be found!!!

Python's modules implement namespaces

All code in Python is associated with a *namespace*.

Code in your main Python program (and within IDLE's shell) is associated with a namespace called __main__. When you put your code into its own module, Python automatically creates a namespace with the same name as your module. So, the code in your module is associated with a namespace called nester.

← That's a double underscore in front of the word "main" and after it.

> I guess namespaces are like family names? If someone is looking for Chris, we need to know if it's Chris Murray or Chris Larkin, right? The family name helps to qualify what we mean, as do namespace names in Python.

Yes, namespace names are like family names.

When you want to refer to some function from a module namespace other than the one you are currently in, you need to qualify the invocation of the function with the module's namespace name.

So, instead of invoking the function as print_lol(cast) you need to qualify the name as nester.print_lol(cast). That way, the Python interpreter knows where to look. The format for *namespace qualification* is: the module's name, followed by a period, and then the function name.

The module name, which identifies the namespace.

```
nester.print_lol(cast)
```

The function is then invoked as normal, with "cast" provided as the list to process.

A period separates the module namespace name from the function name.

An IDLE Session

Let's test this. Staying at the IDLE shell, import your module, create the list, and then try to invoke the function without a qualifying name. You're expecting to see an error message:

```
>>> import nester
>>> cast = ['Palin', 'Cleese', 'Idle', 'Jones', 'Gilliam', 'Chapman']
>>> print_lol(cast)
Traceback (most recent call last):
  File "<pyshell#4>", line 1, in <module>
    print_lol(cast)
NameError: name 'print_lol' is not defined
```

As expected, your code has caused a NameError, because you didn't qualify the name.

When you qualify the name of the function with the namespace, things improve dramatically:

```
>>> nester.print_lol(cast)
Palin
Cleese
Idle
Jones
Gilliam
Chapman
```

This time, things work as expected...the data items in the list are displayed on screen.

 Geek Bits

When you use a plain import statement, such as `import nester`, the Python interpreter is instructed to allow you to access `nester`'s functions using namespace qualification. However, it is possible to be *more specific*. If you use `from nester import print_lol`, the specified function (`print_lol` in this case) is *added* to the current namespace, effectively *removing* the requirement for you to use namespace qualification. But you need to be **careful**. If you already have a function called `print_lol` defined in your current namespace, the specific import statement overwrites your function with the imported one, which might not be the behavior you want.

Your module is now ready for upload to PyPI.

Register with the PyPI website

In order to upload your distribution to PyPI, you need to register with the PyPI website. This is a relatively straightforward process.

Begin by surfing over to the PyPI website at *http://pypi.python.org/* and requesting a PyPI ID:

Provide the Username you'd like to use.

Enter your chosen password twice for confirmation purposes.

Don't worry about providing a PGP key (unless you actually have one).

Don't forget to click the "I agree" checkbox before clicking on the Register button.

Don't try to use "hfpython," because that Username is already taken.

Provide a valid email address.

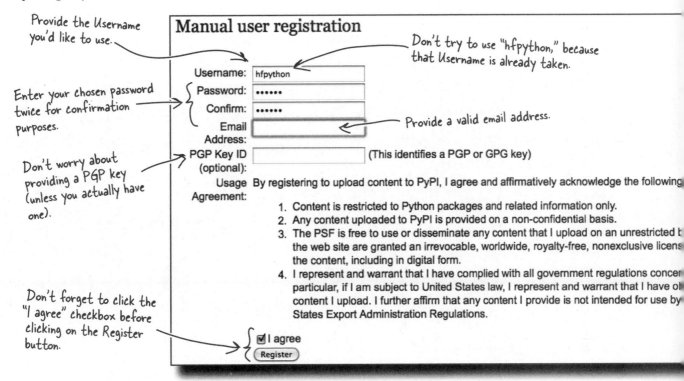

Manual user registration

Username: hfpython
Password: ••••••
Confirm: ••••••
Email Address:
PGP Key ID (optional): (This identifies a PGP or GPG key)
Usage Agreement: By registering to upload content to PyPI, I agree and affirmatively acknowledge the following

1. Content is restricted to Python packages and related information only.
2. Any content uploaded to PyPI is provided on a non-confidential basis.
3. The PSF is free to use or disseminate any content that I upload on an unrestricted b the web site are granted an irrevocable, worldwide, royalty-free, nonexclusive licens the content, including in digital form.
4. I represent and warrant that I have complied with all government regulations concer particular, if I am subject to United States law, I represent and warrant that I have ol content I upload. I further affirm that any content I provide is not intended for use by States Export Administration Regulations.

☑ I agree
(Register)

If all of your registration details are in order, a confirmation message is sent to the email address submitted on the registration form. The email message contains a link you can click to confirm your PyPI registration:

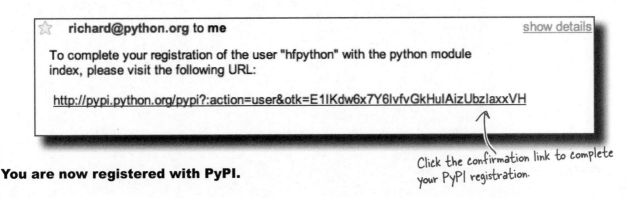

☆ **richard@python.org** to **me**   show details

To complete your registration of the user "hfpython" with the python module index, please visit the following URL:

http://pypi.python.org/pypi?:action=user&otk=E1IKdw6x7Y6IvfvGkHuIAizUbzIaxxVH

Click the confirmation link to complete your PyPI registration.

You are now registered with PyPI.

Upload your code to PyPI

You're ready to rock! The code in your function has been placed in a module, used to create a distribution and installed into your local copy of Python. To upload your distribution to PyPI, complete these two steps: command-line *registration* with PyPI and command-line *uploading*.

It might seem strange to have to register with PyPI *again*, seeing as you just did this with their website. However, the command-line uploading tool needs to be made aware of your PyPI Username and Password, and that's what this registration does. Don't worry: you have to do this only once.

Instruct setup to register your details.

Confirm that you want to use your just-created PyPI credentials.

Use your PyPI settings and save them for future use.

```
File Edit Window Help Register
$ python3 setup.py register
running register
running check
We need to know who you are, so please choose either:
 1. use your existing login,
 2. register as a new user,
 3. have the server generate a new password for you (and email it to you), or
 4. quit
Your selection [default 1]:
1
Username: hfpython
Password:
Registering nester to http://pypi.python.org/pypi
Server response (200): OK
I can store your PyPI login so future submissions will be faster.
(the login will be stored in /Users/barryp/.pypirc)
Save your login (y/N)?y
```

With your registration details entered and saved, you are now ready to upload your distribution to PyPI. Another command line does the trick:

Note: If you try to upload a module called "nester", you'll get an error as that name's already taken. ☺

Instruct setup to upload your software distribution to PyPI.

Setup confirms that the upload is successful. Your distribution is now part of PyPI.

```
File Edit Window Help Upload
$ python3 setup.py sdist upload
running sdist
running check
reading manifest file 'MANIFEST'
creating nester-1.0.0
making hard links in nester-1.0.0...
hard linking nester.py -> nester-1.0.0
hard linking setup.py -> nester-1.0.0
Creating tar archive
removing 'nester-1.0.0' (and everything under it)
running upload
Submitting dist/nester-1.0.0.tar.gz to http://pypi.python.org/pypi
Server response (200): OK
$
```

Welcome to the PyPI community

Congratulations! You are now a full-fledged, card-carrying member of the PyPI community. Your distribution has joined the over 10,000 other uploads on PyPI. Feel free to surf on over to the PyPI website to confirm the upload.

Programmers from all over the globe are now able to download, unpack, and install your module into their local copy of Python, which is pretty cool when you think about it.

Sit back, put your feet up, and wait for the plaudits to begin... ← *You've now written and published your code... how cool is that?*

---

there are no Dumb Questions

Q: **Which is best: plain imports or specific imports?**

A: Neither, really. Most programmers mix and match based on their own personal preference and taste (although there are plenty of programmers willing to argue that their preferred way is the "one true way").

Note that the `from module import function` form pollutes your current namespace: names already defined in your current namespace are *overwritten* by the imported names.

Q: **And when I press F5 in IDLE's edit window, it's as if the module's code is imported with an import statement, right?**

A: Yes, that is essentially what happens. The code in your edit window is compiled and executed by Python, and any names in the edit window are imported into the namespace being used by IDLE's shell. This is handy, because it makes it easy to test functionality with IDLE. But bear in mind that outside of IDLE, you still need to import your module *before* you can use its functionality.

Q: **Is it really necessary for me to install my modules into my local copy of Python? Can't I just put them in any old folder and import them from there?**

A: Yes, it is possible. Just bear in mind that Python looks for modules in a very specific list of places (recall the `import sys; sys.path` trick from earlier in this chapter). If you put your modules in a folder not listed in Python's path list, chances are the interpreter won't find them, resulting in ImportErrors. Using the distribution utilities to build and install your module into your local copy of Python avoids these types of errors.

Q: **I noticed the distribution utiliites created a file called** `nester.pyc`. **What's up with that?**

A: That's a very good question. When the interpreter executes your module code for the first time, it reads in the code and translates it into an internal bytecode format which is ultimately executed. (This idea is very similar to the way the Java JVM works: your Java code is turned into a class file as a result of your Java technologies compiling your code.) The Python interpreter is smart enough to skip the translation phase the next time your module is used, because it can determine when you've made changes to the original module code file. If your module code hasn't changed, no translation occurs and the "compiled" code is executed. If your code has changed, the translation occurs (creating a new `pyc` file) as needed. The upshot of all this is that when Python sees a `pyc` file, it tries to use it because doing so *makes everything go much faster*.

Q: **Cool. So I can just provide my users with the pyc file?**

A: No, don't do that, because the use of the `pyc` file (if found) is primarily a runtime optimization performed by the interpreter.

Q: **So, can I delete the pyc file if I don't need it?**

A: Sure, if you really want to. Just be aware that you lose any potential runtime optimization.

With success comes responsibility

Lots of programmers from many different locations are using your module. And some of these programmers are looking for more features.

> We really love your code, but is there any chance this thing could print the data to screen and indent each nested list whenever one is found?

> Hang on a second. I kinda like the way it works right now. I vote NOT to change it.

Likes what you've done, but could be happier. →

← Any changes to the way your function works are likely to annoy this guy.

Requests for change are inevitable

You need to keep your current users happy by maintaining the existing functionality, while at the same time providing enhanced functionality to those users that require it. This could be tricky.

What are your options here?

Life's full of choices

When it comes to deciding what to do here, there's
no shortage of suggestions.

> That's soooo easy. Simply create
> another function called "print_lol2",
> right? You could then import the
> function you want using the specific
> form of the import statement. It's not
> that hard, really...

Yeah, that might just work.

You could edit your module's code and define a new function called
`print_lol2`, then code up the function to perform the nested printing
When you want to use the original function, use this specific form of the
import statement: `from nester import print_lol`. When you want
to use the new, improved version of the function, use this import statement:
`from nester import print_lol2`.

Which would work, but...

> But that suggestion is twice
> the work...which might be OK
> sometimes...but the creation of a
> second, almost identical, function
> seems wasteful to me.

Right. A second function is wasteful.

Not only are you introducing an almost identical function to your
module, which might create a potential maintenance nightmare, but
you're also making things much more difficult for the users of your
module, who must decide *ahead of time* which version of the function
they need. Adding a second function makes your module's *application
programming interface* (API) more complex than it needs to be.

There has to be a better strategy, doesn't there?

Control behavior with an extra argument

If you add an extra argment to your function, you can handle indentation within your current code without too much trouble.

> Yikes! I should've thought about that myself... I probably need to go easy on the coffee. Of course, it's clear to me now: adding another argument to your function gives you options.

Take your function to the next level

At the moment, your function has a single argument: `the_list`. If you add a second argument called `level`, you can use it to control indentation. A positive value for `level` indicates the number of tab-stops to include when displaying a line of data on screen. If `level` is 0, no indentation is used; if it's 1, use a single tab-stop; if it's 2, use two tab-stops; and so on.

It's clear you are looking at some sort of looping mechanism here, right? You already know how to iterate over a variably sized list, but how do you iterate a fixed number of times in Python?

Does Python provide any functionality that can help?

Before your write new code, think BIF

When you come across a need that you think is *generic*, ask yourself if there's a built-in function (BIF) that can help. After all, iterating a fixed number of times is something you'll need to do *all the time*.

And remember: Python 3 includes over 70 BIFs, so there's a lot of functionality waiting to be discovered.

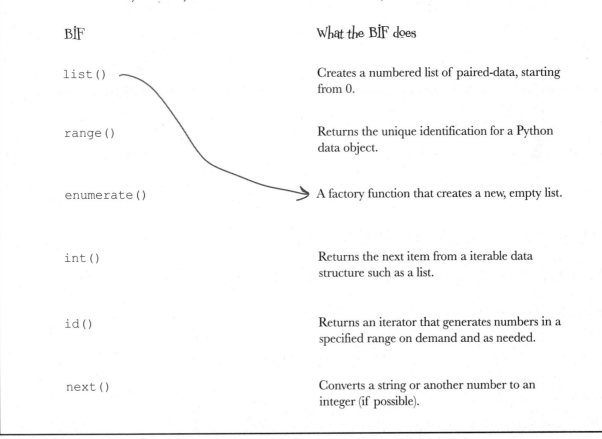

Use your pencil to draw a line matching each BIF to the correct description. The first one is done for you. Once you have all your lines drawn, circle the BIF you think you need to use in the next version of your function.

BIF	What the BIF does
list()	Creates a numbered list of paired-data, starting from 0.
range()	Returns the unique identification for a Python data object.
enumerate()	A factory function that creates a new, empty list.
int()	Returns the next item from a iterable data structure such as a list.
id()	Returns an iterator that generates numbers in a specified range on demand and as needed.
next()	Converts a string or another number to an integer (if possible).

WHO DOES WHAT?
SOLUTION

You were to use your pencil to draw a line matching each BIF to the correct description. Once you had all your lines drawn, you were to circle the BIF you think you need to use in the next version of your function.

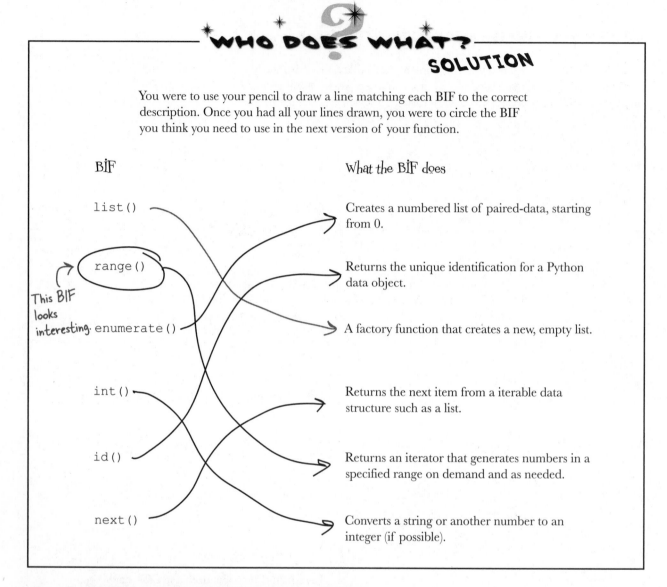

BIF

list()

range()

This BIF looks interesting. enumerate()

int()

id()

next()

What the BIF does

Creates a numbered list of paired-data, starting from 0.

Returns the unique identification for a Python data object.

A factory function that creates a new, empty list.

Returns the next item from a iterable data structure such as a list.

Returns an iterator that generates numbers in a specified range on demand and as needed.

Converts a string or another number to an integer (if possible).

The range() BIF iterates a fixed number of times

The range() BIF gives you the control you need to iterate a specific number of times and can be used to generate a list of numbers from zero up-to-but-not-including some number. Here's how to use it:

Generate numbers up-to-but-not-including 4.

"num" is the target identifier and is assigned each of the numbers generated by "range()" in turn.

```
for num in range(4):
    print(num)
```

The numbers 0, 1, 2, and 3 will appear on screen.

there are no Dumb Questions

Q: Don't I need to import the BIFs in order to use them in my program?

A: No. For all intents and purposes, the BIFs are specifically imported into every Python program as well as IDLE.

Q: So the BIFs must belong to the __main__ namespace, right?

A: No. They are automatically imported into the __main__ namespace, but the BIFs have their very own namespace called (wait for it) __builtins__.

Q: I get how range() works, but surely I could just as easily use a while loop to do the same thing?

A: Yes, you can, but it's not as elegant as using range(). Seriously, though, the while equivalent not only requires you to write more code, but it also makes it your responsibility to worry about loop state, whereas range() worries about this for you. As a general rule, Python programmers look for ways to reduce the amount of code they need to write and worry about, which leads to better code robustness, fewer errors, and a good night's sleep.

Q: So BIFs are actually good for me?

A: BIFs exist to make your programming experience as straightforward as possible by providing a collection of functions that provide common solutions to common problems. Since they are included with Python, you are pretty much assured that they have been tested to destruction and do "exactly what it says on the tin." You can depend on the BIFs. Using them gives your program a leg up and makes you look good. So, yes, the BIFs are good for you!

Exercise

Now that you know a bit about the range() BIF, amend your function to use range() to indent any nested lists a specific number of tab-stops.

Hint: To display a TAB character on screen using the print() BIF yet avoid taking a new-line (which is print()'s default behavior), use this Python code: print("\t", end='').

```
"""This is the "nester.py" module and it provides one function called print_lol()
    which prints lists that may or may not include nested lists."""

def print_lol(the_list, .................................):
```
Include the name of the extra argument.
```
    """This function takes a positional argument called "the_list", which
        is any Python list (of - possibly - nested lists). Each data item in the
        provided list is (recursively) printed to the screen on it's own line."""

    .......................................................................

    for each_item in the_list:
        if isinstance(each_item, list):
            print_lol(each_item)
        else:
```
Don't forget to edit the comment.
```
            ...........................................................

            .......................................................
        print(each_item)
```
Add code here to take the required number of tab-stops.

Exercise Solution

Now that you know a bit about the range() BIF, you were to amend your function to use range() to indent any nested lists a specific number of tab-stops.

Hint: To display a TAB character on screen using the print() BIF yet avoid taking a new-line (which is print()'s default behavior), use this Python code: print("\t", end='').

```python
"""This is the "nester.py" module and it provides one function called print_lol()
    which prints lists that may or may not include nested lists."""


def print_lol(the_list, level):
    """This function takes a positional argument called "the_list", which
        is any Python list (of - possibly - nested lists). Each data item in the
        provided list is (recursively) printed to the screen on it's own line.
        A second argument called "level" is used to insert tab-stops when a nested list is encountered."""
    for each_item in the_list:
        if isinstance(each_item, list):
            print_lol(each_item)
        else:
            for tab_stop in range(level):
                print("\t", end='')
            print(each_item)
```

Use the value of "level" to control how many tab-stops are used.

Display a TAB character for each level of indentation.

An IDLE Session

It's time to test the new version of your function. Load your module file into IDLE, press F5 to import the function into IDLE's namespace, and then invoke the function on your movies list with a second argument:

```
>>> print_lol(movies, 0)
The Holy Grail
1975
Terry Jones & Terry Gilliam
91
Traceback (most recent call last):
  File "<pyshell#2>", line 1, in <module>
    print_lol(movies,0)
  File "/Users/barryp/HeadFirstPython/chapter2/nester/nester.py", line 14, in print_lol
    print_lol(each_item)
TypeError: print_lol() takes exactly 2 positional arguments (1 given)
```

Invoke your function, being sure to provide a second argument.

The data in "movies" starts to appear on screen...

...then all hell breaks loose! Something is not right here.

Here's your clue as to what's gone wrong.

Your code has a TypeError, which caused it to crash.

Python tries its best to run your code

Unlike compiled languages (such as C, Java, C#, and others), Python doesn't *completely* check the validity of your code *until it runs*. This allows Python to do some rather cool things that just aren't possible in those other languages, such as dynamically defining functions at runtime. This, of course, can be very flexible and powerful.

The cost to you, however, is that you need to be very careful when writing your code, because something that typically would be caught and flagged as an "error" by a traditional, statically typed, compiled language often goes unnoticed in Python.

> ...OK, C++ syntax fine...continuing to parse...whoops! You're trying to use a function before it's declared?!? That's NOT allowed around here... I'm outta here.

Please wait. Compiling your C++ code...

> Ah ha! The old "calling a function before you've defined it yet" trick, eh? I'll just make a note in case you define it later at runtime. You are planning to do that, right? Please don't disappoint me, or I'll give you an error...

Running your Python code right now...

⚛ BRAIN POWER

Take another look at the error on the opposite page. Why do you think Python is giving you this particular error? What do you think is wrong?

Trace your code

When you're trying to work out what went wrong with a program that looks
like it should be OK, a useful technique is to trace what happens as each line
of code executes. Here's the code that you are currently working with. At
only three lines long (remember: the creation of the list is one line of code), it
doesn't look like it should cause any trouble:

```
import nester          ←——— Thes two lines look OK.

                              ↙
movies = [ "The Holy Grail", 1975, "Terry Jones & Terry Gilliam",
           91,["Graham Chapman", ["Michael Palin",
           "John Cleese", "Terry Gilliam", "Eric Idle",
           "Terry Jones"]]]

                                              You are invoking the function with two arguments,
nester.print_lol(movies, 0) ←————             so that's OK, too.
```

With the data assigned to the function's arguments, the function's code starts
to execute on each data item contained within the passed-in list:

The "movies" list is assigned to
"the_list", and the value 0 is
assigned to "level".

To save space, the
entire comment is
not shown.

Process each item in
the list...

...then decide what
to do next based on
whether or not the
data item is a list.

If the data item is a
list, recursively invoke
the function...hang on
a second, that doesn't
look right!?

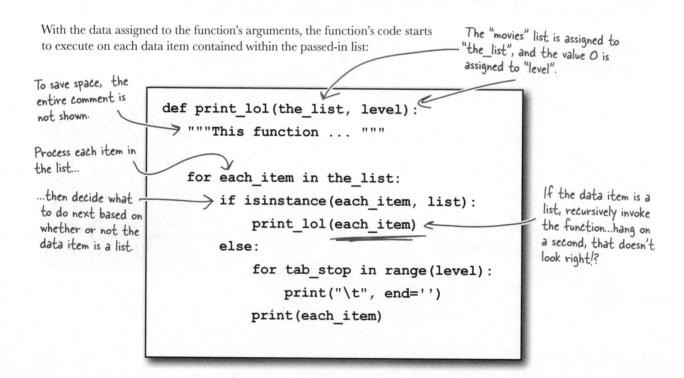

```
def print_lol(the_list, level):
    """This function ... """

    for each_item in the_list:
        if isinstance(each_item, list):
            print_lol(each_item)
        else:
            for tab_stop in range(level):
                print("\t", end='')
            print(each_item)
```

Work out what's wrong

There's your problem: the recursive invocation of your function is using the old *function signature* that required only one argument. The new version of your function requires two arguments.

The fix is easy: provide the correct number of arguments when calling the new version of your function. So, this snippet of code from your function:

```
if isinstance(each_item, list):
    print_lol(each_item)
```

needs to be rewritten to specify the correct number of arguments:

```
if isinstance(each_item, list):
    print_lol(each_item, level)
```

> Not so fast. Surely the nested list needs to be printed after a specific number of tab-stops? At the moment, your code sets "level" to 0 but never changes the value, so "level" never has any impact on your displayed output...

Right. Your use of "level" needs one final tweak.

The whole point of having `level` as an argument is to allow you to control the nested output. Each time you process a nested list, you need to increase the value of `level` by 1. Your code snippet needs to look like this:

```
if isinstance(each_item, list):
    print_lol(each_item, level+1)
```

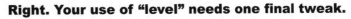

Simply increment the value of level by 1 each time you recursively invoke your function.

It's time to perform that update.

Update PyPI with your new code

Go ahead and edit your `nester.py` module (in the `nester` folder) to invoke your function properly. Now that you have a new version of your module, it's a good idea to update the distribution that you uploaded to PyPI.

With your code amended, there's also a small change needed to your distribution's `setup.py` program. You've changed your API, so adjust the value associated with `version` in `setup.py`. Let's move from version 1.0.0 to 1.1.0:

```
from distutils.core import setup

setup(
        name         = 'nester',
        version      = '1.1.0',
        py_modules   = ['nester'],
        author       = 'hfpython',
        author_email = 'hfpython@headfirstlabs.com',
        url          = 'http://www.headfirstlabs.com',
        description  = 'A simple printer of nested lists',
     )
```

Change the value associated with "version" to indicate to PyPI that this is indeed a new version.

Just as you did when you created and uploaded your distribution, invoke the `setup.py` program within your distribution folder to perform the upload:

```
File  Edit  Window  Help  UploadAgain
$ python3 setup.py sdist upload
running sdist
running check
reading manifest file 'MANIFEST'
creating nester-1.1.0
making hard links in nester-1.1.0...
hard linking nester.py -> nester-1.1.0
hard linking setup.py -> nester-1.1.0
Creating tar archive
removing 'nester-1.1.0' (and everything under it)
running upload
Submitting dist/nester-1.1.0.tar.gz to http://pypi.python.org/pypi
Server response (200): OK
$
```

Don't you just love those "200 OK" messages?

Your new distribution is now available on PyPI.

Cool. There's a new version of "nester" on PyPI. Take a look.

Bob   Mark   Laura

Mark: Take a look at this, guys…the `nester` module has been updated on PyPI.

Bob: Version 1.1.0…

Laura: I wonder what's changed?

Mark: It still works with nested lists of lists, but now you can see the nested structure on screen, which I think is pretty cool.

Laura: And useful. I've been waiting for that feature.

Bob: Eh…OK…but how do I upgrade my existing local copy?

Mark: Just follow the same steps as when you downloaded and installed `nester` from PyPI the first time.

Bob: So I download the package file, unpack it, and ask `setup.py` to install it into my Python for me?

Mark: Yes. It couldn't be any easier.

Laura: And what about my existing version of `nester`; what happens to that "old" version?

Bob: Yeah…do I have two `nester` modules now?

Mark: No. When you use `setup.py` to install the latest version it becomes the current version and effectively replaces the previous module, which was the 1.0.0 release.

Bob: And PyPI knows to give you the latest version of the module, too, right?

Mark: Yes, when you surf the PyPI website and search for `nester`, you are always provided with the latest version of the module.

Laura: Well, I use this module all the time and I've been waiting for this feature. I think I'll update right away.

Mark: I've already upgraded mine, and it works a treat.

Bob: Yeah, I use it a lot, too, so I guess I'll keep my system up to date and install the latest version. It's probably not a good idea to rely on out-of-date software, right?

Mark: I'd say. And, there's nothing quite like progress.

Laura: Catch you later, guys, I've got work to do.

Bob: Me, too. I'm off to PyPI to grab the latest `nester` and install it into my local copy of Python. I'll give it a quick test to confirm all is OK.

Mark: Later, dudes…

You've changed your API

Your new version of `nester` is indeed better, but not for all your users.

Ah, phooey! I can't believe it... I installed the latest version of "nester" from PyPI, and now all of my code that uses your function is not working. What did you do?!?

Get with the program, Bob. You have TypeError's everywhere...

In your rush to release the lates and greatest version of your module, you forgot about *some* of your existing users. Recall that not all of your users want the new nested printing feature. However, by adding the second argument to `print_lol()`, you've changed your function's signature, which means your module has a different API. Anyone using the old API is going to have problems.

The ideal solution would be to provide **both** APIs, one which switches on the new feature and another that doesn't. Maybe the feature could be optional?

But how would that work?

Use optional arguments

To turn a required argument to a function into an *optional* argument, provide the argument with a default value. When no argument value is provided, the default value is used. When an argument value is provided, it is used *instead of* the default. The key point is, of course, that the default value for the argument effectively makes the argument optional.

To provide a default value for any function argument, specify the default value *after* the argument name:

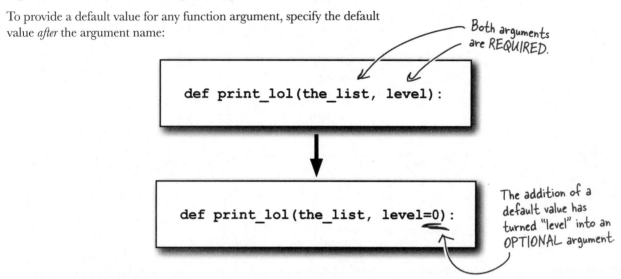

Both arguments are REQUIRED.

```
def print_lol(the_list, level):
```

```
def print_lol(the_list, level=0):
```

The addition of a default value has turned "level" into an OPTIONAL argument.

With the default value for the argument defined, you can now invoke the function in a number of different ways:

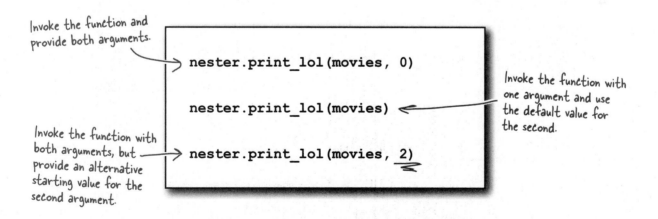

Invoke the function and provide both arguments.

```
nester.print_lol(movies, 0)
```

```
nester.print_lol(movies)
```

Invoke the function with one argument and use the default value for the second.

Invoke the function with both arguments, but provide an alternative starting value for the second argument.

```
nester.print_lol(movies, 2)
```

Your function now supports different signatures, but the functonality remains as it was.

An IDLE Session

Amend your code to give the `level` argument a default value of 0 and then load your code into the IDLE editor. Press F5 to load the code into the shell and then follow along to confirm that the latest version of your function works as expected. Start be defining a short list of lists and use the function to display the the list on screen:

```
>>> names = ['John', 'Eric', ['Cleese', 'Idle'], 'Michael', ['Palin']]
>>> print_lol(names, 0)
John
Eric
        Cleese
        Idle
Michael
        Palin
```

The standard behavior works as expected, with nested lists indented.

Now try to do the same thing without specifiying the second argument. Let's rely on the default value kicking in:

```
>>> print_lol(names)
John
Eric
        Cleese
        Idle
Michael
        Palin
```

Without specifying the second argument, the default is used and works, too.

Now specify a value for the second argument and note the change in the function's behavior:

```
>>> print_lol(names, 2)
        John
        Eric
            Cleese
            Idle
        Michael
            Palin
```

Specify an alternative value for the second argument and the indenting starts from that level.

One final example provides what looks like a silly value for the second argument. Look what happens:

```
>>> print_lol(names, -9)
John
Eric
Cleese
Idle
Michael
Palin
```

Using a negative value effectively switches OFF the indenting, as the count for "level" is unlikely to become a positive integer. This looks exactly like the original output from version 1.0.0, right?

Your module supports both APIs

Well done! It looks like your module is working well, as both APIs, the original
1.0.0 API *and* the newer 1.1.0 API, can now be used.

Let's take a moment to create and upload a new distibution for PyPI. As
before, let's amend the `version` setting in the `setup.py` program:

```
name        = 'nester',
version     = '1.2.0',
py_modules  = ['nester'],
```

Once again, be sure to change the value associated with "version" in "setup.py".

And with the code changes applied, upload this new version of your
distribution to PyPI:

```
File Edit Window Help UploadThree
$ python3 setup.py sdist upload
running sdist
running check
reading manifest file 'MANIFEST'
creating nester-1.2.0
making hard links in nester-1.2.0...
hard linking nester.py -> nester-1.2.0
hard linking setup.py -> nester-1.2.0
Creating tar archive
removing 'nester-1.2.0' (and everything under it)
running upload
Submitting dist/nester-1.2.0.tar.gz to http://pypi.python.org/pypi
Server response (200): OK
$
```

This all looks fine and dandy.

Success! The messages from `setup.py` confirm that the your latest version
of `nester` is up on PyPI. Let's hope this one satisfies all of your users.

Consider your code carefully. How might some of
your users still have a problem with this version of
your code?

Your API is still not right

Although the API lets your users invoke the function in its original form, *the nesting is switched on by default.* This behavior is not required by everyone and some people aren't at all happy.

Of course, if you have some functionality that really ought to be optional (that is, *not* the default), you should adjust your code to make it so. But how?

One solution is to **add a third argument** which is set to True when the indenting is required and False otherwise. If you ensure that this argument is False by default, the original functonality becomes the default behavior and users of your code have to request the new indenting feature explicitly.

Let's look at adding this final revision.

Exercise

1 Amend your module one last time to add a third argument to your function. Call your argument `indent` and set it initially to the value `False`—that is, do not switch on indentation by default. In the body of your function, use the value of `indent` to control your indentation code.

Note: to save a bit of space, the comments from the module are not shown here. Of course, *you* need to make the necessary adjustments to your comments to keep them in sync with your code.

Put the extra argument here.

```
def print_lol(the_list, ........................ , level=0):

    for each_item in the_list:
        if isinstance(each_item, list):
            print_lol(each_item, ........................ , level+1)
        else:
            ..................................................
                for tab_stop in range(level):
                    print("\t", end='')
            print(each_item)
```

What needs to go in here?

Add a line of code to control when indenting occurs.

2 With your new code additions in place, provide the edit you would recommend making to the `setup.py` program prior to uploading this latest version of your module to PyPI:

....

....

3 Provide the command you would use to upload your new distribution to PyPI:

....

....

Exercise Solution

1 You were to amend your module one last time to add a third argument to your function. You were to call your argument `indent` and set it initially to the value `False`—that is, do not switch on indentation by default. In the body of your function, you were to use the value of `indent` to control your indentation code.

Did you include the default value?

```
def print_lol(the_list,  indent=False  , level=0):

    for each_item in the_list:
        if isinstance(each_item, list):
            print_lol(each_item,  indent  , level+1)
        else:
            if indent :
                for tab_stop in range(level):
                    print("\t", end='')
            print(each_item)
```

Your signature has changed, so be sure to update this invocation.

Don't forget the colon at the end of the "if" line.

A simple "if" statement does the trick.

A sweet alternative to this "for" loop is this code: print("\t" * level, end=").

2 With your new code additions in place, you were to provide the edit you would recommend making to the `setup.py` program prior to uploading this latest version of your module to PyPI:

Edit "setup.py" so that it reads: version = '1.3.0',

It's a new version of your module, so be sure to change the value associated with "version" in your "setup.py" file.

3 You were to provide the command you would use to upload your new distribution to PyPI:

python3 setup.py sdisk upload

Remember: if you are on Windows use "C:\Python31\python.exe" instead of "python3".

An IDLE Session

A final test of the functionality should convince you that your module is now working exactly the way you and your users want it to. Let's start with the original, default behavior:

```
>>> names = ['John', 'Eric', ['Cleese', 'Idle'], 'Michael', ['Palin']]
>>> print_lol(names)
John
Eric
Cleese
Idle
Michael
Palin
```

The original, default functionality is restored (that should please Bob).

Next, turn on indentation by providing True as the second argument:

```
>>> names = ['John', 'Eric', ['Cleese', 'Idle'], 'Michael', ['Palin']]
>>> print_lol(names, True)
John
Eric
        Cleese
        Idle
Michael
        Palin
```

By providing a second argument, it's possible to switch on indented output (keeping Laura happy).

And, finally, control where indentation begins by providing a third argument value:

```
>>> names = ['John', 'Eric', ['Cleese', 'Idle'], 'Michael', ['Palin']]
>>> print_lol(names, True, 4)
                John
                Eric
                        Cleese
                        Idle
                Michael
                        Palin
```

Indenting from a specific tab-stop is also possible.

Do this! ➞

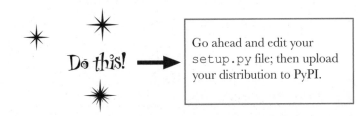
Go ahead and edit your `setup.py` file; then upload your distribution to PyPI.

Your module's reputation is restored

Congratulations! Word of your new and improved module is spreading fast.

Lots of PyPI hits already. I told you this was good.

My programs are back to working the way I want them to, so I'm a happy guy. Thanks!

Great work! I love that I can switch indentation on and off.

← This is as close as Bob gets to a smile. But trust us, he's happy. ☺

Your Python skills are starting to build

You've created a useful module, made it shareable, and uploaded it to the PyPI website. Programmers all over the world are downloading and using your code in their projects.

Keep up the good work.

Your Python Toolbox

You've got Chapter 2 under your belt and you've added some key Python goodies to your toolbox.

BULLET POINTS

- A **module** is a text file that contains Python code.

- The **distribution utilities** let you turn your module into a shareable package.

- The `setup.py` program provides *metadata* about your module and is used to build, install, and upload your packaged distribution.

- Import your module into other programs using the **import** statement.

- Each module in Python provides its own **namespace**, and the namespace name is used to qualify the module's functions when invoking them using the `module.function()` form.

- Specifically import a function from a module into the current namespace using the `from module import function` form of the import statement.

- Use # to comment-out a line of code or to add a short, one-line comment to your program.

- The built-in functions (BIFs) have their own namespace called `__builtins__`, which is automatically included in every Python program.

- The `range()` BIF can be used with **for** to iterate a fixed number of times.

- Including `end=' '` as a argument to the `print()` BIF switches off its automatic inclusion of a new-line on output.

- Arguments to your functions are **optional** if you provide them with a **default value**.

Python Lingo

- Use a "triple-quoted string" to include a multiple-line comment in your code.

- "PyPI" is the Python Package Index and is well worth a visit.

- A "namespace" is a place in Python's memory where names exist.

- Python's main namespace is known as `__main__`.

IDLE Notes

- Press F5 to "run" the code in the IDLE edit window.

- When you press F5 to "load" a module's code into the IDLE shell, the module's names are specifically imported into IDLE's namespace. This is a convenience when using IDLE. Within your code, you need to use the import statement explicitly.

3 files and exceptions

Dealing with errors

I always thought he was exceptional...especially when it comes to processing my files.

It's simply not enough to process your list data in your code.

You need to be able to get your data *into* your programs with ease, too. It's no surprise then that Python makes reading data from **files** easy. Which is great, until you consider what can go *wrong* when interacting with data *external* to your programs...and there are lots of things waiting to trip you up! When bad stuff happens, you need a strategy for getting out of trouble, and one such strategy is to deal with any exceptional situations using Python's **exception handling** mechanism showcased in this chapter.

Data is external to your program

Most of your programs conform to the *input-process-output model*: data comes in, gets manipulated, and then is stored, displayed, printed, or transferred.

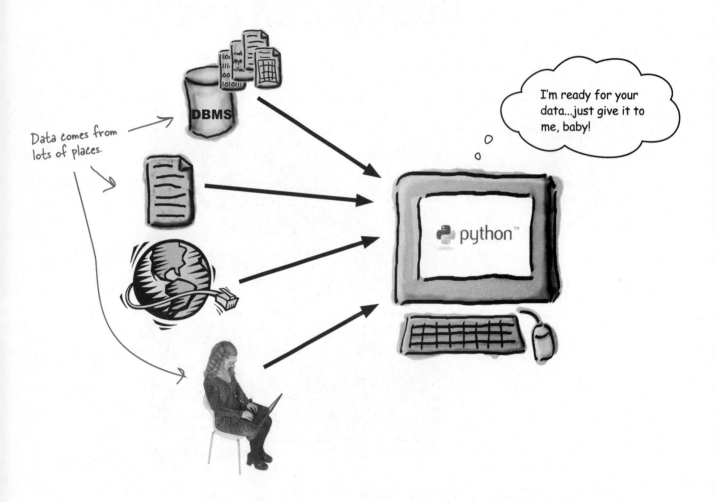

So far, you've learned how to **process** data as well as **display** it on screen. But what's involved in getting data into your programs? Specifically, what's involved in reading data from a file?

How does Python read data from a file?

It's all lines of text

The basic input mechanism in Python is **line based**: when read into your program from a text file, data arrives one line at a time.

Python's open() BIF lives to interact with files. When combined with a **for** statement, reading files is straightforward.

Your data in a text file called "sketch.txt".

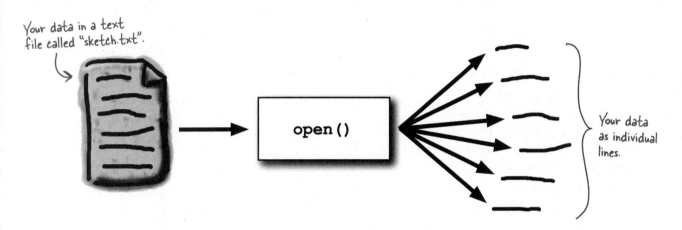

Your data as individual lines.

When you use the open() BIF to access your data in a file, an **iterator** is created to feed the lines of data from your file to your code one line at a time. But let's not get ahead of ourselves. For now, consider the standard *open-process-close* code in Python:

Do this!

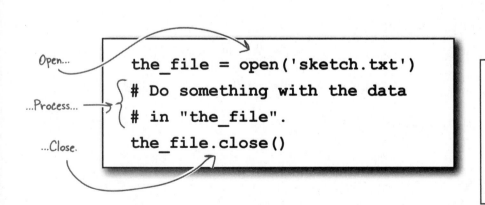

Open...

```python
the_file = open('sketch.txt')
# Do something with the data
# in "the_file".
the_file.close()
```

...Process...

...Close.

Create a folder called HeadFirstPython and a subfolder called chapter3. With the folders ready, download sketch.txt from the Head First Python support website and save it to the chapter3 folder.

Let's use IDLE to get a feel for Python's file-input mechanisms.

An IDLE Session

Start a new IDLE sesson and import the os module to change the current working directory to the folder that contains your just-downloaded data file:

```
>>> import os          ←——— Import "os" from the Standard Library.
>>> os.getcwd()        }← What's the current working directory?
'/Users/barryp/Documents'
>>> os.chdir('../HeadFirstPython/chapter3')  ←——— Change to the folder that contains your data file.
>>> os.getcwd()        }← Confirm you are now in the right place.
'/Users/barryp/HeadFirstPython/chapter3'
```

Now, open your data file and read the first two lines from the file, displaying them on screen:

```
>>> data = open('sketch.txt')  ←——— Open a named file and assign the file to a file object called "data".
>>> print(data.readline(), end='')
Man: Is this the right room for an argument?  }  Use the "readline()" method to grab a
>>> print(data.readline(), end='')               line from the file, then use the "print()"
Other Man: I've told you once.                   BIF to display it on screen.
```

Let's "rewind" the file back to the start, then use a **for** statement to process every line in the file:

```
>>> data.seek(0)    ←— Use the "seek()" method to return to the start of the file.
0                      And yes, you can use "tell()" with Python's files, too.
>>> for each_line in data:
        print(each_line, end='')  }← This code should look familiar: it's a standard
                                     iteration using the file's data as input.
Man: Is this the right room for an argument?
Other Man: I've told you once.
Man: No you haven't!
Other Man: Yes I have.
Man: When?                              Every line of the data is
Other Man: Just now.                    displayed on screen (although
Man: No you didn't!                  ← for space reasons, it is
    ...                                 abridged here).
Man: (exasperated) Oh, this is futile!!
(pause)
Other Man: No it isn't!
Man: Yes it is!
>>> data.close()   ←——— Since you are now done with the file, be sure to close it.
```

Take a closer look at the data

Look closely at the data. It appears to conform to a specific format:

The cast member's role

A colon, followed by a space character

The line spoken by the cast member

```
Man: Is this the right room for an argument?
Other Man: I've told you once.
Man: No you haven't!
Other Man: Yes I have.
Man: When?
Other Man: Just now.
Man: No you didn't!
```

With this format in mind, you can process each line to *extract* parts of the line as required. The `split()` method can help here:

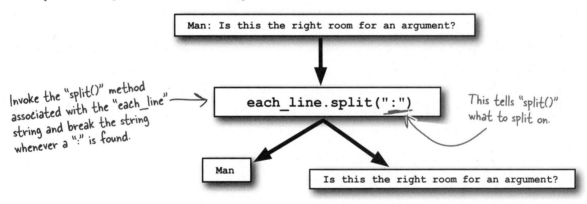

```
Man: Is this the right room for an argument?
```

Invoke the "split()" method associated with the "each_line" string and break the string whenever a ":" is found.

```
each_line.split(":")
```

This tells "split()" what to split on.

```
Man
```

```
Is this the right room for an argument?
```

The `split()` method returns a list of strings, which are assigned to a list of target identifiers. This is known as *multiple assignment*:

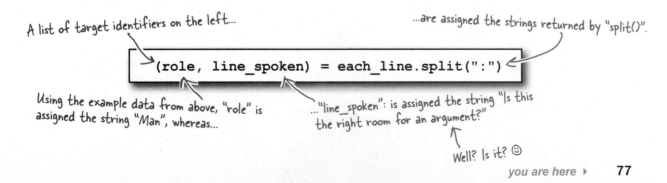

A list of target identifiers on the left...

...are assigned the strings returned by "split()".

```
(role, line_spoken) = each_line.split(":")
```

Using the example data from above, "role" is assigned the string "Man", whereas...

..."line_spoken": is assigned the string "Is this the right room for an argument?"

Well? Is it? ☺

An IDLE Session

Let's confirm that you can still process your file while splitting each line. Type the following code into IDLE's shell:

```
>>> data = open('sketch.txt')    ← Open the data file.
>>> for each_line in data:
        (role, line_spoken) = each_line.split(':')
        print(role, end='')
        print(' said: ', end='')
        print(line_spoken, end='')
```

Process the data, extracting each part from each line and displaying each part on screen.

```
Man said:  Is this the right room for an argument?
Other Man said:  I've told you once.
Man said:  No you haven't!
Other Man said:  Yes I have.
Man said:  When?
Other Man said:  Just now.
Man said:  No you didn't!
Other Man said:  Yes I did!
Man said:  You didn't!
Other Man said:  I'm telling you, I did!
Man said:  You did not!
Other Man said:  Oh I'm sorry, is this a five minute argument, or the full half hour?
Man said:  Ah! (taking out his wallet and paying) Just the five minutes.
Other Man said:  Just the five minutes. Thank you.
Other Man said:  Anyway, I did.
Man said:  You most certainly did not!
Traceback (most recent call last):
  File "<pyshell#10>", line 2, in <module>
    (role, line_spoken) = each_line.split(':')
ValueError: too many values to unpack
```

This all looks OK.

Whoops! There's something seriously wrong here.

It's a ValueError, so that must mean there's something wrong with the data in your file, right?

Know your data

Your code worked fine for a while, then crashed with a *runtime error*. The problem occurred right after the line of data that had the *Man* saying, "You most certainly did not!"

Let's look at the data file and see what comes after this successfully processed line:

```
Man: You didn't!
Other Man: I'm telling you, I did!
Man: You did not!
Other Man: Oh I'm sorry, is this a five minute argument, or the full half hour?
Man: Ah! (taking out his wallet and paying) Just the five minutes.
Other Man: Just the five minutes. Thank you.
Other Man: Anyway, I did.
Man: You most certainly did not!
Other Man: Now let's get one thing quite clear: I most definitely told you!
Man: Oh no you didn't!
Other Man: Oh yes I did!
```

The error occurs AFTER this line of data.

Notice anything?

Notice anything about the *next* line of data?

The next line of data has two colons, not one. This is enough extra data to upset the `split()` method due to the fact that, as your code currently stands, `split()` expects to break the line into two parts, assigning each to `role` and `line_spoken`, respectively.

When an extra colon appears in the data, the `split()` method breaks the line into *three parts*. Your code hasn't told `split()` what to do with the third part, so the Python interpreter *raises* a `ValueError`, complains that you have "too many values," and terminates. A **runtime error** has occurred.

Do this!

To help diagnose this problem, let's put your code into its own file called `sketch.py`. You can copy and paste your code from the IDLE shell into a new IDLE edit window.

What approach might you take to solve this data-processing problem?

Know your methods and ask for help

It might be useful to see if the `split()` method includes any functionality that might help here. You can ask the IDLE shell to tell you more about the `split()` method by using the `help()` BIF.

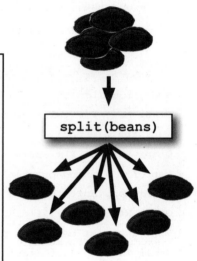

An IDLE Session

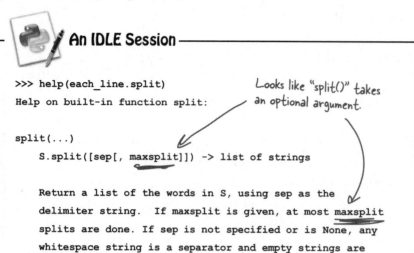

```
>>> help(each_line.split)
Help on built-in function split:

split(...)
    S.split([sep[, maxsplit]]) -> list of strings

    Return a list of the words in S, using sep as the
    delimiter string.  If maxsplit is given, at most maxsplit
    splits are done. If sep is not specified or is None, any
    whitespace string is a separator and empty strings are
    removed from the result.
```

Looks like "split()" takes an optional argument.

`split(beans)`

The optional argument to `split()` controls how many breaks occur within your line of data. By default, the data is broken into as many parts as is possible. But you need only two parts: the name of the character and the line he spoke.

If you set this optional argument to 1, your line of data is only ever broken into two pieces, effectively negating the effect of any extra colon on any line.

Let's try this and see what happens.

Geek Bits

IDLE gives you searchable access to the entire Python documentation set via its Help → Python Docs menu option (which will open the docs in your web browser). If all you need to see is the documentation associated with a single method or function, use the **help()** BIF within IDLE's shell.

`split(beans, 1)`

An IDLE Session

Here's the code in the IDLE edit window. Note the extra argument to the `split()` method.

sketch.py – /Users/barryp/HeadFirstPython/chapter4/sketch.py

```
data = open('sketch.txt')

for each_line in data:
    (role, line_spoken) = each_line.split(':', 1)
    print(role, end='')
    print(' said: ', end='')
    print(line_spoken, end='')

data.close()
```

Ln: 11 Col: 0

The extra argument controls how "split()" splits.

With the edit applied and saved, press F5 (or select **Run Module** from IDLE's **Run** menu) to try out this version of your code:

```
>>> ============================ RESTART ============================
>>>
Man said:  Is this the right room for an argument?
Other Man said:  I've told you once.
Man said:  No you haven't!
Other Man said:  Yes I have.
Man said:  When?
Other Man said:  Just now.
   ...
Other Man said:  Anyway, I did.
Man said:  You most certainly did not!
Other Man said:  Now let's get one thing quite clear: I most definitely told you!
Man said:  Oh no you didn't!
Other Man said:  Oh yes I did!
Man said:  Oh no you didn't!
Other Man said:  Oh yes I did!
Man said:  Oh look, this isn't an argument!
Traceback (most recent call last):
  File "/Users/barryp/HeadFirstPython/chapter4/sketch.py", line 5, in <module>
    (role, line_spoken) = each_line.split(':', 1)
ValueError: need more than 1 value to unpack
```

The displayed output is abridged to allow the important stuff to fit on this page.

Cool. You made it past the line with two colons...

...but your joy is short lived. There's ANOTHER ValueError!!

That's enough to ruin your day. What could be wrong now?

Know your data (better)

Your code has raised another `ValueError`, but this time, instead of complaining that there are "too many values," the Python interpreter is complaining that it doesn't have enough data to work with: "need more than 1 value to unpack." Hopefully, another quick look at the data will clear up the mystery of the missing data.

```
Other Man: Now let's get one thing quite clear: I most definitely told you!
Man: Oh no you didn't!
Other Man: Oh yes I did!
Man: Oh no you didn't!
Other Man: Oh yes I did!
Man: Oh look, this isn't an argument!
(pause)
Other Man: Yes it is!
Man: No it isn't!
(pause)
Man: It's just contradiction!
Other Man: No it isn't!
```

What's this?!? Some of the data doesn't conform to the expected format...which can't be good.

The case of the missing colon

Some of the lines of data contain no colon, which causes a problem when the `split()` method goes looking for it. The lack of a colon prevents `split()` from doing its job, causes the runtime error, which then results in the complaint that the interpreter needs "more than 1 value."

> It looks like you still have problems with the data in your file. What a shame it's not in a standard format.

Two very different approaches

When you have to deal with a bunch of exceptional situations, the best approach is to add extra logic. If there's more stuff to worry about, you need more code.

Or you could decide to let the errors occur, then simply handle each error if and when it happens. That would be exceptional.

Jill

Joe

Jill's suggested approach certainly works: add the extra logic required to work out whether it's worth invoking split() on the line of data. All you need to do is work out how to check the line of data.

Joe's approach works, too: let the error occur, spot that it has happened, and then recover from the runtime error...somehow.

Which approach works best here?

Add extra logic

Let's try *each* approach, then decide which works best here.

In addition to the `split()` method, every Python string has the `find()` method, too. You can ask `find()` to try and locate a substring in another string, and if it can't be found, the `find()` method returns the value −1. If the method locates the substring, `find()` returns the index position of the substring in the string.

 An IDLE Session

Assign a string to the `each_line` variable that does not contain a colon, and then use the `find()` method to try and locate a colon:

```
>>> each_line = "I tell you, there's no such thing as a flying circus."
>>> each_line.find(':')
-1
```

−1 ← ──────── The string does NOT contain a colon, so "find()" returns −1 for NOT FOUND.

Press **Alt-P** *twice* to recall the line of code that assigns the string to the variable, but this time edit the string to include a colon, then use the `find()` method to try to locate the colon:

```
>>> each_line = "I tell you: there's no such thing as a flying circus."
>>> each_line.find(':')
10
```

10 ← ──────────── The string DOES contain a colon, so "find()" returns a positive index value.

> And you thought this approach wouldn't work? Based on this IDLE session, I think this could do the trick.

Exercise

Adjust your code to use the extra logic technique demonstrated on the previous page to deal with lines that don't contain a colon character.

```
data = open('sketch.txt')

for each_line in data:
    if ..............................................................................
        (role, line_spoken) = each_line.split(':', 1)
        print(role, end='')
        print(' said: ', end='')
        print(line_spoken, end='')

data.close()
```

What condition needs to go here?

Sharpen your pencil

Can you think of any potential problems with this technique?
Grab your pencil and write down any issues you might have with this approach in the space provided below:

....

....

....

....

....

....

....

....

....

....

....

....

Exercise Solution

You were to adjust your code to use the extra logic technique to deal with lines that don't contain a colon character:

```
data = open('sketch.txt')

for each_line in data:
    if not each_line.find(':') == -1:
        (role, line_spoken) = each_line.split(':', 1)
        print(role, end='')
        print(' said: ', end='')
        print(line_spoken, end='')

data.close()
```

It takes a few seconds to get your head around this condition, but it does work.

Note the use of the "not" keyword, which negates the value of the condition.

Sharpen your pencil Solution

You were to think of any potential problems with this technique, grabbing your pencil to write down any issues you might have with this approach.

It's OK if your issues are different. Just so long as they are similar to these.

There might be a problem with this code if the format of the data file changes, which will require changes to the condition.

The condition used by the if statement is somewhat hard to read and understand.

This code is a little "fragile"...it will break if another exceptional situation arises.

Test Drive

Amend your code within IDLE's edit window, and press F5 to see if it works.

```
○○○                              Python Shell
>>> ================================ RESTART ================================
>>>
Man said:  Is this the right room for an argument?
Other Man said:  I've told you once.
Man said:  No you haven't!
Other Man said:  Yes I have.
Man said:  When?
Other Man said:  Just now.
Man said:  No you didn't!
Other Man said:  Yes I did!
Man said:  You didn't!
Other Man said:  I'm telling you, I did!
Man said:  You did not!
Other Man said:  Oh I'm sorry, is this a five minute argument, or the full half hour?
Man said:  Ah! (taking out his wallet and paying) Just the five minutes.
Other Man said:  Just the five minutes. Thank you.
Other Man said:  Anyway, I did.
Man said:  You most certainly did not!
Other Man said:  Now let's get one thing quite clear: I most definitely told you!
Man said:  Oh no you didn't!
Other Man said:  Oh yes I did!
Man said:  Oh no you didn't!
Other Man said:  Oh yes I did!
Man said:  Oh look, this isn't an argument!
Other Man said:  Yes it is!
Man said:  No it isn't!
Man said:  It's just contradiction!
Other Man said:  No it isn't!
Man said:  It IS!
Other Man said:  It is NOT!
Man said:  You just contradicted me!
Other Man said:  No I didn't!
Man said:  You DID!
Other Man said:  No no no!
Man said:  You did just then!
Other Man said:  Nonsense!
Man said:  (exasperated) Oh, this is futile!!
Other Man said:  No it isn't!
Man said:  Yes it is!
>>> |
                                                          Ln: 149 Col: 4
```

No errors this time.

Your program works…although it is **fragile**.

If the format of the file changes, your code will need to change, too, and *more code* generally means *more complexity*. Adding extra logic to handle exceptional situations works, but it might cost you in the long run.

Maybe it's time for a different approach? One that doesn't require extra logic, eh?

Handle exceptions

Have you noticed that when something goes wrong with your code, the Python interpreter displays a *traceback* followed by an error message?

The **traceback** is Python's way of telling you that something *unexpected* has occurred during runtime. In the Python world, runtime errors are called **exceptions**.

Whoooah! I don't know what to do with this error, so I'm gonna raise an exception...this really is someone else's problem.

Oooh, yuck! It looks like there's a bug.

```
>>> if not each_
Traceback (most r
    File "<pyshell
    (role, line_
ValueError: too m
```

Of course, if you decide to *ignore* an exception when it occurs, your program crashes and burns.

But here's the skinny: Python let's you *catch* exceptions as they occur, which gives you with a chance to possibly recover from the error and, critically, **not** crash.

By controlling the runtime behavior of your program, you can ensure (as much as possible) that your Python programs are robust in the face of *most* runtime errors.

Try the code first. Then deal with errors as they happen.

Try first, then recover

Rather than adding extra code and logic to guard against bad things happening, Python's **exception handling** mechanism lets the error occur, spots that it has happened, and then gives you an opportunity to recover.

During the *normal flow of control*, Python tries your code and, if nothing goes wrong, your code continues as normal. During the *exceptional flow of control*, Python tries your code only to have something go wrong, your recovery code executes, and then your code continues as normal.

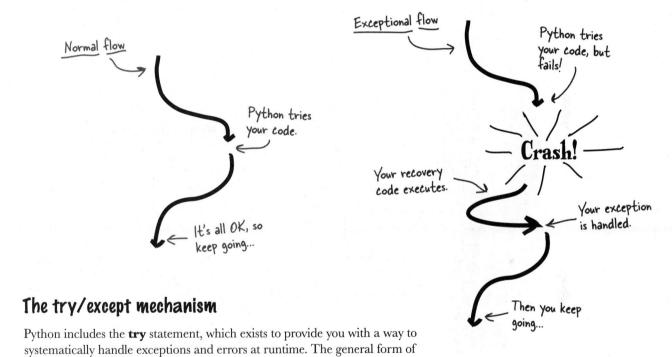

The try/except mechanism

Python includes the **try** statement, which exists to provide you with a way to systematically handle exceptions and errors at runtime. The general form of the **try** statement looks like this:

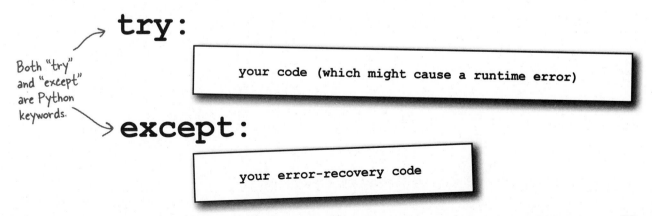

Both "try" and "except" are Python keywords.

```
try:
```
your code (which might cause a runtime error)

```
except:
```
your error-recovery code

Hang on, here! Are you actually letting errors occur on purpose? ARE YOU MAD?!?

No. Not mad. And, yes. Letting errors occur.

If you try to code for every possible error, you'll be at it for a long time, because all that extra logic takes a while to work out.

Paradoxically, when you worry less about covering *every* possible error condition, your coding task actually gets *easier*.

Identify the code to protect

In order to plug into the Python exception handling mechanism, take a
moment to identify the code that you need to *protect*.

✏️ Sharpen your pencil

Study your program and circle the line or lines of code that you
think you need to protect. Then, in the space provided, state why.

```
data = open('sketch.txt')

for each_line in data:
        (role, line_spoken) = each_line.split(':', 1)
        print(role, end='')
        print(' said: ', end='')
        print(line_spoken, end='')

data.close()
```

*State your reason
why here.*

....
....
....
....
....

there are no Dumb Questions

Q: Something has been bugging me for a while. When the split() method executes, it passes back a list, but the target identifiers are enclosed in regular brackets, not square brackets, so how is this a list?

A: Well spotted. It turns out that there are **two** types of list in Python: those that can change (enclosed in square brackets) and those that cannot be changed once they have been created (enclosed in regular brackets). The latter is an *immutable* list, more commonly referred to as a *tuple*. Think of tuples as the same as a list, except for one thing: once created, the data they hold **cannot** be changed under any circumstances. Another way to think about tuples is to consider them to be a *constant list*. At Head First, we pronounce "tuple" to rhyme with "couple." Others pronounce "tuple" to rhyme with "rupal." There is no clear concensus as to which is correct, so pick one and stick to it.

Sharpen your pencil
Solution

You were to study your program and circle the line or lines of code that you think you need to protect. Then, in the space provided, you were to state why.

```
data = open('sketch.txt')

for each_line in data:
        (role, line_spoken) = each_line.split(':', 1)
        print(role, end='')
        print(' said: ', end='')
        print(line_spoken, end='')

data.close()
```

These four lines of code all need to be protected.

If the call to "split()" fails, you don't want the three "print()" statements executing, so it's best to protect all four lines of the "if" suite, not just the line of code that calls "split()".

OK. I get that the code can be protected from an error. But what do I do when an error actually occurs?

Yeah...good point. It's probably best to ignore it, right? I wonder how...

Take a pass on the error

With this data (and this program), it is best if you ignore lines that don't conform to the expected format. If the call to the `split()` method causes an exception, let's simply **pass** on reporting it as an error.

When you have a situation where you might be expected to provide code, but don't need to, use Python's `pass` statement (which you can think of as the *empty* or *null* statement.)

Here's the `pass` statement combined with `try`:

```
data = open('sketch.txt')

for each_line in data:
    try:
        (role, line_spoken) = each_line.split(':', 1)
        print(role, end='')
        print(' said: ', end='')
        print(line_spoken, end='')
    except:
        pass

data.close()
```

This code is protected from runtime errors.

If a runtime error occurs, this code is executed.

Now, no matter what happens when the `split()` method is invoked, the `try` statement *catches* any and all exceptions and *handles* them by ignoring the error with `pass`.

Let's see this code in action.

Do this!

Make the required changes to your code in the IDLE edit window.

An IDLE Session

With your code in the IDLE edit window, press F5 to run it.

```
○ ○ ○   sketch-try.py – /Users/barryp/HeadFirstPython/chapter4/sketch-try.py

data = open('sketch.txt')

for each_line in data:
    try:
        (role, line_spoken) = each_line.split(':', 1)
        print(role, end='')
        print(' said: ', end='')
        print(line_spoken, end='')
    except:
        pass

data.close()

                                                          Ln: 14 Col: 0
```

```
>>> =============================== RESTART ================================
>>>
Man said:  Is this the right room for an argument?
Other Man said:  I've told you once.
Man said:  No you haven't!
Other Man said:  Yes I have.
Man said:  When?
    ...
OOther Man said:  Nonsense!
Man said:  (exasperated) Oh, this is futile!!
Other Man said:  No it isn't!
Man said:  Yes it is!
```

This code works, and there are no runtime errors, either.

So...both approaches work. But which is better?

Fireside Chats

Tonight's talk: **Approaching runtime errors with extra code and exception handlers**

Extra Code:	**Exception Handler:**
By making sure runtime errors never happen, I keep my code safe from tracebacks.	
Complexity never hurt anyone.	At the cost of added complexity….
	I'll be sure to remind you of that the next time you're debugging a complex piece of code at 4 o'clock in the morning.
I just don't get it. You're more than happy for your code to explode in your face…then you decide it's probably a good idea to put out the fire?!?	
	Yes. I concentrate on getting my work done first and foremost. If bad things happen, I'm ready for them.
But the bad things *still* happen to you. They never happen with me, because I don't let them.	Until something else happens that you weren't expecting. Then you're toast.
Well…that depends. If you're smart enough—and, believe me, I am—you can think up all the possible runtime problems and code around them.	
	Sounds like a whole heap of extra work to me.
Hard work never hurt anyone.	You did hear me earlier about debugging at 4 AM, right? Sometimes I think you actually enjoy writing code that you don't need…
Of course all my code is needed! How else can you code around all the runtime errors that are going to happen?	
Um, uh…most of them, I guess.	Yeah…how many?
	You don't know, do you? You've no idea what will happen when an unknown or unexpected runtime error occurs, do you?
Look: just cut it out. OK?	

What about other errors?

It is true that both approaches work, but let's consider what happens when other errors surface.

Handling missing files

Frank's posed an interesting question and, sure enough, the problem caused by the removal of the data file makes life more complex for Jill and Joe. When the data file is missing, *both* versions of the program crash with an IOError.

Rename the data file, then run both versions of your program again to confirm that they do indeed raise an IOError and generate a traceback.

Add more error-checking code...

If you're a fan of the "let's not let errors happen" school of thinking, your first reaction will be to *add extra code* to check to see if the data file exists before you try to open it, right?

Let's implement this strategy. Python's os module has some facilities that can help determine whether a data file exists, so we need to import it from the Standard Library, then add the required check to the code:

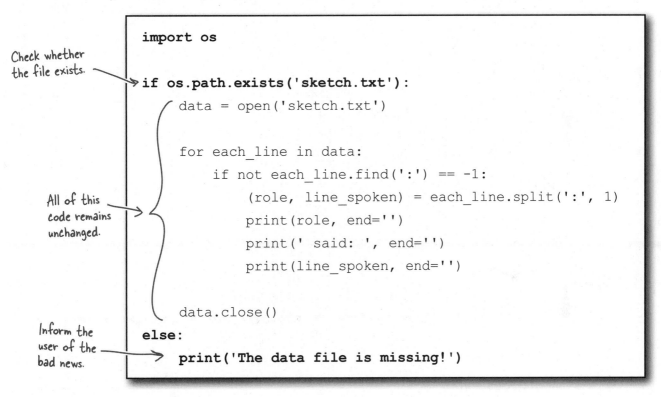

Check whether the file exists.

All of this code remains unchanged.

Inform the user of the bad news.

```python
import os

if os.path.exists('sketch.txt'):
    data = open('sketch.txt')

    for each_line in data:
        if not each_line.find(':') == -1:
            (role, line_spoken) = each_line.split(':', 1)
            print(role, end='')
            print(' said: ', end='')
            print(line_spoken, end='')

    data.close()
else:
    print('The data file is missing!')
```

 An IDLE Session

A quick test of the code confirms that this new problem is dealt with properly. With this new version of your code in IDLE's edit window, press F5 to confirm all is OK.

```
>>> =============================== RESTART ===============================
>>>
The data file is missing!        ← Exactly what was expected. Cool.
>>>
```

...Or add another level of exception handling

If you are a fan of the "handle exceptions as they occur" school of thinking, you'll simply wrap your code within another **try** statement.

Add another
"try" statement.

As with the
other program,
all of this
code remains
unchanged.

Give the user
the bad news.

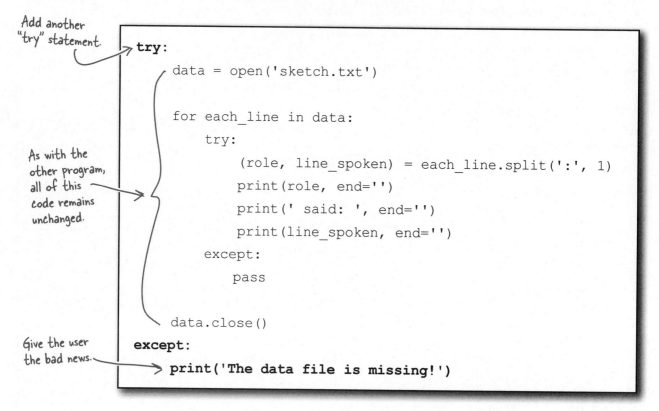

```
try:
    data = open('sketch.txt')

    for each_line in data:
        try:
            (role, line_spoken) = each_line.split(':', 1)
            print(role, end='')
            print(' said: ', end='')
            print(line_spoken, end='')
        except:
            pass

    data.close()
except:
    print('The data file is missing!')
```

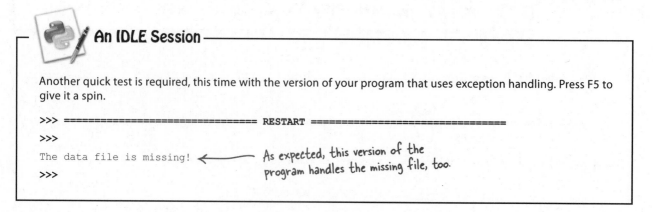

An IDLE Session

Another quick test is required, this time with the version of your program that uses exception handling. Press F5 to give it a spin.

```
>>> =============================== RESTART ===============================
>>>
The data file is missing!
>>>
```

As expected, this version of the
program handles the missing file, too.

So, which approach is best?

Well…it depends on who you ask! Here are both versions of your code:

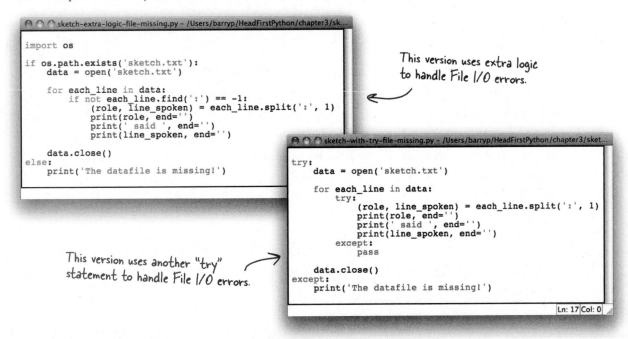

```
import os

if os.path.exists('sketch.txt'):
    data = open('sketch.txt')

    for each_line in data:
        if not each_line.find(':') == -1:
            (role, line_spoken) = each_line.split(':', 1)
            print(role, end='')
            print(' said ', end='')
            print(line_spoken, end='')

    data.close()
else:
    print('The datafile is missing!')
```

This version uses extra logic to handle File I/O errors.

```
try:
    data = open('sketch.txt')

    for each_line in data:
        try:
            (role, line_spoken) = each_line.split(':', 1)
            print(role, end='')
            print(' said ', end='')
            print(line_spoken, end='')
        except:
            pass

    data.close()
except:
    print('The datafile is missing!')
```

Ln: 17 Col: 0

This version uses another "try" statement to handle File I/O errors.

Let's ask a simple question about these two versions of your program: *What do each of these programs do?*

Sharpen your pencil

Grab your pencil. In box 1, write down what you think the program on the left does. In box 2, write down what you think the program on the right does.

1 ....

....

....

2 ....

....

....

Sharpen your pencil
Solution

There's a lot to write, so you actually need more space for your description than was provided on the previous page.

You were to grab your pencil, then in box 1, write down what you thought the program on the left does. In box 2, write down what you thought the program on the right does.

1 The code on the right starts by importing the "os" library, and then it uses "path.exists" to make sure the data file exists, before it attempts to open the data file. Each line from the file is then processed, but only after it has determined that the line conforms to the required format by checking first for a single ":" character in the line. If the ":" is found, the line is processed; otherwise, it's ignored. When we're all done, the data file is closed. And you get a friendly message at the end if the file is not found.

Now...that's more like it.

2 The code on the right opens a data file, processes each line in that file, extracts the data of interest and displays it on screen. The file is closed when done. If any exceptions occur, this code handles them.

Complexity is rarely a good thing

Do you see what's happening here?

As the list of errors that you have to worry about grows, the **complexity** of the "add extra code and logic" solution increases to the point where it starts to *obscure the actual purpose of the program*.

This is not the case with the exceptions handling solution, in which it's *obvious* what the main purpose of the program is.

By using Python's exception-handling mechanism, you get to concentrate on what your code *needs to do*, as opposed to worrying about what can go wrong and writing extra code to avoid runtime errors.

Prudent use of the `try` statement leads to code that is easier to read, easier to write, and—perhaps most important—easier to fix when something goes wrong.

Concentrate on what your code needs to do.

You're done...except for one small thing

Your exception-handling code is good. In fact, your code might be *too good* in that it is *too general*.

At the moment, no matter what error occurs at runtime, it is handled by your code because it's *ignored* or a error message is *displayed*. But you really need to worry only about IOErrors and ValueErrors, because those are the types of exceptions that occurred earlier when your were developing your program.

Although it is great to be able to handle all runtime errors, it's probably unwise to be too generic...you will want to know if something other than an IOError or ValueError occurs as a result of your code executing at runtime. If something else does happen, your code might be handling it in an *inappropriate* way.

```python
try:
    data = open('sketch.txt')

    for each_line in data:
        try:
            (role, line_spoken) = each_line.split(':', 1)
            print(role, end='')
            print(' said: ', end='')
            print(line_spoken, end='')
        except:
            pass

    data.close()
except:
    print('The data file is missing!')
```

This code and this code runs when ANY runtime error occurs within the code that is being tried.

As your code is currently written, it is too generic. Any runtime error that occurs is handled by one of the except suites. This is unlikely to be what you want, because this code has the potential to *silently ignore runtime errors*.

You need to somehow use except in a less generic way.

Be specific with your exceptions

If your exception-handling code is designed to deal with a specific type of
error, be sure to specify the error type on the except line. In doing so, you'll
take your exception handling code from *generic* to *specific*.

```
try:

    data = open('sketch.txt')

    for each_line in data:
        try:
            (role, line_spoken) = each_line.split(':', 1)
            print(role, end='')
            print(' said: ', end='')
            print(line_spoken, end='')
        except ValueError:
            pass

    data.close()
except IOError:
    print('The data file is missing!')
```

Specify the type of runtime error you are handling.

Of course, if an *different* type of runtime error occurs, it is no longer handled
by your code, but at least now you'll get to hear about it. When you are
specific about the runtime errors your code handles, your programs no longer
silently ignore some runtime errors.

Using "try/except"
lets you concentrate
on what your code
needs to do...

...and it lets you avoid
adding unnecessary code
and logic to your programs.
That works for me!

Your Python Toolbox

You've got Chapter 3 under your belt and you've added some key Python techiques to your toolbox.

BULLET POINTS

- Use the `open()` BIF to open a disk file, creating an iterator that reads data from the file one line at a time.

- The `readline()` method reads a single line from an opened file.

- The `seek()` method can be used to "rewind" a file to the beginning.

- The `close()` method closes a previously opened file.

- The `split()` method can break a string into a list of parts.

- An unchangeable, constant list in Python is called a **tuple**. Once list data is assigned to a tuple, it cannot be changed. Tuples are *immutable*.

- A `ValueError` occurs when your data does not conform to an expected format.

- An `IOError` occurs when your data cannot be accessed properly (e.g., perhaps your data file has been moved or renamed).

- The `help()` BIF provides access to Python's documentation within the IDLE shell.

- The `find()` method locates a specific substring within another string.

- The `not` keyword negates a condition.

- The `try`/`except` statement provides an exception-handling mechanism, allowing you to protect lines of code that might result in a runtime error.

- The `pass` statement is Python's empty or null statement; it does nothing.

Python Lingo

- An "exception" occurs as a result of a runtime error, producing a traceback.

- A "traceback" is a detailed description of the runtime error that has occurred.

IDLE Notes

- Access Python's documentation by choosing Python Docs from IDLE's Help menu. The Python 3 documentation set should open in your favorite web browser.

4 persistence

Saving data to files

I'm in a bit of a pickle...my data is not as persistent as it could be.

It is truly great to be able to process your file-based data.

But what happens to your data when you're done? Of course, it's best to save your data to a disk file, which allows you to use it again at some later date and time. Taking your memory-based data and storing it to disk is what **persistence** is all about. Python supports all the usual tools for writing to files and also provides some cool facilities for *efficiently* storing Python data. So…flip the page and let's get started learning them.

Programs produce data

It's a rare program that reads data from a disk file, processes the data, and then throws away the processed data. Typically, programs **save** the data they process, **display** their output on screen, or **transfer** data over a network.

Before you learn what's involved in writing data to disk, let's process the data from the previous chapter to work out who said what to whom.

When that's done, you'll have something worth saving.

Code Magnets

Add the code magnets at the bottom of this page to your existing code to satisfy the following requirements:

1. Create an empty list called man.
2. Create an empty list called other.
3. Add a line of code to remove unwanted whitespace from the line_spoken variable.
4. Provide the conditions and code to add line_spoken to the correct list based on the value of role.
5. Print each of the lists (man and other) to the screen.

```
..........................
..........................
try:
    data = open('sketch.txt')
    for each_line in data:
        try:
            (role, line_spoken) = each_line.split(':', 1)

            ................................................................
            ........................................
            ..................................................
            ........................................
            ..................................................

        except ValueError:
            pass
    data.close()
except IOError:
    print('The datafile is missing!')

..........................
..........................
```

Here are your magnets.

```
elif role == 'Other Man':
if role == 'Man':
man = []
line_spoken = line_spoken.strip()
other = []
other.append(line_spoken)
man.append(line_spoken)
print(man)
print(other)
```

Code Magnets Solution

Your were to add the code magnets to your existing code to satisfy the following requirements:

1. Create an empty list called man.
2. Create an empty list called other.
3. Add a line of code to remove unwanted whitespace from the line_spoken variable.
4. Provide the conditions and code to add line_spoken to the correct list based on the value of role.
5. Print each of the lists (man and other) to the screen.

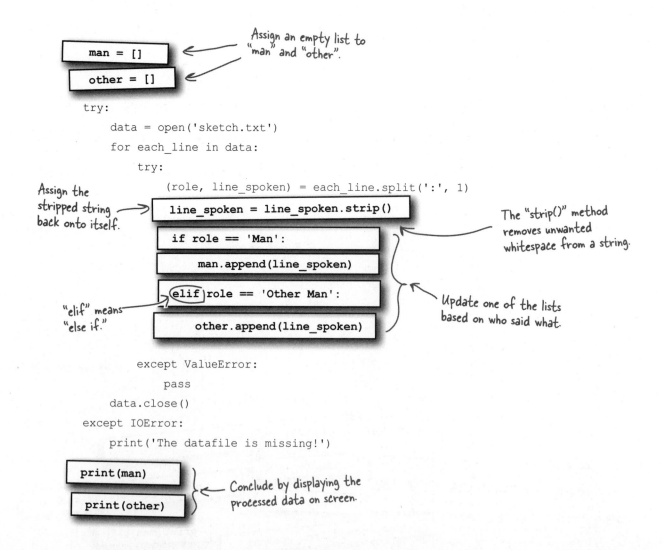

Assign an empty list to "man" and "other".

```
man = []

other = []
try:
    data = open('sketch.txt')
    for each_line in data:
        try:
            (role, line_spoken) = each_line.split(':', 1)
            line_spoken = line_spoken.strip()
            if role == 'Man':
                man.append(line_spoken)
            elif role == 'Other Man':
                other.append(line_spoken)
        except ValueError:
            pass
    data.close()
except IOError:
    print('The datafile is missing!')

print(man)
print(other)
```

Assign the stripped string back onto itself.

The "strip()" method removes unwanted whitespace from a string.

"elif" means "else if."

Update one of the lists based on who said what.

Conclude by displaying the processed data on screen.

Test Drive

Load your code into IDLE's edit window and take it for a spin by pressing F5. Be sure to save your program into the same folder that contains `sketch.txt`.

```
2-open-into-lists-cleaned-up.py - /Users/barryp/HeadFirstPython/chapter4/2-o...

man = []
other = []

try:
    data = open('sketch.txt')

    for each_line in data:
        try:
            (role, line_spoken) = each_line.split(':', 1)
            line_spoken = line_spoken.strip()
            if role == 'Man':
                man.append(line_spoken)
            elif role == 'Other Man':
                other.append(line_spoken)
        except ValueError:
            pass

    data.close()
except IOError:
    print('The datafile is missing!')

print(man)
print(other)
```

The code in IDLE's edit window

```
Python Shell

Python 3.1.2 (r312:79360M, Mar 24 2010, 01:33:18)
[GCC 4.0.1 (Apple Inc. build 5493)] on darwin
Type "copyright", "credits" or "license()" for more information.
>>> ================================ RESTART ================================
>>>
['Is this the right room for an argument?', "No you haven't!", 'When?', "No yo
u didn't!", "You didn't!", 'You did not!', 'Ah! (taking out his wallet and pay
ing) Just the five minutes.', 'You most certainly did not!', "Oh no you didn't
!", "Oh no you didn't!", "Oh look, this isn't an argument!", "No it isn't!", "
It's just contradiction!", 'It IS!', 'You just contradicted me!', 'You DID!',
'You did just then!', '(exasperated) Oh, this is futile!!', 'Yes it is!']
["I've told you once.", 'Yes I have.', 'Just now.', 'Yes I did!', "I'm telling
you, I did!", "Oh I'm sorry, is this a five minute argument, or the full half
hour?", 'Just the five minutes. Thank you.', 'Anyway, I did.', "Now let's get
one thing quite clear: I most definitely told you!", 'Oh yes I did!', 'Oh yes
I did!', 'Yes it is!', "No it isn't!", 'It is NOT!', "No I didn't!", 'No no no
!', 'Nonsense!', "No it isn't!"]
>>>

Ln: 8 Col: 4
```

And here's what appears on screen: the contents of the two lists.

It worked, as expected.

Surely Python's open() BIF can open files for writing as well as reading, eh?

Yes, it can.

When you need to **save** data to a file, the open() BIF is all you need.

Open your file in write mode

When you use the open() BIF to work with a disk file, you can specify an *access mode* to use. By default, open() uses mode r for *reading*, so you don't need to specify it. To open a file for *writing*, use mode w:

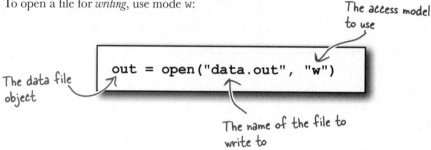

The access model to use

The data file object

The name of the file to write to

By default, the print() BIF uses standard output (usually the screen) when displaying data. To write data to a file instead, use the file argument to specify the data file object to use:

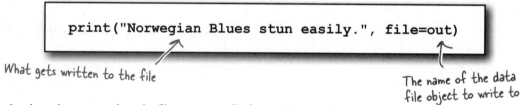

```
print("Norwegian Blues stun easily.", file=out)
```

What gets written to the file

The name of the data file object to write to

When you're done, be sure to close the file to ensure all of your data is written to disk. This is known as **flushing** and is very important:

```
out.close()
```

This is VERY important when writing to files.

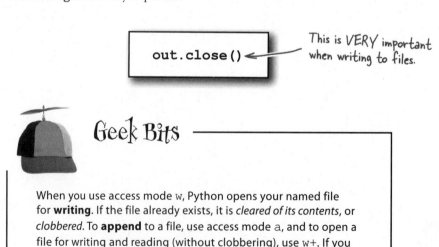

Geek Bits

When you use access mode w, Python opens your named file for **writing**. If the file already exists, it is *cleared of its contents*, or *clobbered*. To **append** to a file, use access mode a, and to open a file for writing and reading (without clobbering), use w+. If you try to open a file for writing that does not already exist, it is first created for you, and then opened for writing.

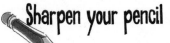
Sharpen your pencil

At the bottom of your program, two calls to the `print()` BIF display your processed data on screen. Let's amend this code to save the data to two disk files instead.

Call your disk files `man_data.txt` (for what the man said) and `other_data.txt` (for what the other man said). Be sure to both **open** and **close** your data files, as well as protect your code against an `IOError` using **try/except**.

```
man = []
other = []


try:
    data = open('sketch.txt')
    for each_line in data:
        try:
            (role, line_spoken) = each_line.split(':', 1)
            line_spoken = line_spoken.strip()
            if role == 'Man':
                man.append(line_spoken)
            elif role == 'Other Man':
                other.append(line_spoken)
        except ValueError:
            pass
    data.close()
except IOError:
    print('The datafile is missing!')
```

Go on, try.
↳..........

....
.... }← Open your two data files here.

```
print(man, ...........................)
print(other, ..........................)
```
}← Specify the files to write to when you invoke "print()".

Be sure to close your files. ↘ { ....
....

....
.... ← Handle any exceptions here.

Sharpen your pencil
Solution

At the bottom of your program, two calls to the `print()` BIF display your processed data on screen. You were to amend this code to save the data to two disk files instead.

You were to call your disk files `man_data.txt` (for what the man said) and `other_data.txt` (for what the other man said). You were to make sure to both **open** and **close** your data files, as well as protect your code against an `IOError` using **try/except**.

```python
man = []
other = []

try:
    data = open('sketch.txt')
    for each_line in data:
        try:
            (role, line_spoken) = each_line.split(':', 1)
            line_spoken = line_spoken.strip()
            if role == 'Man':
                man.append(line_spoken)
            elif role == 'Other Man':
                other.append(line_spoken)
        except ValueError:
            pass
    data.close()
except IOError:
    print('The datafile is missing!')
```

All of this code is unchanged.

```python
try:
    man_file = open('man_data.txt', 'w')
    other_file = open('other_data.txt', 'w')

    print(man, file=man_file )
    print(other, file=other_file )

    man_file.close()
    other_file.close()
except IOError:
    print('File error.')
```

Did you remember to open your files in WRITE mode?

Open your two files, and assign each to file objects.

Use the "print()" BIF to save the named lists to named disk files.

Don't forget to close BOTH files.

Handle an I/O exception, should one occur.

TEST DRIVE

Perform the edits to your code to replace your two `print()` calls with your new file I/O code. Then, run your program to confirm that the data files are created:

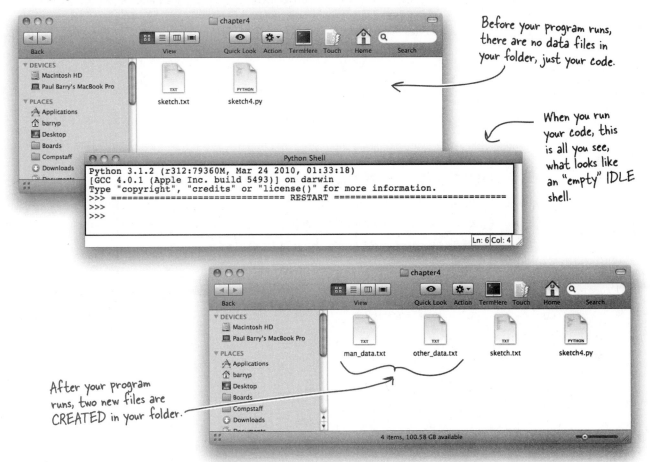

Before your program runs, there are no data files in your folder, just your code.

When you run your code, this is all you see, what looks like an "empty" IDLE shell.

After your program runs, two new files are CREATED in your folder.

That code worked, too. You've created two data files, each holding the data from each of your lists. Go ahead and open these files in your favorite editor to confirm that they contain the data you expect.

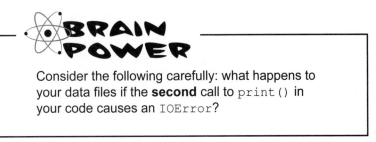

BRAIN POWER

Consider the following carefully: what happens to your data files if the **second** call to `print()` in your code causes an `IOError`?

you are here ▸ **113**

Files are left open after an exception!

When all you ever do is read data from files, getting an `IOError` is annoying, but rarely dangerous, because your data is still in your file, even though you might be having trouble getting at it.

It's a different story when writing data to files: if you need to handle an `IOError` *before* a file is closed, your written data might become corrupted and there's no way of telling until *after* it has happened.

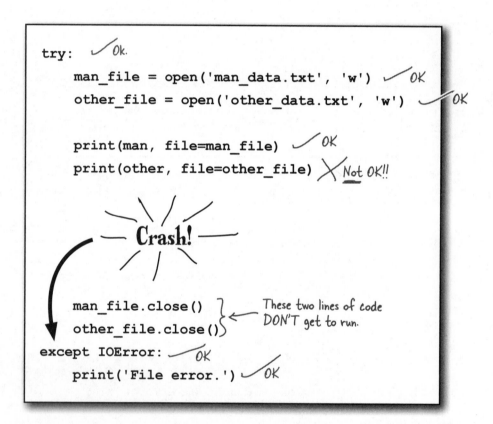

```
try:          ✓ Ok.
    man_file = open('man_data.txt', 'w')      ✓ OK
    other_file = open('other_data.txt', 'w')      ✓ OK

    print(man, file=man_file)      ✓ OK
    print(other, file=other_file)   ✗ Not OK!!

                    — Crash! —

    man_file.close()        ⎤  These two lines of code
    other_file.close()      ⎦  DON'T get to run.
except IOError:   ✓ OK
    print('File error.')   ✓ OK
```

Your exception-handling code is doing its job, but you now have a situation where your data could *potentially* be corrupted, which can't be good.

What's needed here is something that lets you run some code regardless of whether an `IOError` has occured. In the context of your code, you'll want to make sure the files are closed *no matter what*.

Extend try with finally

When you have a situation where code must *always* run no matter what errors occur, add that code to your try statement's finally suite:

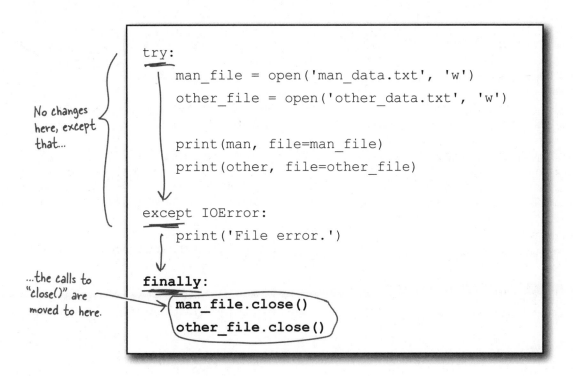

No changes here, except that...

...the calls to "close()" are moved to here.

```
try:
    man_file = open('man_data.txt', 'w')
    other_file = open('other_data.txt', 'w')

    print(man, file=man_file)
    print(other, file=other_file)

except IOError:
    print('File error.')

finally:
    man_file.close()
    other_file.close()
```

If no runtime errors occur, any code in the finally suite executes. Equally, if an IOError occurs, the except suite executes and *then* the finally suite runs.

No matter what, the code in the finally suite *always* runs.

By moving your file closing code into your finally suite, you are reducing the possibility of data corruption errors.

This is a big improvement, because you're now ensuring that files are closed properly (even when write errors occur).

But what about *those* errors?

How do you find out the specifics of the error?

there are no
Dumb Questions

Q: I'm intrigued. When you stripped the line_spoken data of unwanted whitespace, you assigned the result back to the line_spoken variable. Surely invoking the strip() method on line_spoken changed the string it refers to?

A: No, that's not what happens. Strings in Python are *immutable*, which means that once a string is created, it **cannot** be changed.

Q: But you did change the line_spoken string by removing any unwanted whitespace, right?

A: Yes and no. What actually happens is that invoking the `strip()` method on the `line_spoken` string creates a new string with leading and trailing whitespace removed. The new string is then assigned to `line_spoken`, replacing the data that was referred to before. In effect, it is as if you changed `line_spoken`, when you've actually completely replaced the data it refers to.

Q: So what happens to the replaced data?

A: Python's built-in memory management technology reclaims the RAM it was using and makes it available to your program. That is, unless some other Python data object is also referring to the string.

Q: What? I don't get it.

A: It is conceivable that another data object is referring to the string referred to by `line_spoken`. For example, let's assume you have some code that contains two variables that refer to the same string, namely "Flying Circus." You then decide that one of the variables needs to be in all UPPERCASE, so you invoke the `upper()` method on it. The Python interperter takes a copy of the string, converts it to uppercase, and returns it to you. You can then assign the uppercase data back to the variable that used to refer to the original data.

Q: And the original data cannot change, because there's another variable referring to it?

A: Precisely. That's why strings are immutable, because you never know what other variables are referring to any particular string.

Q: But surely Python can work out how many variables are referring to any one particular string?

A: It does, but only for the purposes of garbage collection. If you have a line of code like `print('Flying Circus')`, the string is not referred to by a variable (so any variable reference counting that's going on isn't going to count it) but is still a valid string object (which might be referred to by a variable) and it cannot have its data changed under any circumstances.

Q: So Python variables don't actually contain the data assigned to them?

A: That's correct. Python variables contain a reference to a data object. The data object contains the data and, because you can conceivably have a string object used in many different places throughout your code, it is safest to make all strings immutable so that no nasty side effects occur.

Q: Isn't it a huge pain not being able to adjust strings "in place"?

A: No, not really. Once you get used to how strings work, it becomes less of an issue. In practice, you'll find that this issue rarely trips you up.

Q: Are any other Python data types immutable?

A: Yes, a few. There's the tuple, which is an immutable list. Also, all of the number types are immutable.

Q: Other than learning which is which, how will I know when something is immutable?

A: Don't worry: you'll know. If you try to change an immutable value, Python raises a `TypeError` exception.

Q: Of course: an exception occurs. They're everywhere in Python, aren't they?

A: Yes. Exceptions make the world go 'round.

Knowing the type of error is not enough

When a file I/O error occurs, your code displays a generic "File Error" message. This is too generic. How do you know what actually happened?

Maybe the problem is that you can't open the file?

It could be that the file can be opened but not written to?

Yeah, or it could be a permission error, or maybe your disk is full?

Who knows?

It turns out that the Python interpreter knows…and it will give up the details if only you'd ask.

When an error occurs at runtime, Python raises an exception of the specific type (such as `IOError`, `ValueError`, and so on). Additionally, Python creates an **exception object** that is passed *as an argument* to your **except** suite.

Let's use IDLE to see how this works.

An IDLE Session

Let's see what happens when you try to open a file that doesn't exist, such as a disk file called `missing.txt`. Enter the following code at IDLE's shell:

```
>>> try:
        data = open('missing.txt')
        print(data.readline(), end='')
except IOError:
        print('File error')
finally:
        data.close()
```

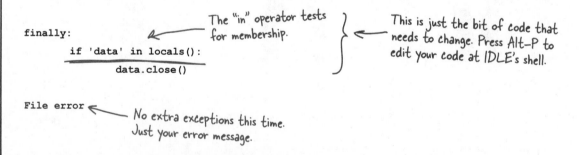

```
File error       ←——— There's your error message, but...
Traceback (most recent call last):
  File "<pyshell#8>", line 7, in <module>
    data.close()
NameError: name 'data' is not defined
```
...what's this?!? Another exception was raised and it killed your code.

As the file doesn't exist, the `data` file object **wasn't** created, which subsequently makes it impossible to call the `close()` method on it, so you end up with a `NameError`. A quick fix is to add a small test to the `finally` suite to see if the `data` name exists *before* you try to call `close()`. The `locals()` BIF returns a collection of names defined in the current scope. Let's exploit this BIF to only invoke `close()` when it is safe to do so:

```
finally:                    ←——— The "in" operator tests for membership.
        if 'data' in locals():
                data.close()
```
This is just the bit of code that needs to change. Press Alt-P to edit your code at IDLE's shell.

```
File error ←——
```
No extra exceptions this time. Just your error message.

Here you're searching the collection returned by the `locals()` BIF for the string `data`. If you find it, you can assume the file was opened successfully and safely call the `close()` method.

If some other error occurs (perhaps something awful happens when your code calls the `print()` BIF), your exception-handling code **catches** the error, **displays** your "File error" message and, finally, **closes** any opened file.

But you still are none the wiser as to *what actually caused the error.*

When an exception is raised and handled by your `except` suite, the Python interpreter passes an *exception object* into the suite. A small change makes this exception object available to your code as an identifier:

```
except IOError as err:
        print('File error: ' + err)
```

Give your exception object a name...

...then use it as part of your error message.

But when you try to run your code with this change made, another exception is raised:

```
Traceback (most recent call last):
  File "<pyshell#18>", line 5, in <module>
    print('File error:' + err)
TypeError: Can't convert 'IOError' object to str implicitly
```

Whoops! Yet another exception; this time it's a "TypeError".

This time your error message didn't appear *at all*. It turns out exception objects and strings are not *compatible* types, so trying to concatenate one with the other leads to problems. You can convert (or *cast*) one to the other using the `str()` BIF:

```
except IOError as err:
        print('File error: ' + str(err))
```

Use the "str()" BIF to force the exception object to behave like a string.

Now, with this final change, your code is behaving exactly as expected:

```
File error: [Errno 2] No such file or directory: 'missing.txt'
```

And you now get a specific error message that tells you exactly what went wrong.

Of course, all this extra logic is starting to obscure the real meaning of your code.

Wouldn't it be dreamy if there were a way to take advantage of these mechanisms without the code bloat? I guess it's just a fantasy...

Use with to work with files

Because the use of the **try/except/finally** pattern is so common when it comes to working with files, Python includes a statement that abstracts away some of the details. The `with` statement, when used with files, can dramatically reduce the amount of code you have to write, because it negates the need to include a `finally` suite to handle the closing of a *potentially* opened data file. Take a look:

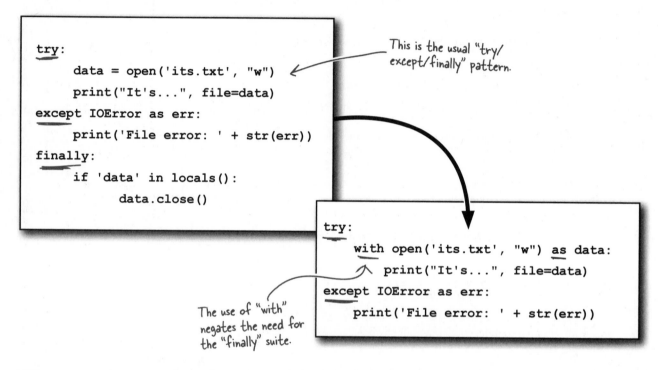

```python
try:
    data = open('its.txt', "w")
    print("It's...", file=data)
except IOError as err:
    print('File error: ' + str(err))
finally:
    if 'data' in locals():
        data.close()
```

This is the usual "try/except/finally" pattern.

```python
try:
    with open('its.txt', "w") as data:
        print("It's...", file=data)
except IOError as err:
    print('File error: ' + str(err))
```

The use of "with" negates the need for the "finally" suite.

When you use `with`, you no longer have to worry about closing any opened files, as the Python interpreter automatically takes care of this for you. The `with` code on the the right is *identical* in function to that on the left. At Head First Labs, we know which approach we prefer.

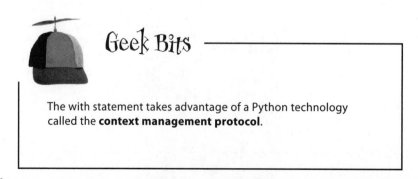

Geek Bits

The with statement takes advantage of a Python technology called the **context management protocol**.

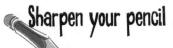

Sharpen your pencil

Grab your pencil and rewrite this **try/except/finally** code to use `with` instead. Here's your code with the appropriate `finally` suite added:

```python
try:
    man_file = open('man_data.txt', 'w')
    other_file = open('other_data.txt', 'w')

    print(man, file=man_file)
    print(other, file=other_file)
except IOError as err:
    print('File error: ' + str(err))
finally:
    if 'man_file' in locals():
        man_file.close()
    if 'other_file' in locals():
        other_file.close()
```

Write your "with" code here.

....

....

....

....

....

....

....

....

....

....

....

....

....

Sharpen your pencil
Solution

You were to grab your pencil and rewrite this **try/except/finally** code to use `with` instead. Here's your code with the appropriate `finally` suite added:

```
try:
    man_file = open('man_data.txt', 'w')
    other_file = open('other_data.txt', 'w')

    print(man, file=man_file)
    print(other, file=other_file)
except IOError as err:
    print('File error: ' + str(err))
finally:
    if 'man_file' in locals():
        man_file.close()
    if 'other_file' in locals():
        other_file.close()
```

```
try:
    with open('man_data.txt', 'w') as man_file:
        print(man, file=man_file)
        with open('other_data.txt', 'w') as other_file:
            print(other, file=other_file)
except IOError as err:
    print('File error: ' + str(err))
```

Using two "with" statements to rewrite the code without the "finally" suite.

Or combine the two "open()" calls into one "with" statement.

Note the use of the comma.

```
    with open('man_data.txt', 'w') as man_file, open('other_data.txt', 'w') as other_file:
        print(man, file=man_file)
        print(other, file=other_file)
```

Test Drive

Add your `with` code to your program, and let's confirm that it continues to function as expected. Delete the two data files you created with the previous version of your program and then load your newest code into IDLE and give it a spin.

No errors in the IDLE shell appears to indicate that the program ran successfully.

```
Python 3.1.2 (r312:79360M, Mar 24 2010, 01:33:18)
[GCC 4.0.1 (Apple Inc. build 5493)] on darwin
Type "copyright", "credits" or "license()" for more information.
>>> ================================ RESTART ================================
>>>
>>>
```

If you check your folder, your two data files should've reappeared. Let's take a closer look at the data file's contents by opening them in your favorite text editor (or use IDLE).

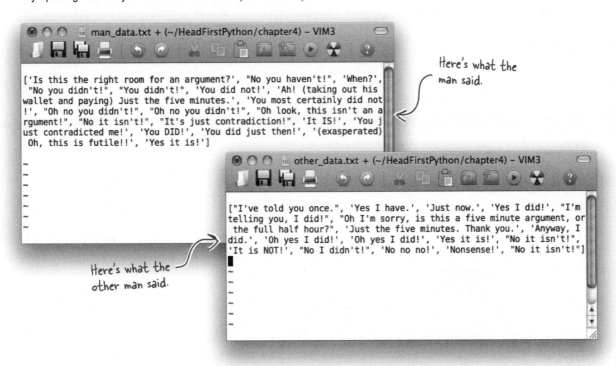

Here's what the man said.

```
['Is this the right room for an argument?', "No you haven't!", 'When?',
 "No you didn't!", "You didn't!", 'You did not!', 'Ah! (taking out his
wallet and paying) Just the five minutes.', 'You most certainly did not
!', "Oh no you didn't!", "Oh no you didn't!", "Oh look, this isn't an a
rgument!", "No it isn't!", "It's just contradiction!", 'It IS!', 'You j
ust contradicted me!', 'You DID!', 'You did just then!', '(exasperated)
 Oh, this is futile!!', 'Yes it is!']
```

Here's what the other man said.

```
["I've told you once.", 'Yes I have.', 'Just now.', 'Yes I did!', "I'm
telling you, I did!", "Oh I'm sorry, is this a five minute argument, or
 the full half hour?", 'Just the five minutes. Thank you.', 'Anyway, I
did.', 'Oh yes I did!', 'Oh yes I did!', 'Yes it is!', "No it isn't!",
'It is NOT!', "No I didn't!", 'No no no!', 'Nonsense!', "No it isn't!"]
```

You've saved the lists in two files containing what the *Man* said and what the *Other man* said. Your code is smart enough to handle any exceptions that Python or your operating system might throw at it.

Well done. This is really coming along.

Default formats are unsuitable for files

Although your data is now stored in a file, it's not really in a useful format.
Let's experiment in the IDLE shell to see what impact this can have.

An IDLE Session

Use a `with` statement to open your data file and display a single line from it:

```
>>> with open('man_data.txt') as mdf:
        print(mdf.readline())
```

Note: no need to close your file, because "with" does that for you.

```
['Is this the right room for an argument?', "No you haven't!", 'When?', "No you didn't!", "You
didn't!", 'You did not!', 'Ah! (taking out his wallet and paying) Just the five minutes.',
'You most certainly did not!', "Oh no you didn't!", "Oh no you didn't!", "Oh look, this isn't
an argument!", "No it isn't!", "It's just contradiction!", 'It IS!', 'You just contradicted
me!', 'You DID!', 'You did just then!', '(exasperated) Oh, this is futile!!', 'Yes it is!']
```

Yikes! It would appear your list is converted to a large string by `print()`
when it is saved. Your experimental code reads a single line of data from the
file and gets *all* of the data as one large chunk of text…so much for your code
saving your *list* data.

What are your options for dealing with this problem?

Geek Bits

By default, `print()` displays your data in a format that mimics
how your list data is actually stored by the Python interpreter.
The resulting output is not really meant to be processed further…
its primary purpose is to show you, the Python programmer,
what your list data "looks like" in memory.

> I guess I could write some custom parsing code to process the "internal format" used by "print()". It shouldn't take me all that long...

> It might be worth looking at using something other than a plain "print()" to format the data prior to saving it to the data file? I'd certainly look into it.

Parsing the data in the file is a possibility…although it's *complicated* by all those square brackets, quotes, and commas. Writing the required code is doable, but it is a lot of code just to read back in your saved data.

Of course, if the data is in a *more easily parseable format*, the task would likely be easier, so maybe the second option is worth considering, too?

BRAIN POWER

Can you think of a function you created from earlier in this book that might help here?

Why not modify print_lol()?

Recall your `print_lol()` function from Chapter 2, which takes any list (or list of lists) and displays it on screen, one line at a time. And nested lists can be indented, if necessary.

This functionality sounds perfect! Here's your code from the `nester.py` module (last seen at the end of Chapter 2):

```
nester.py – /Users/barryp/Downloads/nester-1.3.0/nester.py

"""This is the "nester.py" module and it provides one function called print_lol()
    which prints lists that may or may not include nested lists."""

def print_lol(the_list, indent=False, level=0):
    """ Prints a list of (possibly) nested lists.

        This function takes a positional argument called "the_list", which
        is any Python list (of - possibly - nested lists). Each data item in the
        provided list is (recursively) printed to the screen on it's own line.
        A second argument called "indent" controls whether or not indentation is
        shown on the display. This defaults to False: set it to True to switch on.
        A third argument called "level" (which defaults to 0) is used to insert
        tab-stops when a nested list is encountered."""

    for each_item in the_list:
        if isinstance(each_item, list):
            print_lol(each_item, indent, level+1)
        else:
            if indent:
                for tab_stop in range(level):
                    print("\t", end='')
            print(each_item)
```

`Ln: 24 Col: 0`

This code currently displays your data on the screen.

Amending this code to print to a disk file instead of the screen (known as *standard output*) should be relatively straightforward. You can then save your data in a more usable format.

the Scholar's Corner

Standard Output The default place where your code writes its data when the "print()" BIF is used. This is typically the screen. In Python, standard output is referred to as "sys.stdout" and is importable from the Standard Library's "sys" module.

① Exercise Let's add a fourth argument to your `print_lol()` function to identify a place to write your data to. Be sure to give your argument a default value of `sys.stdout`, so that it continues to write to the screen if no file object is specified when the function is invoked.

Fill in the blanks with the details of your new argument. (**Note:** to save on space, the comments have been removed from this cod, but be sure to update your comments in your `nester.py` module after you've amended your code.)

```
def print_lol(the_list, indent=False, level=0, .....................................):

    for each_item in the_list:
        if isinstance(each_item, list):
            print_lol(each_item, indent, level+1, ................)
        else:
            if indent:
                for tab_stop in range(level):
                    print("\t", end='', ...........................)
            print(each_item, .....................................)
```

② What needs to happen to the code in your `with` statement now that your amended `print_lol()` function is available to you?

....

....

....

③ List the name of the module(s) that you now need to import into your program in order to support your amendments to `print_lol()`.

....

....

Exercise
Solution

① You were to add a fourth argument to your `print_lol()` function to identify a place to write your data to, being sure to give your argument a default value of `sys.stdout` so that it continues to write to the screen if no file object is specified when the function is invoked.

You were to fill in the blanks with the details of your new argument. (**Note:** to save on space, the comments have been removed from this code, but be sure to update those in your `nester.py` module after you've amended your code).

Add the fourth argument and give it a default value.

```
def print_lol(the_list, indent=False, level=0,    fh=sys.stdout    ):

    for each_item in the_list:
        if isinstance(each_item, list):
            print_lol(each_item, indent, level+1,    fh    )
        else:
            if indent:
                for tab_stop in range(level):
                    print("\t", end='',    file=fh    )
            print(each_item,    file=fh    )
```

Note: the signature has changed.

Adjust the two calls to "print()" to use the new argument.

② What needs to happen to the code in your `with` statement now that your amended `print_lol()` function is available to you?

The code needs to be adjusted so that instead of using the "print()" BIF, the code needs to invoke "print_lol()" instead.

③ List the name of the module(s) that you now need to import into your program in order to support your amendments to `print_lol()`.

The program needs to import the amended "nester" module.

Before taking your code for a test drive, you need to do the following:

1. Make the necessary changes to `nester` and install the amended module into your Python environment (see Chapter 2 for a refresher on this). You might want to upload to PyPI, too.

2. Amend your program so that it imports `nester` and uses `print_lol()` instead of `print()` within your **with** statement. **Note:** your `print_lol()` invocation should look something like this:
   ```
   print_lol(man, fh=man_file).
   ```

When you are ready, take your latest program for a test drive and let's see what happens:

As before, there's no output on screen.

```
Python Shell

Python 3.1.2 (r312:79360M, Mar 24 2010, 01:33:18)
[GCC 4.0.1 (Apple Inc. build 5493)] on darwin
Type "copyright", "credits" or "license()" for more information.
>>> ================================ RESTART ================================
>>>
>>>
                                                                    Ln: 6 Col: 4
```

Let's check the contents of the files to see what they look like now.

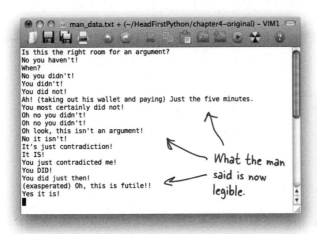

```
man_data.txt + (~/HeadFirstPython/chapter4-original) – VIM1

Is this the right room for an argument?
No you haven't!
When?
No you didn't!
You didn't!
You did not!
Ah! (taking out his wallet and paying) Just the five minutes.
You most certainly did not!
Oh no you didn't!
Oh no you didn't!
Oh look, this isn't an argument!
No it isn't!
It's just contradiction!
It IS!
You just contradicted me!
You DID!
You did just then!
(exasperated) Oh, this is futile!!
Yes it is!
```

What the man said is now legible.

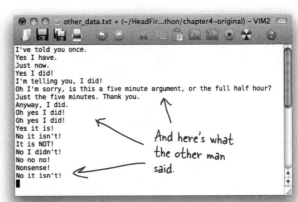

```
other_data.txt + (~/HeadFir...thon/chapter4-original) – VIM2

I've told you once.
Yes I have.
Just now.
Yes I did!
I'm telling you, I did!
Oh I'm sorry, is this a five minute argument, or the full half hour?
Just the five minutes. Thank you.
Anyway, I did.
Oh yes I did!
Oh yes I did!
Yes it is!
No it isn't!
It is NOT!
No I didn't!
No no no!
Nonsense!
No it isn't!
```

And here's what the other man said.

This is looking good. By amending your `nester` module, you've provided a facility to save your list data in a legible format. It's now way easier on the eye.

But does this make it any easier to read the data back in?

Hang on a second...haven't you been here before? You've already written code to read in lines from a data file and put 'em into lists...do you like going around in circles?!?

That's a good point.

This problem is not unlike the problem from the beginning of the chapter, in that you've got lines of text in a disk file that you need to process, only now you have *two* files instead of one.

You know how to write the code to process your new files, but writing custom code like this is specific to the format that you've created for this problem. This is *brittle*: if the data format changes, your custom code will have to change, too.

Ask yourself: *is it worth it?*

Custom Code Exposed

**This week's interview:
When is custom code appropriate?**

Head First: Hello, CC, how are you today?

Custom Code: Hi, I'm great! And when I'm not great, there's always something I can do to fix things. Nothing's too much trouble for me. Here: have a seat.

Head First: Why, thanks.

Custom Code: Let me get that for you. It's my new custom *SlideBack&Groove™*, the 2011 model, with added cushions and lumbar support…and it automatically adjusts to your body shape, too. How does that feel?

Head First: Actually [relaxes], that feels kinda groovy.

Custom Code: See? Nothing's too much trouble for me. I'm your "go-to guy." Just ask; absolutely anything's possible when it's a custom job.

Head First: Which brings me to why I'm here. I have a "delicate" question to ask you.

Custom Code: Go ahead, shoot. I can take it.

Head First: When is custom code appropriate?

Custom Code: Isn't it obvious? It's *always* appropriate.

Head First: Even when it leads to problems down the road?

Custom Code: Problems?!? But I've already told you: nothing's too much trouble for me. I live to customize. If it's broken, I fix it.

Head First: Even when a readymade solution might be a better fit?

Custom Code: Readymade? You mean (I hate to say it): *off the shelf*?

Head First: Yes. Especially when it comes to writing complex programs, right?

Custom Code: What?!? That's where I excel: creating beautifully crafted custom solutions for folks with complex computing problems.

Head First: But if something's been done before, why reinvent the wheel?

Custom Code: But everything I do is custom-made; that's why people come to me…

Head First: Yes, but if you take advantage of other coders' work, you can build your own stuff in half the time *with less code*. You can't beat that, can you?

Custom Code: "Take advantage"…isn't that like *exploitation*?

Head First: More like collaboration, sharing, participation, *and* working together.

Custom Code: [shocked] You want me to give my code…*away*?

Head First: Well…more like share and share alike. I'll scratch your back if you scratch mine. How does that sound?

Custom Code: That sounds disgusting.

Head First: Very droll [laughs]. All I'm saying is that it is not always a good idea to create everything from scratch with custom code when a good enough solution to the problem might already exist.

Custom Code: I guess so…although it won't be as perfect a fit as that chair.

Head First: But I will be able to sit on it!

Custom Code: [laughs] You should talk to my buddy **Pickle**…he's forever going on about stuff like this. And to make matters worse, he lives in a library.

Head First: I think I'll give him a shout. Thanks!

Custom Code: Just remember: you know where to find me if you need any custom work done.

Pickle your data

Python ships with a standard library called `pickle`, which can save and load almost any Python data object, including lists.

Once you *pickle* your data to a file, it is **persistent** and ready to be read into another program at some later date/time:

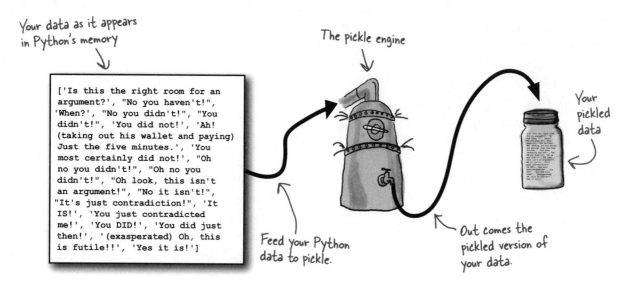

Your data as it appears in Python's memory

The pickle engine

```
['Is this the right room for an
argument?', "No you haven't!",
'When?', "No you didn't!", "You
didn't!", 'You did not!', 'Ah!
(taking out his wallet and paying)
Just the five minutes.', 'You
most certainly did not!', "Oh
no you didn't!", "Oh no you
didn't!", "Oh look, this isn't
an argument!", "No it isn't!",
"It's just contradiction!", 'It
IS!', 'You just contradicted
me!', 'You DID!', 'You did just
then!', '(exasperated) Oh, this
is futile!!', 'Yes it is!']
```

Your pickled data

Feed your Python data to pickle.

Out comes the pickled version of your data.

You can, for example, **store** your pickled data on disk, **put** it in a database, or **transfer** it over a network to another computer.

When you are ready, reversing this process unpickles your persistent pickled data and **recreates** your data *in its original form* within Python's memory:

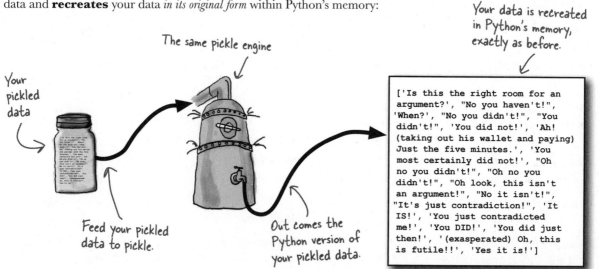

Your data is recreated in Python's memory, exactly as before.

The same pickle engine

Your pickled data

```
['Is this the right room for an
argument?', "No you haven't!",
'When?', "No you didn't!", "You
didn't!", 'You did not!', 'Ah!
(taking out his wallet and paying)
Just the five minutes.', 'You
most certainly did not!', "Oh
no you didn't!", "Oh no you
didn't!", "Oh look, this isn't
an argument!", "No it isn't!",
"It's just contradiction!", 'It
IS!', 'You just contradicted
me!', 'You DID!', 'You did just
then!', '(exasperated) Oh, this
is futile!!', 'Yes it is!']
```

Feed your pickled data to pickle.

Out comes the Python version of your pickled data.

Save with <u>dump</u> and restore with <u>load</u>

Using `pickle` is straightforward: import the required module, then use `dump()` to save your data and, some time later, `load()` to restore it. The only requirement when working with pickled files is that they have to be opened in *binary access mode*:

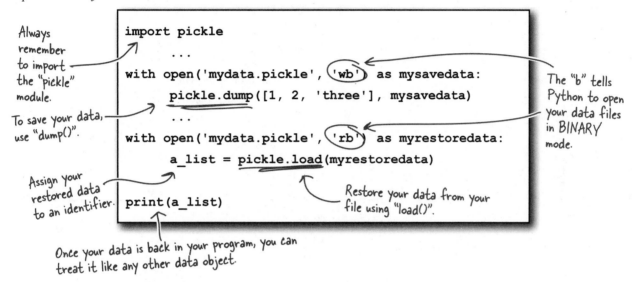

Always remember to import the "pickle" module.

To save your data, use "dump()".

```
import pickle
    ...
with open('mydata.pickle', 'wb') as mysavedata:
    pickle.dump([1, 2, 'three'], mysavedata)
    ...
with open('mydata.pickle', 'rb') as myrestoredata:
    a_list = pickle.load(myrestoredata)

print(a_list)
```

The "b" tells Python to open your data files in BINARY mode.

Assign your restored data to an identifier.

Restore your data from your file using "load()".

Once your data is back in your program, you can treat it like any other data object.

What if something goes wrong?

If something goes wrong when pickling or unpickling your data, the `pickle` module raises an exception of type `PickleError`.

Sharpen your pencil

Here's a snippet of your code as it currently stands. Grab your pencil and strike out the code you no longer need, and then replace it with code that uses the facilities of `pickle` instead. Add any additional code that you think you might need, too.

```
try:
    with open('man_data.txt', 'w') as man_file, open('other_data.txt', 'w') as other_file:
        nester.print_lol(man, fh=man_file)
        nester.print_lol(other, fh=other_file)
except IOError as err:
    print('File error: ' + str(err))
```

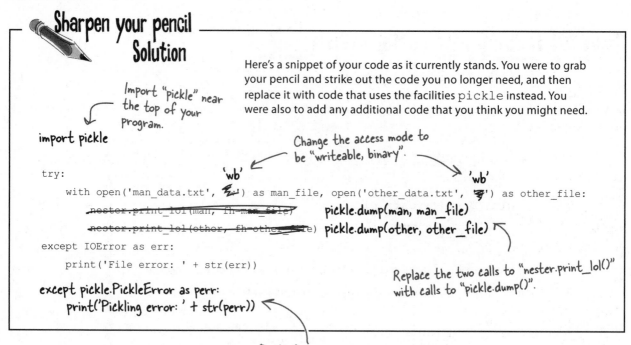

Sharpen your pencil
Solution

Here's a snippet of your code as it currently stands. You were to grab your pencil and strike out the code you no longer need, and then replace it with code that uses the facilities `pickle` instead. You were also to add any additional code that you think you might need.

Import "pickle" near the top of your program.

```
import pickle
```

Change the access mode to be "writeable, binary".

`'wb'`　　　　　　　　　　　　`'wb'`

```
try:
    with open('man_data.txt', 'wb') as man_file, open('other_data.txt', 'wb') as other_file:
        nester.print_lol(man, fh=man_file)      pickle.dump(man, man_file)
        nester.print_lol(other, fh=other_file)  pickle.dump(other, other_file)
except IOError as err:
    print('File error: ' + str(err))
except pickle.PickleError as perr:
    print('Pickling error: ' + str(perr))
```

Replace the two calls to "nester.print_lol()" with calls to "pickle.dump()".

Don't forget to handle any exceptions that can occur.

---

there are no
Dumb Questions

Q: When you invoked print_lol() earlier, you provided only two arguments, even though the function signature requires you to provide four. How is this possible?

A: When you invoke a Python function in your code, you have options, especially when the function provides default values for some arguments. If you use positional arguments, the position of the argument in your function invocation dictates what data is assigned to which argument. When the function has arguments that also provide default values, you do not need to always worry about positional arguments being assigned values.

Q: OK, you've completely lost me. Can you explain?

A: Consider `print()`, which has this signature: `print(value, sep=' ', end='\n', file=sys.stdout)`. By default, this BIF displays to standard output (the screen), because it has an argument called `file` with a default value of `sys.stdout`. The file argument is the fourth positional argument. However, when you want to send data to something other than the screen, you do not need to (nor want to have to) include values for the second and third positional arguments. They have default values anyway, so you need to provide values for them only if the defaults are not what you want. If all you want to do is to send data to a file, you invoke the `print()` BIF like this: `print("Dead Parrot Sketch", file='myfavmonty.txt')` and the fourth positional argument uses the value you specify, while the other positional arguments use their defaults. In Python, not only do the BIFs work this way, but your custom functions support this mechanism, too.

TEST DRIVE

Let's see what happens now that your code has been amended to use the standard `pickle` module instead of your custom `nester` module. Load your amended code into IDLE and press F5 to run it.

```
Python Shell
Python 3.1.2 (r312:79360M, Mar 24 2010, 01:33:18)
[GCC 4.0.1 (Apple Inc. build 5493)] on darwin
Type "copyright", "credits" or "license()" for more information.
>>> ============================= RESTART =============================
>>>
>>>
                                                              Ln: 6 Col: 4
```

Once again, you get no visual clue that something has happened.

So, once again, let's check the contents of the files to see what they look like now:

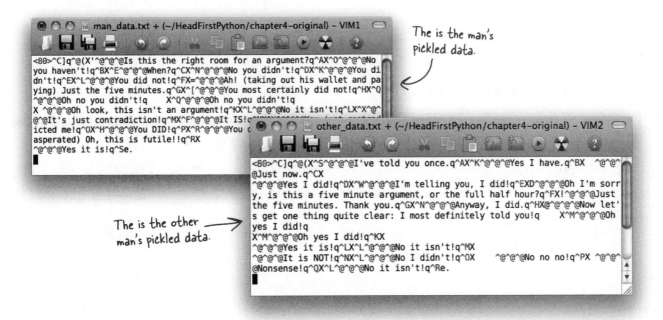

The is the man's pickled data.

```
man_data.txt + (~/HeadFirstPython/chapter4-original) – VIM1
<80>^C]q^@(X'^@^@^@Is this the right room for an argument?q^AX^O^@^@^@No
you haven't!q^BX^E^@^@^@When?q^CX^N^@^@^@No you didn't!q^DX^K^@^@^@You di
dn't!q^EX^L^@^@^@You did not!q^FX=^@^@^@Ah! (taking out his wallet and pa
ying) Just the five minutes.q^GX^[^@^@^@You most certainly did not!q^HX^Q
^@^@^@Oh no you didn't!q      X^Q^@^@^@Oh no you didn't!q
X ^@^@^@Oh look, this isn't an argument!q^KX^L^@^@^@No it isn't!q^LX^X^@^
@^@It's just contradiction!q^MX^F^@^@^@It IS!q...
icted me!q^OX^H^@^@^@You DID!q^PX^R^@^@^@You c
asperated) Oh, this is futile!!q^RX
^@^@^@Yes it is!q^Se.
```

The is the other man's pickled data.

```
other_data.txt + (~/HeadFirstPython/chapter4-original) – VIM2
<80>^C]q^@(X^S^@^@^@I've told you once.q^AX^K^@^@^@Yes I have.q^BX  ^@^@^
@Just now.q^CX
^@^@^@Yes I did!q^DX^W^@^@^@I'm telling you, I did!q^EXD^@^@^@Oh I'm sorr
y, is this a five minute argument, or the full half hour?q^FX!^@^@^@Just
the five minutes. Thank you.q^GX^N^@^@^@Anyway, I did.q^HX@^@^@^@Now let'
s get one thing quite clear: I most definitely told you!q    X^M^@^@^@Oh
yes I did!q
X^M^@^@^@Oh yes I did!q^KX
^@^@^@Yes it is!q^LX^L^@^@^@No it isn't!q^MX
^@^@^@It is NOT!q^NX^L^@^@^@No I didn't!q^OX   ^@^@^@No no no!q^PX ^@^@^
@Nonsense!q^QX^L^@^@^@No it isn't!q^Re.
```

It appears to have worked…but these files look like *gobbledygook*! What gives?

Recall that Python, not you, is pickling your data. To do so efficiently, Python's `pickle` module uses a custom binary format (known as its **protocol**). As you can see, viewing this format in your editor looks decidedly *weird*.

Don't worry: it is supposed to look like this.

An IDLE Session

`pickle` really shines when you load some previously pickled data into another program. And, of course, there's nothing to stop you from using `pickle` with `nester`. After all, each module is designed to serve different purposes. Let's demonstrate with a handful of lines of code within IDLE's shell. Start by importing any required modules:

```
>>> import pickle
>>> import nester
```

No surprises there, eh?

Next up: create a new identifier to hold the data that you plan to unpickle.Create an empty list called `new_man`:

```
>>> new_man = []
```

Yes, almost too exciting for words, isn't it? With your list created. let's load your pickled data into it. As you are working with external data files, it's best if you enclose your code with **try/except**:

```
>>> try:
        with open('man_data.txt', 'rb') as man_file:
                new_man = pickle.load(man_file)
except IOError as err:
        print('File error: ' + str(err))
except pickle.PickleError as perr:
        print('Pickling error: ' + str(perr))
```

This code is not news to you either. However, at this point, your data has been unpickled and assigned to the `new_man` list. It's time for `nester` to do its stuff:

```
>>> nester.print_lol(new_man)
Is this the right room for an argument?
No you haven't!
When?
No you didn't!
    . . .
You did just then!
(exasperated) Oh, this is futile!!
Yes it is!
```

Not all the data is shown here, but trust us: it's all there.

And to finish off, let's display the first line spoken as well as the last:

```
>>> print(new_man[0])
Is this the right room for an argument?
>>> print(new_man[-1])
Yes it is!
```

See: after all that, it is the right room! ☺

Generic file I/O with pickle is the way to go!

Now, no matter what data you create and process in your Python programs, you have a simple, tested, tried-and-true mechanism for saving and restoring your data. How cool is that?

Python takes care of your file I/O details, so you can concentrate on what your code actually does or needs to do.

As you've seen, being able to work with, save, and restore data in lists is a breeze, thanks to Python. But what other **data structures** does Python support *out of the box*?

Let's dive into Chapter 5 to find out.

Your Python Toolbox

You've got Chapter 4 under your belt and you've added some key Python techiques to your toolbox.

Python Lingo

- "Immutable types" – data types in Python that, once assigned a value, cannot have that value changed.
- "Pickling" – the process of saving a data object to persistence storage.
- "Unpickling" – the process of restoring a saved data object from persistence storage.

BULLET POINTS

- The `strip()` method removes unwanted whitespace from strings.

- The `file` argument to the `print()` BIF controls where data is sent/saved.

- The `finally` suite is always executed no matter what exceptions occur within a **try/except** statement.

- An exception object is passed into the `except` suite and can be assigned to an identifier using the `as` keyword.

- The `str()` BIF can be used to access the stringed representation of any data object that supports the conversion.

- The `locals()` BIF returns a collection of variables within the current scope.

- The `in` operator tests for membership.

- The "+" operator concatenates two strings when used with strings but adds two numbers together when used with numbers.

- The `with` statement automatically arranges to close all opened files, even when exceptions occur. The `with` statement uses the `as` keyword, too.

- `sys.stdout` is what Python calls "standard output" and is available from the standard library's `sys` module.

- The standard library's `pickle` module lets you easily and efficiently save and restore Python data objects to disk.

- The `pickle.dump()` function saves data to disk.

- The `pickle.load()` function restores data from disk.

5 comprehending data

 Work that data!

Life could be so much easier if only she'd let me help her extract, sort, and comprehend her data...

Data comes in all shapes and sizes, formats and encodings.

To work effectively with your data, you often have to manipulate and transform it into a common format to allow for efficient processing, sorting, and storage. In this chapter, you'll explore Python goodies that help you work your data up into a sweat, allowing you to achieve data-munging greatness. So, flip the page, and let's not keep the coach waiting…

Coach Kelly needs your help

I'm too busy on the track to waste time fiddling with my computer. Can you help me process my athlete data?

The coach is an old friend, and you'd love to help. His crack squad of U10 athletes has been training hard. With each 600m run they do, Coach Kelly has recorded their time in a text file on his computer. There are four files in all, one each for James, Sarah, Julie, and Mikey.

james.txt

`2-34,3:21,2.34,2.45,3.01,2:01,2:01,3:10,2-22`

julie.txt

`2.59,2.11,2:11,2:23,3-10,2-23,3:10,3.21,3-21`

`2:22,3.01,3:01,3.02,3:02,3.02,3:22,2.49,2:38`

`2:58,2.58,2:39,2-25,2-55,2:54,2.18,2:55,2:55`

sarah.txt

mikey.txt

Initially, the coach needs a quick way to know the *top three fastest times* for each athlete.

Can you help?

Do this!

Before proceeding with this chapter, take a few moments to download the four data files from the *Head First Python* support website.

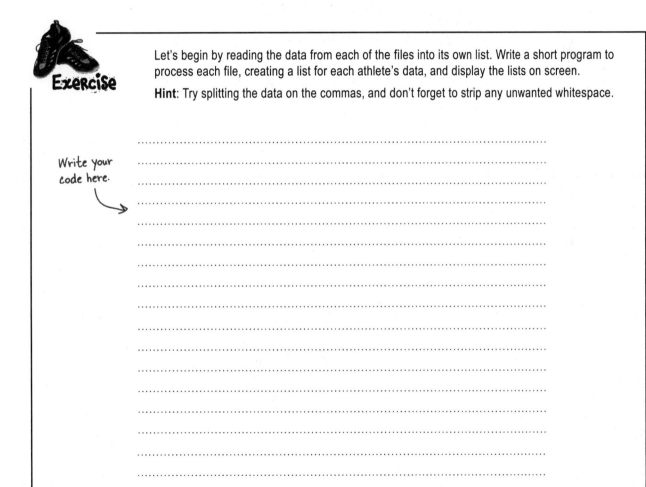

Exercise

Let's begin by reading the data from each of the files into its own list. Write a short program to process each file, creating a list for each athlete's data, and display the lists on screen.

Hint: Try splitting the data on the commas, and don't forget to strip any unwanted whitespace.

Write your code here.

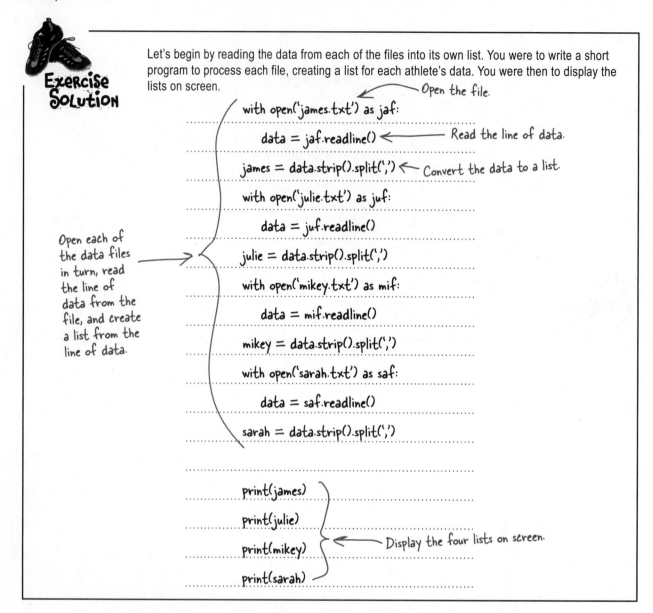

Let's begin by reading the data from each of the files into its own list. You were to write a short program to process each file, creating a list for each athlete's data. You were then to display the lists on screen.

Open the file.

```
with open('james.txt') as jaf:
    data = jaf.readline()        ← Read the line of data.
    james = data.strip().split(',')  ← Convert the data to a list.
    with open('julie.txt') as juf:
        data = juf.readline()
        julie = data.strip().split(',')
        with open('mikey.txt') as mif:
            data = mif.readline()
            mikey = data.strip().split(',')
            with open('sarah.txt') as saf:
                data = saf.readline()
                sarah = data.strip().split(',')


print(james)
print(julie)
print(mikey)      ← Display the four lists on screen.
print(sarah)
```

Open each of the data files in turn, read the line of data from the file, and create a list from the line of data.

there are no Dumb Questions

Q: That `data.strip().split(',')` line looks a little weird. Can you explain what's going on?

A: That's called *method chaining*. The first method, `strip()`, is applied to the line in `data`, which removes any unwanted whitespace from the string. Then, the results of the stripping are processed by the second method, `split(',')`, creating a list. The resulting list is then applied to the target identifier in the previous code. In this way, the methods are **chained together** to produce the required result. It helps if you read method chains from left to right.

Test Drive

Load your code into IDLE and run it to confirm that it's all OK for now:

Here's your program as displayed in IDLE.

```
coach.py – /Users/barryp/HeadFirstPython/chapter5/coach.py

with open('james.txt') as jaf:
    data = jaf.readline()
james = data.strip().split(',')

with open('julie.txt') as juf:
    data = juf.readline()
julie = data.strip().split(',')

with open('mikey.txt') as mif:
    data = mif.readline()
mikey = data.strip().split(',')

with open('sarah.txt') as saf:
    data = saf.readline()
sarah = data.strip().split(',')

print(james)
print(julie)
print(mikey)
print(sarah)
```

And here's the output produced by running your code.

```
Python Shell

Python 3.1.2 (r312:79360M, Mar 24 2010, 01:33:18)
[GCC 4.0.1 (Apple Inc. build 5493)] on darwin
Type "copyright", "credits" or "license()" for more information.
>>> ================================ RESTART ================================
>>>
['2-34', '3:21', '2.34', '2.45', '3.01', '2:01', '2:01', '3:10', '2-22']
['2.59', '2.11', '2:11', '2:23', '3-10', '2-23', '3:10', '3.21', '3-21']
['2:22', '3.01', '3:01', '3.02', '3:02', '3.02', '3:22', '2.49', '2:38']
['2:58', '2.58', '2:39', '2-25', '2-55', '2:54', '2.18', '2:55', '2:55']
>>> |

                                                          Ln: 10  Col: 4
```

So far, so good. Coach Kelly's data is now represented by four lists in Python's memory. Other than the use of method chaining, there's nothing much new here, because you've pretty much mastered reading data from files and using it to populate lists.

There's nothing to show the coach yet, so no point in disturbing him until his data is arranged in ascending order, which requires you to *sort* it.

Let's look at your sorting options in Python.

Sort in one of two ways

When it comes to sorting your data using Python, you have two options.

In-place sorting takes your data, *arranges* it in the order you specify, and then *replaces* your original data with the sorted version. The original ordering is lost. With lists, the sort() method provides in-place sorting:

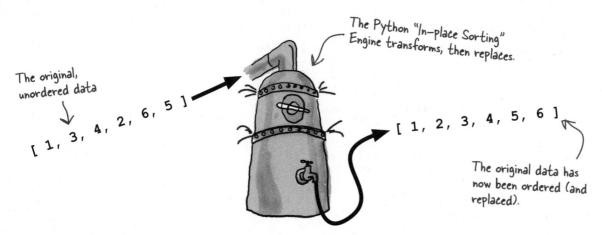

The original, unordered data

[1, 3, 4, 2, 6, 5]

The Python "In-place Sorting" Engine transforms, then replaces.

[1, 2, 3, 4, 5, 6]

The original data has now been ordered (and replaced).

Copied sorting takes your data, arranges it in the order you specify, and then *returns a sorted copy* of your original data. Your original data's ordering is maintained and only the copy is sorted. In Python, the sorted() BIF supports copied sorting.

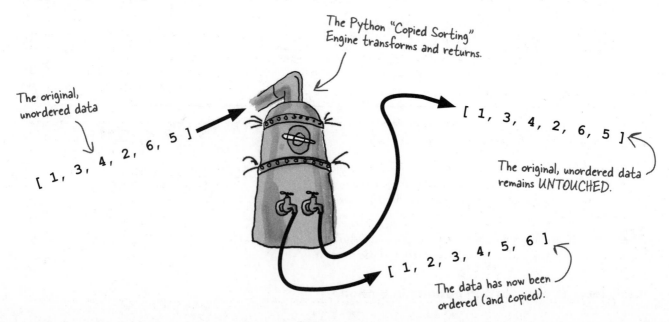

The original, unordered data

[1, 3, 4, 2, 6, 5]

The Python "Copied Sorting" Engine transforms and returns.

[1, 3, 4, 2, 6, 5]

The original, unordered data remains UNTOUCHED.

[1, 2, 3, 4, 5, 6]

The data has now been ordered (and copied).

An IDLE Session

Let's see what happens to your data when each of Python's sorting options is used. Start by creating an unordered list at the IDLE shell:

```
>>> data = [6, 3, 1, 2, 4, 5]
>>> data
[6, 3, 1, 2, 4, 5]
```

Create a list of unordered data and assign to a variable.

Perform an in-place sort using the `sort()` method that is built in as standard to every Python list:

```
>>> data.sort()
>>> data
[1, 2, 3, 4, 5, 6]
```

Perform IN-PLACE sorting on the data.

The data's ordering has changed.

Reset `data` to its original unordered state, and then perform a copied sort using the `sorted()` BIF:

```
>>> data = [6, 3, 1, 2, 4, 5]
>>> data
[6, 3, 1, 2, 4, 5]
>>> data2 = sorted(data)
>>> data
[6, 3, 1, 2, 4, 5]
>>> data2
[1, 2, 3, 4, 5, 6]
```

The data's ordering has been reset.

Perform COPIED sorting on the data.

Same as it ever was.

The copied data is ordered from lowest to highest.

Sharpen your pencil

Either sorting option works with the coach's data, but let's use a copied sort for now to arrange to sort the data on output. In the space below, provide four amended `print()` statements to replace those at the bottom of your program.

....
....
....
....
....
....

Sharpen your pencil
Solution

Either sorting option works with the coach's data, but let's use a copied sort for now to arrange to sort the data on output. You were to provide four amended `print()` statements to replace those at the bottom of your program.

Simply call "sorted()" on the data BEFORE you display it on screen.

```
print(sorted(james))

print(sorted(julie))

print(sorted(mikey))

print(sorted(sarah))
```

---

there are no
Dumb Questions

Q: What happens to the unsorted data when I use sort()?

A: For all intents and purposes, it disappears. Python takes a copy, sorts it, and then replaces your original data with the sorted version.

Q: And there's no way to get the original data back?

A: No. If the ordering of the original data is important to you, use the `sorted()` BIF to transform your data into a sorted copy.

Geek Bits

You've already seen *method chaining*, and now it's time to say "hello" to *function chaining*. Function chaining allows you to apply a series of functions to your data. Each function takes your data, performs some operation on it, and then passes the transformed data on to the next function. Unlike method chains, which read from left to right, function chains read from **right to left** (just to keep things interesting).

—TEST DRIVE—

Let's see if this improves your output in any way. Make the necessary amendments to your code and run it.

```
○ ○ ○  coach2.py – /Users/barryp/HeadFirstPython/chapter5/coach2.py
with open('james.txt') as jaf:
    data = jaf.readline()
james = data.strip().split(',')

with open('julie.txt') as juf:
    data = juf.readline()
julie = data.strip().split(',')

with open('mikey.txt') as mif:
    data = mif.readline()
mikey = data.strip().split(',')

with open('sarah.txt') as saf:
    data = saf.readline()
sarah = data.strip().split(',')

print(sorted(james))
print(sorted(julie))
print(sorted(mikey))
print(sorted(sarah))
```

Here's the updates to the code.

But look at THIS! The data is not at all sorted...which is, like, weird.

```
○ ○ ○                              Python Shell
>>> ============================ RESTART ============================
>>>
['2-22', '2-34', '2.34', '2.45', '2:01', '2:01', '3.01', '3:10', '3:21']
['2-23', '2.11', '2.59', '2:11', '2:23', '3-10', '3-21', '3.21', '3:10']
['2.49', '2:22', '2:38', '3.01', '3.02', '3.02', '3:01', '3:02', '3:22']
['2-25', '2-55', '2.18', '2.58', '2:39', '2:54', '2:55', '2:55', '2:58']
>>> |
                                                              Ln: 10 Col: 4
```

Look at this: 2–55 is coming BEFORE 2.18...now that is weird.

> Hey, it looks like your data values are not uniform. Is the problem with all those periods, dashes, and colons?

Yes. The minute and seconds separators are confusing Python's sorting technology.

When recording his athletes' times in each of their files, Coach Kelly sometimes used a different character to separate minutes from seconds. It looks like you need to fix your data.

The trouble with time

Well...there's never enough of it, is there?

Let's look closely at the coach's data to see what the problem is. Here's Sarah *raw data* again:

```
2:58,2.58,2:39,2-25,2-55,2:54,2.18,2:55,2:55
```

← sarah.txt

Oh, look: what a lovely bunch of strings...

Recall that data read from a file comes into your program *as text*, so Sarah's data looks like this once you turn it into a list of "times":

```
['2:58', '2.58', '2:39', '2-25', '2-55', '2:54', '2.18', '2:55', '2:55']
```

These are all strings, even though the coach thinks they're times.

And when you sort Sarah's data, it ends up in this order (which isn't quite what you were expecting):

```
['2-25', '2-55', '2.18', '2.58', '2:39', '2:54', '2:55', '2:55', '2:58']
```

Whoops! That's not right. How can 2.18 come after 2-55?

Whoops again. 2:39 can't come between 2.58 and 2:54, can it?

I don't get what the problem is...they're all times to me.

Python sorts the strings, and when it comes to strings, a dash comes *before* a period, which itself comes *before* a colon. As all the strings start with 2, the next character in each string acts like a grouping mechanism, with the dashed times grouped and sorted, then the period times, and finally the colon times.

Nonuniformity in the coach's data is causing the sort to fail.

Code Magnets

Let's create a function called `sanitize()`, which takes as input a string from each of the athlete's lists. The function then processes the string to replace any dashes or colons found with a period and returns the sanitized string. **Note:** if the string already contains a period, there's no need to sanitize it.

Rearrange the code magnets at the bottom of the page to provide the required functionality.

```
def sanitize(time_string):
    ............................................................
    ............................................................
    ............................................................
    ............................................................
    ............................................................
    ............................................................
    ............................................................
    ............................................................
    return(mins + '.' + secs)
```

↑
Return the sanitized time string to the caller of this function.

Your magnets are waiting.

```
time_string.split(splitter)
```

```
elif ':' in time_string:
```

```
return(time_string)
```

```
if '-' in time_string:
```

```
else:
```

```
(mins, secs) =
```

```
splitter = ':'
```

```
splitter = '-'
```

Code Magnets Solution

You were to create a function called `sanitize()`, which takes as input a string from each of the athlete's lists. The function then processes the string to replace any dashes or colons found with a period and returns the sanitized string. **Note:** if the string already contains a period, there's no need to sanitize it.

You were to rearrange the code magnets at the bottom of the previous page to provide the required functionality.

```
def sanitize(time_string):
```

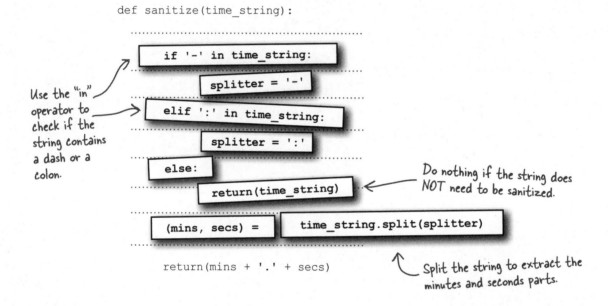

Use the "in" operator to check if the string contains a dash or a colon.

```
if '-' in time_string:
    splitter = '-'
elif ':' in time_string:
    splitter = ':'
else:
    return(time_string)
(mins, secs) = time_string.split(splitter)
```

Do nothing if the string does NOT need to be sanitized.

Split the string to extract the minutes and seconds parts.

```
return(mins + '.' + secs)
```

Of course, on its own, the `sanitize()` function is not enough. You need to iterate over each of your lists of data and use your new function to convert each of the athlete's times into the correct format.

Let's put your new function to work right away.

Exercise

Let's write the code to convert your existing data into a sanitized version of itself. Create four new lists to hold the sanitized data. Iterate over each athlete's list data and append each sanitized string from each list to the appropriate new list. Conclude your program by printing a sorted copy of each new list to the screen.

The code that reads the data from the data files remains unchanged (and has been compressed to fit on this page).

```
with open('james.txt') as jaf: data = jaf.readline()
james = data.strip().split(',')
with open('julie.txt') as juf: data = juf.readline()
julie = data.strip().split(',')
with open('mikey.txt') as mif: data = mif.readline()
mikey = data.strip().split(',')
with open('sarah.txt') as saf: data = saf.readline()
sarah = data.strip().split(',')
```

Add your new code here.

```
................................................................
................................................................
................................................................
................................................................
................................................................
................................................................
................................................................
................................................................
................................................................
................................................................
................................................................
................................................................
................................................................
................................................................
................................................................
................................................................
................................................................
```

What happens to the four "print()" statements?

```
print( ..................................... )
print( ..................................... )
print( ..................................... )
print( ..................................... )
```

Exercise Solution

Let's write the code to convert your existing data into a sanitized version of itself. You were to create four new lists to hold the sanitized data. You were then to iterate over each athlete's data and append each sanitized string from each list to an appropriate new list. You were to conclude your program by printing a sorted copy of each new list to the screen.

```
with open('james.txt') as jaf: data = jaf.readline()
james = data.strip().split(',')
with open('julie.txt') as juf: data = juf.readline()
julie = data.strip().split(',')
with open('mikey.txt') as mif: data = mif.readline()
mikey = data.strip().split(',')
with open('sarah.txt') as saf: data = saf.readline()
sarah = data.strip().split(',')
```

Create four new, initially empty lists. →

```
clean_james = []
clean_julie = []
clean_mikey = []
clean_sarah = []
```

```
for each_t in james:
    clean_james.append(sanitize(each_t))
for each_t in julie:
    clean_julie.append(sanitize(each_t))
for each_t in mikey:
    clean_mikey.append(sanitize(each_t))
for each_t in sarah:
    clean_sarah.append(sanitize(each_t))
```

Take each of the data items in the original lists, sanitize them, and then append the sanitized data to the appropriate new list.

The four "print()" statements now display the new lists, which are sorted, too. →

```
print(    sorted(clean_james)    )
print(    sorted(clean_julie)    )
print(    sorted(clean_mikey)    )
print(    sorted(clean_sarah)    )
```

TEST DRIVE

Combine your `sanitize()` function with your amended code from the previous page, and then press F5 in IDLE to confirm the sorting is now working as expected.

The sanitized data only contains '.' as a separator.

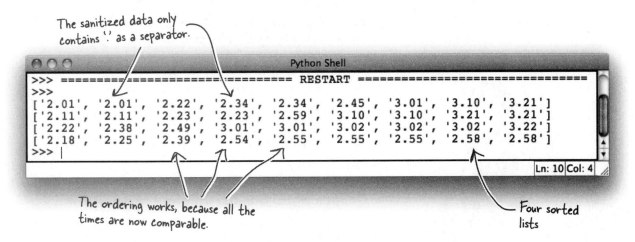

```
Python Shell
>>> ================================ RESTART ================================
>>>
['2.01', '2.01', '2.22', '2.34', '2.34', '2.45', '3.01', '3.10', '3.21']
['2.11', '2.11', '2.23', '2.23', '2.59', '3.10', '3.10', '3.21', '3.21']
['2.22', '2.38', '2.49', '3.01', '3.01', '3.02', '3.02', '3.02', '3.22']
['2.18', '2.25', '2.39', '2.54', '2.55', '2.55', '2.55', '2.58', '2.58']
>>> |
                                                              Ln: 10 Col: 4
```

The ordering works, because all the times are now comparable.

Four sorted lists

This output looks *much better*.

It's taken a bit of work, but now the data from each of the four files is both **sorted** and **uniformly formatted**. By preprocessing your data *before* you sort it, you've helped ensure Python's sorting technology performs correctly.

Geek Bits

By default, both the `sort()` method and the `sorted()` BIF order your data in **ascending** order. To order your data in **descending** order, pass the `reverse=True` argument to either `sort()` or `sorted()` and Python will take care of things for you.

Hang on a sec! Something doesn't feel quite right...look at all that duplicated code, as well as all those duplicated lists. This duplication is bad, right? Is this really the best you can do?

That's right. Duplicated code is a problem.

As things stand, your code creates four lists to hold the data as read from the data files. Then your code creates *another* four lists to hold the sanitized data. And, of course, you're iterating all over the place...

There has to be a better way to write code like this.

Transforming lists is such a common requirement that Python provides a tool to make the transformation as painless as possible. This tool goes by the rather unwieldy name of **list comprehension**. And list comprehensions are designed to reduce the amount of code you need to write when *transforming* one list into another.

Comprehending lists

Consider what you need to do when you transform one list into another. Four things have to happen. You need to:

1 Create a new list to hold the transformed data.

2 Iterate each data item in the original list.

3 With each iteration, perform the transformation.

4 Append the transformed data to the new list.

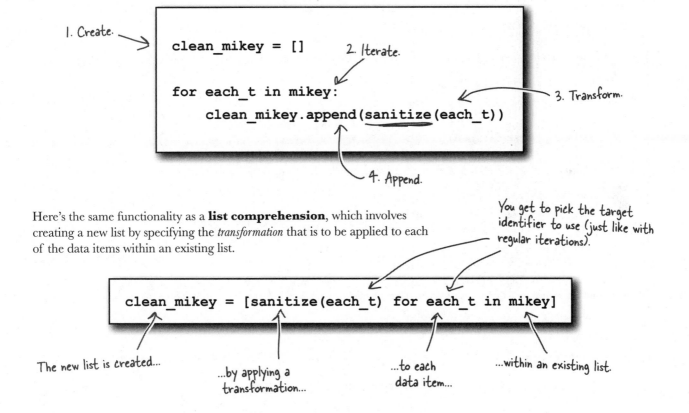

1. Create.

```
clean_mikey = []        2. Iterate.

for each_t in mikey:
    clean_mikey.append(sanitize(each_t))
```

3. Transform.

4. Append.

Here's the same functionality as a **list comprehension**, which involves creating a new list by specifying the *transformation* that is to be applied to each of the data items within an existing list.

You get to pick the target identifier to use (just like with regular iterations).

```
clean_mikey = [sanitize(each_t) for each_t in mikey]
```

The new list is created...

...by applying a transformation...

...to each data item...

...within an existing list.

What's interesting is that the transformation has been reduced to a *single line of code*. Additionally, there's no need to specify the use of the `append()` method as this action is implied within the list comprehension. Neat, eh?

An IDLE Session

Let's see some other list comprehension examples. Open up your IDLE shell and follow along with these one-liner transformations.

Start by transforming a list of minutes into a list of seconds:

```
>>> mins = [1, 2, 3]
>>> secs = [m * 60 for m in mins]
>>> secs
[60, 120, 180]
```

Simply multiply the minute values by 60.

How about meters into feet?

```
>>> meters = [1, 10, 3]
>>> feet = [m * 3.281 for m in meters]
>>> feet
[3.281, 32.81, 9.843]
```

Yes, there are 3.281 feet in a meter.

Given a list of strings in mixed and lowercase, it's a breeze to transform the strings to UPPERCASE:

```
>>> lower = ["I", "don't", "like", "spam"]
>>> upper = [s.upper() for s in lower]
>>> upper
['I', "DON'T", 'LIKE', 'SPAM']
```

Every string comes with the "upper()" method.

Let's use your `sanitize()` function to transform some list data into correctly formatted times:

```
>>> dirty = ['2-22', '2:22', '2.22']
>>> clean = [sanitize(t) for t in dirty]
>>> clean
['2.22', '2.22', '2.22']
```

It's never been so easy to turn something dirty into something clean. ☺

It's also possible to assign the results of the list transformation back onto the original target identifier. This example transforms a list of strings into floating point numbers, and then replaces the original list data:

```
>>> clean = [float(s) for s in clean]
>>> clean
[2.22, 2.22, 2.22]
```

The "float()" BIF converts to floating point.

And, of course, the transformation can be a function chain, if that's what you need:

```
>>> clean = [float(sanitize(t)) for t in ['2-22', '3:33', '4.44']]
>>> clean
[2.22, 3.33, 4.44]
```

Combining transformations on the data items is supported, too!

Sharpen your pencil

Now that you know about list comprehensions, let's write four of them to process the coach's four lists of timing values. Transform each of your lists into sorted, sanitized version of themselves. Grab your pencil and in the space provided, scribble the list comprehensions you plan to use.

....

....

....

....

....

....

there are no Dumb Questions

Q: So...let me get this straight: list comprehensions are good and list iterations are bad, right?

A: No, that's not the best way to look at it. If you have to perform a transformation on every item in a list, using a list comprehension is the way to go, especially when the transformation is easily specified on one line (or as a function chain). List iterations can do everything that list comprehensions can, they just take more code, but iterations do provide more flexibility should you need it.

Geek Bits

Python's list comprehension is an example of the language's support for *functional programming concepts*. There's plenty of debate about the **best way** to develop program code: either procedurally, using functional programming techniques, or using object orientation. At Head First Labs, we try not to get involved in this debate, other than to rejoice in the fact that Python supports, in one way or another, all three of these programming practices.

Sharpen your pencil
Solution

Now that you know about list comprehensions, you were to write four of them to process the coach's four lists of timing values. You were to transform each of your lists into sorted, sanitized version of themselves. You were to grab your pencil and in the space provided, scribble the list comprehensions you plan to use.

The list comprehension performs the transformation, and the new list is then ordered by the "sorted()" BIF.

sorted([sanitize(t) for t in james])

sorted([sanitize(t) for t in julie])

sorted([sanitize(t) for t in mikey])

sorted([sanitize(t) for t in sarah])

Rinse and repeat for the other lists.

Be careful about where you use the sorted() BIF when defining your list comprehensions.

Watch it!

You may have been tempted to use the function chain `sorted(sanitize(t))` *within your list comprehension. Don't be. Recall that the transformation works on one list item at a time, **not** the entire list. In this example, the* `sorted()` *BIF expects to sort a list, not an individual data item.*

The beauty of list comprehensions

The use of list comprehensions with the coach's athlete data has resulted in a lot less code for you to maintain. Additionally, as you get used to list comprehension syntax and usage, you'll find that their use is natural and matches the way your brain thinks about your data and the transformations that you might want to apply.

Let's confirm that your new code is working as expected.

Test Drive

Replace your list iteration code from earlier with your four new (beautiful) list comprehensions. Run your program to confirm that the results have not changed.

```
○ ○ ○  coach4.py – /Users/barryp/HeadFirstPython/chapter5/coach4.py

def sanitize(time_string):
    if '-' in time_string:
        splitter = '-'
    elif ':' in time_string:
        splitter = ':'
    else:
        return(time_string)
    (mins, secs) = time_string.split(splitter)
    return(mins + '.' + secs)

with open('james.txt') as jaf:
    data = jaf.readline()
james
```

```
○ ○ ○                          Python Shell
>>> ============================= RESTART =============================
>>>
['2.01', '2.01', '2.22', '2.34', '2.34', '2.45', '3.01', '3.10', '3.21']
['2.11', '2.11', '2.23', '2.23', '2.59', '3.10', '3.10', '3.21', '3.21']
['2.22', '2.38', '2.49', '3.01', '3.01', '3.02', '3.02', '3.02', '3.22']
['2.18', '2.25', '2.39', '2.54', '2.55', '2.55', '2.55', '2.58', '2.58']
>>>
                                                              Ln: 10 Col: 4
```

```
with
    d
julie
with
    d
mikey
with open('sarah.txt') as saf:
    data = saf.readline()
sarah = data.strip().split(',')

print(sorted([sanitize(t) for t in james]))
print(sorted([sanitize(t) for t in julie]))
print(sorted([sanitize(t) for t in mikey]))
print(sorted([sanitize(t) for t in sarah]))
                                                              Ln: 27 Col: 0
```

Your new list comprehensions produce EXACTLY the same output as your earlier list iterations.

As expected, the outout matches that from earlier.

You've written a program that reads Coach Kelly's data from his data files, stores his raw data in lists, sanitizes the data to a uniform format, and then sorts and displays the coach's data on screen. And all in 25 lines of code.

It's probably safe to let the coach take a look at your output now.

What will the coach think?

Have you not been drinking enough water? I wanted the three fastest times for each athlete...but you've given me everything and it contains duplicates!

In your haste to sanitize and sort your data, you forgot to worry about what you were actually supposed to be doing: *producing the three fastest times for each athlete*. And, of course, there's no place for any duplicated times in your output.

Accessing the first three data items from any list is easy. Either specify each list item *individually* using the standard notation or use a **list slice**:

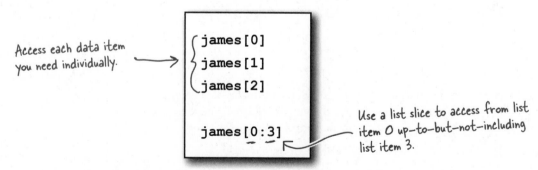

Access each data item you need individually.

```
james[0]
james[1]
james[2]

james[0:3]
```

Use a list slice to access from list item 0 up-to-but-not-including list item 3.

But...what about removing duplicates from your list?

Iterate to remove duplicates

Processing a list to remove duplicates is one area where a list comprehension can't help you, because duplicate removal is *not* a transformation; it's more of a *filter*. And a duplicate removal filter needs to examine the list being created *as it is being created*, which is not possible with a list comprehension.

To meet this new requirement, you'll need to revert to regular list iteration code.

Exercise

Assume that the fourth from last line of code from your current program is changed to this:

```
james = sorted([sanitize(t) for t in james])
```

That is, instead of printing the sanitized and sorted data for James to the screen, this line of code replaces James's unordered and nonuniform data with the sorted, sanitized copy.

Your next task is to write some code to remove any duplicates from the `james` list produced by the preceding line of code. Start by creating a new list called `unique_james`, and then populate it with the unique data items found in `james`. Additionally, provide code to display only the top three fastest times for James.

Hint: you might want to consider using the `not in` operator.

....

....

....

....

....

....

....

....

....

....

....

....

Exercise Solution

Assume that the fourth from last line of code from your current program is changed to this:

```
james = sorted([sanitize(t) for t in james])
```

That is, instead of printing the sanitized and sorted data for James to the screen, this line of code replaces James's unordered and non-uniform data with the sorted, sanitized copy.

Your next task was to write some code to remove any duplicates from the `james` list produced by the preceding line of code. You were to start by creating a new list called `unique_james` and then populate it with the unique data items found in `james`. Additionally, you were to provide code to only display the top three fastest times for James.

Create the empty list to hold the unique data items. →
```
unique_james = []
```

— Iterate over the existing data... ↙

```
for each_t in james:
```

...and if the data item ISN'T already in the new list... ↙
```
    if each_t not in unique_james:
```

```
        unique_james.append(each_t)
```
...append the unique data item to the new list. ↙

Slice the first three data items from the list and display them on screen. →
```
print(unique_james[0:3])
```

Do this!

Repeat the code on this page for the rest of the coach's lists: `julie`, `mikey` & `sarah`. Add all of your new code to your existing program.

TEST DRIVE

Take all of the recent amendments and apply them to your program. Run this latest code within IDLE when you are ready.

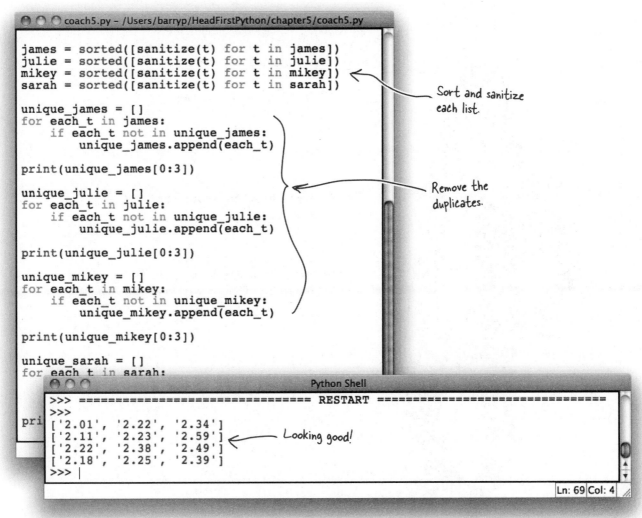

coach5.py – /Users/barryp/HeadFirstPython/chapter5/coach5.py

```
james = sorted([sanitize(t) for t in james])
julie = sorted([sanitize(t) for t in julie])
mikey = sorted([sanitize(t) for t in mikey])
sarah = sorted([sanitize(t) for t in sarah])

unique_james = []
for each_t in james:
    if each_t not in unique_james:
        unique_james.append(each_t)

print(unique_james[0:3])

unique_julie = []
for each_t in julie:
    if each_t not in unique_julie:
        unique_julie.append(each_t)

print(unique_julie[0:3])

unique_mikey = []
for each_t in mikey:
    if each_t not in unique_mikey:
        unique_mikey.append(each_t)

print(unique_mikey[0:3])

unique_sarah = []
for each_t in sarah:
```

Sort and sanitize each list.

Remove the duplicates.

Python Shell

```
>>> ================================ RESTART ================================
>>>
['2.01', '2.22', '2.34']
['2.11', '2.23', '2.59']
['2.22', '2.38', '2.49']
['2.18', '2.25', '2.39']
>>>
```

Looking good!

Ln: 69 Col: 4

It worked!

You are now displaying only the top three times for each athlete, and the duplicates have been successfully removed.

The list iteration code is what you need in this instance. There's a little bit of duplication in your code, but it's not too bad, is it?

"Not too bad"...you're kidding, right?!?
Surely there's something that can be done
with all that duplicated duplicate code?

The irony is hard to avoid, isn't it?

The code that removes duplicates from your lists is itself
duplicated.

Sometimes such a situation is unavoidable, and sometimes
creating a small function to factor out the duplicated code can
help. But something still doesn't feel quite right here...

Remove duplicates with sets

In addition to lists, Python also comes with the **set** data structure, which behaves like the sets you learned all about in math class.

The overriding characteristics of sets in Python are that the data items in a set are *unordered* and *duplicates are not allowed*. If you try to add a data item to a set that already contains the data item, Python simply ignores it.

Create an empty set using the set() BIF, which is an example of a *factory function*:

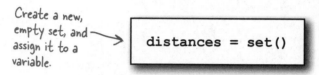

Create a new, empty set, and assign it to a variable.

```
distances = set()
```

It is also possible to *create* and *populate* a set in one step. You can provide a list of data values between curly braces or specify an existing list as an argument to the set() BIF, which is the *factory function*:

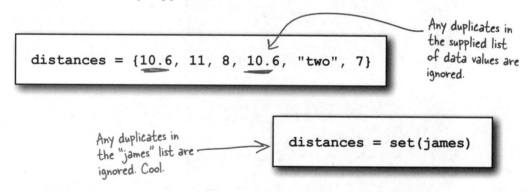

```
distances = {10.6, 11, 8, 10.6, "two", 7}
```

Any duplicates in the supplied list of data values are ignored.

Any duplicates in the "james" list are ignored. Cool.

```
distances = set(james)
```

the Scholar's Corner

Factory Function: A factory function is used to make new data items of a particular type. For instance, "set()" is a factory function because it makes a new set. In the real world, factories make things, hence the name.

Fireside Chats

Tonight's talk: **Does list suffer from set envy?**

List:

[sings] "Anything you can do, I can do better. I can do anything better than you."

Can you spell "d-a-t-a l-o-s-s"? Getting rid of data automatically sounds kinda *dangerous* to me.

Seriously?

And that's *all* you do?

And they pay you for that?!?

Have you ever considered that I like my duplicate values. I'm very fond of them, you know.

Which isn't very often. And, anyway, I can always rely on the kindness of others to help me out with any duplicates that I don't need.

Set:

I'm resisting the urge to say, "No, you can't." Instead, let me ask you: what about handling duplicates? When I see them, I throw them away *automatically*.

But that's what I'm supposed to do. Sets aren't allowed duplicate values.

Yes. That's why I exist…to store sets of values. Which, when it's needed, is a real lifesaver.

That's all I need to do.

Very funny. You're just being smug in an effort to hide from the fact that you can't get rid of duplicates on your own.

Yeah, right. Except when you *don't* need them.

I think you meant to say, "the kindness of `set()`", didn't you?

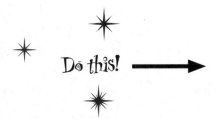

Do this! ⟶

To extract the data you need, replace all of that list iteration code in your current program with four calls to `sorted(set(...))[0:3]`.

Head First Code Review

The Head First Code Review Team has taken your code and annotated it in the only way they know how: *they've scribbled all over it*. Some of their comments are confirmations of what you might already know. Others are suggestions that might make your code better. Like all code reviews, these comments are an attempt to improve the quality of your code.

I think we can make a few improvements here.

```python
def sanitize(time_string):
    if '-' in time_string:
        splitter = '-'
    elif ':' in time_string:
        splitter = ':'
    else:
        return(time_string)
    (mins, secs) = time_string.split(splitter)
    return(mins + '.' + secs)
```

A comment would be nice to have here.

Meet the Head First Code Review Team.

What happens if one of these files is missing?!? Where's your exception handling code?

```python
with open('james.txt') as jaf:
    data = jaf.readline()
james = data.strip().split(',')

with open('julie.txt') as juf:
    data = juf.readline()
julie = data.strip().split(',')

with open('mikey.txt') as mif:
    data = mif.readline()
mikey = data.strip().split(',')

with open('sarah.txt') as saf:
    data = saf.readline()
sarah = data.strip().split(',')
```

There's a bit of duplication here. You could factor out the code into a small function; then, all you need to do is call the function for each of your athlete data files, assigning the result to an athlete list.

There's a lot going on here, but we find it's not too hard to understand if you read it from the inside out.

```python
print(sorted(set([sanitize(t) for t in james]))[0:3])
print(sorted(set([sanitize(t) for t in julie]))[0:3])
print(sorted(set([sanitize(t) for t in mikey]))[0:3])
print(sorted(set([sanitize(t) for t in sarah]))[0:3])
```

Ah, OK. We get it. The slice is applied to the list produced by "sorted()", right?

ExeRcise

Let's take a few moments to implement the review team's suggestion to turn those four `with` statements into a function. Here's the code again. In the space provided, create a function to abstract the required functionality, and then provide one example of how you would call your new function in your code:

```
with open('james.txt') as jaf:
    data = jaf.readline()
james = data.strip().split(',')

with open('julie.txt') as juf:
    data = juf.readline()
julie = data.strip().split(',')

with open('mikey.txt') as mif:
    data = mif.readline()
mikey = data.strip().split(',')

with open('sarah.txt') as saf:
    data = saf.readline()
sarah = data.strip().split(',')
```

Write your new
function here.
↘

....

....

....

....

....

....

....

Provide one
example call.
↗

....

....

Exercise Solution

You were to take a few moments to implement the review team's suggestion to turn those four `with` statements into a function. In the space provided, your were to create a function to abstract the required functionality, then provide one example of how you would call your new function in your code:

```
with open('james.txt') as jaf:
    data = jaf.readline()
james = data.strip().split(',')

with open('julie.txt') as juf:
    data = juf.readline()
julie = data.strip().split(',')

with open('mikey.txt') as mif:
    data = mif.readline()
mikey = data.strip().split(',')

with open('sarah.txt') as saf:
    data = saf.readline()
sarah = data.strip().split(',')
```

Accept a filename as the sole argument.

Create a new function.

```
def get_coach_data(filename):
    try:
        with open(filename) as f:
            data = f.readline()
            return(data.strip().split(','))
    except IOError as ioerr:
        print('File error: ' + str(ioerr))
        return(None)
```

Add the suggested exception-handling code.

Open the file, and read the data.

Perform the split/strip trick on the data prior to returning it to the calling code.

Tell your user about the error (if it occurs) and return "None" to indicate failure.

Calling the function is straightforward.

```
sarah = get_coach_data('sarah.txt')
```

Provide the name of the file to process.

TEST DRIVE

It's time for one last run of your program to confirm that your use of sets produces the same results as your list-iteration code. Take your code for a spin in IDLE and see what happens.

```
⊙ ⊙ ⊙    coach5.py – /Users/barryp/HeadFirstPython/chapter5/coach5.py

def sanitize(time_string):
    if '-' in time_string:
        splitter = '-'
    elif ':' in time_string:
        splitter = ':'
    else:
        return(time_string)
    (mins, secs) = time_string.split(splitter)
    return(mins + '.' + secs)

with open('james.txt') as jaf:
    data = jaf.readline()
james = data.strip().split(',')
```

```
⊙ ⊙ ⊙                              Python Shell
>>> ================================ RESTART ================================
>>>
['2.01', '2.22', '2.34']
['2.11', '2.23', '2.59']
['2.22', '2.38', '2.49']
['2.18', '2.25', '2.39']
>>> |
                                                                    Ln: 69 Col: 4
```

```
sarah = data.strip().split(',')

print(sorted(set([sanitize(t) for t in james]))[0:3])
print(sorted(set([sanitize(t) for t in julie]))[0:3])
print(sorted(set([sanitize(t) for t in mikey]))[0:3])
print(sorted(set([sanitize(t) for t in sarah]))[0:3])

                                                            Ln: 32 Col: 0
```

As expected, your latest code does the business. Looking good!

Excellent!

You've processed the coach's data perfectly, while taking advantage of the `sorted()` BIF, *sets*, and *list comprehensions*. As you can imagine, you can apply these techniques to many different situations. You're well on your way to becoming a Python *data-munging master*!

That's great work, and just what I need. Thanks! I'm looking forward to seeing you on the track soon...

Your Python Toolbox

You've got Chapter 5 under your belt and you've added some more Python techiques to your toolbox.

Python Lingo

- "In-place" sorting – transforms and then replaces.
- "Copied" sorting – transforms and then returns.
- "Method Chaining" – reading from left to right, applies a collection of methods to data.
- "Function Chaining" – reading from right to left, applies a collection of functions to data.

More Python Lingo

- "List Comprehension" – specify a transformation on one line (as opposed to using an iteration).
- A "slice" – access more than one item from a list.
- A "set" – a collection of unordered data items that contains no duplicates.

BULLET POINTS

- The `sort()` method changes the ordering of lists *in-place*.

- The `sorted()` BIF sorts most any data structure by providing *copied sorting*.

- Pass `reverse=True` to either `sort()` or `sorted()` to arrange your data in **descending** order.

- When you have code like this:
  ```
  new_l = []
  for t in old_l:
      new_l.append(len(t))
  ```
  rewrite it to use a **list comprehension**, like this:
  ```
  new_l = [len(t) for t in old_l]
  ```

- To access more than one data item from a list, use a slice. For example:
  ```
  my_list[3:6]
  ```
  accesses the items from index location 3 up-to-but-not-including index location 6.

- Create a **set** using the `set()` factory function.

6 custom data objects

Bundling code with data

The object of my desire [sigh] is in a class of her own.

It's important to match your data structure choice to your data.

And that choice can make a big difference to the complexity of your code. In Python, although really useful, lists and sets aren't the only game in town. The Python **dictionary** lets you organize your data for speedy lookup by *associating your data with names*, not numbers. And when Python's built-in data structures don't quite cut it, the Python **class** statement lets you define your own. This chapter shows you how.

Coach Kelly is back
(with a new file format)

I love what you've done, but I can't tell which line of data belongs to which athlete, so I've added some information to my data files to make it easy for you to figure it out. I hope this doesn't mess things up much.

The output from your last program in Chapter 5 was exactly what the coach was looking for, but for the fact that no one can tell which athlete belongs to which data. Coach Kelly thinks he has the solution: he's added identification data to each of his data files:

This is "sarah2.txt", with extra data added.

```
Sarah Sweeney,2002-6-17,2:58,2.58,2:39,2-25,2-55,2:54,2.18,2:55,2:55,2:22,2-21,2.22
```

Sarah's full name   Sarah's date of birth   Sarah's timing data

If you use the split() BIF to extract Sarah's data into a list, the first data item is Sarah's name, the second is her date of birth, and the rest is Sarah's timing data.

Let's exploit this format and see how well things work.

Do this!

Grab the updated files from the *Head First Python* website.

Code Magnets

Let's look at the code to implement the strategy outlined at the bottom of the previous page. For now, let's concentrate on Sarah's data. Rearrange the code magnets at the bottom of this page to implement the list processing required to extract and process Sarah's three fastest times from Coach Kelly's raw data.

Hint: the pop () method removes and returns a data item from the specified list location.

```
def sanitize(time_string):
    if '-' in time_string:
        splitter = '-'
    elif ':' in time_string:
        splitter = ':'
    else:
        return(time_string)
    (mins, secs) = time_string.split(splitter)
    return(mins + '.' + secs)
```
← The "sanitize()" function is as it was in Chapter 5.

```
def get_coach_data(filename):
    try:
        with open(filename) as f:
            data = f.readline()
        return(data.strip().split(','))
    except IOError as ioerr:
        print('File error: ' + str(ioerr))
        return(None)
```
← The "get_coach_data()" function is also from the last chapter.

Rearrange the magnets here.

....

....

....

....

`(sarah_name, sarah_dob)`

`sarah`

`"'s fastest times are: " +`

`=`

`print(sarah_name +`

`get_coach_data('sarah2.txt')`

`=`

`sarah.pop(0), sarah.pop(0)`

`str(sorted(set([sanitize(t) for t in sarah]))[0:3]))`

Code Magnets Solution

Let's look at the code to implement the strategy outlined earlier. For now, let's concentrate on Sarah's data.

You were to rearrange the code magnets at the bottom of the previous page to implement the list processing required to extract and process Sarah's three fastest times from Coach Kelly's raw data.

```python
def sanitize(time_string):
    if '-' in time_string:
        splitter = '-'
    elif ':' in time_string:
        splitter = ':'
    else:
        return(time_string)
    (mins, secs) = time_string.split(splitter)
    return(mins + '.' + secs)


def get_coach_data(filename):
    try:
        with open(filename) as f:
            data = f.readline()
        return(data.strip().split(','))
    except IOError as ioerr:
        print('File error: ' + str(ioerr))
        return(None)
```

Use the function to turn Sarah's data file into a list, and then assign it to the "sarah" variable.

```python
sarah  =  get_coach_data('sarah2.txt')
(sarah_name, sarah_dob)  =  sarah.pop(0), sarah.pop(0)
print(sarah_name + "'s fastest times are: " +
str(sorted(set([sanitize(t) for t in sarah]))[0:3]))
```

The "pop(0)" call returns and removes data from the front of a list. Two calls to "pop(0)" remove the first two data values and assigns them to the named variables.

A custom message within the call to "print()" is used to display the results you're after.

TEST DRIVE

Let's run this code in IDLE and see what happens.

```
coach2.py – /Users/barryp/HeadFirstPython/chapter6/coach2.py

def sanitize(time_string):
    if '-' in time_string:
        splitter = '-'
    elif ':' in time_string:
        splitter = ':'
    else:
        return(time_string)
    (mins, secs) = time_string.split(splitter)
    return(mins + '.' + secs)

def get_coach_data(filename):
    try:
        with open(filename) as f:
            data = f.readline()
        return(data.strip().split(','))
    except IOError as ioerr:
        print('File error: ' + str(ioerr))
        return(None)

sarah = get_coach_data('sarah2.txt')

(sarah_name, sarah_dob) = sarah.pop(0), sarah.pop(0)

print(sarah_name + "'s fastest times are: " +
        str(sorted(set([sanitize(t) for t in sarah]))[0:3]))
```

Your latest code

```
Python Shell

Python 3.1.2 (r312:79360M, Mar 24 2010, 01:33:18)
[GCC 4.0.1 (Apple Inc. build 5493)] on darwin
Type "copyright", "credits" or "license()" for more information.
>>> ================================ RESTART ================================
>>>
Sarah Sweeney's fastest times are: ['2.18', '2.21', '2.22']
>>>
                                                                      Ln: 7 Col: 4
```

This output is much more understandable.

This program works as expected, and is *fine*…except that you have to name and create Sarah's three variables in such as way that it's possible to identify *which* name, date of birth, and timing data relate to Sarah. And if you add code to process the data for James, Julie, and Mikey, you'll be up to 12 variables that need juggling. This just about works for now with four athletes. But what if there are 40, 400, or 4,000 athletes to process?

Although the data is related in "real life," within your code things are **disjointed**, because the three related pieces of data representing Sarah are stored in *three separate variables*.

Use a dictionary to associate data

Lists are *great*, but they are not always the best data structure for every situation. Let's take another look at Sarah's data:

Sarah's full name   Sarah's date of birth   Sarah's timing data

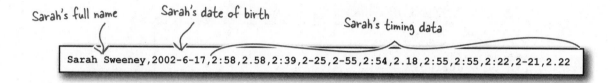

```
Sarah Sweeney,2002-6-17,2:58,2.58,2:39,2-25,2-55,2:54,2.18,2:55,2:55,2:22,2-21,2.22
```

There's a definite **structure** here: the athlete's name, the date of birth, and then the list of times.

Let's continue to use a list for the timing data, because that still makes sense. But let's make the timing data part of *another* data structure, which associates all the data for an athlete with a single variable.

We'll use a Python **dictionary**, which *associates data values with keys*:

The "keys"

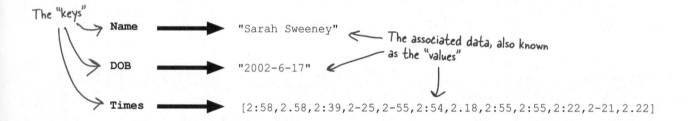

Name ➡ "Sarah Sweeney"   The associated data, also known as the "values"

DOB ➡ "2002-6-17"

Times ➡ [2:58,2.58,2:39,2-25,2-55,2:54,2.18,2:55,2:55,2:22,2-21,2.22]

^{the} Scholar's Corner

Dictionary A built-in data structure (included with Python) that allows you to associate data with keys, as opposed to numbers. This lets your in-memory data closely match the structure of your actual data.

Fireside Chats

Tonight's talk: **To use a list or not to use a list?**

Dictionary:

Hi there, List. I hear you're great, but not always the best option for complex data. That's where I come in.

True. But when you do, you lose any structure associated with the data you are processing.

Isn't it always?

You *guess* so? When it comes to modeling your data in code, it's best not to guess. Be firm. Be strong. Be assertive. Use a dictionary.

[laughs] Oh, I do love your humor, List, even when you know you're on thin ice. Look, the rule is simple: *if your data has structure, use a dictionary, not a list.* How hard is that?

Which *rarely* makes sense. Knowing when to use a list and when to use a dictionary is what separates the good programmers from the great ones, right?

List:

What?!? Haven't you heard? You can put *anything* into a list, anything at all.

Well…assuming, of course, that structure is important to you.

Ummm, uh…I guess so.

That sounds like a slogan from one of those awful self-help conferences. Is that where you heard it?

Not that hard, really. Unless, of course, you are a list, and you miss being used for every piece of data in a program…

I guess so. Man, I do hate it when you're right!

Geek Bits

The Python **dictionary** is known by different names in other programming languages. If you hear other programmers talking about a "mapping," a "hash," or an "associative array," they are talking about a "dictionary."

An IDLE Session

Let's see the Python dictionary in action. Follow along with this IDLE session on your computer, ensuring that you get the same results as shown.

Start by creating two empty dictionaries, one using curly braces and the other using a factory function:

```
>>> cleese = {}
>>> palin = dict()
>>> type(cleese)
<class 'dict'>
>>> type(palin)
<class 'dict'>
```

Both techniques create an empty dictionary, as confirmed.

Add some data to both of these dictionaries by *associating values with keys*. Note the actual structure of the data is presenting itself here, as each dictionary has a `Name` and a list of `Occupations`. Note also that the `palin` dictionary is being created at the same time:

```
>>> cleese['Name'] = 'John Cleese'
>>> cleese['Occupations'] = ['actor', 'comedian', 'writer', 'film producer']
>>> palin = {'Name': 'Michael Palin', 'Occupations': ['comedian', 'actor', 'writer', 'tv']}
```

With your data associated with keys (which are strings, in this case), it is possible to access an individual data item using a notation similar to that used with lists:

```
>>> palin['Name']
'Michael Palin'
>>> cleese['Occupations'][-1]
'film producer'
```

Use square brackets to index into the dictionary to access data items, but instead of numbers, index with keys.

Use numbers to access a list item stored at a particular dictionary key. Think of this as "index-chaining" and read from right to left: "...the last item of the list associated with Occupations...".

As with lists, a Python dictionary can grow dynamically to store additional key/value pairings. Let's add some data about birthplace to each dictionary:

```
>>> palin['Birthplace'] = "Broomhill, Sheffield, England"
>>> cleese['Birthplace'] = "Weston-super-Mare, North Somerset, England"
```

Provide the data associated with the new key.

Unlike lists, a Python dictionary **does not maintain insertion order**, which can result in some unexpected behavior. The key point is that the dictionary *maintains the associations*, not the ordering:

```
>>> palin
{'Birthplace': 'Broomhill, Sheffield, England', 'Name': 'Michael Palin', 'Occupations':
['comedian', 'actor', 'writer', 'tv']}
>>> cleese
{'Birthplace': 'Weston-super-Mare, North Somerset, England', 'Name': 'John Cleese',
'Occupations': ['actor', 'comedian', 'writer', 'film producer']}
```

The ordering maintained by Python is different from how the data was inserted. Don't worry about it; this is OK.

EXERCISE

It's time to apply what you now know about Python's dictionary to your code. Let's continue to concentrate on Sarah's data for now. Strike out the code that you no longer need and replace it with new code that uses a dictionary to hold and process Sarah's data.

```python
def sanitize(time_string):
    if '-' in time_string:
        splitter = '-'
    elif ':' in time_string:
        splitter = ':'
    else:
        return(time_string)
    (mins, secs) = time_string.split(splitter)
    return(mins + '.' + secs)


def get_coach_data(filename):
    try:
        with open(filename) as f:
            data = f.readline()
        return(data.strip().split(','))
    except IOError as ioerr:
        print('File error: ' + str(ioerr))
        return(None)
```

Strike out the code you no longer need.

→
```python
sarah = get_coach_data('sarah2.txt')
(sarah_name, sarah_dob) = sarah.pop(0), sarah.pop(0)
print(sarah_name + "'s fastest times are: " +
        str(sorted(set([sanitize(t) for t in sarah]))[0:3]))
```

Add your dictionary using and processing code here. →

....
....
....
....
....
....
....
....
....

Exercise Solution

It's time to apply what you now know about Python's dictionary to your code. Let's continue to concentrate on Sarah's data for now. You were to strike out the code that you no longer needed and replace it with new code that uses a dictionary to hold and process Sarah's data.

```python
def sanitize(time_string):
    if '-' in time_string:
        splitter = '-'
    elif ':' in time_string:
        splitter = ':'
    else:
        return(time_string)
    (mins, secs) = time_string.split(splitter)
    return(mins + '.' + secs)


def get_coach_data(filename):
    try:
        with open(filename) as f:
            data = f.readline()
        return(data.strip().split(','))
    except IOError as ioerr:
        print('File error: ' + str(ioerr))
        return(None)


sarah = get_coach_data('sarah2.txt')
```

You don't need this code anymore.

~~(sarah_name, sarah_dob) = sarah.pop(0), sarah.pop(0)~~
~~print(sarah_name + "'s fastest times are: " +~~
~~str(sorted(set([sanitize(t) for t in sarah]))[0:3]))~~

Create an empty dictionary.
```python
sarah_data = {}
```

```python
sarah_data['Name'] = sarah.pop(0)
sarah_data['DOB'] = sarah.pop(0)
sarah_data['Times'] = sarah
```
Populate the dictionary with the data by associating the data from the file with the dictionary keys..

```python
print(sarah_data['Name'] + "'s fastest times are: " +
      str(sorted(set([sanitize(t) for t in sarah_data['Times']]))[0:3]))
```
Refer to the dictionary when processing the data.

TEST DRIVE

Let's confirm that this new version of your code works exactly as before by testing your code within the IDLE environment.

```
                     coach3.py - /Users/barryp/HeadFirstPython/chapter6/coach3.py

def sanitize(time_string):
    if '-' in time_string:
        splitter = '-'
    elif ':' in time_string:
        splitter = ':'
    else:
        return(time_string)
    (mins, secs) = time_string.split(splitter)
    return(mins + '.' + secs)

def get_coach_data(filename):
    try:
        with open(filename) as f:
            data = f.readline()
        return(data.strip().split(','))
    except IOError as ioerr:
        print('File error: ' + str(ioerr))
        return(None)

sarah = get_coach_data('sarah2.txt')          ⟵

sarah_data = {}
sarah_data['Name'] = sarah.pop(0)    ⟵
sarah_data['DOB'] = sarah.pop(0)     ⟵
sarah_data['Times'] = sarah

print(sarah_data['Name'] + "'s fastest times are: " +
        str(sorted(set([sanitize(t) for t in sarah_data['Times']]))[0:3]))
```

Your dictionary code produces the same results as earlier.

```
                                    Python Shell
>>> ================================ RESTART ================================
>>>
Sarah Sweeney's fastest times are: ['2.18', '2.21', '2.22']
>>> |
                                                                    Ln: 43 Col: 4
```

Which, again, works as expected…the difference being that you can now more easily determine and control which identification data **associates** with which timing data, because they are *stored in a single dictionary*.

Although, to be honest, it does take *more* code, which is a bit of a bummer. Sometimes the extra code is worth it, and sometimes it isn't. In this case, it most likely is.

Let's review your code to see if we can improve anything.

Head First Code Review

The Head First Code Review Team has been at it again: *they've scribbled all over your code.* Some of their comments are confirmations; others are suggestions. Like all code reviews, these comments are an attempt to improve the quality of your code.

It's great to see you taking some of our suggestions on board. Here are a few more...

```python
def sanitize(time_string):
    if '-' in time_string:
        splitter = '-'
    elif ':' in time_string:
        splitter = ':'
    else:
        return(time_string)
    (mins, secs) = time_string.split(splitter)
    return(mins + '.' + secs)


def get_coach_data(filename):
    try:
        with open(filename) as f:
            data = f.readline()
        return(data.strip().split(','))
    except IOError as ioerr:
        print('File error: ' + str(ioerr))
        return(None)

sarah = get_coach_data('sarah2.txt')

sarah_data = {}
sarah_data['Name'] = sarah.pop(0)
sarah_data['DOB'] = sarah.pop(0)
sarah_data['Times'] = sarah

print(sarah_data['Name'] + "'s fastest times are: " +
    str(sorted(set([sanitize(t) for t in sarah_data['Times']]))[0:3]))
```

Rather than building the dictionary as you go along, why not do it all in one go? In fact, in this situation, it might even make sense to do this processing within the get_coach_data() function and have the function return a populated dictionary as opposed to a list.

Then, all you need to do is create the dictionary from the data file using an appropriate function call, right?

You might want to consider moving this code into the get_coach_data() function, too, because doing so would rather nicely abstract away these processing details. But whether you do or not is up to you. It's your code, after all!

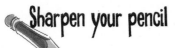

Sharpen your pencil

Actually, those review comments are really useful. Let's take the time to apply them to your code. There are four suggestions that you need to adjust your code to support:

1. Create the dictionary all in one go.

2. Move the dictionary creation code into the `get_coach_data()` function, returning a dictionary as opposed to a list.

3. Move the code that determines the top three times for each athlete into the `get_coach_data()` function.

4. Adjust the invocations within the main code to the new version of the `get_coach_data()` function to support it's new mode of operation.

Grab your pencil and write your new `get_coach_data()` function in the space provided below. Provide the four calls that you'd make to process the data for each of the athletes and provide four amended `print()` statements:

....

....

....

....

....

....

....

....

....

....

....

....

....

....

....

Sharpen your pencil
Solution

You were to take the time to apply the code review comments to your code. There were four suggestions that you needed to adjust your code to support:

1. Create the dictionary all in one go.

2. Move the dictionary creation code into the get_coach_data() function, returning a dictionary as opposed to a list.

3. Move the code that determines the top three times for each athlete into the get_coach_data() function.

4. Adjust the invocations within the main code to the new version of the get_coach_data() function to support its new mode of operation.

You were to grab your pencil and write your new get_coach_data() function in the space provided below, as well as provide the four calls that you'd make to process the data for each of the athletes and provide four amended print() statements:

```
def get_coach_data(filename):
    try:
        with open(filename) as f:
            data = f.readline()
        templ = data.strip().split(',')
        return({'Name' : templ.pop(0),
                'DOB' : templ.pop(0),
                'Times': str(sorted(set([sanitize(t) for t in templ]))[0:3])})
    except IOError as ioerr:
        print('File error: ' + str(ioerr))
        return(None)
```

1. Create a temporary list to hold the data BEFORE creating the dictionary all in one go.

2. The dictionary creation code is now part of the function.

3. The code that determines the top three scores is part of the function, too.

4. Call the function for an athlete and adjust the "print()" statement as needed.

```
james = get_coach_data('james2.txt')
```

We are showing only these two lines of code for one athlete (because repeating it for the other three is a trivial exercise).

```
print(james['Name'] + "'s fastest times are: " + james['Times'])
```

Test Drive

Let's confirm that *all* of the re-factoring suggestions from the Head First Code Review Team are working as expected. Load your code into IDLE and take it for a spin.

coach3c.py – /Users/barryp/HeadFirstPython/chapter6/coach3c.py

```python
def sanitize(time_string):
    if '-' in time_string:
        splitter = '-'
    elif ':' in time_string:
        splitter = ':'
    else:
        return(time_string)
    (mins, secs) = time_string.split(splitter)
    return(mins + '.' + secs)

def get_coach_data(filename):
    try:
        with open(filename) as f:
            data = f.readline()
        templ = data.strip().split(',')
        return({'Name' : templ.pop(0),
                'DOB'  : templ.pop(0),
                'Times': str(sorted(set([sanitize(t) for t in templ]))[0:3])})
    except IOError as ioerr:
        print('File error: ' + str(ioerr))
        return(None)

james = get_coach_data('james2.txt')
julie = get_coach_data('julie2.txt')
mikey = get_coach_data('mikey2.txt')
sarah = get_coach_data('sarah2.txt')

print(james['Name'] + "'s fastest times are: " + james['Times'])
print(julie['Name'] + "'s fastest times are: " + julie['Times'])
print(mikey['Name'] + "'s fastest times are: " + mikey['Times'])
print(sarah['Name'] + "'s fastest times are: " + sarah['Times'])
```

All of the data processing is moved into the function.

This code has been considerably tidied up and now displays the name of the athlete associated with their times.

Python Shell

```
>>> ================================ RESTART ================================
>>>
James Lee's fastest times are: ['2.01', '2.16', '2.22']
Julie Jones's fastest times are: ['2.11', '2.23', '2.59']
Mikey McManus's fastest times are: ['2.22', '2.31', '2.38']
Sarah Sweeney's fastest times are: ['2.18', '2.21', '2.22']
>>>
```

Looking good!

Ln: 19 Col: 4

To process additional athletes, all you need is two lines of code: the first invokes the get_coach_data() function and the second invokes print().

And if you require additional functionality, it's no big deal to write more functions to provide the required functionality, is it?

> Wait a minute...you're using a dictionary to keep your data all in one place, but now you're proposing to write a bunch of custom functions that work on your data but **aren't** associated with it. Does that really make sense?

Keeping your code and its data together is good.

It does indeed make sense to try and associate the functions with the data they are meant to work on, doesn't it? After all, the functions are only going to make sense when *related* to the data—that is, the functions will be *specific* to the data, not general purpose. Because this is the case, it's a great idea to try and bundle the code with its data.

But how? Is there an easy way to associate custom code, in the form of functions, with your custom data?

Bundle your code and its data in a class

Like the majority of other modern programming languages, Python lets you create and define an object-oriented **class** that can be used to *associate code with the data that it operates on*.

Why would anyone want to do this?

Using a class helps reduce complexity.

By associating your code with the data it works on, you reduce complexity as your code base grows.

So what's the big deal with that?

Reduced complexity means fewer bugs.

Reducing complexity results in fewer bugs in your code. However, it's a fact of life that your programs will have functionality added over time, which will result in additional complexity. Using classes to **manage** this complexity is a *very good thing*.

Yeah? But...who really cares?

Fewer bugs means more maintainable code.

Using classes lets you keep your code and your data together in one place, and as your code base grows, this really can make quite a difference. Especially when it's 4 AM and you're under a deadline...

Define a class

Python follows the standard object-oriented programming model of providing a means for you to define the code and the data it works on as a *class*. Once this definition is in place, you can use it to create (or *instantiate*) **data objects**, which inherit their characteristics from your class.

Within the object-oriented world, your code is often referred to as the class's **methods**, and your data is often referred to as its **attributes**. Instantiated data objects are often referred to as **instances**.

The "raw" data

```
"Sarah Sweeney","2002-6-17",[2:58,2.58,2:39,2-25,2-55,2:54,2.18,2:55,2:55,2:22,2-21,2.22]
```

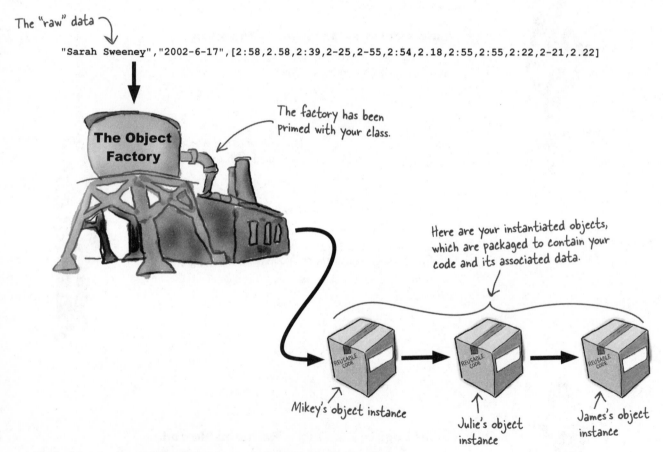

The factory has been primed with your class.

The Object Factory

Here are your instantiated objects, which are packaged to contain your code and its associated data.

Mikey's object instance

Julie's object instance

James's object instance

Each object is **created from** the class and **shares** a similar set of characteristics. The methods (your code) are the *same* in each instance, but each object's attributes (your data) *differ* because they were created from your raw data.

Let's look at how classes are defined in Python.

Use <u>class</u> to define classes

Python uses **class** to create objects. Every defined class has a *special method* called __init__(), which allows you to control how objects are initialized.

Methods within your class are defined in much the same way as functions, that is, using def. Here's the basic form:

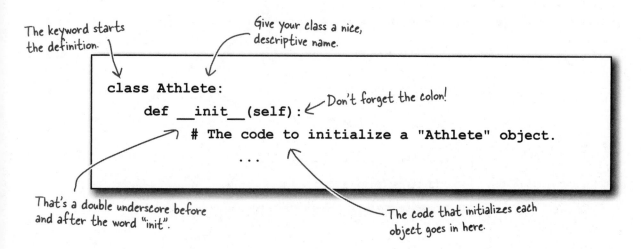

The keyword starts the definition.

Give your class a nice, descriptive name.

```
class Athlete:
    def __init__(self):
        # The code to initialize a "Athlete" object.
        ...
```

Don't forget the colon!

That's a double underscore before and after the word "init".

The code that initializes each object goes in here.

Creating object instances

With the class in place, it's easy to create object instances. Simply assign a *call* to the class name to each of your variables. In this way, the class (together with the __init__() method) provides a mechanism that lets you create a **custom factory function** that you can use to create as many object instances as you require:

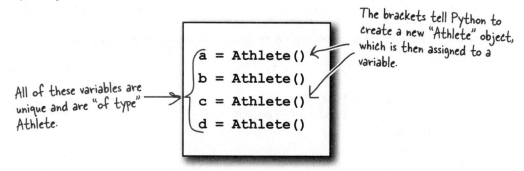

The brackets tell Python to create a new "Athlete" object, which is then assigned to a variable.

All of these variables are unique and are "of type" Athlete.

```
a = Athlete()
b = Athlete()
c = Athlete()
d = Athlete()
```

Unlike in C++-inspired languages, Python has no notion of defining a constructor called "new." Python does object contruction for you, and then lets you customize your object's initial state using the __init__() method.

The importance of self

To confirm: when you define a class you are, in effect, defining a *custom factory function* that you can then use in your code to create instances:

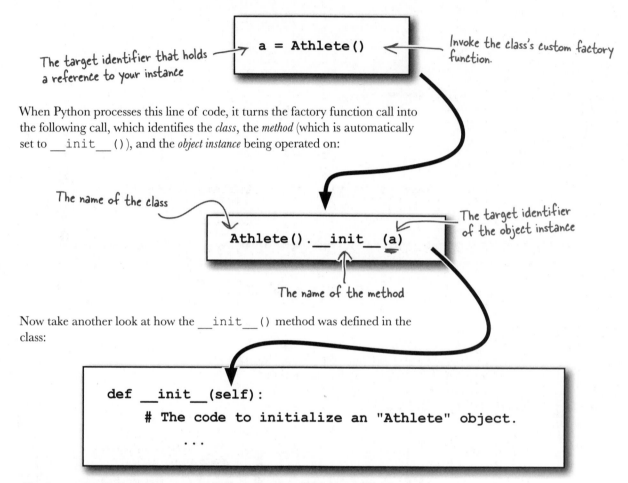

The target identifier that holds a reference to your instance

`a = Athlete()`

Invoke the class's custom factory function.

When Python processes this line of code, it turns the factory function call into the following call, which identifies the *class*, the *method* (which is automatically set to __init__()), and the *object instance* being operated on:

The name of the class

`Athlete().__init__(a)`

The target identifier of the object instance

The name of the method

Now take another look at how the __init__() method was defined in the class:

```
def __init__(self):
        # The code to initialize an "Athlete" object.
        ...
```

Check out what Python turns your object creation invocation into. Notice anything?

The target identifer is assigned to the self argument.

This is a very important argument assignment. Without it, the Python interpreter can't work out which object instance to apply the method invocation to. Note that the class code is designed to be *shared* among all of the object instances: the methods are shared, the attributes are **not**. The self argument helps identify which object instance's data to work on.

Every method's first argument is <u>self</u>

In fact, not only does the __init__() method require self as its first argument, but *so does every other method defined within your class*.

Python arranges for the first argument of every method to be the invoking (or *calling*) object instance. Let's extend the sample class to store a value in a object attribute called thing with the value set during initialization. Another method, called how_big(), returns the length of thing due to the use of the len() BIF:

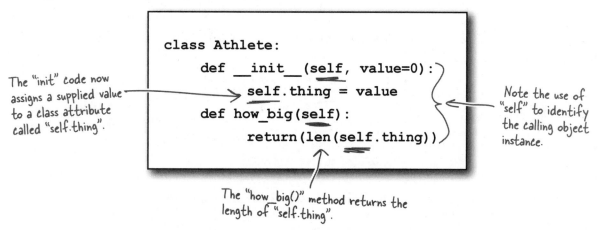

The "init" code now assigns a supplied value to a class attribute called "self.thing".

```
class Athlete:
    def __init__(self, value=0):
        self.thing = value
    def how_big(self):
        return(len(self.thing))
```

Note the use of "self" to identify the calling object instance.

The "how_big()" method returns the length of "self.thing".

When you invoke a class method on an object instance, Python arranges for the first argument to be the invoking object instance, which is *always* assigned to each method's self argument. This fact alone explains why self is so important and also why self needs to be the *first argument to every object method you write*:

What you write:

```
d = Athlete("Holy Grail")
```

```
d.how_big()
```

What Python executes:

```
Athlete.__init__(d, "Holy Grail")
```

The class   The method   The target indentifer (or instance)

```
Athlete.how_big(d)
```

An IDLE Session

Let's use IDLE to create some object instances from a new class that you'll define. Start by creating a small class called `Athlete`:

```
>>> class Athlete:
        def __init__(self, a_name, a_dob=None, a_times=[]):
            self.name = a_name
            self.dob = a_dob
            self.times = a_times
```

Note the default values for two of the arguments.

Three attributes are initialized and assigned to three class attributes using the supplied argument data.

With the class defined, create two unique object instances which derive their characteristcs from the `Athlete` class:

```
>>> sarah = Athlete('Sarah Sweeney', '2002-6-17', ['2:58', '2.58', '1.56'])
>>> james = Athlete('James Jones')
>>> type(sarah)
<class '__main__.Athlete'>
>>> type(james)
<class '__main__.Athlete'>
```

Create two unique athletes (with "james" using the default argument values).

Confirm that both "sarah" and "james" are athletes.

Even though `sarah` and `james` are both athletes and were created by the `Athlete` class's factory function, they are stored at different memory addreses:

```
>>> sarah
<__main__.Athlete object at 0x14d23f0>
>>> james
<__main__.Athlete object at 0x14cb7d0>
```

These are the memory addresses on our computer, which will differ from the values reported on yours. The key point is the memory address for "sarah" and "james" differ.

Now that `sarah` and `james` exist as object instances, you can use the familiar dot notation to access the attributes associated with each:

```
>>> sarah.name
'Sarah Sweeney'
>>> james.name
'James Jones'
>>> sarah.dob
'2002-6-17'
>>> james.dob
>>> sarah.times
['2:58', '2.58', '1.56']
>>> james.times
[]
```

The "james" object instance has no value for "dob", so nothing appears on screen.

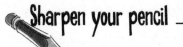
Sharpen your pencil

Here's your code (except for the santize() function, which doesn't need to change). With your pencil, write code to define the Athlete class. In addition to the __init__() method, define a new method called top3() that, when invoked, returns the top three times.

Be sure to adjust the get_coach_data() function to return an Athlete object as opposed to a dictionary, and don't forget to amend your print() statements, too.

....

.... *Write your Athlete class code here.*

....

....

....

....

....

....

....

....

....

```python
def get_coach_data(filename):
    try:
        with open(filename) as f:
            data = f.readline()
        templ = data.strip().split(',')
        return({'Name' : templ.pop(0),
                'DOB'  : templ.pop(0),
                'Times': str(sorted(set([sanitize(t) for t in templ]))[0:3])})
    except IOError as ioerr:
        print('File error: ' + str(ioerr))
        return(None)

james = get_coach_data('james2.txt')

print(james['Name'] + "'s fastest times are: " + james['Times'])
```

What needs to change here to ensure this function returns an Athlete object as opposed to a dictionary?

This line of code needs to change, too.

Sharpen your pencil
Solution

Here's your code (except for the `santize()` function, which doesn't need to change). With your pencil, you were to write code to define the `Athlete` class. In addition to the `__init__()` method, you were to define a new method called `top3()` that, when invoked, returns the top three times. You were to be sure to adjust the `get_coach_data()` function to return an `Athlete` object as opposed to a dictionary, and you weren't to forget to amend `print()`, too.

```
class Athlete:
    def __init__(self, a_name, a_dob=None, a_times=[]):
        self.name = a_name
        self.dob = a_dob
        self.times = a_times
```

There's nothing new here as this code is taken straight from the most recent IDLE session.

Did you remember to use "self"?

```
    def top3(self):
        return(sorted(set([sanitize(t) for t in self.times]))[0:3])
```

```
def get_coach_data(filename):
    try:
        with open(filename) as f:
            data = f.readline()
        templ = data.strip().split(',')
        return(  'Name' : templ.pop(0),
                 'DOB' : templ.pop(0),  Athlete(templ.pop(0), templ.pop(0), templ)
                 'Times': str(sorted(set([sanitize(t) for t in templ]))[0:3]) )
    except IOError as ioerr:
        print('File error: ' + str(ioerr))
        return(None)
```

Remove the dictionary creation code and replace it with Athlete object creation code instead.

```
james = get_coach_data('james2.txt')
```

james.name

Use the dot notation to get at your data.

Invoke the "top3()" method and convert its results to a string prior to its display on screen.

str(james.top3())

```
print(james['Name'] + "'s fastest times are: " + james['Times'])
```

TEST DRIVE

With these changes applied to your program, let's ensure you continue to get the same results as earlier. Load your code into IDLE and run it.

```
                    coach4.py – /Users/barryp/HeadFirstPython/chapter6/coach4.py
class Athlete:
    def __init__(self, a_name, a_dob=None, a_times=[]):
        self.name = a_name
        self.dob = a_dob
        self.times = a_times

    def top3(self):
        return(sorted(set([sanitize(t) for t in self.times]))[0:3])

def get_coach_data(filename):
    try:
        with open(filename) as f:
            data = f.readline()
        templ = data.strip().split(',')
        return(Athlete(templ.pop(0), templ.pop(0), templ))
    except IOError as ioerr:
        print('File error: ' + str(ioerr))
        return(None)

james = get_coach_data('james2.txt')
julie = get_coach_data('julie2.txt')
mikey = get_coach_data('mikey2.txt')
sarah = get_coach_data('sarah2.txt')

print(james.name + "'s fastest times are: " + str(james.top3()))
print(julie.name + "'s fastest times are: " + str(julie.top3()))
print(mikey.name + "'s fastest times are: " + str(mikey.top3()))
print(sarah.name + "'s fastest times are: " + str(sarah.top3()))
```

The code to the "sanitize()" function is not shown here, but it is still part of this program.

```
                                    Python Shell
>>> ================================ RESTART ================================
>>>
James Lee's fastest times are: ['2.01', '2.16', '2.22']
Julie Jones's fastest times are: ['2.11', '2.23', '2.59']
Mikey McManus's fastest times are: ['2.22', '2.31', '2.38']
Sarah Sweeney's fastest times are: ['2.18', '2.21', '2.22']
>>> |
                                                                  Ln: 30 Col: 4
```

Cool! There's no change here.

And to make objects do more, I just add more methods, right?

Yes, that's correct: more functionality = more methods.

Simply add methods to **encapsulate** the new functionality you need within your class. There's no limit to how many methods a class can have, so feel free to knock yourself out!

there are no
Dumb Questions

Q: I'm not sure I see why the top3() method is coded to return a three-item list, as opposed to a string? Surely a string would make the print() statement in the main program easier to write?

A: It would, but it wouldn't be as flexible. By returning a list (albeit a small one), the `top3()` method lets the calling code decide what happens *next*, as opposed to forcing the caller to work with a string. Granted, the current program needs to treat the list like a string, but not all programs will want or need to.

Q: Why does the class even need the top3() method? Why not store the top three times as an attribute within the class and create it as part of the object's creation?

A: Again, better not to, because doing so is *less flexible*. If you compute and store the top three times at object creation, you make it harder to extend the list of timing data associated with the object.

For instance, if you add more timing data **after** the object is created, you'll need to arrange to recompute the top three (because the new times might be fast) and update the attribute. However, when you compute the top three times "on the fly" using a call to the `top3()` method, you always ensure you're using the most up-to-date data.

Q: OK, I get that. But, with a little extra work, I could do it during object creation, right?

A: Well, yes...but we really don't advise that. By preserving the original data in each object's attributes, you are supporting the extension of the class to support additional requirements in the future (whatever they might be). If you process the data as part of the object initialization code, the assumptions you make about how programmers will use your class might just come back to bite you.

Q: But what if I'm the only programmer that'll ever use a custom class that I write?

A: Trust us: you'll thank yourself for coding your class to be as flexible as possible when you come to use it for some other purpose in a future project. When you are creating a class, you have no idea how it will be used by other programmers in their projects. And, if you think about, you have no idea how you might use it in the future, too.

Q: OK, I think I'm convinced. But tell me: how do I go about adding more times to my existing Athlete objects?

A: To do more, add more methods. With your `Athlete` class created, it's a breeze to extend it to do more work for you: simply add more methods.

So, if you want to add a single new timing value to your `times` attribute, define a method called `add_time()` to do it for you. Additionally, you can add a list of times by defining a method called `add_times()`.Then all you need to do in your code is say something like this:

```
sarah.add_time('1.31')
```
to add a single time to Sarah's timing data, or say this:

```
james.add_times(['1.21','2.22'])
```
to add a bunch of times to James's data.

Q: But surely, knowing that times is a list, I could write code like this to do the same thing?

```
sarah.times.append('1.31')
james.times.append(['1.21','2.22'])
```

A: You could, but that would be a *disaster*.

Q: What?!? Why do you say that? There's nothing wrong with my suggestion, is there?

A: Well...it does indeed work. However, the **problem** with writing code like that is that it exposes (and exploits) that fact that the timing data is stored in a list within the `Athlete` class. If you later change your class implementation to use (for instance) a string *instead of* a list, you may well break all of the existing code that uses your class and that exploits the fact that the timing data is a list.

By defining your own API with `add_time()` and `add_times()`, you leave open the possibility that the way the data is stored within your class can change in the future (obviously, only if such a change makes sense). It is worth noting that one of the reasons for using object orientation is to hide away the details of a class's implementation from the users of that class. Defining your own API *directly* supports this design ideal. Exposing the internals of your class's implementation and expecting programmers to exploit it **breaks** this fundamental ideal in a very big way.

Exercise

Let's add two methods to your class. The first, called `add_time()`, appends a single additional timing value to an athlete's timing data. The second, `add_times()`, extends an athlete's timing data with one or more timing values supplied as a list.

Here's your current class: add the code to implement these two new methods.

```
class Athlete:
    def __init__(self, a_name, a_dob=None, a_times=[]):
        self.name = a_name
        self.dob = a_dob
        self.times = a_times

    def top3(self):
        return(sorted(set([sanitize(t) for t in self.times]))[0:3])
```

Add your new methods here. →

....

....

....

....

....

....

....

....

Sharpen your pencil

Don't put down the pencil just yet! Provide a few lines of code to test your new functionality:

....

....

....

....

....

Exercise Solution

Let's add two methods to your class. The first, called `add_time()`, appends a single additional timing value to an athlete's timing data. The second, `add_times()`, extends an athlete's timing data with one of more timing values supplied as a list.

Here's your current class: you were to add the code to implement these two new methods.

```
class Athlete:
    def __init__(self, a_name, a_dob=None, a_times=[]):
        self.name = a_name
        self.dob = a_dob
        self.times = a_times

    def top3(self):
        return(sorted(set([sanitize(t) for t in self.times]))[0:3])
```

```
def add_time(self, time_value):

    self.times.append(time_value)
```
Take the supplied argument and append it to the existing list of timing values.

Don't forget to use "self"!!!

```
def add_times(self, list_of_times):

    self.times.extend(list_of_times)
```
Take the list of supplied arguments and extend the existing list of timing values with them.

Sharpen your pencil Solution

While still holding on firmly to your pencil, you were to provide a few lines of code to test your new functionality:

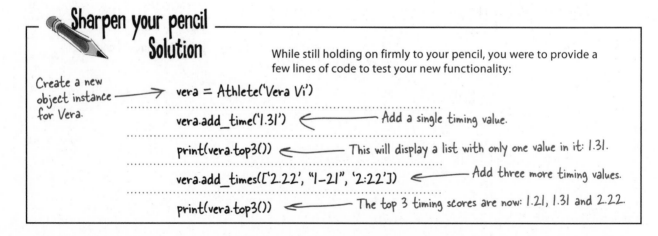

Create a new object instance for Vera. → `vera = Athlete('Vera Vi')`

`vera.add_time('1.31')` ← Add a single timing value.

`print(vera.top3())` ← This will display a list with only one value in it: 1.31.

`vera.add_times(['2.22', "1-21", '2:22'])` ← Add three more timing values.

`print(vera.top3())` ← The top 3 timing scores are now: 1.21, 1.31 and 2.22.

Do this!

Amend your code with the updated version
of your `Athlete` class *before* proceeding
with this Test Drive.

TEST DRIVE

After running your existing program, try out your test code in the IDLE shell to confirm that
everything is working as expected.

```
○ ○ ○                              Python Shell
>>> ================================ RESTART ================================
>>>
James Lee's fastest times are: ['2.01', '2.16', '2.22']    }
Julie Jones's fastest times are: ['2.11', '2.23', '2.59']  }  ← As expected.
Mikey McManus's fastest times are: ['2.22', '2.31', '2.38'] }
Sarah Sweeney's fastest times are: ['2.18', '2.21', '2.22'] }
>>>
>>> vera = Athlete('Vera Vi')  ← Create a new athlete.
>>> vera.add_time('1.31')  ← Add one timing value.
>>> print(vera.top3())
['1.31']  ← Display the top three times (there's only one, so that's all you see).
>>>
>>> vera.add_times(['2.22', "1-21", '2:22'])  ← Add three more timing values.
>>> print(vera.top3())
['1.21', '1.31', '2.22']  ← Display the top three times (which, now, makes a little more sense).
>>>
                                                            Ln: 179 Col: 4
```

Great: it worked.

You've **packaged** your code with your data and created a custom class
from which you can create objects that share behaviors. And when extra
functionality is required, **add more methods** to implement the required
functionality.

By **encapsulating** your athlete code and data within a custom class, you've
created a much more **maintainable** piece of software. You will thank
yourself for doing this when, in six months, you need to amend your code.

Well done. This is really coming along!

Emmm...maybe I'm missing something, but isn't your Athlete class wasteful? I mean, you've extended it with functionality that's **already** in lists, which feels a little like reinventing the wheel to me...

Yes, your Athlete class is much like a list.

Your `Athlete` class does indeed behave like a **list** *most of the time*, and you've added methods to expose some list functionality to the users of your class. But it's true: *you are* reinventing the wheel here. Your `add_time()` method is a thin wrapper around the list `append()` method and your `add_times()` method is list's `extend()` method in disguise.

In fact, your `Athlete` class only differs from Python's list due to the inclusion of the `name` and `dob` object attributes.

Wouldn't it be dreamy if there were a way to extend a built-in class with custom attributes? But I know it's just a fantasy...

Inherit from Python's built-in list

Python's **class** lets you create a custom class *from scratch*, just like you did with your Athlete class. However, **class** also lets you create a class by *inheriting* from any other existing class, including Python's built-in data structure classes that provide you with list, set, and dict. Such classes are referred to as *subclasses*.

What's really nice is that when you inherit from an existing class (such as list), you are given all of the existing functionality for free.

As your existing class is really nothing more than a **list** with added attributes, perhaps a better design is to kill off your Athlete class and replace it with a class that inherits from the built-in list class? It's certainly worth considering, isn't it?

Sorry to hear about your Athlete class. But, according to my files, you're in line to inherit a mountain of functionality from the built-in list class. Congratulations, you're rich!

Slippery lawyer-type

R.I.P.

Herein lies the Athlete class.

A short, but glittering, career.

Will be missed by all who knew and loved him.

Taken in his prime...

Fireside Chats

Tonight's talk: **Inheritance, a.k.a. He looks just like his father.**

Custom Class:	**Inherited Class:**
Programmers like me because they get to control *everything* in their code…and you know programmers: *they love to code*.	
	Yes, they do. But sometimes writing everything from scratch is not the best design decision.
Design! Phooey! Real programmers eat, sleep, dream, snore, and exhale code. All that design talk is for people who *can't* code!	
	Is it really? So, you're saying it's much better to do everything from scratch and repeat the work of others, because your way is the best way. Are you serious?!?
No, no, no: you're not listening. It's all done with control. When you build everything from the ground up, you're in control, as *it's all your code*.	
	And you're happy to reinvent the wheel, even though someone else solved that problem eons ago?
Of course, especially when there are custom requirements to be taken into consideration. In that case, a brand-spanking new custom class is the only way to go.	
	Not if you can extend someone else's class to handle your custom requirements. That way, you get the best of both worlds: inherited functionality (so you're not reinventing the wheel) together with the custom bits. It's a win-win situation.
Yeah, right…it's a win-win for you, not me.	
	But it's not about us: it's to do with making the life of the programmer easier, even the ones that live to code, right?
I guess so, although I'm still a fan of custom code…	

An IDLE Session

Let's see what's involved in inheriting from Python's built-in `list` class. Working in IDLE's shell, start by creating a custom list derived from the built-in `list` class that also has an attribute called `name`:

```
>>> class NamedList(list):
        def __init__(self, a_name):
            list.__init__([])
            self.name = a_name
```

Provide the name of the class that this new class derives from.

Initialize the derived from class, and then assign the argument to the attribute.

With your `NamedList` class defined, use it to create an object instance, check the object's type (using the `type()` BIF), and see what it provides (using the `dir()` BIF):

```
>>> johnny = NamedList("John Paul Jones")
```
Create a new "NamedList" object instance.
```
>>> type(johnny)
<class '__main__.NamedList'>
```
Yes, "johnny" is a "NamedList".
```
>>> dir(johnny)
['__add__', '__class__', '__contains__', '__delattr__', '__delitem__', '__dict__', '__doc__',
'__eq__', '__format__', '__ge__', '__getattribute__', '__getitem__', '__gt__', '__hash__',
'__iadd__', '__imul__', '__init__', '__iter__', '__le__', '__len__', '__lt__', '__module__',
'__mul__', '__ne__', '__new__', '__reduce__', '__reduce_ex__', '__repr__', '__reversed__',
'__rmul__', '__setattr__', '__setitem__', '__sizeof__', '__str__', '__subclasshook__',
'__weakref__', 'append', 'count', 'extend', 'index', 'insert', 'name', 'pop', 'remove',
'reverse', 'sort']
```

"johnny" can do everything a list can, as well as store data in the "name" attribute.

Use some of the functionality supplied by the `list` class to add to the data stored in `johnny`:

```
>>> johnny.append("Bass Player")
>>> johnny.extend(['Composer', "Arranger", "Musician"])
```
Add data to the "NamedList" using the methods provided by the list built in.
```
>>> johnny
['Bass Player', 'Composer', 'Arranger', 'Musician']
>>> johnny.name
'John Paul Jones'
```
Access the list data, as well as the attribute data.

Because `johnny` is a **list**, it's quite OK to do list-type things to it:

```
>>> for attr in johnny:
        print(johnny.name + " is a " + attr + ".")
```
"johnny" is like any other list, so feel free to use it wherever you'd use a list.

```
John Paul Jones is a Bass Player.
John Paul Jones is a Composer.
John Paul Jones is a Arranger.
John Paul Jones is a Musician.
```

Confirmation: John's a busy boy. ☺

Exercise

Here is the code for the now defunct `Athlete` class. In the space provided below, rewrite this class to inherit from the built-in `list` class. Call your new class `AthleteList`. Provide a few lines of code to exercise your new class, too:

```python
class Athlete:
    def __init__(self, a_name, a_dob=None, a_times=[]):
        self.name = a_name
        self.dob = a_dob
        self.times = a_times

    def top3(self):
        return(sorted(set([sanitize(t) for t in self.times]))[0:3])

    def add_time(self, time_value):
        self.times.append(time_value)

    def add_times(self, list_of_times):
        self.times.extend(list_of_times)
```

Write your new class code here. →

....
....
....
....
....
....
....
....
....
....
....

Exercise your code here. →

....
....
....

Exercise Solution

Here is the code for the now defunct `Athlete` class. In the space provided below, you were to rewrite this class to inherit from the built-in `list` class. You were to call your new class `AthleteList`, as well as provide a few lines of code to exercise your new class:

```python
class Athlete:
    def __init__(self, a_name, a_dob=None, a_times=[]):
        self.name = a_name
        self.dob = a_dob
        self.times = a_times

    def top3(self):
        return(sorted(set([sanitize(t) for t in self.times]))[0:3])

    def add_time(self, time_value):
        self.times.append(time_value)

    def add_times(self, list_of_times):
        self.times.extend(list_of_times)
```

These methods aren't needed anymore.

The class name has changed.

Inherit from the built-in list class.

```python
class AthleteList(list):

    def __init__(self, a_name, a_dob=None, a_times=[]):
        list.__init__([])
        self.name = a_name
        self.dob = a_dob
        self.extend(a_times)

    def top3(self):
        return(sorted(set([sanitize(t) for t in self]))[0:3])
```

Nothing new here... this code is very similar to the "NamedList" init code.

The data itself is the timing data, so the "times" attribute is gone.

Use the new class's name.

```python
vera = AthleteList('Vera Vi')
vera.append('1.31')
print(vera.top3())
vera.extend(['2.22', '1-21', '2:22'])
print(vera.top3())
```

This code does a good job of exercising your new class.

Now that you're inheriting from the built-in list, you can use its methods to get your work on.

Do this!

> In your code, replace your `Athlete` class code with your new `AthleteList` class code, and don't forget to change `get_coach_data()` to return an `AthleteList` object instance as opposed to an `Athlete` object instance.

there are no Dumb Questions

Q: Sorry...but not three minutes ago you were telling me not to expose the inner workings of my class to its users, because that was fundamentally a bad idea. Now you're doing the exact opposite! What gives?

A: Well spotted. In this particular case, it's OK to expose the fact that the class is built on top of **list**. This is due to the fact that the class is deliberately called `AthleteList` to distinguish it from the more generic `Athlete` class. When programmers see the word "list" in a class name, they are likely to expect the class to work like a **list** and then some. This is the case with `AthleteList`.

Q: And I can inherit from any of the built-in types?

A: Yes.

Q: What about inheriting from more than one class...does Python support multiple interitance?

A: Yes, but it's kind of scary. Refer to a good Python reference text for all the gory details.

Q: Can I inherit from my own custom classes?

A: Of course, that's the whole idea. You create a generic class that can then be "subclassed" to provide more specific, targeted functionality.

Q: Can I put my class in a module file?

A: Yes, that's a really good idea, because it lets you share your class with many of your own programs and with other programmers. For instance, if you save your `AthleteList` class to a file called `athletelist.py`, you can import the into your code using this line of code:

```
from athletelist import AthleteList
```

then use the class as if it was defined in your current program. And, of course, if you create a really useful class, pop it into its own module and upload it to PyPI for the whole world to share.

Test Drive

One last run of your program should confirm that it's working to specification now. Give it a go in IDLE to confirm.

```
coach6.py – /Users/barryp/HeadFirstPython/chapter6/coach6.py
def sanitize(time_string):
    if '-' in time_string:
        splitter = '-'
    elif ':' in time_string:
        splitter = ':'
    else:
        return(time_string)
    (mins, secs) = time_string.split(splitter)
    return(mins + '.' + secs)

class AthleteList(list):

    def __init__(self, a_name, a_dob=None, a_times=[]):
        list.__init__([])
        self.name = a_name
        self.dob = a_dob
        self.extend(a_times)

    def top3(self):
        return(sorted(set([sanitize(t) for t in self]))[0:3])

def get_coach_data(filename):
    try:
        with open(filename) as f:
            data = f.readline()
        templ = data.strip().split(',')
        return(AthleteList(templ.pop(0), templ.pop(0), templ))
    except IOError as ioerr:
        print('File error: ' + str(ioerr))
        return(None)

james = get_coach_data('james2.txt')
julie = get_coach_data('julie2.txt')
mikey = get_coach_data('mikey2.txt')
sarah = get_coach_data('sarah2.txt')

print(james.name + "'s fastest times are: " + str(james.top3()))
print(julie.name + "'s fastest times are: " + str(julie.top3()))
print(mikey.name + "'s fastest times are: " + str(mikey.top3()))
print(sarah.name + "'s fastest times are: " + str(sarah.top3()))
```

Your entire program now produces the output the coach wants.

```
Python Shell
>>> ================================ RESTART ================================
>>>
James Lee's fastest times are: ['2.01', '2.16', '2.22']
Julie Jones's fastest times are: ['2.11', '2.23', '2.59']
Mikey McManus's fastest times are: ['2.22', '2.31', '2.38']
Sarah Sweeney's fastest times are: ['2.18', '2.21', '2.22']
>>>
                                                              Ln: 306 Col: 4
```

Coach Kelly is impressed

That looks great! I can't wait to show this to my young athletes and see their reaction...

By basing your class on built-in functionality, you've leveraged the power of Python's data structures while providing the custom solution your application needs.

You've **engineered** a much more *maintainable solution* to Coach Kelly's data processing needs.

Good job!

Your Python Toolbox

You've got Chapter 6 under your belt and you've added some key Python techiques to your toolbox.

Python Lingo

- "Dictionary" – a built-in data structure that allows you to associate data values with keys.

- "Key" – the look-up part of the dictionary.

- "Value" – the data part of the dictionary (which can be any value, including another data structure).

More Python Lingo

- "self" – a method argument that always refers to the current object instance.

BULLET POINTS

- Create a empty **dictionary** using the `dict()` factory function or using `{}`.

- To access the value associated with the key `Name` in a dictionary called `person`, use the familiar square bracket notation: `person['Name']`.

- Like **list** and **set**, a Python's dictionary dynamically grows as new data is added to the data structure.

- Populate a dictionary as you go: `new_d = {}` or `new_d = dict()` and then `d['Name'] = 'Eric Idle'` or do the same thing all in the one go: `new_d = {'Name': 'Eric Idle'}`

- The `class` keyword lets you define a class.

- Class **methods** (your code) are defined in much the same way as functions, that is, with the `def` keyword.

- Class **attributes** (your data) are just like variables that exist within object instances.

- The `__init__()` method can be defined within a class to initialize object instances.

- Every method defined in a class must provide `self` as its first argument.

- Every attribute in a class must be prefixed with `self.` in order to associate it data with its instance.

- Classes can be built from scratch or can **inherit** from Python's built-in classes or from other custom classes.

- Classes can be put into a Python module and **uploaded** to PyPI.

7 web development

Putting it all together

> This Web thing will never catch on...especially now that I have my trusty Underwood to keep me company...

Sooner or later, you'll want to share your app with lots of people.

You have many options for doing this. Pop your code on PyPI, send out lots of emails, put your code on a CD or USB, or simply install your app manually on the computers of those people who need it. Sounds like a lot of work...not to mention boring. Also, what happens when you produce the next best version of your code? What happens then? How do you manage the update? Let's face it: it's such a pain that you'll think up really creative excuses not to. Luckily, you don't have to do any of this: just create a webapp instead. And, as this chapter demonstrates, using Python for web development is a breeze.

It's good to share

The coach showed us your program running on his laptop...any chance me and my friends could also get access to our list of times? I'd love to show them to my dad...

Coach Kelly's young athletes

You're a victim of your own success.

The new requests come flooding in right after Coach Kelly starts showing off your latest program. It appears that everyone wants access to the coach's data!

The thing is: what's the "best way" to do this?

You can put your program on the Web

You'll want to be able to share your functionality with lots of people...

...but you probably want only one version of your program "out there" that everyone accesses...

...and you need to make sure updates to your program are easy to apply.

A "webapp" is what you want.

If you develop your program as a *Web-based application* (or *webapp*, for short), your program is:

- Available to everyone who can get to your website

- In one place on your web server

- Easy to upate as new functionality is needed

But...how do webapps actually work?

Webapps Up Close

No matter what you do on the Web, it's all about *requests* and *responses*. A **web request** is sent from a web browser to a web server as the result of some user interaction. On the web server, a **web response** (or *reply*) is formulated and *sent back* to the web browser. The entire process can be summarized in five steps.

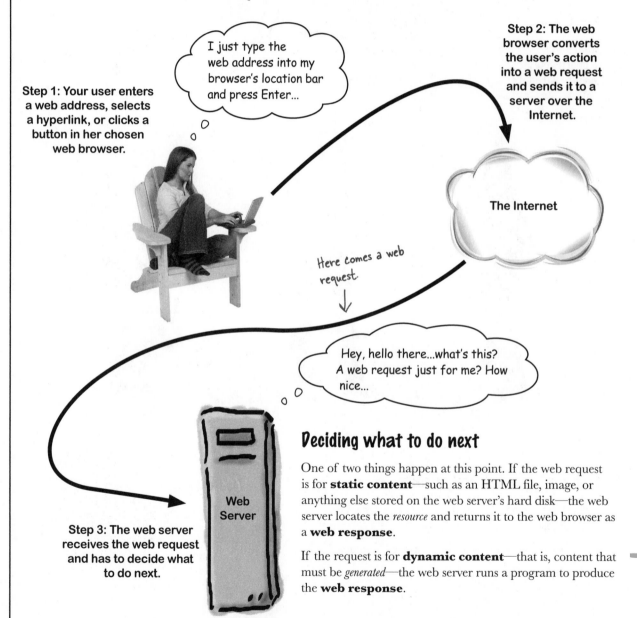

Step 1: Your user enters a web address, selects a hyperlink, or clicks a button in her chosen web browser.

I just type the web address into my browser's location bar and press Enter...

Step 2: The web browser converts the user's action into a web request and sends it to a server over the Internet.

The Internet

Here comes a web request.

Hey, hello there...what's this? A web request just for me? How nice...

Web Server

Step 3: The web server receives the web request and has to decide what to do next.

Deciding what to do next

One of two things happen at this point. If the web request is for **static content**—such as an HTML file, image, or anything else stored on the web server's hard disk—the web server locates the *resource* and returns it to the web browser as a **web response**.

If the request is for **dynamic content**—that is, content that must be *generated*—the web server runs a program to produce the **web response**.

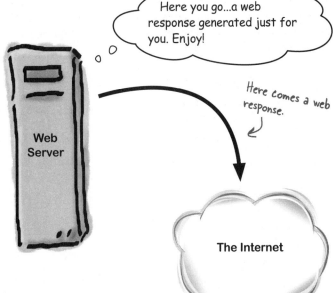

Step 4: The web server processes the web request, creating a web response, which is sent back over the Internet to the waiting web browser.

Here you go...a web response generated just for you. Enjoy!

Here comes a web response.

Web Server

The Internet

The (potentially) many substeps of step 4

In practice, step 4 can involve multiple *substeps*, depending on what the web server has to do to produce the response. Obviously, if all the server has to do is locate static content and sent it back to the browser, the substeps aren't too taxing, because it's all just file I/O.

However, when dynamic content must be *generated*, the substeps involve the web server *locating* the program to execute, *executing* the located program, and then *capturing* the output from the program as the web response...which is then sent back to the waiting web browser.

This dynamic content generation process has been standardized since the early days of the Web and is known as the **Common Gateway Interface** (CGI). Programs that conform to the standard are often referred to as *CGI scripts*.

That's exactly what I need. Thanks!

Step 5: The web browser receives the web response and displays it on your user's screen.

What does your webapp need to do?

Let's take a moment to consider what you want your webapp to look like and how it should behave on your user's web browser. You can then use this information to help you specify what your webapp needs to do.

I guess I need a nice, friendly home page to kick things off, eh?

Yeah...and I want to be able to get at my times easily...

...and once I've selected mine, I want them to look nice on my screen, so I can print them for my mom.

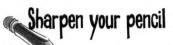

Sharpen your pencil

There's nothing like grabbing your pencil and a few blank paper napkins to quickly sketch a simple web design. You probably need three web pages: a "welcome" page, a "select an athlete" page, and a "display times" page. Go ahead and draw out a rough design on the napkins on this page, and don't forget to draw any linkages between the pages (where it makes sense).

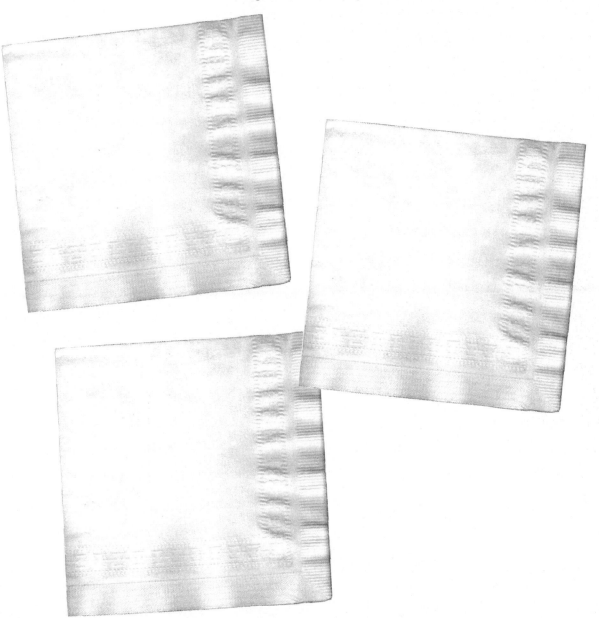

Sharpen your pencil
Solution

There's nothing like grabbing your pencil and a few blank paper napkins to quickly sketch a simple web design. You probably need three web pages: a "welcome" page, a "select an athlete" page, and a "display times" page. You were to draw out a rough design on the napkins. You were to draw any linkages between the pages (where it made sense).

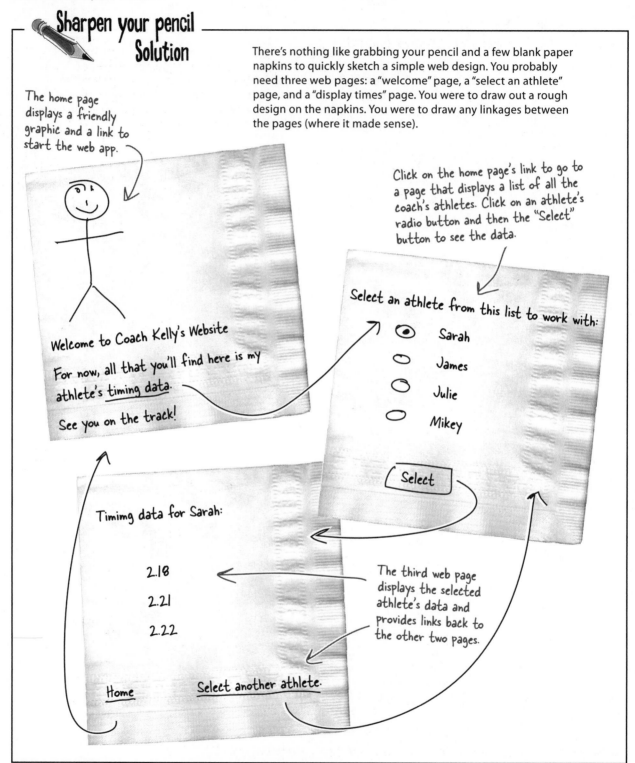

The home page displays a friendly graphic and a link to start the web app.

Welcome to Coach Kelly's Website

For now, all that you'll find here is my athlete's timing data.

See you on the track!

Click on the home page's link to go to a page that displays a list of all the coach's athletes. Click on an athlete's radio button and then the "Select" button to see the data.

Select an athlete from this list to work with:

- ◉ Sarah
- ○ James
- ○ Julie
- ○ Mikey

[Select]

Timimg data for Sarah:

2.18

2.21

2.22

Home   Select another athlete.

The third web page displays the selected athlete's data and provides links back to the other two pages.

Design your webapp with MVC

Now that you have an idea of the pages your webapp needs to provide, your next question should be: *what's the best way to build this thing?*

Ask 10 web developers that question and you'll get 10 different answers; the answer often depends on whom you ask.

Despite this, the general consensus is that great webapps conform to the *Model-View-Controller* pattern, which helps you segment your webapp's code into easily manageable functional chunks (or *components*):

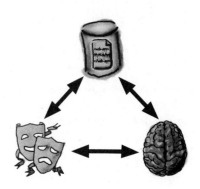

The Model
The code to store (and sometimes process) your webapp's data

The View
The code to format and display your webapp's user interface(s)

The Controller
The code to glue your webapp together and provide its business logic

By following the MVC pattern, you build your webapp in such as way as to enable your webapp to grow as new requirements dictate. You also open up the possibility of splitting the workload among a number of people, one for each component.

Let's build each of the MVC components for your webapp.

Model your data

Your web server needs to store a single copy of your data, which in this case is Coach Kelly's timing values (which start out in his text files).

When your webapp starts, the data in the text files needs to be converted to `AthleteList` object instances, stored within a dictionary (indexed by athlete name), and then saved as a pickle file. Let's put this functionality in a new function called `put_to_store()`.

While your webapp runs, the data in the pickle needs to be available to your webapp as a dictionary. Let's put this functionality in another new function called `get_from_store()`.

When your webapp starts:

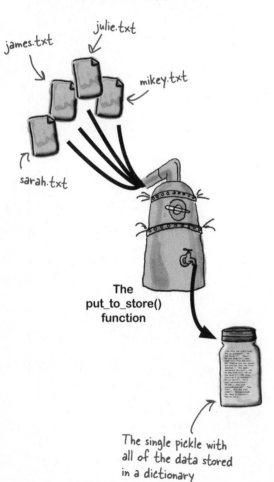

james.txt

julie.txt

mikey.txt

sarah.txt

The
put_to_store()
function

The single pickle with all of the data stored in a dictionary

While your webapp runs:

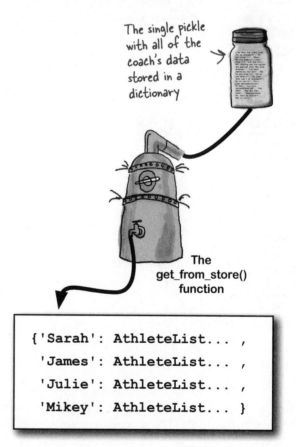

The single pickle with all of the coach's data stored in a dictionary

The
get_from_store()
function

```
{'Sarah': AthleteList... ,
 'James': AthleteList... ,
 'Julie': AthleteList... ,
 'Mikey': AthleteList... }
```

A dictionary of AthleteLists returned from the "get_from_store()" function

Exercise

Here is the outline for a new module called `athletemodel.py`, which provides the functionality described on the previous page. Some of the code is already provided for you. Your job is to provide the rest of the code to the `put_to_store()` and `get_from_store()` functions. Don't forget to protect any file I/O calls.

```
import pickle
from athletelist import AthleteList

def get_coach_data(filename):
    # Not shown here as it has not changed since the last chapter.

def put_to_store(files_list):
    all_athletes = {}
```

This function is called with a list of filenames as its sole argument.

You need code in here to populate the dictionary with the data from the files.

And don't forget to save the dictionary to a pickle (and check for file I/O errors).

```
    return(all_athletes)

def get_from_store():
    all_athletes = {}
```

Both functions need to return a dictionary of AthleteLists.

Get the dictionary from the file, so that it can be returned to the caller.

```
    return(all_athletes)
```

Exercise Solution

Here is the outline for a new module called `athletemodel.py`, which provides the functionality described on the previous page. Some of the code is already provided for you. Your job was to provide the rest of the code to the `put_to_store()` and `get_from_store()` functions. You were not to forget to protect any file I/O calls.

```python
import pickle
from athletelist import AthleteList

def get_coach_data(filename):
    # Not shown here as it has not changed since the last chapter.

def put_to_store(files_list):
    all_athletes = {}
    for each_file in files_list:
        ath = get_coach_data(each_file)
        all_athletes[ath.name] = ath
    try:
        with open('athletes.pickle', 'wb') as athf:
            pickle.dump(all_athletes, athf)
    except IOError as ioerr:
        print('File error (put_and_store): ' + str(ioerr))
    return(all_athletes)

def get_from_store():
    all_athletes = {}
    try:
        with open('athletes.pickle', 'rb') as athf:
            all_athletes = pickle.load(athf)
    except IOError as ioerr:
        print('File error (get_from_store): ' + str(ioerr))
    return(all_athletes)
```

Take each file, turn it into an AthleteList object instance, and add the athlete's data to the dictionary.

Each athlete's name is used as the "key" in the dictionary. The "value" is the AthleteList object instance.

Save the entire dictionary of AthleteLists to a pickle.

And don't forget a try/except to protect your file I/O code.

Simply read the entire pickle into the dictionary. What could be easier?

Again...don't forget your try/except.

An IDLE Session

Let's test your code to ensure that it is working to specification. Type your code into an IDLE edit window and save your code into a folder that also includes the coach's text files. Press F5 to import your code to the IDLE shell, and then use the `dir()` command to confirm that the import has been successful:

```
>>> dir()
['AthleteList', '__builtins__', '__doc__', '__name__', '__package__', 'get_coach_data',
'get_from_store', 'pickle', 'put_to_store']
```

Create a list of files to work with, and then call the `put_to_store()` function to take the data in the list of files and turn them into a dictionary stored in a pickle:

```
>>> the_files = ['sarah.txt', 'james.txt', 'mikey.txt', 'julie.txt']
>>> data = put_to_store(the_files)
>>> data
```

Here's all of the AthleteLists.

```
{'James Lee': ['2-34', '3:21', '2.34', '2.45', '3.01', '2:01', '2:01', '3:10', '2-22', '2-
01', '2.01', '2:16'], 'Sarah Sweeney': ['2:58', '2.58', '2:39', '2-25', '2-55', '2:54', '2.18',
'2:55', '2:55', '2:22', '2-21', '2.22'], 'Julie Jones': ['2.59', '2.11', '2:11', '2:23', '3-
10', '2-23', '3:10', '3.21', '3-21', '3.01', '3.02', '2:59'], 'Mikey McManus': ['2:22', '3.01',
'3:01', '3.02', '3:02', '3.02', '3:22', '2.49', '2:38', '2:40', '2.22', '2-31']}
```

At this point, the `athletes.pickle` file should appear in the same folder as your code and text files. Recall that this file is a *binary* file, so trying to view it in IDLE or in your editor is not going to make much sense. To access the data, use the dictionary returned by the `put_to_store()` or `get_from_store()` functions.

Use the existing data in the `data` dictionary to display each athlete's name and date of birth:

```
>>> for each_athlete in data:
        print(data[each_athlete].name + ' ' + data[each_athlete].dob)
```

```
James Lee 2002-3-14
Sarah Sweeney 2002-6-17
Julie Jones 2002-8-17
Mikey McManus 2002-2-24
```

By accessing the "name" and "dob" attributes, you can get at the rest of the AthleteList data.

Use the `get_from_store()` function to load the pickled data into another dictionary, then confirm that the results are as expected by repeating the code to display each athlete's name and date of birth:

```
>>> data_copy = get_from_store()
>>> for each_athlete in data_copy:
        print(data_copy[each_athlete].name + ' ' + data_copy[each_athlete].dob)
```

```
James Lee 2002-3-14
Sarah Sweeney 2002-6-17
Julie Jones 2002-8-17
Mikey McManus 2002-2-24
```

The data in the returned dictionary is as expected, exactly the same as that produced by put_to_store().

View your interface

With your model code written and working, it's time to look at your view code, which creates your webapp's user interface (UI).

On the Web, UIs are created with HTML, the Web's markup technology. If you are new to HTML, it is worth taking some time to become familiar with this *critical* web development technology. There's lots of material on the Web and more than a few good books out there.

[Note from Marketing: This is the book that we recommend for quickly getting up to speed with HTML...not that we're biased or anything. ☺ J.

(Most of) the Head First Code Review Team

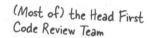

Hey, we hear you are getting into web development? We have a small module that we put together that might help you generate HTML. It's a little rough, but it works. You're more than welcome to use it for your projects, if you like.

YATE: Yet Another Template Engine

Your friends over at the Head First Code Review Team heard you're planning to write some code to generate HTML for your webapp's UI. They've sent over some code that they swear will make your life easier. It's a small library of HTML-generating helper functions called `yate`. The code was produced quickly and was originally designed to be "throw away," so the team has provided it *as is*. It's somewhat raw, but it should be OK.

```
from string import Template

def start_response(resp="text/html"):
    return('Content-type: ' + resp + '\n\n')

def include_header(the_title):
    with open('templates/header.html') as headf:
        head_text = headf.read()
    header = Template(head_text)
    return(header.substitute(title=the_title))

def include_footer(the_links):
    with open('templates/footer.html') as footf:
        foot_text = footf.read()
    link_string = ''
    for key in the_links:
        link_string += '<a href="' + the_links[key] + '">' + key + '</a>    '
    footer = Template(foot_text)
    return(footer.substitute(links=link_string))

def start_form(the_url, form_type="POST"):
    return('<form action="' + the_url + '" method="' + form_type + '">')

def end_form(submit_msg="Submit"):
    return('<p></p><input type=submit value="' + submit_msg + '">')

def radio_button(rb_name, rb_value):
    return('<input type="radio" name="' + rb_name +
                        '" value="' + rb_value + '"> ' + rb_value + '<br />')

def u_list(items):
    u_string = '<ul>'
    for item in items:
        u_string += '<li>' + item + '</li>'
    u_string += '</ul>'
    return(u_string)

def header(header_text, header_level=2):
    return('<h' + str(header_level) + '>' + header_text +
            '</h' + str(header_level) + '>')

def para(para_text):
    return('<p>' + para_text + '</p>')
```

There's not much help here, just the code. No comments, explanations, documentation, or anything!

Long Exercise

Let's get to know the `yate` code before proceeding with the rest of this chapter. For each chunk of code presented, provide a written description of what you think it does in the spaces provided:

```
from string import Template
```

Take a moment to look up the "Template" module in Python's documentation set.

Write your explanations in the spaces.

....

....

```
def start_response(resp="text/html"):
    return('Content-type: ' + resp + '\n\n')
```

One has already been done for you. → This function takes a single (optional) string as its argument and uses it to create a CGI "Content-type:" line, with "text/html" as the default.

....

```
def include_header(the_title):
    with open('templates/header.html') as headf:
        head_text = headf.read()
    header = Template(head_text)
    return(header.substitute(title=the_title))
```

....

....

....

```
def include_footer(the_links):
    with open('templates/footer.html') as footf:
        foot_text = footf.read()
    link_string = ''
    for key in the_links:
        link_string += '<a href="' + the_links[key] + '">' + key +
                              '</a>    '
    footer = Template(foot_text)
    return(footer.substitute(links=link_string))
```

....

....

....

```
def start_form(the_url, form_type="POST"):
    return('<form action="' + the_url + '" method="' + form_type + '">')

...............................................................................................

...............................................................................................

def end_form(submit_msg="Submit"):
    return('<p></p><input type=submit value="' + submit_msg + '"></form>')

...............................................................................................

...............................................................................................

def radio_button(rb_name, rb_value):
    return('<input type="radio" name="' + rb_name +
                    '" value="' + rb_value + '"> ' + rb_value + '<br />')

...............................................................................................

...............................................................................................

def u_list(items):
    u_string = '<ul>'
    for item in items:
        u_string += '<li>' + item + '</li>'
    u_string += '</ul>'
    return(u_string)

...............................................................................................

...............................................................................................

...............................................................................................

def header(header_text, header_level=2):
    return('<h' + str(header_level) + '>' + header_text +
            '</h' + str(header_level) + '>')

...............................................................................................

...............................................................................................

def para(para_text):
    return('<p>' + para_text + '</p>')

...............................................................................................

...............................................................................................
```

Long Exercise Solution

Let's get to know the `yate` code before proceeding with the rest of this chapter. For each chunk of code presented, you were to provide a written description of what you think it does:

```python
from string import Template
```

Import the "Template" class from the standard library's "string" module. This allows for simple string-substitution templates.

Note the default for "resp". →

```python
def start_response(resp="text/html"):
    return('Content-type: ' + resp + '\n\n')
```

This function takes a single (optional) string as its argument and uses it to create a CGI "Content-type:" line, with "text/html" as the default.

Open the template file (which is HTML), read it in, and substitute in the provided "title". →

```python
def include_header(the_title):
    with open('templates/header.html') as headf:
        head_text = headf.read()
    header = Template(head_text)
    return(header.substitute(title=the_title))
```

This function takes a single string as its argument and uses at the title for the start of a HTML page. The page itself is stored within a separate file in "templates/header.html", and the title is substituted in as needed.

Open the template file (which is HTML), read it in, and substitute in the provided dictionary of HTML links in "the_links". →

```python
def include_footer(the_links):
    with open('templates/footer.html') as footf:
        foot_text = footf.read()
    link_string = ''
    for key in the_links:
        link_string += '<a href="' + the_links[key] + '">' + key +
                        '</a>        '
    footer = Template(foot_text)
    return(footer.substitute(links=link_string))
```

Turn the dictionary of links into a string, which is then substituted into the template.

This looks a little weird, but it's an HTML hack for forcing spaces into a string. ←

Similar to the "include_header" function, this one uses its single string as its argument to create the end of a HTML page. The page itself is stored within a separate file in "templates/footer.html", and the argument is used to dynamically create a set of HTML link tags. Based on how they are used, it looks like the argument needs to be a dictionary.

This is typically either
"POST" or "GET".

```
def start_form(the_url, form_type="POST"):
    return('<form action="' + the_url + '" method="' + form_type + '">')
```

This function returns the HTML for the start of a form and lets the caller
specify the URL to send the form's data to, as well as the method to use.

```
def end_form(submit_msg="Submit"):
    return('<p></p><input type=submit value="' + submit_msg + '"></form>')
```

This function returns the HTML markup, which terminates the form while
allowing the caller to customize the text of the form's "submit" button.

```
def radio_button(rb_name, rb_value):
    return('<input type="radio" name="' + rb_name +
                    '" value="' + rb_value + '"> ' + rb_value + '<br />')
```

Given a radio-button name and value, create a HTML radio button (which is
typically included within a HTML form). Note: both arguments are required.

A simple "for"
loop does the
trick. →

```
def u_list(items):
    u_string = '<ul>'
    for item in items:
        u_string += '<li>' + item + '</li>'
    u_string += '</ul>'
    return(u_string)
```

Given a list of items, this function turns the list into a HTML unnumbered
list. A simple "for" loop does all the work, adding a LI to the UL element
with each iteration.

```
def header(header_text, header_level=2):
    return('<h' + str(header_level) + '>' + header_text +
        '</h' + str(header_level) + '>')
```

Create and return a HTML header tag (H1, H2, H2, and so on) with level 2
as the default. The "header_text" argument is required.

```
def para(para_text):
    return('<p>' + para_text + '</p>')
```

Enclose a paragraph of text (a string) in HTML paragraph tags. Almost not
worth the effort, is it?

there are no
Dumb Questions

Q: Where are the HTML templates used in the include_header() and include_footer() functions?

A: They are included with the `yate` module's download. Go ahead and grab them from the *Head First Python* support website, and put them into a folder of your choice.

Q: Why do I need yate at all? Why not include the HTML that I need right in the code and generate it with print() as needed?

A: You could, but it's not as flexible as the approach shown here. And (speaking from bitter experience) using a collection of `print()` statements to generate HTML works, but it turns your code into an *unholy mess.*

Q: And you did this because you are using MVC?

A: Partly, yes. The reason the MVC pattern is being followed is to ensure that the model code is separate from the view code, which are both separate from the controller code. No matter the size of the project, following MVC can make your life easier.

Q: But surely MVC is overkill for something this small?

A: We don't think so, because you can bet that your webapp will grow, and when you need to add more features, the MVC "separation of duties" really shines.

 An IDLE Session

Let's get to know the `yate` module even more. With the code downloaded and tucked away in an easy-to-find folder, load the module into IDLE and press F5 to take it for a spin. Let's start by testing the `start_response()` function. The CGI standard states that every web response must start with a header line that indictes the *type* of the data included in the request, which `start_response()` lets you control:

```
>>> start_response()
'Content-type: text/html\n\n'
>>> start_response("text/plain")
'Content-type: text/plain\n\n'
>>> start_response("application/json")
'Content-type: application/json\n\n'
```

The default CGI response header, plus variations on a theme.

The `include_header()` function generates the start of a web page and let's you customizee its title:

```
>>> include_header("Welcome to my home on the web!")
'<html>\n<head>\n<title>Welcome to my home on the web!</title>\n<link type="text/css"
rel="stylesheet" href="/coach.css" />\n</head>\n<body>\n<h1>Welcome to my home on the web!</
h1>\n'
```

This all looks a little bit messy, but don't worry; it's meant to be processed by your web browser, NOT by you. Your web browser will have no difficulty working with this HTML. Note the inclusion of a link to a CSS file (more on this in a bit).

The `include_footer()` function produces HTML that terminates a web page, providing links (if provided as a dictionary). An empty dictionary switches off the inclusion of the linking HTML:

```
>>> include_footer({'Home': '/index.html', 'Select': '/cgi-bin/select.py'})
'<p>\n<a href="/index.html">Home</a>    <a href="/cgi-bin/select.
py">Select</a>    \n</p>\n</body>\n</html>\n'
>>> include_footer({})
'<p>\n\n</p>\n</body>\n</html>\n'
```

With links included, and without.

The `start_form()` and `end_form()` functions bookend a HTML form, with the parameter (if supplied) adjusting the contents of the generated HTML:

```
>>> start_form("/cgi-bin/process-athlete.py")
'<form action="/cgi-bin/process-athlete.py" method="POST">'
>>> end_form()
'<p></p><input type=submit value="Submit"></form>'
>>> end_form("Click to Confirm Your Order")
'<p></p><input type=submit value="Click to Confirm Your Order"></form>'
```

The argument allows you to specify the name of the program on the server to send the form's data to.

HTML radio buttons are easy to create with the `radio_button()` function:

```
>>> for fab in ['John', 'Paul', 'George', 'Ringo']:
        radio_button(fab, fab)


'<input type="radio" name="John" value="John"> John<br />'
'<input type="radio" name="Paul" value="Paul"> Paul<br />'
'<input type="radio" name="George" value="George"> George<br />'
'<input type="radio" name="Ringo" value="Ringo"> Ringo<br />'
```

Which one is your favorite? Select from the list of radio buttons.

Unordered list are a breeze with the `u_list()` function:

```
u_list(['Life of Brian', 'Holy Grail'])
'<ul><li>Life of Brian</li><li>Holy Grail</li></ul>'
```

Again, not too easy on your eye, but fine as far as your web browser is concerned.

The `header()` function lets you quickly format HTML headings at a selected level (with 2 as the default):

```
>>> header("Welcome to my home on the web")
'<h2>Welcome to my home on the web</h2>'
>>> header("This is a sub-sub-sub-sub heading", 5)
'<h5>This is a sub-sub-sub-sub heading</h5>'
```

Nothing too exciting here, but it works as expected. Same goes for here.

Last, but not least, the `para()` function encloses a chunk of text within HTML paragraph tags:

```
>>> para("Was it worth the wait? We hope it was...")
'<p>Was it worth the wait? We hope it was...</p>'
```

Control your code

Your **model** code is ready, and you have a good idea of how the `yate` module can help you with your **view** code. It's time to glue it all together with some **controller** code.

First things first: you need to arrange your wedapp's directory structure to help keep things organized. To be honest, anything goes here, although by giving it a little thought, you can enhance your ability to extend your webapp over time. Here's one folder structure that *Head First Labs* recommends.

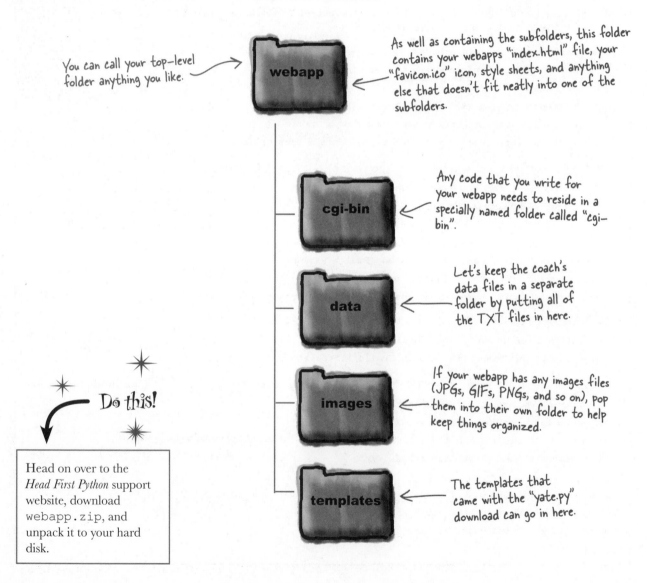

You can call your top-level folder anything you like.

As well as containing the subfolders, this folder contains your webapps "index.html" file, your "favicon.ico" icon, style sheets, and anything else that doesn't fit neatly into one of the subfolders.

webapp

cgi-bin

Any code that you write for your webapp needs to reside in a specially named folder called "cgi-bin".

data

Let's keep the coach's data files in a separate folder by putting all of the TXT files in here.

images

If your webapp has any images files (JPGs, GIFs, PNGs, and so on), pop them into their own folder to help keep things organized.

templates

The templates that came with the "yate.py" download can go in here.

Do this!

Head on over to the *Head First Python* support website, download `webapp.zip`, and unpack it to your hard disk.

CGI lets your web server run programs

The Common Gateway Interface (CGI) is an Internet standard that allows for a web server to run a **server-side program**, known as a *CGI script*.

Typically, CGI scripts are placed inside a special folder called cgi-bin, so that the web server knows where to find them. On some operating systems (most notably UNIX-styled systems), CGI scripts must be set to *executable* before the web server can execute them when responding to a web request.

More on this in a little bit.

So...to run my webapp, I need a web server with CGI enabled.

I'm all fired up and ready to go! I live to serve-up HTML and run CGIs...

CGI Web Server

All webapps need to run on web servers.

Practically every web server on the planet supports CGI. Whether your running *Apache*, *IIS*, *nginx*, *Lighttpd*, or any of the others, they all support running CGI scripts written in Python.

But using one of these tools here is *overkill*. There's no way the coach is going to agree to download, unpack, install, configure, and manage one of these industry heavyweights.

As luck would have it, Python comes with its very own web server, included in the http.server library module. Check the contents of the webapp.zip download: it comes with a CGI-enabled web server called simplehttpd.py.

Here are the five lines of code needed to build a web server in Python.

Import the HTTP server and CGI modules.

Specify a port.

Create a HTTP server.

Display a friendly message and start your server.

```python
from http.server import HTTPServer, CGIHTTPRequestHandler

port = 8080
httpd = HTTPServer(('', port), CGIHTTPRequestHandler)
print("Starting simple_httpd on port: " + str(httpd.server_port))
httpd.serve_forever()
```

Display the list of athletes

Let's create a program called `generate_list.py` which, when executed by the web server, dynamically generates a HTML web page that looks something like this:

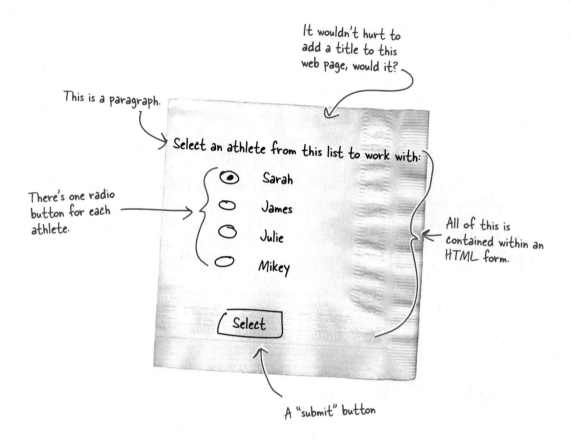

It wouldn't hurt to add a title to this web page, would it?

This is a paragraph.

Select an athlete from this list to work with:

○ Sarah

○ James

○ Julie

○ Mikey

There's one radio button for each athlete.

All of this is contained within an HTML form.

Select

A "submit" button

When your user selects an athlete by clicking on her radio button and clicking Select, a *new* web request is sent to the web server. This new web request contains data about which radio button was pressed, *as well as the name of a CGI script to send the form's data to.*

Recall that all of your CGI scripts need to reside in the `cgi-bin` folder on your web server. With this in mind, let's make sure your `generate_list.py` CGI script sends its data to another program called:

cgi-bin/generate_timing_data.py

Pööl Puzzle

Your **job** is to take the code from the pool and place them into the blank lines in the CGI script. You may **not** use the same line of code more than once. Your **goal** is to make a CGI script that will generate a HTML page that matches the hand-drawn design from the previous page.

I've started things off for you.

```
import athletemodel
import yate
import glob
```

Import the modules that you need. You've already met "athletemodel" and "yate". The "glob" module lets you query your operating system for a list of file names.

```
data_files = glob.glob("data/*.txt")
athletes = athletemodel.put_to_store(data_files)
```

Use your "put_to_store()" function to create a dictionary of athletes from the list of data files.

....
....
....
....

Let's add a link to the bottom of the generated HTML page that takes your user home.

....
....
....
....

```
print(yate.include_footer({"Home": "/index.html"}))
```

Note: each thing from the pool can be used once!

```
print(yate.start_form("generate_timing_data.py"))
print(yate.para("Select an athlete from the list to work with:"))
print(yate.include_header("Coach Kelly's List of Athletes"))
print(yate.radio_button("which_athlete", athletes[each_athlete].name))
for each_athlete in athletes:
print(yate.start_response())        print(yate.end_form("Select"))
```

Pool Puzzle Solution

Your **job** was to take the code from the pool and place them into the blank lines in the CGI script. You were **not** to use the same line of code more than once. Your **goal** was to make a CGI script that generates a HTML page that matches the hand-drawn design.

```python
import athletemodel
import yate
import glob

data_files = glob.glob("data/*.txt")
athletes = athletemodel.put_to_store(data_files)

print(yate.start_response())
print(yate.include_header("Coach Kelly's List of Athletes"))
print(yate.start_form("generate_timing_data.py"))
print(yate.para("Select an athlete from the list to work with:"))

for each_athlete in athletes:
    print(yate.radio_button("which_athlete", athletes[each_athlete].name))
print(yate.end_form("Select"))

print(yate.include_footer({"Home": "/index.html"}))
```

Always start with a Content-type line.

Start generating the form, providing the name of the server-side program to link to.

Generate a radio-button for each of your athletes.

Start generating the web page, providing an appropriate title.

A paragraph telling your user what to do

End the form generation with a custom "Submit" button.

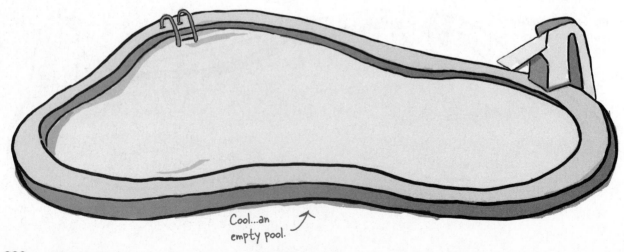

Cool...an empty pool.

Watch it!

What you need to do next depends on the operating system you're running your web server on.

If you are running on Windows, stop reading right now and proceed to the Test Drive. However, if you are running a Unix-based system (such as Linux, Mac OS X, or BSD) you need to do two things to prepare your CGI script for execution:

1. *Set the **executable bit** for your CGI using the **chmod +x** command.*

2. *Add the following line of code to the very top of your program:*

```
#! /usr/local/bin/python3
```

From your terminal window, type chmod +x generate_list.py to set the executable bit. You need do this only once.

Test Drive

To test drive your CGI script, you need to have a web server up and running. The code to `simplehttpd.py` is included as part of the `webapp.zip` download. After you unpack the ZIP file, open a terminal window in the `webapp` folder and start your web server:

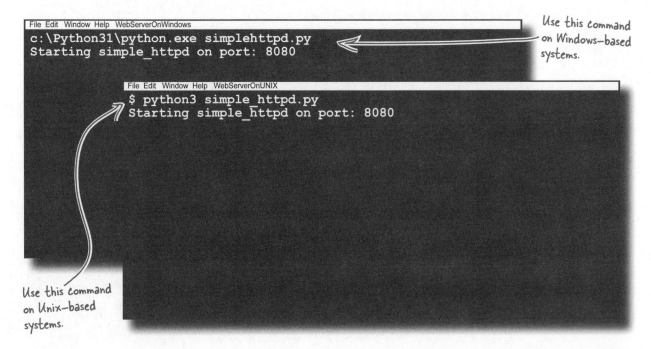

File Edit Window Help WebServerOnWindows
```
c:\Python31\python.exe simplehttpd.py
Starting simple_httpd on port: 8080
```

Use this command on Windows-based systems.

File Edit Window Help WebServerOnUNIX
```
$ python3 simple_httpd.py
Starting simple_httpd on port: 8080
```

Use this command on Unix-based systems.

TEST DRIVE, CONTINUED

With your web server running, let's load up Coach Kelly's home page and get things going. You've started your web server running on port 8080 on your computer, so you need to use the following web address in your web browser: `http://localhost:8080`.

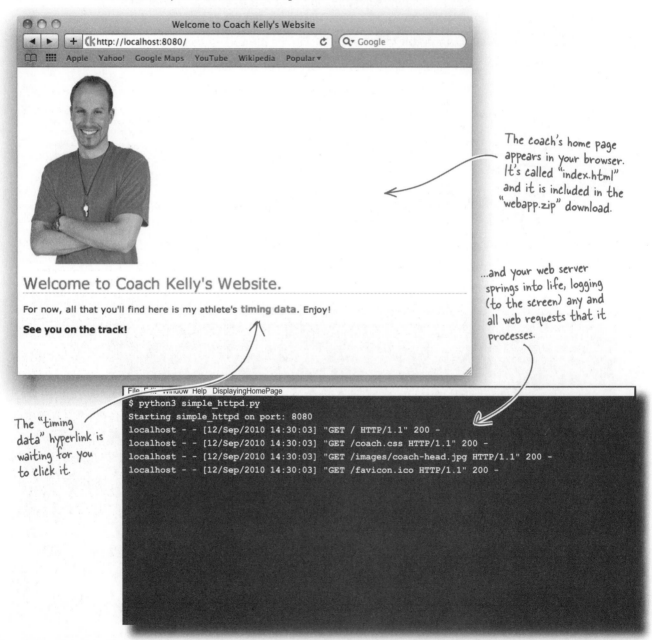

The coach's home page appears in your browser. It's called "index.html" and it is included in the "webapp.zip" download.

...and your web server springs into life, logging (to the screen) any and all web requests that it processes.

The "timing data" hyperlink is waiting for you to click it.

Sure enough, clicking on the home page's link runs the `generate_list.py` program on the web server, which displays Coach Kelly's athletes as a list of radio buttons.

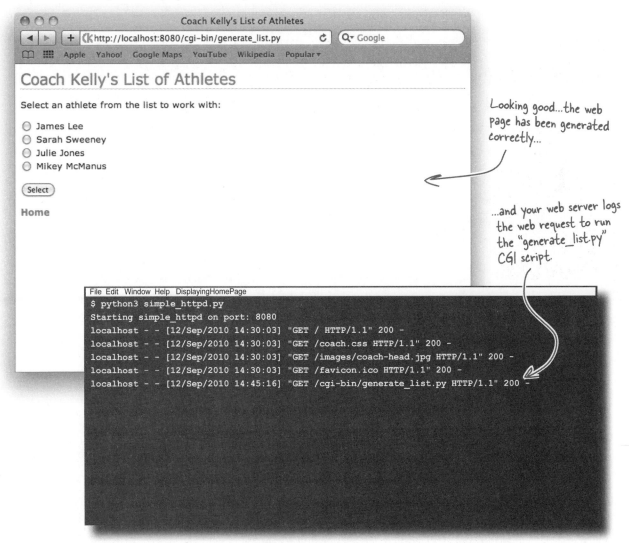

Looking good...the web page has been generated correctly...

...and your web server logs the web request to run the "generate_list.py" CGI script.

You can click the Home hyperlink to return to the coach's home page, or select an athlete from the list (by clicking on their radio-button), before pressing the Select button to continue.

Select an athlete and press Select. What happens?

The dreaded 404 error!

Whoops! Your web server has responded with a "404" error code, which is its way of telling you that something was wrong with *your* request. The web server is in fact telling you that it can't locate the resource that your web browser requested, so it's telling you that *you* made a mistake:

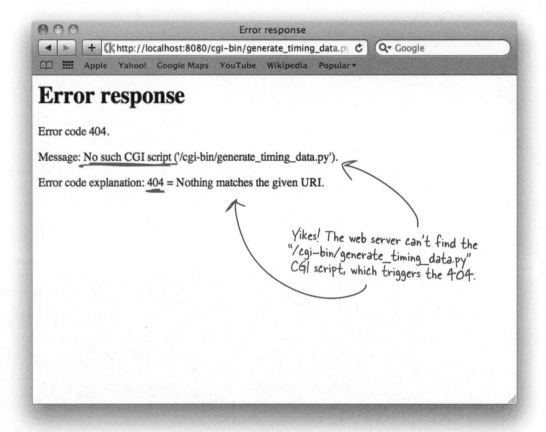

Check the web server's console window to confirm that your attempt to post your form's data to `generate_timing_data.py` resulted in failure.

Which isn't really that surprising seeing as *you have yet to write that code!* So...things aren't as bad as they first appear. The "404" error is *exactly* what you would expect to be displayed in this situation, so your `generate_list.py` CGI is working fine. What's needed is the code to the *other* CGI script.

If you create the required CGI script, you'll be back on track.

Fireside Chats

Tonight's talk: To be CGI or not to be CGI, that is the question.

A Python Program:

Listen: you're really not all that different than me; you just work on a web server, whereas I can work *anywhere*.

Special?!? But you only work on the Web, nowhere else. How's that "special"?

Nonsense! The truth is that you work *only* on the Web and break pretty quickly when used elsewhere. You don't even have control over your own I/O.

Like [sniggers] generating text in the form of HTML? That's really taxing…

Oh, get over yourself! You're a regular program, just like me. I can generate HTML, too, I just choose not to.

I guess so…

Ummmm…I guess so.

A Python CGI Script:

Yes. I like to think of myself as *special*.

Because all the cool stuff works on the Web these days and I'm designed, optimized, tailored, and engineered for the Web. Because the Web's a cool place, it follows that I must be cool, too. See: *special*.

I don't need control over my input and output. I have a friendly web server to take care of that for me. My input *comes from* the web server and my output *goes to* the web server. This arrangement allows me to concentrate on the important stuff.

Smirk all you want; HTML makes the World Wide Web go around and I'm a master at generating it *dynamically*, *on demand*, and *as needed*. Without me, the Web would be a pretty static place.

And if you did generate HTML, you'd want it displayed somewhere…like in a browser?

And to do that you'd need to rely on the services of a friendly web server, right?

Which would make you a CGI script. So, you'd be *special*, too. Q.E.D.

Create another CGI script

Let's take a moment to recall what is required from the `generate_timing_data.py` CGI script. Based on your hand-drawn sketch from earlier, your need to generate a new HTML page that contains the top three times for the selected athlete:

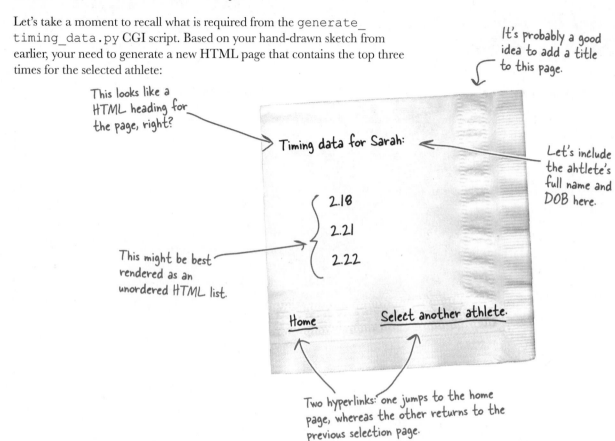

It's probably a good idea to add a title to this page.

This looks like a HTML heading for the page, right?

Timing data for Sarah:

Let's include the ahtlete's full name and DOB here.

2.18

2.21

2.22

This might be best rendered as an unordered HTML list.

Home

Select another athlete.

Two hyperlinks: one jumps to the home page, whereas the other returns to the previous selection page.

But how do you know which athlete is selected?

When you click on a radio-button and then press the Select button, a new web request is sent to the server. The web request identifies the CGI script to execute (in this case, that's `generate_timing_data.py`), together with the form's data. The web server arranges to send the form's data to your CGI script *as its input*. Within your code, you can access the form data using Python's `cgi` module, which is part of the standard library:

Import the "cgi" library.

Grab all of the form data and put it in a dictionary.

```
import cgi
form_data = cgi.FieldStorage()
athlete_name = form_data['which_athlete'].value
```

Access a named piece of data from the form's data.

Sharpen your pencil

Write the code to your new CGI script here.

It's time to exercise your newly acquired web-coding chops. Grab your pencil and write the code for the `generate_timing_data.py` CGI script. It's not too different from the `generate_list.py` code, so you should be able to reuse a lot of your existing code.

....

....

....

....

....

....

....

....

....

....

....

....

....

....

....

....

....

....

....

....

....

Sharpen your pencil
Solution

It's time to exercise your newly acquired web-coding chops. You were to grab your pencil and write the code for the `generate_timing_data.py` CGI script. It's not too different from the `generate_list.py` code, so you should be able to reuse a lot of your existing code.

```
#! /usr/local/bin/python3
```
← This line is needed on Unix—based systems only.

Import the libraries and modules you intend to use. →
```
import cgi

import athletemodel

import yate
```

Get the data from the model. →
```
athletes = athletemodel.get_from_store()
```

Which athlete's data are you working with? →
```
form_data = cgi.FieldStorage()

athlete_name = form_data['which_athlete'].value
```

Nothing new here → or here.
```
print(yate.start_response())

print(yate.include_header("Coach Kelly's Timing Data"))

print(yate.header("Athlete: " + athlete_name + ", DOB: " +

                  athletes[athlete_name].dob + "."))
```
← Grab the athlete's name and DOB.

```
print(yate.para("The top times for this athlete are:"))

print(yate.u_list(athletes[athlete_name].top3()))
```
← Turn the top three list into an unordered HTML list.

The bottom of this web page → has two links.
```
print(yate.include_footer({"Home": "/index.html",

                           "Select another athlete": "generate_list.py"}))
```

↖ A link back to the previous CGI script.

Note: If you are on a Unix-based system, don't forget to add "chmod +x generate_timing_data.py" to set the executable bit.

TEST DRIVE

Your web server should still be running from earlier. If it isn't, start it again. In your web browser, return to the coach's home page, then select the hyperlink to display the list of athletes, select Sarah, and then press the button.

This all looks OK.

Ah, phooey! Something's not quite right here. Where's Sarah's top three times?

Does the web server's logging information tell you anything?

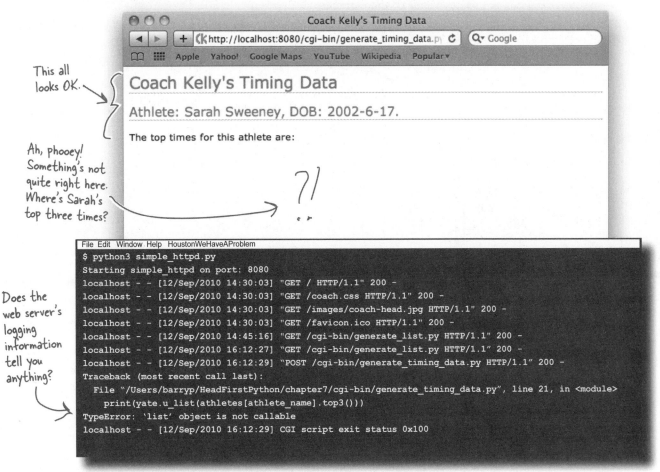

Coach Kelly's Timing Data

Coach Kelly's Timing Data

Athlete: Sarah Sweeney, DOB: 2002-6-17.

The top times for this athlete are:

?!

```
File Edit  Window  Help  HoustonWeHaveAProblem
$ python3 simple_httpd.py
Starting simple_httpd on port: 8080
localhost - - [12/Sep/2010 14:30:03] "GET / HTTP/1.1" 200 -
localhost - - [12/Sep/2010 14:30:03] "GET /coach.css HTTP/1.1" 200 -
localhost - - [12/Sep/2010 14:30:03] "GET /images/coach-head.jpg HTTP/1.1" 200 -
localhost - - [12/Sep/2010 14:30:03] "GET /favicon.ico HTTP/1.1" 200 -
localhost - - [12/Sep/2010 14:45:16] "GET /cgi-bin/generate_list.py HTTP/1.1" 200 -
localhost - - [12/Sep/2010 16:12:27] "GET /cgi-bin/generate_list.py HTTP/1.1" 200 -
localhost - - [12/Sep/2010 16:12:29] "POST /cgi-bin/generate_timing_data.py HTTP/1.1" 200 -
Traceback (most recent call last):
  File "/Users/barryp/HeadFirstPython/chapter7/cgi-bin/generate_timing_data.py", line 21, in <module>
    print(yate.u_list(athletes[athlete_name].top3()))
TypeError: 'list' object is not callable
localhost - - [12/Sep/2010 16:12:29] CGI script exit status 0x100
```

Your CGI has suffered from a `TypeError` exception, but other than looking at the web server's logging screen, it's not clear *on the web browser screen* that anything has gone wrong.

BRAIN BARBELL

What do you think is the problem here? Take a moment to study the error message before flipping the page.

Enable CGI tracking to help with errors

The CGI standard dictates that any output generated by a server-side program (your CGI script) should be captured by the web server and sent to the waiting web browser. Specifically, anything sent to STDOUT (standard output) is captured.

When your CGI script raises an exception, Python arranges for the error message to display on STDERR (standard error). The CGI mechanism is programmed to ignore this output because all it wants is the CGI script's standard output.

When your CGI works, I'll fill your STDOUT with lovely HTML. When your CGI fails, it's a case of—POOF!—gone for good. Sorry, but that's the way the CGI cookie crumbles...

Web Server

This behavior is fine when the webapp is deployed, but *not* when it's being developed. Wouldn't it be useful to see the details of the exception in the browser window, as opposed to constantly having to jump to the web server's logging screen?

Well…guess what? Python's standard library comes with a CGI tracking module (called cgitb) that, when enabled, arranges for detailed error messages to appear in your web browser. These messages can help you work out where your CGI has gone wrong. When you've fixed the error and your CGI is working well, simply switch off CGI tracking:

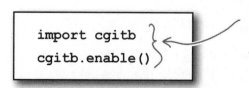

```
import cgitb
cgitb.enable()
```

Add these two lines near the start of your CGI scripts to enable Python's CGI tracking technology.

Test Drive

Add the two CGI tracking lines of code near the top of your `generate_timing_data.py` CGI script. Press the Back button on your web browser and press the Select button again. Let's see what happens this time.

Wow! Look at all of this detail.

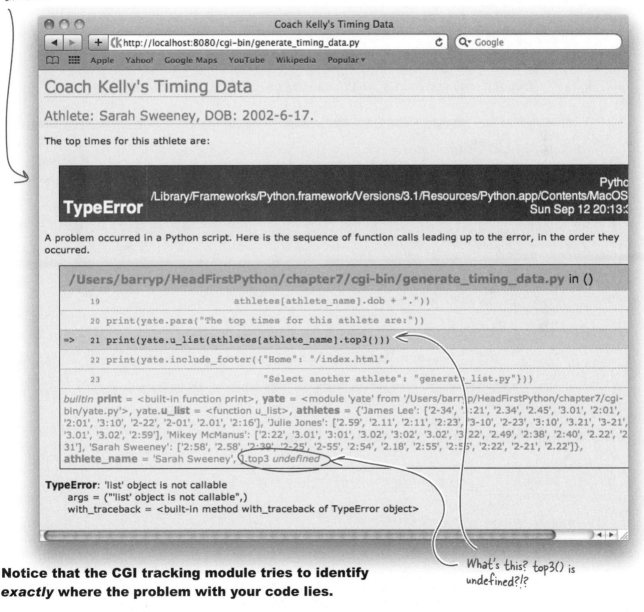

Notice that the CGI tracking module tries to identify *exactly* where the problem with your code lies.

What's this? top3() is undefined?!?

A small change can make all the difference

The CGI tracking output indicates an error with the use of the `top3()` method from the `AthleteList` code.

A quick review of the code to the `AthleteList` class uncovers the source of the error: the `top3()` method has been redesignated as a **class property**.

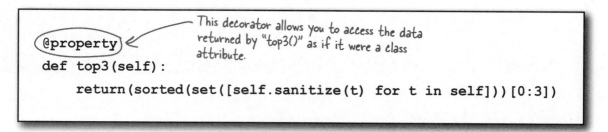

The use of the `@property` decorator allows the `top3()` method to appear like an attribute to users of the class. So, instead of calling the `top3()` method like this:

> *A method call always needs the parentheses...*

```
print(yate.u_list(athletes[athlete_name].top3()))
```

Treat the `top3()` method as if it was another class attribute, and call it like this:

```
print(yate.u_list(athletes[athlete_name].top3))
```

It's a small change, but it's an important one

> *...unless the method is declared to be an "@property", in which case parentheses are NOT required.*

When a change is made to the way a class is used, you need to be careful to consider what impact the change has on existing programs, both yours and those written by others.

At the moment, you are the only one using the `AthleteList` class, so it's not a big deal to fix this. But imagine if thousands of programmers were using and relying on your code…

Let's fix your CGI script and try again.

—Test Drive

Make the small edit to your code to remove the brackets from the call to the `top3()` method, press your web browser's Back button, and press the Select button one last time.

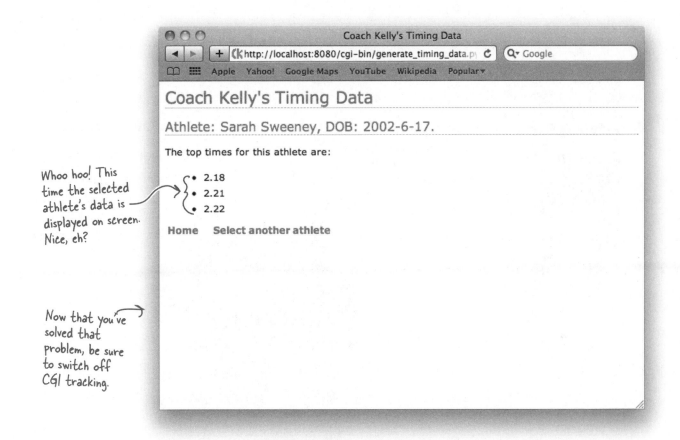

Whoo hoo! This time the selected athlete's data is displayed on screen. Nice, eh?

Now that you've solved that problem, be sure to switch off CGI tracking.

Coach Kelly's Timing Data

http://localhost:8080/cgi-bin/generate_timing_data.py

Coach Kelly's Timing Data

Athlete: Sarah Sweeney, DOB: 2002-6-17.

The top times for this athlete are:

- 2.18
- 2.21
- 2.22

Home   Select another athlete

---

there are no Dumb Questions

Q: What happens if the coach recruits new athletes?

A: All Coach Kelly needs do is create a new text file similar to the others, and your webapp handles the rest by dynamically including the new athlete the next time your webapp runs, which occurs when someone clicks on the home page's "timing data" hyperlink.

Q: Shouldn't the server's data be in a database as opposed to a pickle? Surely that would be better, right?

A: In this case, it's probably overkill to use a database, but it might be worth considering sometime in the future.

Your webapp's a hit!

By moving your program to the Web, you've made it a no-brainer for Coach Kelly to share his data with not only his athletes, but with *anyone* else that needs to access his data.

By conforming to the **MVC** pattern and using **CGI**, you've built a webapp in such a way that it's easy to extend as new requirements are identified.

Congratulations! You're a web developer.

"you are here 253".

Your Python Toolbox

You've got Chapter 7 under your belt and you've added some key Python techiques to your toolbox.

Python Lingo

- "@property" – a decorator that lets you arrange for a class method to appear as if it is a class attribute.

Web Lingo

- "webapp" – a program that runs on the Web.
- "web request" – sent from the web browser to the web server.
- "web response" – sent from the web server to the web browser in repsonse to a web request.
- "CGI" – the Common Gateway Interface, which allows a web server to run a server-side program.
- "CGI script" – another name for a server-side program.

BULLET POINTS

- The *Model-View-Controller* pattern lets you design and build a webapp in a maintainable way.
- The **model** stores your webapp's data.
- The **view** displays your webapp's user interface.
- The **controller** glues everything together with programmed logic.
- The standard library `string` module includes a class called `Template`, which supports simple string substitutions.
- The standard library `http.server` module can be used to build a simple web server in Python.
- The standard library `cgi` module provides support for writing CGI scripts.
- The standard library `glob` module is great for working with lists of filenames.
- Set the **executable** bit with the `chmod +x` command on *Linux* and *Mac OS X*.
- The standard library `cgitb` module, when enabled, lets you see CGI coding errors within your browser.
- Use `cgitb.enable()` to switch on CGI tracking in your CGI code.
- Use `cgi.FieldStorage()` to access data sent to a web server as part of a web request; the data arrives as a Python dictionary.

8 mobile app development

Small devices

This had better be a smartphone running Honeycomb or Mr. Smooth is history!

Putting your data on the Web opens up all types of possibilities.

Not only can anyone from anywhere interact with your webapp, but they are increasingly doing so from a collection of diverse computing devices: PCs, laptops, tablets, palmtops, and even mobile phones. And it's not just humans interacting with your webapp that you have to support and worry about: *bots* are small programs that can automate web interactions and typically want your data, not your human-friendly HTML. In this chapter, you exploit Python on Coach Kelly's mobile phone to write an app that interacts with your webapp's data.

The world is getting smaller

Coach Kelly is continuing to use his webapp every day, but he's having a problem with his new smartphone.

> I can access my timing data over WiFi on my phone, but it's so small it's all but impossible to read, let alone click on links or buttons. Can you take a look at it for me? Gotta dash. I've got another 5K to do before breakfast...

There's more than just desktop computers out there.

Who knew that your users would try to interact with your webapp using something other than a desktop computer or laptop?

It's a diverse computing environment out there.

Coach Kelly is on Android

The coach has a lovely new smartphone that's running Google's Android operating system. Sure enough, when you check it out, the webapp is way too small and not much use on the coach's three-inch screen:

Does anyone have a magnifying glass?

And don't go telling me to do all that two-fingered zoom and double-tapping thing. That just drives me crazy!

Obviously, the coach needs to access his data and run his webapp on his phone…but what's the *best way* to do this if not through the phone's browser?

✏️ Sharpen your pencil

Open your web browser on your desktop computer (or phone) and enter "Python for Android" into your favorite search engine. Make a note in the space below of the most promising site from your search results:

....

....

Sharpen your pencil Solution

You were to open your web browser on your desktop computer (or phone) and enter "Python for Android" into your favorite search engine. You were then to make a note in the space below of the most promising site from your search results:

Is this the one you found?

http://code.google.com/p/android-scripting (the home of the SL4A project.)

Run Python on the coach's smartphone

A quick search of the Web uncovers a pleasant surprise: *Python runs on Android*.

At least a *version* of Python runs on Android. A project called *Scripting Layer for Android* (**SL4A**) provides technology to let you run Python on any Android device. But there's a catch.

Ummmm...I just checked the SL4A website, and it looks like it supports Python 2.6.2, not Python 3. Phooey!

Yes. SL4A ships with Python 2, not 3.

Python 3, this book's preference, is the best version of Python yet, but it achieves its greatness at the cost of a lack of backward compatibility. There's some stuff in 3 that will never work in 2 and vice versa.

Is this fact alone a *show-stopper*?

Don't worry about Python 2

The fact that Python 2 is available for Android and you've learned Python 3 in this book is nothing to lose sleep over. *Python 2 is still Python*, and the differences between Python 2 and Python 3 are easy to manage.

Think about your webapp for a minute. Right now, the model, view, and controller code resides on the web server, which is running Python 3.

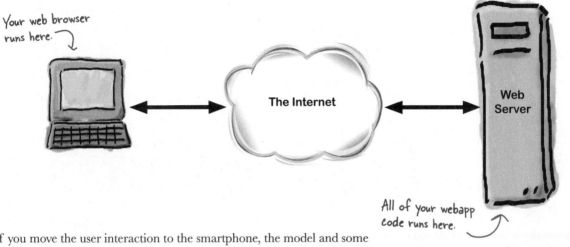

I'm quite happy to run Python 3 all day long...

Your web browser runs here.

The Internet

Web Server

All of your webapp code runs here.

If you move the user interaction to the smartphone, the model and some of the controller code *stay* on the server (and continue to run on Python 3), whereas the view code and the rest of the controller code *move* to the smartphone, where they need to be rewritten to run on Python 2.

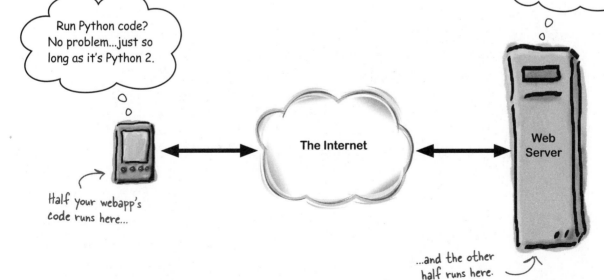

Run Python code? No problem...just so long as it's Python 2.

Python 3 is still going strong...

The Internet

Web Server

Half your webapp's code runs here...

...and the other half runs here.

Set up your development environment

Understandably, the coach won't let your have his phone to work on until you have something that works. Thankfully, *Google* provides a cross-platform **Android emulator** that lets you develop for the phone as needed, even though you don't own any hardware.

Download the Software Development Kit (SDK)

Let's get started developing for Android. Visit this website and download the SDK for your computer and operating system:

http://developer.android.com/sdk/index.html

Do this!

> Follow along with these instructions to ensure you have your Android development environment correctly set up on your computer.

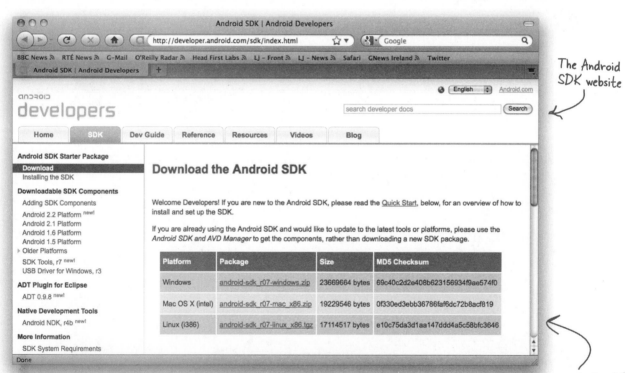

The Android SDK website

Note: This is how the Android SDK download page looks at the time of this writing. It might look a little different for you. No worries: just download the latest version of the SDK.

Despite what this website might look like it's telling you, you do **not** need to install *Eclipse* to run the Android emulator. However, you do need to have a *Java Runtime Environment* installed. If you are unsure about this, don't worry: the Android emulator will advise your best course of action if it spots that Java is missing.

Configure the SDK and emulator

You need to do *two things* to configure the SDK and emulator: add an *Android Platform* and create an *Android Virtual Device* (known as an *AVD*).

Add an Android platform

The coach is running **Android 2.2** on his phone, so let's add a 2.2 platform to mimic this setup. Open up the Android SDK and AVD Manager tool, select Available Packages, and pick 2.2 for installation.

The Android download contains a folder called "tools". Run the "android" program within this folder.

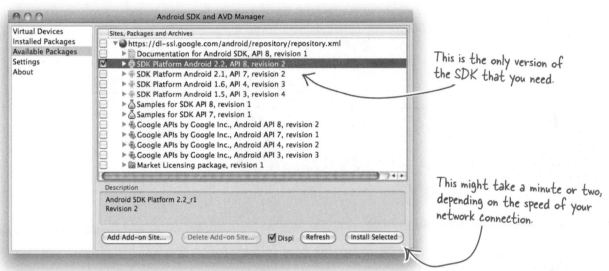

This is the only version of the SDK that you need.

This might take a minute or two, depending on the speed of your network connection.

Create a new Android Virtual Device (AVD)

With the 2.2 platform downloaded and installed, create a new Android Virtual Device.

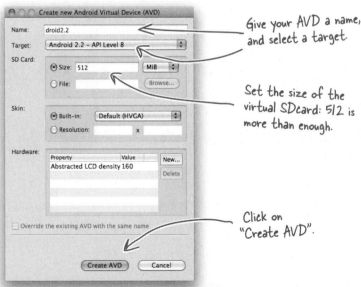

Give your AVD a name, and select a target.

Set the size of the virtual SDcard: 512 is more than enough.

Click on "Create AVD".

Your AVD is a simulated Android phone.

Install and configure Android Scripting

With the emulator ready, use the AVD Manager to start your 2.2 device. Click
on the emulator's browser (the little globe), surf to this web address:

These instructions work on a "real" phone, too. Just be sure to enable "Unknown sources" to allow for non-Market application downloads.

http://code.google.com/p/android-scripting

and tap on the "boxed" bar code near the bottom of the page:

Don't worry if it takes your emulator a minute or two to start. The emulator is slower than the actual phone...

On the emulator, tap on the "boxed" bar code to start the SL4A download.

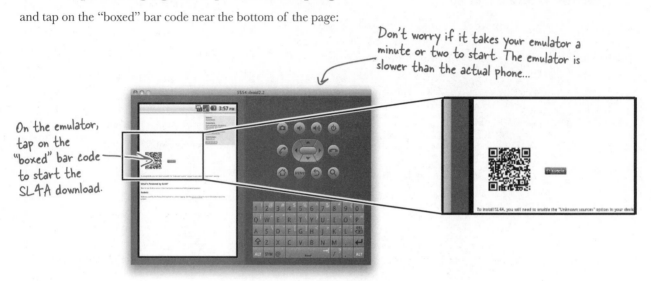

When the download completes, select the emulator's Menu button → More →
Downloads, and then tap on the `sl4a_r2.apk` file to install the SL4A
package on the emulator. When the install completes, tap Done.

The version available to you might be different, but don't worry: download the latest release.

The version you see might be different than this. Don't worry; yours in the most recent.

Add Python to your SL4A installation

Return to the emulator's web browser, double-tap on the screen to zoom in, and select the Downloads tab. Double-tap again and tap the following link:

`python_for_android_r1.apk`

Again, the version you see might be different than this. Select the most recent file.

Tap the download link, and tap on the package name to download it. Select Menu →More → Downloads, and tap on the newly downloaded package.

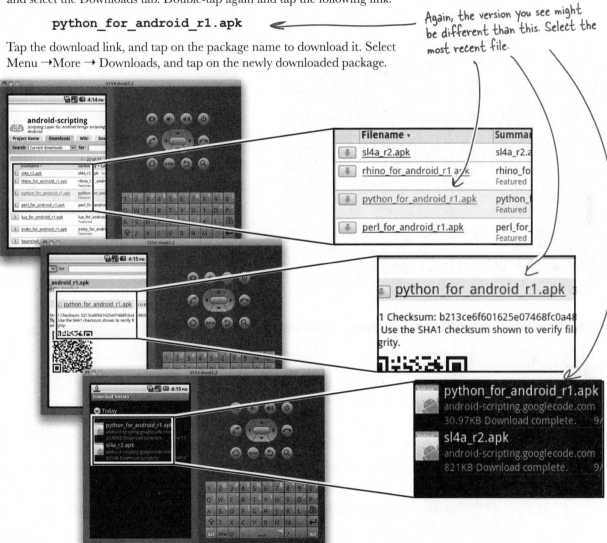

The Python for Android app runs. When you are ready, tap Open -> Install to complete the installation. This downloads, extracts, and installs the Python support files for Android, which can take a few minutes to complete. When it does, Python 2.6.2 and Python for Android are installed on your emulator and ready for action.

This last bit is really important.

Let's confirm everything is working with a quick test.

Test Python on Android

Return to your emulator's main screen and find an app called *SL4A* added to your list of app icons. Tap this app to display the list of Python scripts preinstalled with Python for Android. Simplty tap on any script name to execute it:

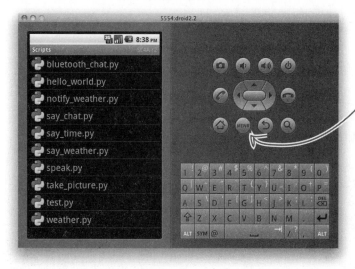

The "menu" button.

Watch it!

Be sure to set the SL4A rotation mode to automatic.

*Your screen might switch to landscape by default the first time you run a script. To fix this, choose Menu → Preferences, scroll down to **Rotation mode**, and set its value to **Automatic**.*

Take your Android emulator for a spin

Here's a four-line Python script that you can create to test your installation. Let's call this script mydroidtest.py:

Import the "android" library and create a new app object instance.

Create an appropriate message and display it on screen.

```
import android
app = android.Android()
msg = "Hello from Head First Python on Android"
app.makeToast(msg)
```

To transfer your script to the emulator, you need to copy it to the emulator's virtual SD card. Another program within the `tools` folder called `adb` helps with this:

Issue this command at your terminal window to transfer your script to the emulator.

```
tools/adb push mydroidtest.py /sdcard/sl4a/scripts
```

Your script should now appear on the list of scripts available to SL4A.

TEST DRIVE

Let's confirm that your Android setup is working. With the SL4A app open, simply tap on your script's name to run it, and then click the *run wheel* from the menu.

Click your app's name...

...then click the "run wheel."

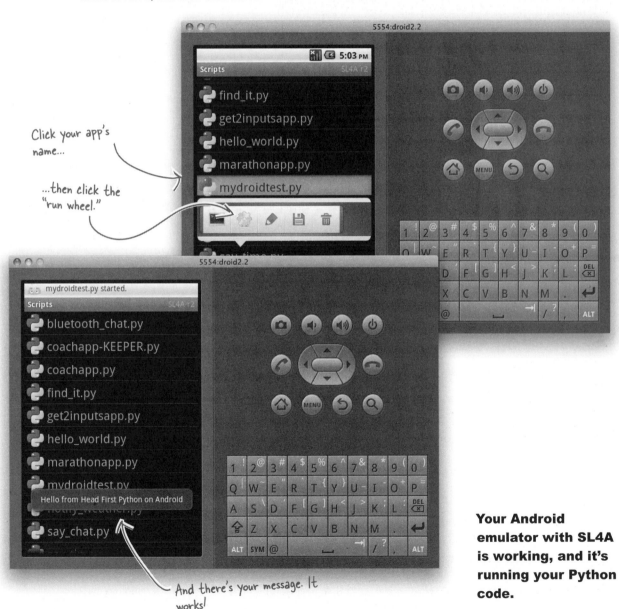

And there's your message. It works!

Your Android emulator with SL4A is working, and it's running your Python code.

Define your app's requirements

Let's think a little bit about what your Android app needs to do.

Nothing's really changed...you just have to get the web data onto the phone.

Frank: Well…first off, the view code no longer has to generate HTML, so that makes things interesting.

Jill: In fact, you need the web server only to supply your data on request, not all that generated HTML.

Joe: Ah ha! I've solved it. Just send the pickle with all the data from the server to the Android phone. It can't be all that hard, can it?

Jill: Sorry, guys, that'll cause problems. The pickle format used by Python 3 is *incompatible* with Python 2. You'll certainly be able to send the pickle to the phone, but the phone's Python won't be able to work with the data in the pickle.

Frank: Darn…what are our options, then? Plain data?

Joe: Hey, good idea: just send the data as one big string and parse it on the phone. Sounds like a workable solution, right?

Jill: No, that's a potential disaster, because you never know in what format that stringed data will arrive. You need an *data interchange format*, something like XML or JSON.

Frank: Hmm…I've heard XML is a hound to work with…and it's probably overkill for this simple app. What's the deal with JSON?

Joe: Yes, of course, I keep hearing about JSON. I think they use it in lots of different places on the Web, especially with AJAX.

Frank: Oh, dear…pickle, XML, JSON, and now AJAX…I think my brain might just explode here.

Jill: Never worry, you only need to know JSON. In fact, you don't even need to worry about understanding JSON at all; you just need to know how to use it. And, guess what? JSON comes standard with Python 2 and with Python 3…and the format is compatible. So, we can use JSON on the web server and on the phone.

Frank & Joe: Bonus! That's the type of technology we like!

JSON Exposed

This week's interview:
The Data Interchange Lowdown

Head First: Hello, JSON. Thanks for agreeing to talk to us today.

JSON: No problem. Always willing to play my part in whatever way I can.

Head First: And what *is* that, exactly?

JSON: Oh, I'm just one of the most widely used data interchange formats on the Web. When you need to transfer data over the Internet, you can rely on me. And, of course, you'll find me *everywhere*.

Head First: Why's that?

JSON: Well…it's really to do with my name. The "JS" in JSON stands for "JavaScript" and the "ON" stands for "Object Notation." See?

Head First: Uh…I'm not quite with you.

JSON: I'm JavaScript's object notation, which means I'm *everywhere*.

Head First: Sorry, but you've completely lost me.

JSON: The first two letters are the key ones: I'm a JavaScript standard, which means you'll find me everywhere JavaScript is…which means I'm in every major web browser on the planet.

Head First: What's that got to do with Python?

JSON: That's where the other two letters come into play. Because I was initially designed to allow JavaScript data objects to be transferred from one JavaScript program to another, I've been extended to allow objects to be transferred regardless of what programming language is used to create the data. By using the JSON library provided by your favorite programming language, you can create data that is interchangeable. If you can read a JSON data stream, you can recreate data as you see fit.

Head First: So I could take an object in, say, Python, use JSON to convert it to JSON's object notation, and then send the converted data to another computer running a program written in C#?

JSON: And as long as C# has a JSON library, you can recreate the Python data as C# data. Neat, eh?

Head First: Yes, that sounds interesting…only [winks] why would anyone in their right mind want to program in C#?

JSON: [laughs] Oh, come on now: *be nice*. There's plenty of reasons to use different programming languages for different reasons.

Head First: Which goes some of the way to explain why we have so many great programming titles, like *Head First C#*, *Head First Java*, *Head First PHP and MySQL*, *Head First Rails*, and *Head First JavaScript*.

JSON: Was that a shameless, self-serving plug?

Head First: You know something…I think it might well have been! [laughs].

JSON: [laughs] Yes, it pays to advertise.

Head First: And to share data, right?

JSON: Yes! And that's exactly my point: when you need a *language-neutral data interchange format* that is easy to work with, it's hard to pass me by.

Head First: But how can you be "language neutral" when you have *JavaScript* in your name?

JSON: Oh, that's just my name. It's what they called me when the only language I supported was JavaScript, and it kinda stuck.

Head First: So they should really call you something else, then?

JSON: Yes, but "WorksWithEveryProgramming LanguageUnderTheSunIncludingPythonObject Notation" doesn't have quite the same ring to it!

This is NOT cool... I spent all that time learning to use pickles and now you're abandoning them in favor of this "JSON" thing. You've got to be joking...?

You are not exactly "abandoning" pickle.

The JSON technology is a better fit *here* for a number of reasons. First of all, it's a **text-based** format, so it fits better with the way the Web works. Second, it's a **standard** that works the same on Python 2 and Python 3, so there are no compatibility issues. And third, because JSON is **language-neutral**, you open up the possibility of other web tools written in other programming languages interacting with your server.

If you use `pickle` here, *you lose all this.*

An IDLE Session

JSON is an established web standard that comes preinstalled with Python 2 and Python 3. The JSON API is not that much different to the one used by `pickle`:

Import the JSON library.

```
>>> import json
>>> names = ['John', ['Johnny', 'Jack'], 'Michael', ['Mike', 'Mikey', 'Mick']]
>>> names
```
Create a list of lists.
```
['John', ['Johnny', 'Jack'], 'Michael', ['Mike', 'Mikey', 'Mick']]
```
Transform the Python list-of-lists into a JSON list of lists.
```
>>> to_transfer = json.dumps(names)
>>> to_transfer
```
The format is similar, but different.
```
'["John", ["Johnny", "Jack"], "Michael", ["Mike", "Mikey", "Mick"]]'
```
Transform the JSON list of lists back into one that Python understands.
```
>>> from_transfer = json.loads(to_transfer)
>>> from_transfer
['John', ['Johnny', 'Jack'], 'Michael', ['Mike', 'Mikey', 'Mick']]
```
The new data is exactly the same as the original list of lists.
```
>>> names
['John', ['Johnny', 'Jack'], 'Michael', ['Mike', 'Mikey', 'Mick']]
```

Sharpen your pencil

Add a new function to the `athletemodel` module that, when called, returns the list of athlete names as a string.

Call the new function `get_names_from_store()`.

....

....

....

....

....

....

Sharpen your pencil
Solution

You were to add a new function to the `athletemodel` module that, when called, returns the list of athlete names as a string.

You were to all the new function `get_names_from_store()`.

```
def get_names_from_store():
    athletes = get_from_store()
    response = [athletes[each_ath].name for each_ath in athletes]
    return(response)
```

Get all the data from the pickle.

Extract a list of athlete names from the data.

Return the list to the caller.

So...rather than running a CGI script to create a HTML web page, you want me to deliver just the data, right? That's OK. Not a problem—just be sure to tell me which script to run...

Web Server

Exercise

With your new function written and added to the `athletemodel` module, create a new CGI script that, when called, returns the data from the `get_names_from_store()` function to the web requester as a JSON data stream.

Call your new script `cgi-bin/generate_names.py`.

Hint: Use `application/json` as your `Content-type`.

....

....

....

....

....

....

....

....

....

....

I may be small, but I'm mighty capable. Whether you need a web page or just your data, you can count on me to get the job done.

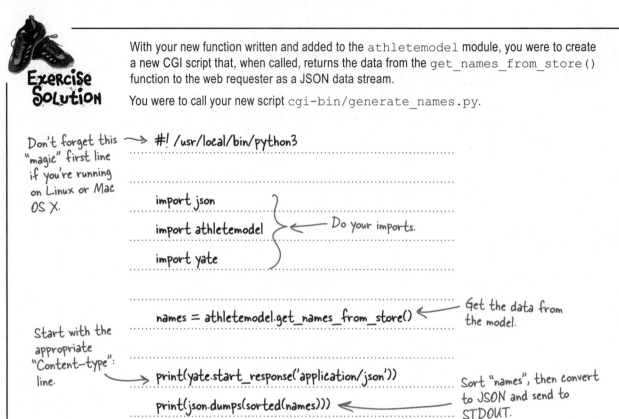

Exercise Solution

With your new function written and added to the `athletemodel` module, you were to create a new CGI script that, when called, returns the data from the `get_names_from_store()` function to the web requester as a JSON data stream.

You were to call your new script `cgi-bin/generate_names.py`.

Don't forget this "magic" first line if you're running on Linux or Mac OS X. →

```
#! /usr/local/bin/python3


import json
import athletemodel      ← Do your imports.
import yate


names = athletemodel.get_names_from_store()   ← Get the data from the model.


print(yate.start_response('application/json'))
print(json.dumps(sorted(names)))   ← Sort "names", then convert to JSON and send to STDOUT.
```

Start with the appropriate "Content-type": line. →

....
Take care testing your JSON-generating CGI code.

Watch it!

The behavior you see when testing your JSON-generating CGI script will differ depending on the web browser you are using. For instance, Firefox might attempt to download the generated data as opposed to display it on screen.
....

Test Drive

If it is not already running, start your web server and be sure to set the executable bit with the `chmod +x cgi-bin/generate_names.py` command (if on Linux or Mac OS X). When you're ready, grab your favorite web browser and take your new CGI for a spin.

Enter the web address of the CGI in your browser's location bar.

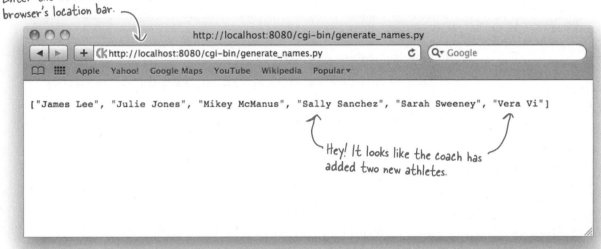

Hey! It looks like the coach has added two new athletes.

The web server's logging information confirms that the CGI executed.

That worked!

Now all you have to do is arrange for the Android emulator to request the data within a Python script and display the list of names on the smartphone's screen. *How hard can that be?*

The SL4A Android API

The SL4A technology provides a high-level API to the low-level Android API, and SL4A's API is documented in the online API reference:

http://code.google.com/p/android-scripting/wiki/ApiReference

Recall the code from earlier, which demonstrated a minimal Android SL4A app:

Import the "android" library and create a new app object instance.

Create an appropriate message and display it on screen.

```
import android
app = android.Android()
msg = "Hello from Head First Python on Android"
app.makeToast(msg)
```

Six calls to the Android API let you create a list of selectable items in a dialog, together with *positive* and *negative* buttons, which are used to indicate the selection your user made. Note how each of the calls to the Android "dialog" API results in something appearing on screen.

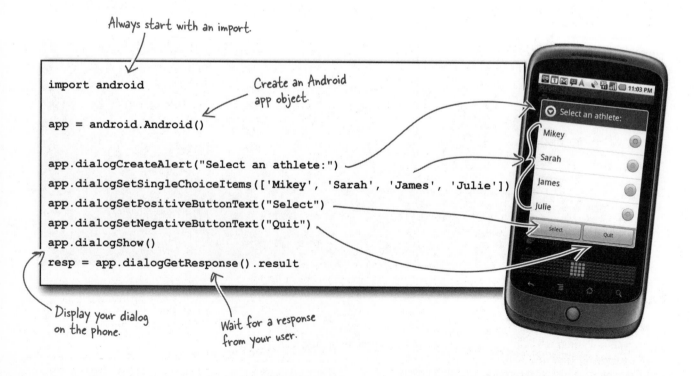

Always start with an import.

```
import android

app = android.Android()

app.dialogCreateAlert("Select an athlete:")
app.dialogSetSingleChoiceItems(['Mikey', 'Sarah', 'James', 'Julie'])
app.dialogSetPositiveButtonText("Select")
app.dialogSetNegativeButtonText("Quit")
app.dialogShow()
resp = app.dialogGetResponse().result
```

Create an Android app object.

Display your dialog on the phone.

Wait for a response from your user.

Android Code Magnets

Here is the code to a program that queries your web server for the list of names as a JSON array and then displays the list on the smartphone. The only trouble is, the second half of the program is a bunch of mixed-up code magnets at the bottom of the screen. Your job is to rearrange the magnets to complete the program.

```python
import android
import json
import time
```

Do the usual imports...these ones pull in web client functionality.

```python
from urllib import urlencode
from urllib2 import urlopen
```

All of this program's messages are in one place.

```python
hello_msg     = "Welcome to Coach Kelly's Timing App"
list_title    = 'Here is your list of athletes:'
quit_msg      = "Quitting Coach Kelly's App."
web_server    = 'http://192.168.1.33:8080'
get_names_cgi = '/cgi-bin/generate_names.py'
```

The name of the CGI script to run on the web server

Change this to the web address that's running your web server.

```python
def send_to_server(url, post_data=None):
    if post_data:
        page = urlopen(url, urlencode(post_data))
    else:
        page = urlopen(url)
    return(page.read().decode("utf8"))
```

This function takes both a web address (url) and some optional data (post_data) and sends a web request to your web server. The web response is returned to the caller.

This code's a mess...can you fix it?

```python
athlete_names = sorted(json.loads(send_to_server(web_server + get_names_cgi)))
```

```python
status_update(quit_msg)
```

```python
resp = app.dialogGetResponse().result
```

```python
app.dialogShow()
```

```python
app.dialogCreateAlert(list_title)
```

```python
status_update(hello_msg)
```

```python
def status_update(msg, how_long=2):
    app.makeToast(msg)
    time.sleep(how_long)
```

```python
app.dialogSetPositiveButtonText('Select')
```

```python
app = android.Android()
```

```python
app.dialogSetNegativeButtonText('Quit')
```

```python
app.dialogSetSingleChoiceItems(athlete_names)
```

Android Code Magnets Solution

Here is the code to a program that queries your web server for the list of names as a JSON array and then displays the list on the smartphone. The only trouble is, the second half of the program is a bunch of mixed-up code magnets at the bottom of the screen. Your job was to rearrange the magnets to complete the program.

```python
import android
import json
import time
from urllib import urlencode
from urllib2 import urlopen

hello_msg      = "Welcome to Coach Kelly's Timing App"
list_title     = 'Here is your list of athletes:'
quit_msg       = "Quitting Coach Kelly's App."
web_server     = 'http://192.168.1.33:8080'
get_names_cgi = '/cgi-bin/generate_names.py'

def send_to_server(url, post_data=None):
    if post_data:
        page = urlopen(url, urlencode(post_data))
    else:
        page = urlopen(url)
    return(page.read().decode("utf8"))
```

Create an Android app object.

```python
app = android.Android()

def status_update(msg, how_long=2):
    app.makeToast(msg)
    time.sleep(how_long)
```

This is a little function for displaying short messages on the phone.

Send the web request to your server, then turn the JSON response into a sorted list.

Say "hello".

```python
status_update(hello_msg)

athlete_names = sorted(json.loads(send_to_server(web_server + get_names_cgi)))

app.dialogCreateAlert(list_title)
app.dialogSetSingleChoiceItems(athlete_names)
app.dialogSetPositiveButtonText('Select')
app.dialogSetNegativeButtonText('Quit')
app.dialogShow()
```

Create a two-buttoned dialog from the list of athlete names.

```python
resp = app.dialogGetResponse().result
```

Wait for the user to tap a button, then assign the result to "resp".

```python
status_update(quit_msg)
```

Say "bye bye."

TEST DRIVE

Recall that (for now) your Android Python scripts run within the emulator, not within IDLE. So use the `tools/adb` program to copy your program to the emulator. Call your program `coachapp.py`. When the code is copied over, start SL4A on your emulator, and then tap your script's name.

Tap your app's name, and then tap the "run wheel."

And there they are...Coach Kelly's athletes.

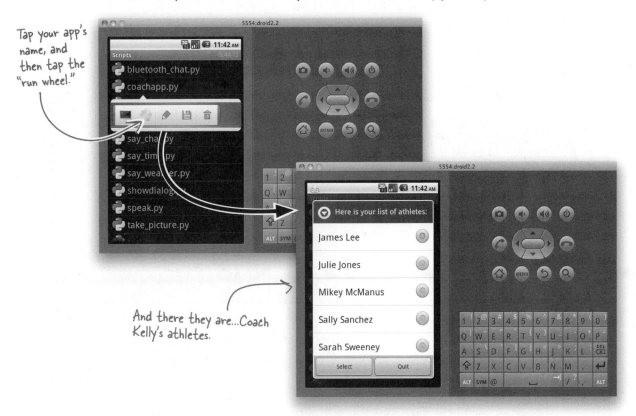

This is looking really good! Your app has communicated with your web server, requested and received the list of athlete names, and displayed the list on your emulator.

If you app doesn't run, don't panic. Check your code for typos.

Run your app again in the Python terminal by tapping on the little terminal icon to the left of the "run wheel" within SL4A. If your code raises an error, you'll see any messages on the emulator's screen, which should give you a good idea of what went wrong.

Select from a list on Android

When your user taps on a button, the "result" of the call to `dialogGetResponse()` is set to `positive` if the first button is tapped or `negative` if the second button is tapped. In your code, you can check the value of `resp`, which is a dictionary, and the `which` key is set to either `positive` or `negative`.

A subsequent call to `dialogGetSelectedItems()` returns the index value of the selected list item.

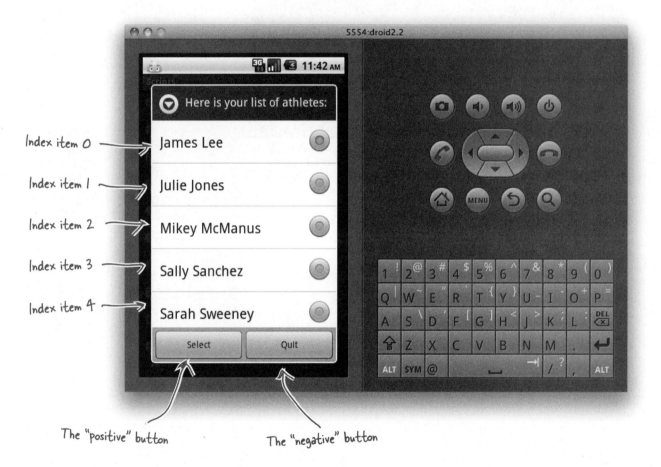

Index item 0 → James Lee

Index item 1 → Julie Jones

Index item 2 → Mikey McManus

Index item 3 → Sally Sanchez

Index item 4 → Sarah Sweeney

The "positive" button

The "negative" button

So...if the `positive` button is tapped, you can index into the list of athlete names to see which athlete was selected from the displayed list. The selected name can then be sent to the web server to request the rest of the athlete's data using the `send_to_server()` function.

You can use this behavior in the next version of your code.

Sharpen your pencil

1 Assume that you have a CGI script called `cgi-bin/generate_data.py`, which, when called, requests the data for a named athlete from the server.

Provide the code (which includes a call to the `send_to_server()` function) to implement this functionality:

....

....

2 Additionally, write the code required to display the list of times returned from the server within an Android dialog.

Hints: Use the `dialogSetItems()` method from the Android API to add a list of items to a dialog. Also, remember that the data arriving over the Internet will be formatted using JSON.

....

....

....

....

....

....

....

....

....

....

....

....

....

....

....

....

Sharpen your pencil
Solution

1 You were to assume that you have a CGI script called `cgi-bin/generate_data.py`, which, when called requests the data for a named athlete from the server.

Provide the name of the CGI to run. → You were to provide the code (which includes a call to the `send_to_server()` function) to implement this functionality:

```
get_data_cgi = '/cgi-bin/generate_data.py'
```

Send the request to the web server, together with the athlete name. →
```
send_to_server(web_server + get_data_cgi, {'which_athlete': which_athlete})
```
⌐Include the data.

2 Additionally, you were to write the code required to display the list of times returned from the server within an Android dialog:

⌐Which button was pressed?

```
if resp['which'] in ('positive'):
```

When your user taps the "positive" button...work out the index value chosen. →
```
    selected_athlete = app.dialogGetSelectedItems().result[0]
```
The index value is in the first element of the list of results returned from the dialog.

Look up the athlete's name using the index value. →
```
    which_athlete = athlete_names[selected_athlete]
```

Dynamically create the dialog's title.
```
    athlete = json.loads(send_to_server(web_server + get_data_cgi,
                                        {'which_athlete': which_athlete}))
```
Send a new web request to the server to fetch the athlete's data.

```
    athlete_title = which_athlete + ' top 3 times:'
```

```
    app.dialogCreateAlert(athlete_title)
```
The user needs to see only the data this time, so you need to use "dialogSetItems()". →
```
    app.dialogSetItems(athlete['Top3'])
```
```
    app.dialogSetPositiveButtonText('OK')
```
Set the single button's text.
```
    app.dialogShow()
```

Wait for a tap from the user. →
```
    resp = app.dialogGetResponse().result
```

The athlete's data CGI script

Here's the code for the `cgi-bin/generate_data.py` CGI script, which takes a web request and returns the indicated athlete's data from the model:

```python
#! /usr/local/bin/python3


import cgi
import json
import athletemodel
import yate


athletes = athletemodel.get_from_store()
form_data = cgi.FieldStorage()
athlete_name = form_data['which_athlete'].value
print(yate.start_response('application/json'))
print(json.dumps(athletes[athlete_name]))
```

Get all the data from the model.

Process the data sent with the request and extract the athlete's name.

Start a web response, with JSON as the data type.

Include the indicated athlete's data in the web response, formatted by JSON.

The complete Android app, so far

You've made quite a few changes to your program at this stage. Before you test it on the Android emulator, take a moment to look at your code *in its entirety*:

```python
import android
import json
import time

from urllib import urlencode
from urllib2 import urlopen

hello_msg       = "Welcome to Coach Kelly's Timing App"
list_title      = 'Here is your list of athletes:'
quit_msg        = "Quitting Coach Kelly's App."

web_server      = 'http://192.168.1.34:8080'

get_names_cgi = '/cgi-bin/generate_names.py'
get_data_cgi  = '/cgi-bin/generate_data.py'
```

The rest of your code is on the following page.

```
def send_to_server(url, post_data=None):
    if post_data:
        page = urlopen(url, urlencode(post_data))
    else:
        page = urlopen(url)
    return(page.read().decode("utf8"))


app = android.Android()


def status_update(msg, how_long=2):
    app.makeToast(msg)
    time.sleep(how_long)


status_update(hello_msg)


athlete_names = sorted(json.loads(send_to_server(web_server + get_names_cgi)))


app.dialogCreateAlert(list_title)
app.dialogSetSingleChoiceItems(athlete_names)
app.dialogSetPositiveButtonText('Select')
app.dialogSetNegativeButtonText('Quit')
app.dialogShow()
resp = app.dialogGetResponse().result


if resp['which'] in ('positive'):
    selected_athlete = app.dialogGetSelectedItems().result[0]
    which_athlete = athlete_names[selected_athlete]
    athlete = json.loads(send_to_server(web_server + get_data_cgi,
                                {'which_athlete': which_athlete}))

    athlete_title = athlete['Name'] + ' (' + athlete['DOB'] + '), top 3 times:'
    app.dialogCreateAlert(athlete_title)
    app.dialogSetItems(athlete['Top3'])
    app.dialogSetPositiveButtonText('OK')
    app.dialogShow()
    resp = app.dialogGetResponse().result


status_update(quit_msg)
```

TEST DRIVE

Let's give the latest version of your app a go. Copy the app to your emulator, and put the new CGI script in your `cgi-bin` folder on your web server (remember to set the executable bit, if needed). What happens when you run your latest app using the emulator's Python shell as opposed to the "run wheel"?

You are dumped into the Python shell with a rather nasty error message.

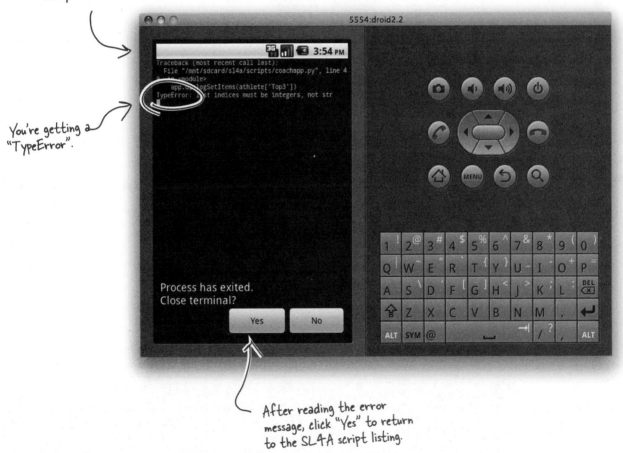

You're getting a "TypeError".

After reading the error message, click "Yes" to return to the SL4A script listing.

Yikes! Your code has a `TypeError`, which is crashing your app when you try to display the selected athlete's timing data. *Why do you think this is happening?*

The data appears to have changed type

Look at the CGI code...it gets the data from the model and sends it to the web browser...

...ummm, I see. But somehow, the data that arrives isn't an AthleteList.

Let's add a debugging line of code to your CGI script to try and determine what's going on. Recall that the CGI mechanism captures any output your script sends to *standard output* by default, so let's use code like this to send your debugging messgage to the web server's console, which is displaying on *standard error*:

Import "sys" from the standard library.

```
import sys


print(json.dumps(athletes[athlete_name]), file=sys.stderr)
```

Redirect the output from "print()" to "stderr", rather than the default, which is "stdout".

Run your app again and, of course, it's still crashes with a `TypeError`. However, if you check your web server's console screen, you'll see that the data being sent as the JSON web response is clearly visible. *Notice anything?*

This is a list of athlete timing values...but where's the name and DOB values?

```
File Edit Window Help JustWhatsInTheData
$ python3 simple_httpd.py
Starting simple_httpd on port: 8080
192.168.1.33 - - [18/Sep/2010 17:40:04] "GET /cgi-bin/generate_names.py HTTP/1.1" 200 -
192.168.1.33 - - [18/Sep/2010 17:40:08] "POST /cgi-bin/generate_data.py HTTP/1.1" 200 -
["2-44", "3:01", "2.44", "2.55", "2.51", "2:41", "2:41", "3:00", "2-32", "2.11", "2:26"]
```

JSON can't handle your custom datatypes

Unlike `pickle`, which is smart enough to pickle your custom classes, the JSON library that comes with Python isn't. This means that the standard library's JSON library can work with Python's built-in types, but not with your `AthleteList` objects.

The solution to this problem is straightforward: add a method to your `AthleteList` class to convert your data into a dictionary, and send *that* back to the app. Because JSON supports Python's dictionary, this should work.

Exercise

Let's create a new method in your `AthleteList` class. Called `to_dict()`, your new method needs to convert the class's attribute data (`name`, `DOB`, and `top3`) into a dictionary. Be sure to decorate your new method with `@property`, so that it appears to be a new attribute to users of your class.

....

....

....

....

....

....

....

there are no Dumb Questions

Q: What's the purpose of this @property thing again?

A: The `@property` *decorator* lets you specify that a method is to be presented to users of your class *as if it were an attribute*. If you think about things, your `to_dict()` method doesn't change the state of your object's data in any way: it merely exists to return the object's attribute data as a dictionary. So, although `to_dict()` is a method, it behaves more like an attribute, and using the `@property` decorator let's you indicate this. Users of your class (that is, other programmers) don't need to know that when they access the `to_dict` attribute they are in fact running a method. All they see is a **unified interface**: attributes access your class's data, while methods manipulate it.

Exercise Solution

Let's create a new method in your `AthleteList` class. Called `to_dict()`, your new method needs to convert the class's attribute data (name, DOB, and top3) into a dictionary. Be sure to decorate your new method with `@property`, so that it appears to be a new attribute to users of your class.

Decorate your new method with "@property".

```
@property
def as_dict(self):
    return({'Name': self.name,
            'DOB':  self.dob,
            'Top3': self.top3})
```

Create a new method.

Return a dictionary of the object's data attributes.

Did you remember to use "self"?

Do this!

As well as updating your `AthleteList` class code, be sure to change `cgi-bin/generate-data.py` to return a dictionary, rather than the object instance, when servicing its web request.

While you're making changes, adjust the `coachapp.py` app code to include the athlete's name and DOB values in the second dialog's title.

TEST DRIVE

With your changes applied to `AthleteList.py`, `cgi-bin/generate_data.py` and `coachapp.py`, use the `adb` tool to copy the latest version of your app to the emulator. Let's see how things work now.

```
coachapp.py – /Users/barryp/HeadFirstPython/chapter8/coachapp.py
if resp['which'] in ('positive'):
    selected_athlete = app.dialogGetSelectedItems().result[0]
    which_athlete = athlete_names[selected_athlete]
    athlete = json.loads(send_to_server(web_server + get_data_cgi,
                                         {'which_athlete': which_athlete}))

    athlete_title = athlete['Name'] + ' (' + athlete['DOB'] + '), top 3 times:'
    app.dialogCreateAlert(athlete_title)
    app.dialogSetItems(athlete['Top3'])
    app.dialogSetPositiveButtonText('OK')
    app.dialogShow()
    resp = app.dialogGetResponse().result

status_update(quit_msg)
```

Here's the code that your app uses in response to an athlete selection.

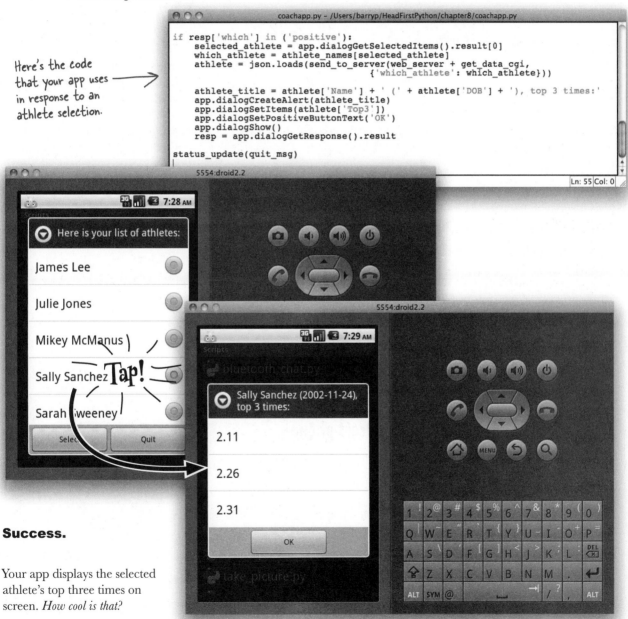

Success.

Your app displays the selected athlete's top three times on screen. *How cool is that?*

Run your app on a real phone

Now that your app is running successfully on your emulator, it's time to try it on a real phone. This is where things get *interesting*.

There are many options when it comes to copying your code to a real device:

- Use file transfer over Bluetooth.
- Use file transfer with a USB connection.
- Use the Android SDK's adb tool with USB.
- Use a file transfer tool over WiFi.

Unfortunately, which technique to use (and which work) depends very much on your phone.

At Head First Labs, we've had the greatest and most consistent success with the last option: *use a file transfer tool over WiFi*.

Watch it!

These instructions do not work on the emulator.

*The Android emulator does not currently support Google's **Android Market**, which you'll need access to use when following along with the instructions on these pages.*

Step 1: Prepare your computer

To transfer files securely between your Android phone and your computer, enable SSH file transfers by running an **SSH server** on your computer. How you do this depends on the operating system you are running:

- **Windows**: download one of the many free SSH servers.
- **Mac OS X**: enable remote logins.
- **Linux**: install and enable OpenSSH Server.

Step 2: Install AndFTP on your Android phone

Use the Android Market on your phone to find and install the **AndFTP** app. This excellent tool lets you transfer files to and from your Android phone over FTP, SFTP, and FTPS.

To use it with the SSH server running on your computer, you'll want to select **SFTP** as the file transfer protocol within the app, because **AndFTP** defaults to using the FTP protocol.

Let's take a look at what's involved.

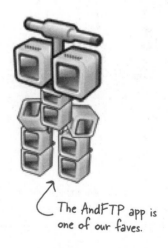

The AndFTP app is one of our faves.

Configure AndFTP

With AndFTP running on your phone, configure it to connect to your computer (*Hostname*) using SFTP as the transfer protocol (*Type*). Leave the *Port, Username, Password,* and *Remote dir* entries as they are, but change the *Local dir* entry to `/sdcard/sl4a/scripts`.

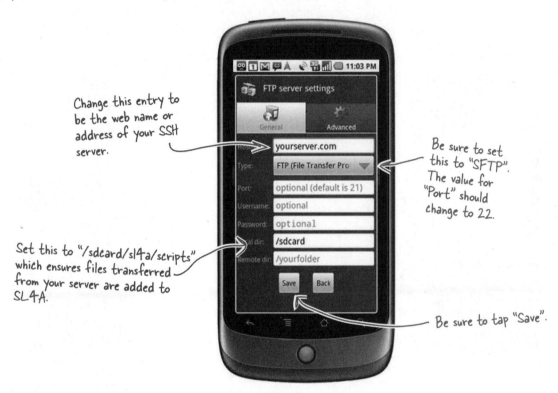

Change this entry to be the web name or address of your SSH server.

Be sure to set this to "SFTP". The value for "Port" should change to 22.

Set this to "/sdcard/sl4a/scripts" which ensures files transferred from your server are added to SL4A.

Be sure to tap "Save".

With the connection set up, tap AndFTP's Connect button to establish a connection to your SSH server, entering your Username and Password when prompted.

With the connection to the server established, navigate to the server folder containing the file(s) you want to transfer to the phone, mark the files for download, and tap the Download button.

When the download completes, click Disconnect to terminate the connection between the phone and your computer. If you transferred a Python program, it should now be added to the list of scripts within SL4A.

It's time to let Coach Kelly take a look.

Your app is ready!

The coach is thrilled with his app

That's looking great! I knew you could do it... now all I need is a way to add a new timing value directly from my phone. That would be awesome!

The coach's app running on the coach's phone.

Welcome to the future!

You've delivered a solution that automates interaction with your website while providing a modern interface on an Android phone. Your app allows your users to access web data *directly* on their mobile device.

The fact that your server code runs on Python 3 and your Android client code runs on Python 2 makes very little difference: *it's all just Python code, after all.*

All that's left to do is write some code to satisfy Coach Kelly's latest request, and you'll get to that in the next chapter.

This is great work.

Your Python Toolbox

You've got Chapter 8 under your belt and you've added some key Python techiques to your toolbox.

Python Lingo

• "Python 2" – the previous release of Python, which has compatibility "issues" with Python 3 (and are not worth getting worked up over).

Android Lingo

• "SL4A" – the Scripting Layer for Android lets you run Python on your Android device.

• "AVD" – an Android Virtual Device which lets you emulate your Android device on your computer.

BULLET POINTS

- The `json` library module lets you convert Python's built-in types to the text-based *JSON* data interchange format.

- Use `json.dumps()` to create a stringed version of a Python type.

- Use `json.loads()` to create a Python type from a JSON string.

- Data sent using *JSON* needs to have its `Content-Type:` set to `application/json`.

- The `urllib` and `urllib2` library modules (both available in Python 2) can be used to send encoded data from a program to a web server (using the `urlencode()` and `urlopen()` functions).

- The `sys` module provides the `sys.stdin`, `sys.stdout` and `sys.stderr` input streams.

9 manage your data

✳ *Handling input* ✳

Input this, input that...that's all I ever hear...input, input, input, input...all day long. It's enough to drive me mad!

The Web and your phone are not just great ways to display data.

They are also great tools to for accepting input from your users. Of course, once your webapp accepts data, it needs to put it somewhere, and the choices you make when deciding what and where this "somewhere" is are often the difference between a webapp that's easy to grow and extend and one that isn't. In this chapter, you'll extend your webapp to accept data from the Web (via a browser or from an Android phone), as well as look at and enhance your back-end data-management services.

Your athlete times app has gone national

We love what you did for Coach Kelly, but it would be great if we could add times for an athlete no matter where we are. Is this possible?

The *National Underage Athletics Committee (NUAC)* took one look at your Android app and realized it's just what they need...almost.

There are many ways to improve your webapp, but for now, let's concentrate on the committee's most pressing need: *adding a new time value to an existing athlete's data set.*

Adding new data to text files isn't going to work: there are just too many coaches around the country adding data. The committee wants something that's user friendly from any web browser or Android phone.

Can you help?

Use a form or dialog to accept input

Simply use the standard <FORM> and <INPUT> tags within your HTML web page to get input from your users...

...or if you are on your phone, a call to the "dialogGetInput()" function will do the trick.

On the Web, your user interacts with your web form and enters data. When she presses the **submit** button, the web browser gathers up all of the form's data and sends it to the web server *as part of the web request*.

On your Android phone, you can use the `dialogGetInput()` method to get input from the user, then mimic the behavior of the web form's **submit** button in code.

In fact, you've done this already: check out this line of code from your `coachapp.py` app, which sends the selected athlete name to your web server:

Here's where the data is included with the web request.

```
athlete = json.loads(send_to_server(web_server + get_data_cgi, {'which_athlete': which_athlete}))
```

Create an HTML form template

Let's extend yate.py to support the creation of a HTML form. Take a look a this simple form, together with the HTML markup used to produce it.

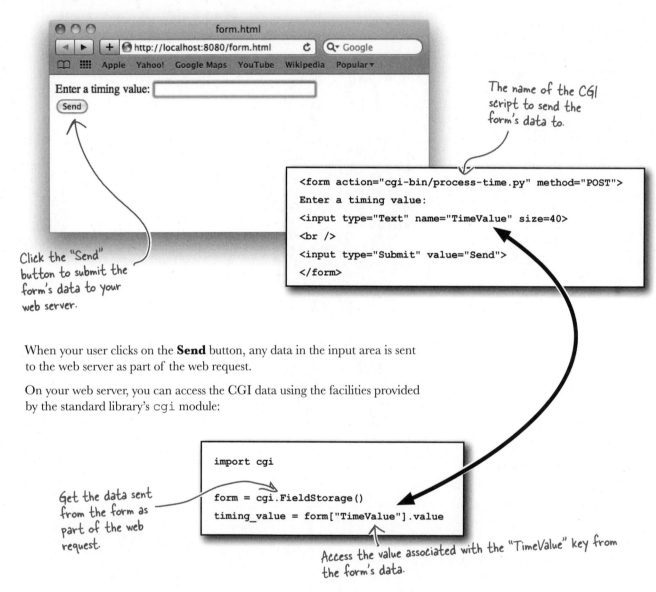

The name of the CGI script to send the form's data to.

Click the "Send" button to submit the form's data to your web server.

```
<form action="cgi-bin/process-time.py" method="POST">
Enter a timing value:
<input type="Text" name="TimeValue" size=40>
<br />
<input type="Submit" value="Send">
</form>
```

When your user clicks on the **Send** button, any data in the input area is sent to the web server as part of the web request.

On your web server, you can access the CGI data using the facilities provided by the standard library's cgi module:

```
import cgi

form = cgi.FieldStorage()
timing_value = form["TimeValue"].value
```

Get the data sent from the form as part of the web request.

Access the value associated with the "TimeValue" key from the form's data.

The cgi module converts the data associated with the web request into a dictionary-like object that you can then query to extract what you need.

Exercise

Let's turn the HTML form from the previous page into a template within the `yate.py` module.

1 Start by creating a new template called `templates/form.html` that allows you to parameterize the form's CGI script name, method, input tags, and submit button text:

....

....

....

2 With the template ready, write the code for two functions you intend to add to `yate.py`.

The first, called `create_inputs()`, takes a list of one of more strings and creates HTML `<INPUT>` tags for each string, similar to the one that accepts `TimeValue` on the previous page.

The second, called `do_form()`, uses the template from Part 1 of this exercise together with the `create_inputs()` function to generate a HTML form.

Given a list of <INPUT> tag names.

```
def create_inputs(inputs_list):
```
....

....

....

....

Return the generated tags to the caller.

....

```
    return(html_inputs)
```

The name of the CGI script and a list of <INPUT> tag names are required arguments.

```
def do_form(name, the_inputs, method="POST", text="Submit"):
```
....

....

The HTTP method and text to the "Submit" button have sensible default values.

....

Substitute the arguments and generated <INPUT> tags into the template to create the form.

....

....

```
    return(form.substitute(cgi_name=name, http_method=method,
                    list_of_inputs=inputs, submit_text=text))
```

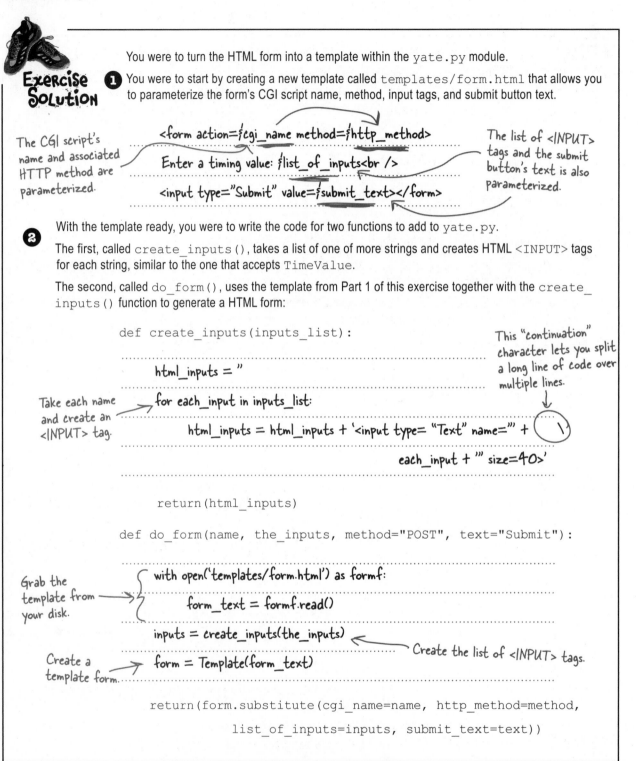

You were to turn the HTML form into a template within the `yate.py` module.

1 You were to start by creating a new template called `templates/form.html` that allows you to parameterize the form's CGI script name, method, input tags, and submit button text.

The CGI script's name and associated HTTP method are parameterized.

```
<form action=$cgi_name method=$http_method>
Enter a timing value: $list_of_inputs<br />
<input type="Submit" value=$submit_text></form>
```

The list of <INPUT> tags and the submit button's text is also parameterized.

2 With the template ready, you were to write the code for two functions to add to `yate.py`.

The first, called `create_inputs()`, takes a list of one of more strings and creates HTML `<INPUT>` tags for each string, similar to the one that accepts `TimeValue`.

The second, called `do_form()`, uses the template from Part 1 of this exercise together with the `create_inputs()` function to generate a HTML form:

```
def create_inputs(inputs_list):
    html_inputs = ''
    for each_input in inputs_list:
        html_inputs = html_inputs + '<input type= "Text" name="' + \
                      each_input + '" size=40>'
    return(html_inputs)

def do_form(name, the_inputs, method="POST", text="Submit"):
    with open('templates/form.html') as formf:
        form_text = formf.read()
    inputs = create_inputs(the_inputs)
    form = Template(form_text)
    return(form.substitute(cgi_name=name, http_method=method,
                           list_of_inputs=inputs, submit_text=text))
```

Take each name and create an <INPUT> tag.

This "continuation" character lets you split a long line of code over multiple lines.

Grab the template from your disk.

Create the list of <INPUT> tags.

Create a template form.

Test Drive

Here's the code to a CGI script called `cgi-bin/test-form.py`, which generates the HTML form from earlier. As you can see, there's nothing to it.

```
#! /usr/local/bin/python3

import yate

print(yate.start_response('text/html'))
print(yate.do_form('add_timing_data.py', ['TimeValue'], text='Send'))
```

Always start with a CGI response.

Dynamically create the form, supplying any arguments as required.

Set the executable bit (if required on your OS) using `chmod + x test_form.py`, and then use your browser to confirm that your HTML form-generating code is working.

Enter the URL for the CGI script into your web browser's location bar.

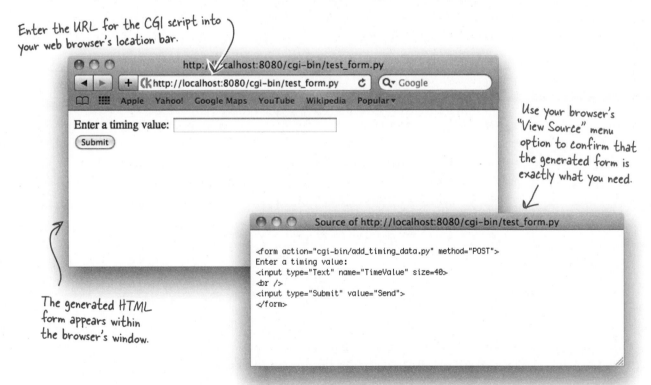

Use your browser's "View Source" menu option to confirm that the generated form is exactly what you need.

```
<form action="cgi-bin/add_timing_data.py" method="POST">
Enter a timing value:
<input type="Text" name="TimeValue" size=40>
<br />
<input type="Submit" value="Send">
</form>
```

The generated HTML form appears within the browser's window.

Great. You've extended `yate.py` to support the creation of a simple data entry form. Now all you need to do is to decide what happens once the data arrives on your server.

The data is delivered to your CGI script

In addition to running your webapp, the web server also arranges to deliver any submitted form data to your waiting CGI script. Python's cgi library converts the data into a dictionary and, as you already know, provides you with convenient access to the submitted data:

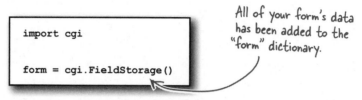

```
import cgi

form = cgi.FieldStorage()
```

All of your form's data has been added to the "form" dictionary.

Additional information about the web request is also available to you via the web server's *environment*. Typically, you won't need to access or use this data directly. However, occasionally, it can be useful to report on some of it.

Here is some code that takes advantage of Python's built-in support for querying your CGI script's environment using the os library, assuming the environment values have been set by a friendly web server. Note that the data in the enviroment is available to your code as a dictionary.

```
import os           Be sure to include the
import time         "os" library in your list of
import sys          imports.

addr = os.environ['REMOTE_ADDR']
host = os.environ['REMOTE_HOST']        Query three environment variables
method = os.environ['REQUEST_METHOD']   and assign their values to variables.

cur_time = time.asctime(time.localtime())   Get the current time.

print(host + ", " + addr + ", " + cur_time + ": " + method, file=sys.stderr)
```

Display the queried data on standard error.

Let's exploit both code snippets on this page to **log** the data sent from a form to your web server's console. When you are convinced that the data is arriving at your web server *intact*, you can extend your code to store the received data in your model.

Let's write a CGI to display your form's data.

CGI Magnets

You need a new CGI script called `add_timing_data.py`, which processes the data from a form and displays the data on your web server's console screen. The CGI needs to query the environment, arranging to display the logged data on one line. The code exists, but most of it is all over the floor. Rearrange the magnets to produce a working program.

Don't forget this line if you are running on Max OS X or Linux.

```
#! /usr/local/bin/python3

import cgi
import os
import time
import sys
import yate
```

There's not much of a response for now...so just send back plain text to the waiting web browser.

There's really nothing new here.

```
print(yate.start_response('text/plain'))
addr = os.environ['REMOTE_ADDR']
host = os.environ['REMOTE_HOST']
method = os.environ['REQUEST_METHOD']
cur_time = time.asctime(time.localtime())
print(host + ", " + addr + ", " + cur_time + ": " + method + ": ",
                end='', file=sys.stderr)
```

```
print('OK.')
```

```
end=' ',
```

```
form = cgi.FieldStorage()
```

```
print(each_form_item + '->' + form[each_form_item].value,
```

```
print(file=sys.stderr)
```

```
for each_form_item in form.keys():
```

```
file=sys.stderr)
```

CGI Magnets Solution

You need a new CGI script called `add_timing_data.py`, which processes the data from a form and displays the data on your web server's console screen. The CGI needs to query the environment, arranging to display the logged data on one line. The code exists, but most of it is all over the floor. You were to rearrange the magnets to produce a working program.

```
#! /usr/local/bin/python3

import cgi
import os
import time
import sys
import yate

print(yate.start_response('text/plain'))
addr = os.environ['REMOTE_ADDR']
host = os.environ['REMOTE_HOST']
method = os.environ['REQUEST_METHOD']
cur_time = time.asctime(time.localtime())
print(host + ", " + addr + ", " + cur_time + ": " + method + ": ",
            end='', file=sys.stderr)
form = cgi.FieldStorage()
for each_form_item in form.keys():
    print(each_form_item + '->' + form[each_form_item].value,
        end=' ', file=sys.stderr)
print(file=sys.stderr)
print('OK.')
```

Ensure that this "print()" function does NOT take a newline.

Take a newline on standard error.

Test Drive

Let's use your form-generating CGI script from earlier to try out `add_timing_data.py`. As you enter data in the form and press the **Send** button, watch what happens on the web server's console.

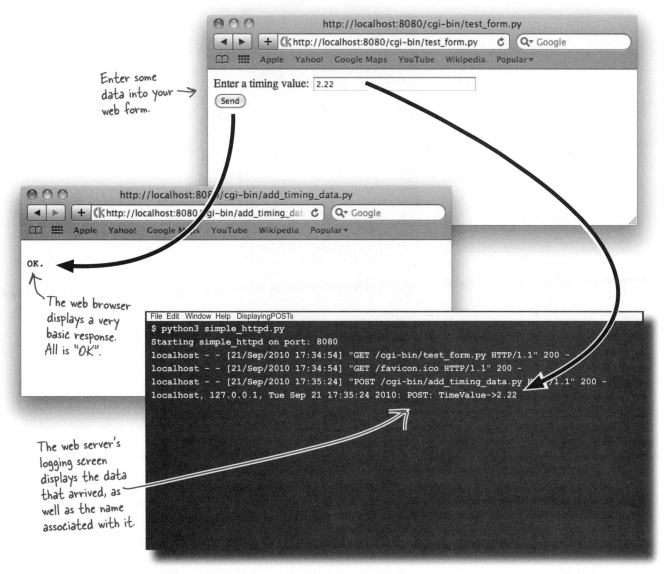

Enter some data into your web form.

Enter a timing value: 2.22
(Send)

http://localhost:8080/cgi-bin/test_form.py
http://localhost:8080/cgi-bin/test_form.py
Apple   Yahoo!   Google Maps   YouTube   Wikipedia   Popular ▼

http://localhost:8080/cgi-bin/add_timing_data.py
http://localhost:8080/cgi-bin/add_timing_dat:
Apple   Yahoo!   Google Maps   YouTube   Wikipedia   Popular ▼

OK.

The web browser displays a very basic response. All is "OK".

```
File Edit Window Help DisplayingPOSTs
$ python3 simple_httpd.py
Starting simple_httpd on port: 8080
localhost - - [21/Sep/2010 17:34:54] "GET /cgi-bin/test_form.py HTTP/1.1" 200 -
localhost - - [21/Sep/2010 17:34:54] "GET /favicon.ico HTTP/1.1" 200 -
localhost - - [21/Sep/2010 17:35:24] "POST /cgi-bin/add_timing_data.py H   /1.1" 200 -
localhost, 127.0.0.1, Tue Sep 21 17:35:24 2010: POST: TimeValue->2.22
```

The web server's logging screen displays the data that arrived, as well as the name associated with it.

That worked perfectly. The data entered into the form is delivered to your CGI script on the your server. Your next challenge is to provide the same user input experience on an Android phone.

Ask for input on your Android phone

When you ask for user input on Android, the dialog that your user sees looks something like this example, which asks your user to confirm or change the web address and port for your server.

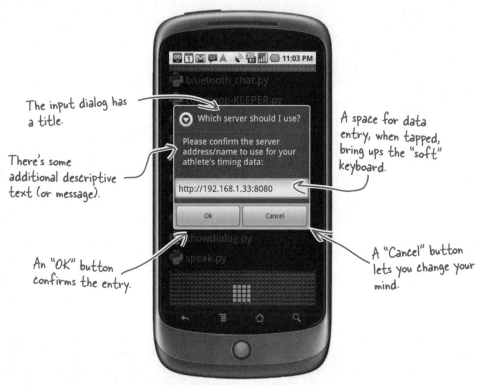

The input dialog has a title.

There's some additional descriptive text (or message).

A space for data entry, when tapped, bring ups the "soft" keyboard.

An "OK" button confirms the entry.

A "Cancel" button lets you change your mind.

A single Android call creates this interface for you using the `dialogGetInput()` method:

```
title = 'Which server should I use?'
message = "Please confirm the server address/name to use for your athlete's timing data:"
data = 'http://192.168.1.33:8080'
resp = app.dialogGetInput(title, message, data).result
```

The result of your user's interaction with the dialog is assigned to "resp".

Pressing the **Ok** button sets `resp` to the data entered into the input area.

Pressing the **Cancel** button sets `resp` to None, which is Python's internal null-value.

Let's create some Android data-entry dialogs.

Exercise

Let's create a small Android app that interacts with your user *twice*. The first dialog asks the user to confirm the web address and port to use for the web server. Assuming your user taps the OK button on your dialog, a second dialog pops up to request the timing value to send to the server. As with the first dialog, tapping the OK button continues execution by sending the newly acquired timing value to the web server. Tapping Cancel at any time causes your app to exit.

Some of the code is provided for you. Your job is to complete the program. Write the code you think you need under this code, and call your program `get2inputsapp.py`:

There's nothing new here...you've seen all of this code before.

```python
import android
from urllib import urlencode
from urllib2 import urlopen

server_title  = 'Which server should I use?'
server_msg    = "Please confirm the server address/name to use for your athlete's timing data:"
timing_title  = 'Enter data'
timing_msg    = 'Provide a new timing value:'
web_server    = 'http://192.168.1.33:8080'
add_time_cgi  = '/cgi-bin/add_timing_data.py'


app = android.Android()


def send_to_server(url, post_data=None):
    if post_data:
        page = urlopen(url, urlencode(post_data))
    else:
        page = urlopen(url)
    return(page.read().decode("utf8"))
```

....

....

....

....

....

....

....

....

You were to create a small Android app that interacts with your user *twice*. The first dialog asks the user to confirm the web address and port to use for the web server. Assuming your user taps the OK button on your dialog, a second dialog pops up to request the timing value to send to the server. As with the first dialog, tapping the OK button continues execution by sending the newly acquired timing value to the web server. Tapping Cancel at any time causes your app to exit.

Some of the code was provided for you. Your job was to complete the program by writing the code you think you need under this code and call your program `get2inputsapp.py`.

```python
import android
from urllib import urlencode
from urllib2 import urlopen


server_title  = 'Which server should I use?'
server_msg    = "Please confirm the server address/name to use for your athlete's timing data:"
timing_title  = 'Enter data'
timing_msg    = 'Provide a new timing value:'
web_server    = 'http://192.168.1.33:8080'
add_time_cgi  = '/cgi-bin/add_timing_data.py'


app = android.Android()


def send_to_server(url, post_data=None):
    if post_data:
        page = urlopen(url, urlencode(post_data))
    else:
        page = urlopen(url)
    return(page.read().decode("utf8"))
```

```python
resp = app.dialogGetInput(server_title, server_msg, web_server).result
```

The first dialog asks your user to confirm the web address and port to use.

```python
if resp is not None:
```

If your user did NOT tap on the Cancel button...

```python
    web_server = resp
```

...the second dialog asks for a new timing value.

```python
    resp = app.dialogGetInput(timing_title, timing_msg).result
```

```python
    if resp is not None:
```

Again, if your user did NOT tap on the Cancel button...

```python
        new_time = resp
```

...the app sends the data to the web server.

```python
        send_to_server(web_server + add_time_cgi, {'TimingValue': new_time})
```

TEST DRIVE

Let's copy `get2inputsapp.py` to the emulator using the `adb` tool:

```
tools/adb push get2inputsapp.py /sdcard/sl4a/scripts
```

The `get2inputsapp.py` app appears on the list of scripts within SL4A. Go ahead and give it a tap:

Your new app starts, and you can edit the web server address and port.

When you click on the input area, Android's "soft" keyboard pops up.

Enter a new timing value, and then tap "Ok".

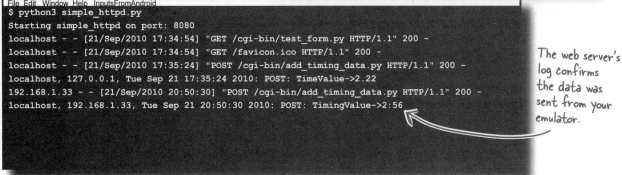

```
File Edit Window Help InputsFromAndroid
$ python3 simple_httpd.py
Starting simple_httpd on port: 8080
localhost - - [21/Sep/2010 17:34:54] "GET /cgi-bin/test_form.py HTTP/1.1" 200 -
localhost - - [21/Sep/2010 17:34:54] "GET /favicon.ico HTTP/1.1" 200 -
localhost - - [21/Sep/2010 17:35:24] "POST /cgi-bin/add_timing_data.py HTTP/1.1" 200 -
localhost, 127.0.0.1, Tue Sep 21 17:35:24 2010: POST: TimeValue->2.22
192.168.1.33 - - [21/Sep/2010 20:50:30] "POST /cgi-bin/add_timing_data.py HTTP/1.1" 200 -
localhost, 192.168.1.33, Tue Sep 21 20:50:30 2010: POST: TimingValue->2:56
```

The web server's log confirms the data was sent from your emulator.

Perfect. That's working, too. Regardless of where your data originates—on the Web or a phone—your app can send it to your web server.

It's time to update your server data

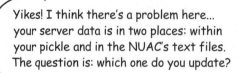

Yikes! I think there's a problem here...
your server data is in two places: within
your pickle and in the NUAC's text files.
The question is: which one do you update?

Which of your two datasets should you update?

If you update the pickle, the next time the `put_to_store()`
function runs, your most recent update will vanish as `put_to_store()` recreates the pickle from the data in the text files.
That's not good.

If you update the appropriate athlete's text file, the data in the
pickle will be **stale** until `put_to_store()` runs again. If
another process calls the `get_from_store()` function in the
meantime, the update to the pickle might not have been applied
and will appear to be *missing* for anyone reading your data. That's
not good, either.

Oh, look, how lovely: I
have a new timing value to add to
the system. Who's going first?

Update me, then
I'll update him.

No, no, no,
he's busy. Just
update me!

Web
Server

Your text file ↗

↖ Your pickle file

Avoid race conditions

> Of course...I could write to the text file and then immediately call "put_to_store()" to update the pickle, right?

Yes, that's one possible solution, but it's a poor one.

You might think it highly unlikely...but it is possible for another process to call the get_from_store() function *between* the text file update and the pickle recreation, resulting in a short period of data inconsistency. These types of situations are known as **race conditions** and are hard to debug when they occur.

It's best to keep them from ever happening if you can.

The basic problem here is that you have *one* update with *one* piece of data that results in *two* file interactions. If nothing else, that's just wasteful.

> Hey, thanks for the update!

Your up-to-date text file

> What update?!? It's been all quiet over here...

Your temporarily inconsistent pickle file

You need a better data storage mechanism

Your initial text files and pickle design is fine when only one user is accessing the data. However, now that more than one person can access the data at any time, and from anywhere, your design is in need of improvement. Above all, you need to *avoid that race condition*.

> This is very upsetting...I appear to be missing an update.

↖ Your inconsistent and upset pickle file

> Listen, bud, it's not my fault...until someone, somewhere runs the "put_to_store()" function without someone, somewhere else running the "get_from_store()" function, you'll have to do without that data update. I'm not a miracle worker...I just do what I'm told.

Web Server

there are no
Dumb Questions

Q: Surely you should have thought about this problem long ago and designed this "properly" from the start?

A: That's certainly one way to look at things, and hindsight is always a wonderful thing! However, programs have a tendency to start out small, then grow to provide more features, which can introduce complexity. Recall that the coach's app started life as a simple "standalone" text-based program, which was then moved to the Web to support multiple users. Part of the app was then redeveloped for use on an Android phone. And yes, if we'd known all of this ahead of time, we might have been designed it differently.

Q: So I'm facing a rewrite of large chunks of my code?

A: Let's see. You did build your program using the MVC pattern, and you are using Python, so those two facts should take the sting out of any potential rewrite, assuming a rewrite is what's required here.

Wouldn't it be dreamy if I could put my data in only one place and support all my app's requirements? But I know it's just a fantasy...

Use a database management system

You need to move away from your text file and pickle combination and use a *real* database management system. You have plenty of choices here…

All of these fine technologies will work, but they are overkill for your app's data requirements. And besides some of these are way beyond the NUAC's budget, let alone their ability to set up, run, and maintain such a system.

What you need is something that's effectively hidden from the NUAC yet lets you take advantage of what a database management system has to offer.

If only such a technology existed…

Python includes SQLite

Python 3 comes preinstalled with Release 3 of **SQLite**, a full-featured, zero-config, SQL-based data management system.

To use SQLite, simply import the `sqlite3` library and use Python's standardized database API to program it. There's really nothing to it: no database setup, no config, and no ongoing maintenance.

With your data stored in SQLite, rewrite your webapp's model code to use SQL to access, manipulate, and query your data. You can plan to move to one of the bigger database systems if and when your application needs dictate such a move.

SQLite sounds perfect for the NUAC's data, doesn't it?

Geek Bits

The material in this chapter assumes you are comfortable with SQL database technology. If you are new to SQL (or just need a quick refresher), take a look at *Head First SQL*, which comes **highly recommended**.

[Note from Marketing: Available anywhere good books are sold and to anyone with a valid credit card.]

Exploit Python's database API

The **Python Database API** provides a standard mechanism for programming a wide variery of database management systems, including SQLite. The process you follow in your code is the same regardless of which back-end database you're using.

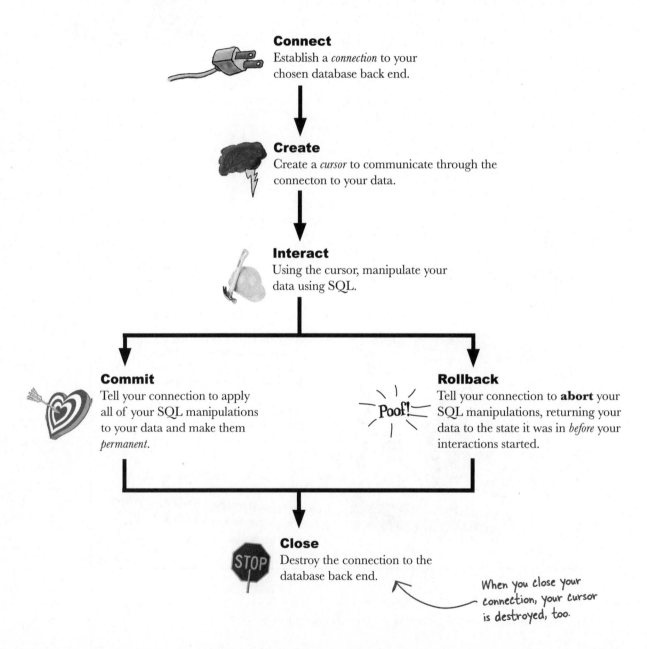

Connect
Establish a *connection* to your chosen database back end.

Create
Create a *cursor* to communicate through the connecton to your data.

Interact
Using the cursor, manipulate your data using SQL.

Commit
Tell your connection to apply all of your SQL manipulations to your data and make them *permanent*.

Rollback
Tell your connection to **abort** your SQL manipulations, returning your data to the state it was in *before* your interactions started.

Poof!

Close
Destroy the connection to the database back end.

When you close your connection, your cursor is destroyed, too.

The database API as Python code

Here's how to implement an interaction with a database using the `sqlite3` module:

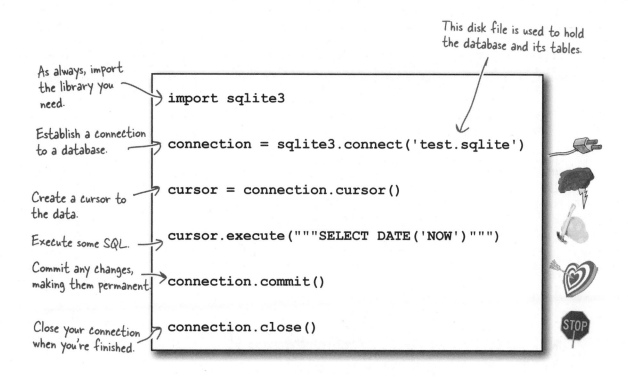

As always, import the library you need.

Establish a connection to a database.

Create a cursor to the data.

Execute some SQL.

Commit any changes, making them permanent.

Close your connection when you're finished.

This disk file is used to hold the database and its tables.

```python
import sqlite3

connection = sqlite3.connect('test.sqlite')

cursor = connection.cursor()

cursor.execute("""SELECT DATE('NOW')""")

connection.commit()

connection.close()
```

Depending on what happens during the **Interact** phase of the process, you either make any changes to your data permanent (`commit`) or decide to abort your changes (`rollback`).

You can include code like this in your program. It is also possible to interact with you SQLite data from within IDLE's shell. Whichever option you choose, you are interacting with your database using Python.

It's great that you can use a database to hold your data. But what schema should you use? Should you use one table, or do you need more? What data items go where? How will you design your database?

Let's start working on the answers to these questions.

A little database design goes a long way

Let's consider how the NUAC's data is currently stored within your pickle.

Each athlete's data is an `AthleteList` object instance, which is associated with the athlete's name in a dictionary. The entire dictionary is pickled.

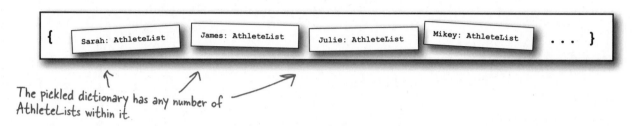

The pickled dictionary has any number of AthleteLists within it.

Each `AthleteList` has the following attributes:

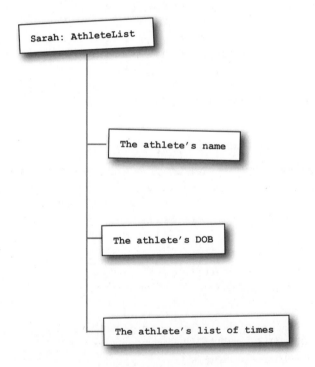

With this arrangement, it is pretty obvious which name, date of birth, and list of times is associated with which individual athlete. But how do you model these relationships within a SQL-compliant database system like *SQLite*?

You need to define your schema and create some tables.

Define your database schema

Here is a suggested SQL schema for the NUAC's data. The database is called `coachdata.sqlite`, and it has two related tables.

The first table, called `athletes`, contains rows of data with a unique ID value, the athlete's name, and a date-of-birth. The second table, called `timing_data`, contains rows of data with an athlete's unique ID and the actual time value.

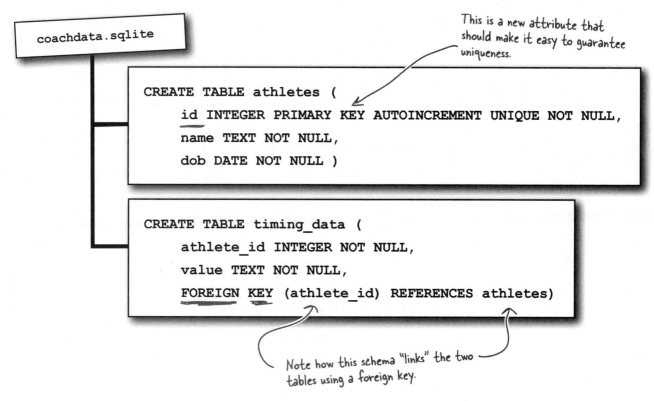

coachdata.sqlite

This is a new attribute that should make it easy to guarantee uniqueness.

```
CREATE TABLE athletes (
    id INTEGER PRIMARY KEY AUTOINCREMENT UNIQUE NOT NULL,
    name TEXT NOT NULL,
    dob DATE NOT NULL )
```

```
CREATE TABLE timing_data (
    athlete_id INTEGER NOT NULL,
    value TEXT NOT NULL,
    FOREIGN KEY (athlete_id) REFERENCES athletes)
```

Note how this schema "links" the two tables using a foreign key.

There can be one *and only one* row of data for each athlete in the `athletes` table. For each athlete, the value of `id` is guaranteed to be *unique*, which ensures that two (or more) athletes with the same name are kept separate within the system, because that have different ID values.

Within the `timing_data` table, each athlete can have any number of time values associated with their unique `athlete_id`, with an individual row of data for each recorded time.

Let's look at some sample data.

What does the data look like?

If the two tables were created and then populated with the data from the NUAC's text files, the data in the tables might look something like this.

id	name	dob
1	James Lee	2002-03-14
2	Sarah Sweeney	2002-06-17
3	Vera Vi	2002-12-25
4	Julie Jones	2002-08-17
5	Sally Sanchez	2002-11-24
6	Mikey McManus	2002-02-24

This is what the data in the "athletes" table might look like, with one row of data for each athlete.

This is what the data in the "timing_data" table might look like, with multiple rows of data for each athlete and one row for each timing value.

athlete_id	value
1	2.01
1	2.16
1	2.22
1	2.34
1	2.45
1	3.01
1	3.1
1	3.21
2	2.18
2	2.21
2	2.22
2	2.25
2	2.39
2	2.54
2	2.55
2	2.58
3	2.41
3	2.49
3	3.01
3	3.02
3	3.11
3	3.23
4	2.11
4	2.23

There's more data in this table than shown here.

If you create these two tables then arrange for your data to be *inserted* into them, the NUAC's data would be in a format that should make it easier to work with.

Looking at the tables, it is easy to see how to add a new timing value for an athlete. Simply add another row of data to the `timing_data` table.

Need to add an athlete? Add a row of data to the `athletes` table.

Want to know the fastest time? Extract the smallest value from the `timing_data` table's `value` column?

Let's create and populate these database tables.

SQLite Magnets

Let's create a small Python program that creates the `coachdata.sqlite` database with the empty `athletes` and `timing_data` tables. Call your program `createDBtables.py`. The code you need is almost ready. Rearrange the magnets at the bottom of the page to complete it.

```
import sqlite3


........................................................................

........................................................................

cursor.execute("""CREATE TABLE athletes (

                ........................................................

                ........................................................

                ........................................................


........................................................................

                athlete_id INTEGER NOT NULL,
                value TEXT NOT NULL,
                FOREIGN KEY (athlete_id) REFERENCES athletes)""")


connection.commit()
connection.close()
```

```
cursor = connection.cursor()
```

```
dob DATE NOT NULL )""")
```

```
cursor.execute("""CREATE TABLE timing_data (
```

```
connection = sqlite3.connect('coachdata.sqlite')
```

```
name TEXT NOT NULL,
```

```
id INTEGER PRIMARY KEY AUTOINCREMENT UNIQUE NOT NULL,
```

SQLite Magnets Solution

Your job was to create a small Python program that creates the
`coachdata.sqlite` database with the empty `athletes`
and `timing_data` tables. You were to call your program
`createDBtables.py`. The code you needed was almost ready,
and you were to rearrange the magnets at the bottom of the page to
complete it.

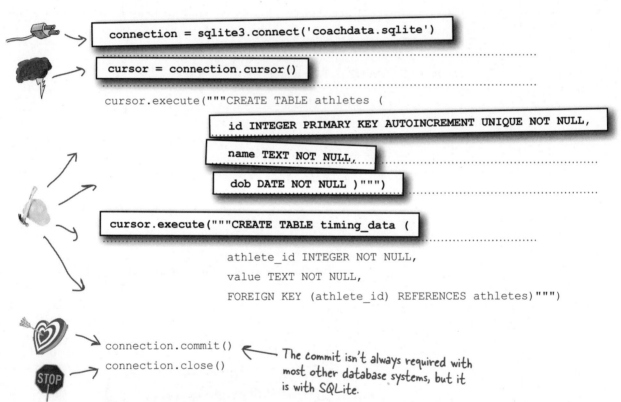

```python
import sqlite3

connection = sqlite3.connect('coachdata.sqlite')

cursor = connection.cursor()

cursor.execute("""CREATE TABLE athletes (

id INTEGER PRIMARY KEY AUTOINCREMENT UNIQUE NOT NULL,

name TEXT NOT NULL,

dob DATE NOT NULL )""")

cursor.execute("""CREATE TABLE timing_data (

athlete_id INTEGER NOT NULL,
value TEXT NOT NULL,
FOREIGN KEY (athlete_id) REFERENCES athletes)""")

connection.commit()
connection.close()
```

The commit isn't always required with
most other database systems, but it
is with SQLite.

Transfer the data from your pickle to SQLite

As well as writing the code to create the tables that you need, you also need to arrange to transfer the data from your existing model (your text files and `pickle` combination) to your new database model. Let's write some code to do that, too.

You can add data to an existing table with the SQL INSERT statement. Assuming you have data in variables called `name` and `dob`, use code like this to add a new row of data to the `athletes` table:

> The data in these variables is substituted in place of the "?" placeholders.

```
cursor.execute("INSERT INTO athletes (name, dob) VALUES (?, ?)",(name, dob))
```

You don't need to worry about supplying a value for the "id" column, because SQLite provides one for you automatically.

READY BAKE PYTHON CODE

Here's a program, called `initDBathletes.py`, which takes your athlete data from your existing model and loads it into your newly created *SQLite* database.

Connect to the new database.

Grab the data from the existing model.

Get the athlete's name and DOB from the pickled data.

Use the INSERT statement to add a new row to the "athletes" table.

```
import sqlite3

connection = sqlite3.connect('coachdata.sqlite')
cursor = connection.cursor()

import glob
import athletemodel
data_files = glob.glob("../data/*.txt")
athletes = athletemodel.put_to_store(data_files)

for each_ath in athletes:

    name = athletes[each_ath].name
    dob = athletes[each_ath].dob

    cursor.execute("INSERT INTO athletes (name, dob) VALUES (?, ?)", (name, dob))
    connection.commit()    <- Make the change(s) permanent.

connection.close()
```

What ID is assigned to which athlete?

You need to query the data in your database table to work out which ID value is automatically assigned to an athlete.

With SQL, the SELECT statement is the *query king*. Here's a small snippet of code to show you how to use it with Python, assuming the name and dob variables have values:

Again, the placeholders indicate where the data values are substituted into the query.

```
cursor.execute("SELECT id from athletes WHERE name=? AND dob=?", (name, dob))
```

If the query succeeds and returns data, it gets added to your cursor. You can call a number of methods on your cursor to access the results:

- cursor.fetchone() returns the next row of data.

- cursor.fetchmany() returns multiple rows of data.

- cursor.fetchall() returns all of the data.

Each of these cursor methods return a <u>list</u> of rows.

> Names alone are not enough anymore...if you want to uniquely identify your athletes, I need to know their IDs.

Web
Server

Insert your timing data

You're on a roll, so let's *keep coding* for now and produce the code to take an athlete's timing values out of the pickle and add them to your database. Specifically, you'll want to arrange to add a new row of data to the `timing_data` table for each time value that is associated with each athlete in your pickle.

Those friendly coders over at the Head First Code Review Team have just announced they've added a `clean_data` attribute to your `AthleteList` class. When you access `clean_data`, you get back a list of timing values that are sanitized, sorted, and free from duplicates. The Head First Code Review Team has excellent timing; that attribute should come in handy with your current coding efforts.

✏️ Sharpen your pencil

Again, it's OK to assume in your code that the "name" and "dob" variables exist and have values assigned to them.

Grab your pencil and write the lines of code needed to query the `athletes` table for an athlete's name and DOB, assigning the result to a variable called `the_current_id`. Write another query to extract the athlete's times from the pickle and add them to the `timing_data` table.

....

....

....

....

....

....

....

....

....

....

Sharpen your pencil
Solution

You were to grab your pencil and write the lines of code needed to query the `athletes` table for an athlete's name and DOB, assigning the result to a variable called `the_current_id`. You were then to write another query to extract the athlete's times from the pickle and add them to the `timing_data` table.

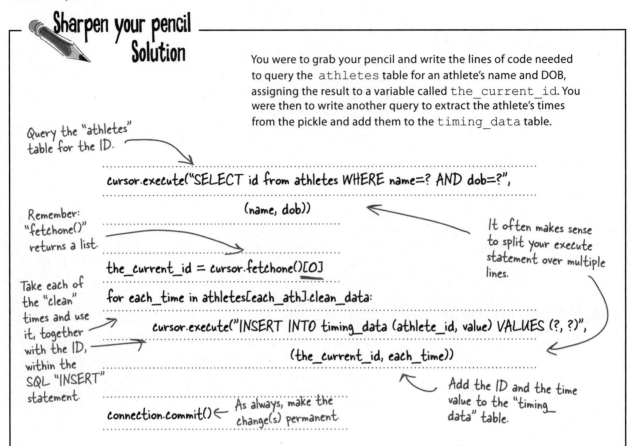

Query the "athletes" table for the ID.

```
cursor.execute("SELECT id from athletes WHERE name=? AND dob=?",
                            (name, dob))
```

Remember: "fetchone()" returns a list.

It often makes sense to split your execute statement over multiple lines.

```
the_current_id = cursor.fetchone()[0]
for each_time in athletes[each_ath].clean_data:
```

Take each of the "clean" times and use it, together with the ID, within the SQL "INSERT" statement.

```
    cursor.execute("INSERT INTO timing_data (athlete_id, value) VALUES (?, ?)",
                            (the_current_id, each_time))
```

Add the ID and the time value to the "timing_data" table.

```
connection.commit()
```
← As always, make the change(s) permanent.

Do this!

Add the code to your `initDBathletes.py` code from earlier, just after the `connection.commit()` call. Rename your program `initDBtables.py`, now that both the `athletes` and `timing_data` tables are populated with data by a single program.

That's enough coding (for now). Let's transfer your pickled data.

Test Drive

You've got two programs to run now: `createDBtables.py` creates an empty database, defining the two tables, and `initDBtables.py` extracts the data from your pickle and populates the tables. Rather than running these programs within IDLE, let's use the Python command-line tool instead.

If you are running Windows, replace "python3" with this: "C:\Python31\python.exe".

Be careful to run both programs ONLY once.

```
File  Edit  Window  Help  PopulateTheTables
$ python3 createDBtables.py
$ python3 initDBtables.py
$
```

Hello? Something happened there, didn't it? I ran the programs but nothing appeared on screen...how do I know if anything worked?

SQLite data management tools

When it comes to checking if your manipulations of the data in your database worked, you have a number of options:

(a) **Write more code to check that the database is in the state that you expect it.**
Which can certainly work, but is error-prone, tedious, and way too much work.

Life really is too short.

(b) **Use the supplied "sqlite3" command-line tool.**
Simply type `sqlite3` within a terminal window to enter the SQLite "shell." To find out which commands are available to you, type `.help` and start reading. The tool is a little basic (and cryptic), but it works.

That's a period, followed by the word "help".

(c) **Use a graphical database browser.**
There are lots of these; just Google "sqlite database browser" for more choices than you have time to review. Our favorite is the SQLite Manager, which installs into the Firefox web browser as an extension.

Works great, but only on Firefox.

This is what SQLite Manager looks like.

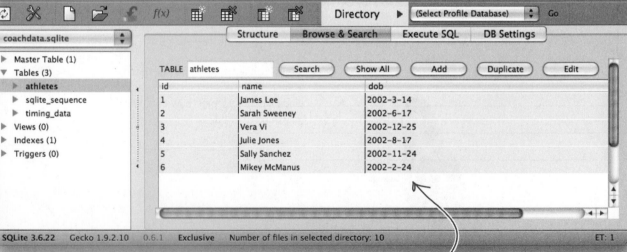

Great, all of the athletes are in the "athletes" table.

But how do you integrate your new database into your webapp?

Integrate SQLite with your existing webapp

So...we just need to change our model code to use SQLite...but what's involved?

Joe: This should be easy. We just have to rewrite the code in `athletemodel.py` to use the database, while keeping the API the same.

Frank: What do you mean by *keeping the API the same?*

Joe: Well...take the `get_from_store()` function, for instance. It returns an `AthleteList` dictionary, so we need to make sure that when we update `get_from_store()` to use our database that it *continues* to return a dictionary, just as it's always done.

Frank: Ah, now I get it: we can query the database, grab all the data, turn it into a big dictionary containing all of our `AthleteList` objects and then return that to the caller, right?

Joe: Yes, exactly! And the best of it is that the calling code doesn't need to change at all. Don't you just love the beauty of MVC?

Frank: Ummm...I guess so.

Jim: [cough, cough]

Frank: What's up, Jim?

Jim: Are you guys crazy?

Joe & Frank: What?!?

Jim: You are bending over backward to maintain compatibility with an API that exists only because of the way your data model was initially designed. Now that you've reimplemented how your data is stored in your model, you need to consider if you need to change your API, too.

Joe & Frank: Change our API? *Are you crazy?!?*

Jim: No, not crazy, just pragmatic. If we can simplify the API by redesigning it to better fit with our database, then we should.

Joe: OK, but we haven't got all day, y'know.

Jim: Don't worry: it'll be worth the effort.

 **LONG EXERCISE** ————————————————————————————

Let's spend some time amending your model code to use your SQLite database as opposed to your pickle. Start with the code to your `athletemodel.py` module. Take a pencil and strike out the lines of code you no longer need.

```python
import pickle


from athletelist import AthleteList


def get_coach_data(filename):
    try:
        with open(filename) as f:
            data = f.readline()
        templ = data.strip().split(',')
        return(AthleteList(templ.pop(0), templ.pop(0), templ))
    except IOError as ioerr:
        print('File error (get_coach_data): ' + str(ioerr))
        return(None)


def put_to_store(files_list):
    all_athletes = {}
    for each_file in files_list:
        ath = get_coach_data(each_file)
        all_athletes[ath.name] = ath
    try:
        with open('athletes.pickle', 'wb') as athf:
            pickle.dump(all_athletes, athf)
    except IOError as ioerr:
        print('File error (put_and_store): ' + str(ioerr))
    return(all_athletes)
```

```
def get_from_store():
    all_athletes = {}
    try:
        with open('athletes.pickle', 'rb') as athf:
            all_athletes = pickle.load(athf)
    except IOError as ioerr:
        print('File error (get_from_store): ' + str(ioerr))
    return(all_athletes)


def get_names_from_store():
    athletes = get_from_store()
    response = [athletes[each_ath].name for each_ath in athletes]
    return(response)
```

Remember: there's no requirement to maintain the existing API.

LONG EXERCISE SOLUTION

Let's spend some time amending your model code to use your SQLite database as opposed to your pickle. Start with the code to your `athletemodel.py` module. You were to take a pencil and strike out the lines of code you no longer need.

```
import pickle


from athletelist import AthleteList


def get_coach_data(filename):
    try:
        with open(filename) as f:
            data = f.readline()
        templ = data.strip().split(',')
        return(AthleteList(templ.pop(0), templ.pop(0), templ))
    except IOError as ioerr:
        print('File error (get_coach_data): ' + str(ioerr))
        return(None)


def put_to_store(files_list):
    all_athletes = {}
    for each_file in files_list:
        ath = get_coach_data(each_file)
        all_athletes[ath.name] = ath
    try:
        with open('athletes.pickle', 'wb') as athf:
            pickle.dump(all_athletes, athf)
    except IOError as ioerr:
        print('File error (put_and_store): ' + str(ioerr))
    return(all_athletes)
```

None of this code is needed anymore, because SQLite provides the data model for you.

```
def get_from_store():
    all_athletes = {}
    try:
        with open('athletes.pickle', 'rb') as athf:
            all_athletes = pickle.load(athf)
    except IOError as ioerr:
        print('File error (get_from_store): ' + str(ioerr))
    return(all_athletes)

def get_names_from_store():
    athletes = get_from_store()
    response = [athletes[each_ath].name for each_ath in athletes]
    return(response)
```

> This might seem a little drastic...but sometimes a redesign requires you to throw away obsolete code.

You still need the list of names

Throwing away all of your "old" model code makes sense, but you still need
to generate a list of names from the model. Your decision to use SQLite is
about to pay off: all you need is a simple SQL SELECT statement.

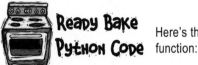

**Ready Bake
Python Code**

Here's the code for your new get_names_from_store()
function:

```python
import sqlite3

db_name = 'coachdata.sqlite'

def get_names_from_store():
    connection = sqlite3.connect(db_name)
    cursor = connection.cursor()
    results = cursor.execute("""SELECT name FROM athletes""")
    response = [row[0] for row in results.fetchall()]
    connection.close()
    return(response)
```

Connect to the
database.

Extract the
data you need.

Formulate a
response.

Return the list of
names to the caller.

> I guess in this case it
> actually makes perfect
> sense to maintain the
> API for this call.

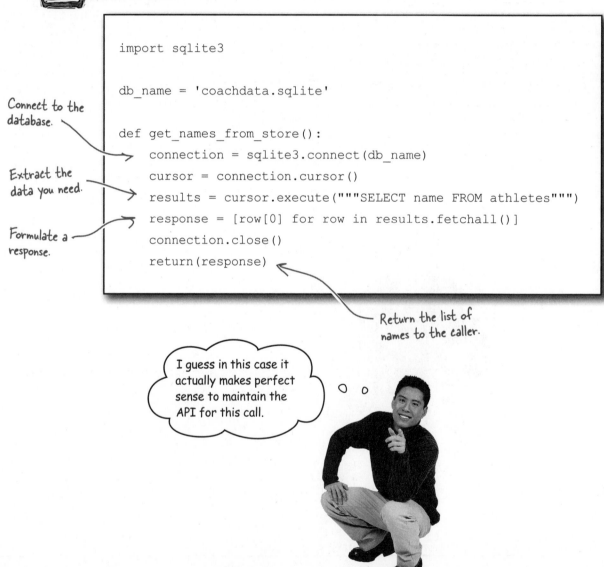

Get an athlete's details based on ID

In addition to the list of names, you need to be able to extract an athlete's
details from the `athletes` table based on ID.

ReaDy Bake PytHon CoDe

Here's the code for another new function called
`get_athlete_from_id()`:

A new function gets the data associated with a specific ID.

Get the "name" and "DOB" values from the athletes table.

Get the list of times from the "timing_data" table.

Return the athlete's data to the caller.

Note the use of the placeholder to indicate where the "athlete_id" argument is inserted into the SQL SELECT query.

Take the data from both query results and turn it into a dictionary.

```python
def get_athlete_from_id(athlete_id):
    connection = sqlite3.connect(db_name)
    cursor = connection.cursor()

    results = cursor.execute("""SELECT name, dob FROM athletes WHERE id=?""",
                                    (athlete_id,))

    (name, dob) = results.fetchone()

    results = cursor.execute("""SELECT value FROM timing_data WHERE athlete_id=?""",
                                    (athlete_id,))

    data = [row[0] for row in results.fetchall()]

    response = {    'Name':    name,
                    'DOB':     dob,
                    'data':    data,
                    'top3':    data[0:3]}
    connection.close()
    return(response)
```

This function is a more involved than `get_names_from_store()`, but
not by much. It still follows the API used with working with data stored in
SQLite. This is coming along. nicely.

With the model code converted, you can revisit your CGI scripts to use your
new model API.

Let's see what's involved with converting the CGIs.

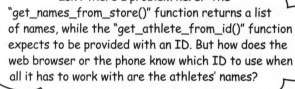

Isn't there a problem here? The "get_names_from_store()" function returns a list of names, while the "get_athlete_from_id()" function expects to be provided with an ID. But how does the web browser or the phone know which ID to use when all it has to work with are the athletes' names?

That's a good point: which ID do you use?

Your current CGIs all operate on the athlete name, not the ID. In order to ensure each athlete is **unique**, you designed your database schema to include a unique ID that allows for your system to properly identify two (or more) athletes with the *same name*, but at the moment, your model code doesn't provide the ID value to either your web browser or your phone.

One solution to this problem is to ensure that the athlete names are displayed to the user within the view, while the IDs are used *internally* by your system to unique identify a specific athlete. For this to work, you need to change `get_names_from_store()`.

Exercise

Here is the current code for your `get_names_from_store()` function. Rather than amending this code, create a new function, called `get_namesID_from_store()`, based on this code but including the ID values as well as the athlete names in its response. Write your new function in the space provided.

```
import sqlite3

db_name = 'coachdata.sqlite'

def get_names_from_store():
    connection = sqlite3.connect(db_name)
    cursor = connection.cursor()
    results = cursor.execute("""SELECT name FROM athletes""")
    response = [row[0] for row in results.fetchall()]
    connection.close()
    return(response)
```

....
....
....
....
....
....
....
....
....
....
....
....
....

Here is your current code for your `get_names_from_store()` function. Rather than amending this code, you were to create a new function, called `get_namesID_from_store()`, based on this code but including the ID values as well as the athlete names in its response. You were to write your new function in the space provided.

```python
import sqlite3

db_name = 'coachdata.sqlite'

def get_names_from_store():
    connection = sqlite3.connect(db_name)
    cursor = connection.cursor()
    results = cursor.execute("""SELECT name FROM athletes""")
    response = [row[0] for row in results.fetchall()]
    connection.close()
    return(response)
```

```python
def get_namesID_from_store():
    connection = sqlite3.connect(db_name)
    cursor = connection.cursor()
    results = cursor.execute("""SELECT name, id FROM athletes""")
    response = results.fetchall()
    connection.close()
    return(response)
```

Arrange to include the value of "id" in the SQL "SELECT" query.

There's no need to process "results" in any way...assign everything returned from the query to "response".

Remember: when you close your connection, your cursor is also destroyed, so you'll generate an exception if you try and use "return(results.fetchall())".

Sharpen your pencil

Part 1: With your model code ready, let's revisit each of your CGI scripts to change them to support your new model. At the moment, all of your code assumes that a list of athlete names or an `AthleteList` is returned from your model. Grab your pencil and amend each CGI to work with athlete IDs where necessary.

This is the "generate_list.py" CGI script.

```
#! /usr/local/bin/python3

import glob
import athletemodel
import yate

data_files = glob.glob("data/*.txt")
athletes = athletemodel.put_to_store(data_files)

print(yate.start_response())
print(yate.include_header("NUAC's List of Athletes"))
print(yate.start_form("generate_timing_data.py"))
print(yate.para("Select an athlete from the list to work with:"))
for each_athlete in sorted(athletes):
    print(yate.radio_button("which_athlete", athletes[each_athlete].name))
print(yate.end_form("Select"))
print(yate.include_footer({"Home": "/index.html"}))
```

Note the change to the title.

This is "generate_timing_data.py".

```
#! /usr/local/bin/python3

import cgi
import athletemodel
import yate

athletes = athletemodel.get_from_store()
form_data = cgi.FieldStorage()
athlete_name = form_data['which_athlete'].value

print(yate.start_response())
print(yate.include_header("NUAC's Timing Data"))
print(yate.header("Athlete: " + athlete_name + ", DOB: " + athletes[athlete_name].dob + "."))
print(yate.para("The top times for this athlete are:"))
print(yate.u_list(athletes[athlete_name].top3))
print(yate.para("The entire set of timing data is: " + str(athletes[athlete_name].clean_data) +
                " (duplicates removed)."))
print(yate.include_footer({"Home": "/index.html", "Select another athlete": "generate_list.py"}))
```

Another title change.

This "Sharpen" is continued on the next page, but no peeking! Don't flip over until you've amended the code on this page.

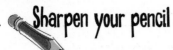
Sharpen your pencil

Part 2: You're not done with that pencil just yet! In addition to amending the code to the CGIs that support your web browser's UI, you also need to change the CGIs that provide your webapp data to your Android app. Amend these CGIs, too.

This is the "generate_names.py" CGI.

```
#! /usr/local/bin/python3

import json

import athletemodel
import yate

names = athletemodel.get_names_from_store()

print(yate.start_response('application/json'))
print(json.dumps(sorted(names)))
```

And here is the "generate_data.py" CGI.

```
#! /usr/local/bin/python3

import cgi
import json
import sys

import athletemodel
import yate

athletes = athletemodel.get_from_store()

form_data = cgi.FieldStorage()
athlete_name = form_data['which_athlete'].value

print(yate.start_response('application/json'))
print(json.dumps(athletes[athlete_name].as_dict))
```

Sharpen your pencil
Solution

Part 1: With your model code ready, you were to revisit each of your CGI scripts to change them to support your new model. At the moment, all of your code assumes that a list of athlete names or an `AthleteList` is returned from your model. You were to grab your pencil and amend each CGI to work with athlete IDs where necessary.

This is the "generate_list.py" CGI script.

```
#! /usr/local/bin/python3

import glob    ←
import athletemodel
import yate

data_files = glob.glob("data/*.txt")
athletes = athletemodel.put_to_store(data_files)


print(yate.start_response())
print(yate.include_header("NUAC's List of Athletes"))
print(yate.start_form("generate_timing_data.py"))
print(yate.para("Select an athlete from the list to work with:"))
for each_athlete in sorted(athletes):
    print(yate.radio_button("which_athlete", athletes[each_athlete].name))
print(yate.end_form("Select"))
print(yate.include_footer({"Home": "/index.html"}))
```

You no longer need the "glob" module, as "get_nameID_from_store()" does all this work for you.

get_namesID_from_store()

The "athletes" are now a list of lists, so amend the code to get at the data you need.

each_athlete[0], each_athlete[1]

radio_button_id() ?!?

It looks like you might need a slightly different "radio_button()" function?!?

The rest of this "Sharpen Solution" is on the next page.

This is "generate_timing_data.py".

```
#! /usr/local/bin/python3

import cgi
import athletemodel
import yate

athletes = athletemodel.get_from_store()
form_data = cgi.FieldStorage()
athlete_name = form_data['which_athlete'].value
athlete = athletemodel.get_athlete_from_id(athlete_id)
print(yate.start_response())
print(yate.include_header("NUAC's Timing Data"))
print(yate.header("Athlete: " + athlete_name + ", DOB: " + athletes[athlete_name].dob + "."))
print(yate.para("The top times for this athlete are:"))
print(yate.u_list(athletes[athlete_name].top3))
print(yate.para("The entire set of timing data is: " + str(athletes[athlete_name].clean_data) +
                " (duplicates removed)."))
print(yate.include_footer({"Home": "/index.html", "Select another athlete": "generate_list.py"}))
```

Get the athlete's data from the model, which returns a dictionary.

Use the returned data as needed, accessing each of the dictionary key/values to get at the athlete's data.

athlete['Name'] + " DOB: " + athlete['DOB']

athlete['top3']

str(athlete['data'])

Sharpen your pencil
Solution

This is the "generate_names.py" CGI.

Part 2: You weren't done with that pencil just yet! In addition to amending the code to the CGIs that support your web browser's UI, you also needed to change the CGIs that provide your webapp data to your Android app. You were to amend these CGIs, too.

```
#! /usr/local/bin/python3

import json

import athletemodel
import yate
```

get_namesID_from_store()

```
names = athletemodel.get_names_from_store()

print(yate.start_response('application/json'))
print(json.dumps(sorted(names)))
```

And here is the "generate_data.py" CGI.

```
#! /usr/local/bin/python3

import cgi
import json
import sys

import athletemodel
import yate

athletes = athletemodel.get_from_store()

form_data = cgi.FieldStorage()
athlete_name = form_data['which_athlete'].value
```
athlete = athletemodel.get_athlete_from_id(athlete_id)
```
print(yate.start_response('application/json'))
print(json.dumps(athletes[athlete_name].as_dict))
```

The tiniest of changes need to be made to these CGIs, because your Android app is only interested in your webapp's data, NOT all of that generated HTML.

Add this code to "yate.py" to support the creation of radio buttons that provide a value for the button that differs from the button text.

A third argument lets you specify an ID to go with the radio button.

```
def radio_button_id(rb_name, rb_value, rb_id):
    return('<input type="radio" name="' + rb_name +
           '" value="' + str(rb_id) + '"> ' + rb_value + '<br />')
```

TEST DRIVE

Before you run your amended webapp, be sure to move you SQLite database into the top-level directory of your webapp (that is, into the same folder your `index.html` file). That way, your model code can find it, so move it into your webapp's root folder *now*. When you are ready, take your SQL-powered webapp for a spin.

Start (or restart) your web server.

```
File Edit Window Help StartYourWebEngine
$ python3 simple_httpd.py
Starting simple_httpd on port: 8080
```

Welcome to the National Underage Athletics Committee's Website

http://localhost:8080/index.html

Apple   Yahoo!   Google Maps   YouTube   Wikipedia   Popular▾

Welcome to the NUAC's Website.

Here is our athlete's timing data. Enjoy!

See you on the track!

Click on the link on the home page.

The NUAC's List of Athletes

http://localhost:8080/cgi-bin/generate_list.py

Apple   Yahoo!   Google Maps   YouTube   Wikipedia   Popular▾

The NUAC's List of Athletes

Select an athlete from the list to work with:

- ○ James Lee
- ○ Julie Jones
- ○ Mikey McManus
- ◉ Sally Sanchez
- ○ Sarah Sweeney
- ○ Vera Vi

(Select)

Display the list of athlete names as radio buttons.

NUAC's Timing Data

http://localhost:8080/cgi-bin/generate_timing_data.py

Apple   Yahoo!   Google Maps   YouTube   Wikipedia   Popular▾

NUAC's Timing Data

Athlete: Sally Sanchez, DOB: 2002-11-24.

The top times for this athlete are:

- 2.11
- 2.26
- 2.31

The entire set of timing data is: ['2.11', '2.26', '2.31', '2.32', '2.41', '2.44', '2.51', '2.55', '3.00', '3.01'] (duplicates removed).

Home   Select another athlete

And there's Sally's timing data.

That worked well. But what about your Android app?

You need to amend your Android app, too

Unlike your HTML-based webapp, where all of your code resides and is executed on your web server, your Android app runs on your phone and it is programmed to work with a list of names, not a list of names *and* athlete IDs.

When you run `coachapp.py` on your emulator, weirdness ensues…

Here's your current Android app running on the emulator.

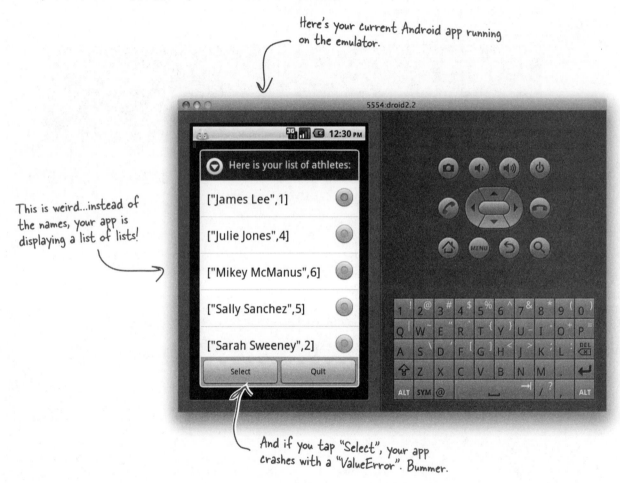

This is weird…instead of the names, your app is displaying a list of lists!

And if you tap "Select", your app crashes with a "ValueError". Bummer.

Just like with the CGI scripts, you need to amend you Android app to work with the data that's now arriving from your web server—that is, a list of lists as opposed to a list.

That shouldn't take too long, should it?

Exercise

Here is your current `coachapp.py` code, which you need to amend to support the way your webapp's model now works. Grab a pencil and make the necessary changes to this code.

```python
import android, json, time

from urllib import urlencode
from urllib2 import urlopen


hello_msg     = "Welcome to NUAC's Timing App"
list_title    = 'Here is your list of athletes:'
quit_msg      = "Quitting NUAC's App."
web_server    = 'http://192.168.1.34:8080'
get_names_cgi = 'cgi-bin/generate_names.py'
get_data_cgi  = '/cgi-bin/generate_data.py'


def send_to_server(url, post_data=None):
    # There is no change to this code from the previous chapter.


app = android.Android()


def status_update(msg, how_long=2):
    # There is no change to this code from the previous chapter.


status_update(hello_msg)
athlete_names = sorted(json.loads(send_to_server(web_server + get_names_cgi)))
app.dialogCreateAlert(list_title)
app.dialogSetSingleChoiceItems(athlete_names)
app.dialogSetPositiveButtonText('Select')
app.dialogSetNegativeButtonText('Quit')
app.dialogShow()
resp = app.dialogGetResponse().result


if resp['which'] in ('positive'):
    selected_athlete = app.dialogGetSelectedItems().result[0]
    which_athlete = athlete_names[selected_athlete]
    athlete = json.loads(send_to_server(web_server + get_data_cgi,{'which_athlete': which_athlete}))
    athlete_title = athlete['Name'] + ' (' + athlete['DOB'] + '), top 3 times:'
    app.dialogCreateAlert(athlete_title)
    app.dialogSetItems(athlete['Top3'])
    app.dialogSetPositiveButtonText('OK')
    app.dialogShow()
    resp = app.dialogGetResponse().result
status_update(quit_msg)
```

Exercise Solution

Here is your current `coachapp.py` code, which you need to amend to support the way your webapp's model now works. You were to grab a pencil and make the necessary changes to this code.

```
import android, json, time
from urllib import urlencode
from urllib2 import urlopen


hello_msg     = "Welcome to NUAC's Timing App"
list_title    = 'Here is your list of athletes:'
quit_msg      = "Quitting NUAC's App."
web_server    = 'http://192.168.1.34:8080'
get_names_cgi = 'cgi-bin/generate_names.py'
get_data_cgi  = '/cgi-bin/generate_data.py'


def send_to_server(url, post_data=None):
    # There is no change to this code from the previous chapter.


app = android.Android()


def status_update(msg, how_long=2):
    # There is no change to this code from the previous chapter.


status_update(hello_msg)
athletes = sorted(json.loads(send_to_server(web_server + get_names_cgi)))
app.dialogCreateAlert(list_title)
athlete_names = [ath[0] for ath in athletes]
app.dialogSetSingleChoiceItems(athlete_names)
app.dialogSetPositiveButtonText('Select')
app.dialogSetNegativeButtonText('Quit')
app.dialogShow()
resp = app.dialogGetResponse().result

if resp['which'] in ('positive'):
    selected_athlete = app.dialogGetSelectedItems().result[0]
    which_athlete = athletes[selected_athlete][1]
    athlete = json.loads(send_to_server(web_server + get_data_cgi,{'which_athlete': which_athlete}))
    athlete_title = athlete['Name'] + ' (' + athlete['DOB'] + '), top 3 times:'
    app.dialogCreateAlert(athlete_title)
    app.dialogSetItems(athlete['top3'])
    app.dialogSetPositiveButtonText('OK')
    app.dialogShow()
    resp = app.dialogGetResponse().result
status_update(quit_msg)
```

Handwritten annotations:

- Extract the athlete names ONLY from the list of lists. → `athletes =`
- `athlete_names = [ath[0] for ath in athletes]`
- This is a cool use of a comprehension.
- Determine the ID associated with the selected athlete. → `athletes[selected_athlete][1]`
- `athlete['top3']`
- A small adjustment to next line is needed to access the "top3" attribute.

Android Pool Puzzle

Your **job** is to take the code from the pool and place it into the blank lines in the program. Your **goal** is to write the code to have your app provide the user with a mechanism to add a timing value to the server for the currently selected athlete. For now, send your data to the `cgi-bin/add_timing_data.py` CGI script.

Hint: the code from `get2inputsapp.py` (from earlier in this chapter) should come in handy here.

```
app.dialogSetNegativeButtonText('Add Time')
```
Add another button to the existing dialog in the current version of your app.

```
    ...

if resp['which'] in ('positive'):
    pass
elif resp['which'] in ('negative'):
```
Based on the button that's tapped, either do nothing ("pass") or start a new dialog with the user.

```
.........................................................................................
.........................................................................................
.........................................................................................
.........................................................................................
.........................................................................................
.........................................................................................
.........................................................................................

        send_to_server(web_server + add_time_cgi,{'Time': new_time, 'Athlete': which_athlete})
```

If some input is supplied, send it to the web server together with the athlete's ID.

Pool contents:

```
new_time = resp

'/cgi-bin/add_timing_data.py'

resp = app.dialogGetInput(timing_title, timing_msg).result

add_time_cgi =

'Provide a new timing value ' + athlete['Name'] + ': '

timing_msg =

timing_title = 'Enter a new time'

if resp is not None:
```

Andröid Pöol Puzzle Sölutiön

Your **job** was to take the code from the pool and place it into the blank lines in the program. Your **goal** was to write the code to have your app provide the user with a mechanism to add a timing value to the server for the currently selected athlete. For now, you were to send your data to the `cgi-bin/add_timing_data.py` CGI script.

Hint: the code from `get2inputsapp.py` (from earlier in this chapter) should come in handy here.

```python
app.dialogSetNegativeButtonText('Add Time')

    ...

if resp['which'] in ('positive'):
    pass
elif resp['which'] in ('negative'):
    timing_title = 'Enter a new time'
    timing_msg =   'Provide a new timing value ' + athlete['Name'] + ': '
    add_time_cgi ='/cgi-bin/add_timing_data.py'

    resp = app.dialogGetInput(timing_title, timing_msg).result

    if resp is not None:
        new_time = resp

        send_to_server(web_server + add_time_cgi,{'Time': new_time, 'Athlete': which_athlete})
```

> Define the dialog's titles and specify the CGI to send the data to.

> Display the dialog and wait for some user input.

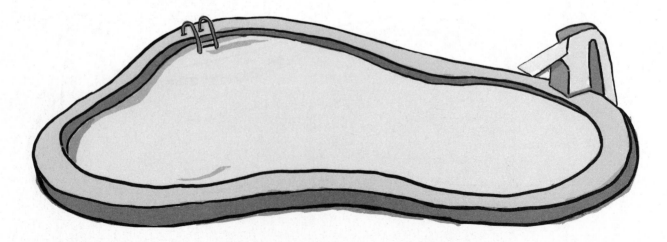

Test Drive

Use the `tools/adb` command to copy your latest app to the emulator, and give your app a go.

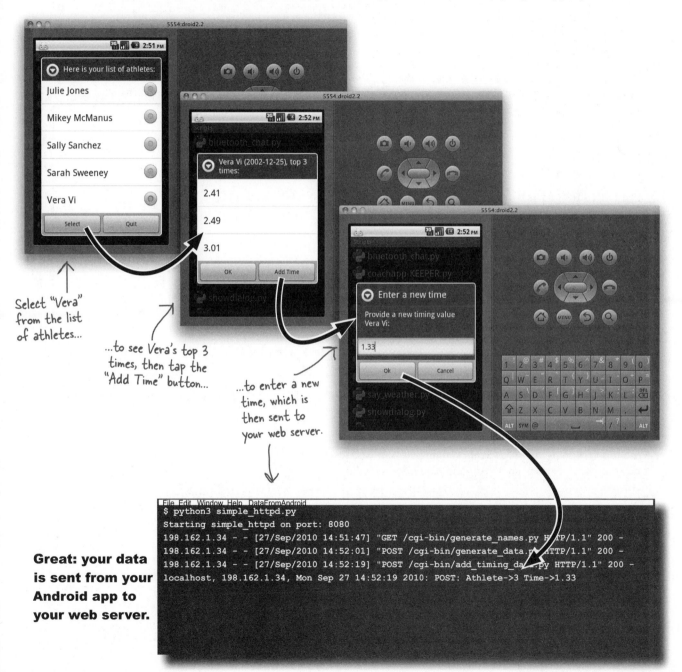

Select "Vera" from the list of athletes...

...to see Vera's top 3 times, then tap the "Add Time" button...

...to enter a new time, which is then sent to your web server.

Great: your data is sent from your Android app to your web server.

```
File Edit Window Help DataFromAndroid
$ python3 simple_httpd.py
Starting simple_httpd on port: 8080
198.162.1.34 - - [27/Sep/2010 14:51:47] "GET /cgi-bin/generate_names.py HTTP/1.1" 200 -
198.162.1.34 - - [27/Sep/2010 14:52:01] "POST /cgi-bin/generate_data.py HTTP/1.1" 200 -
198.162.1.34 - - [27/Sep/2010 14:52:19] "POST /cgi-bin/add_timing_data.py HTTP/1.1" 200 -
localhost, 198.162.1.34, Mon Sep 27 14:52:19 2010: POST: Athlete->3 Time->1.33
```

Update your SQLite-based athlete data

All that's left is to change the `cgi-bin/add_timing_data.py` CGI
script to write your submitted data to your database, as opposed to the web
server's console screen.

At this point, it's a trivial exercise, because a single SQL INSERT statement
will do the heavy lifting.

```
add_timing_data.py - /Users/barryp/HeadFirstPython/chapter9/cgi-bin/add_timing_data.py

#! /usr/local/bin/python3

import cgi
import sqlite3

import yate

print(yate.start_response('text/plain'))

form = cgi.FieldStorage()
the_id = form_data['Athlete'].value
the_time = form_data['Time'].value

connection = sqlite3.connect('coachdata.sqlite')
cursor = connection.cursor()
cursor.execute("INSERT INTO timing_data (athlete_id, value) VALUES (?, ?)",
                    (the_id, the_time))
connection.commit()
connection.close()

print('OK.')
```

Get the data sent to your web browser from your Android app.

INSERT the data into your "timing_data" table.

Ln: 22 Col: 0

With this version of your CGI script running on your web server, any new
times entered by anyone on an Android phone are added to the data in the
database.

The NUAC no longer has to worry about adding data to text files, because
the files are effectively obsoleted by the use of SQLite.

You've produced a robust solution that is more manageable, scalable,
programmable, and extendable. And it's all thanks to the power of Python,
it's database API and the inclusion of `sqlite3` in the standard library.

**All that's left to do is sit back, relax and bask in the
glory of your latest programming creation...**

The NUAC is over the moon!

Of course, your use of SQLite gives you more than just easy insertions of data. With the NUAC's data in tables, it's easy to answer some of the questions that have been on their mind.

> With our data in a database, it's a breeze to work out the fastest time among all our athletes.

> And if we need to know who had the fastest time, that's easy, too.

> This is just great! I can get instant answers to my many questions in the blink of an eye. All thanks to Python and SQLite.

To answer these and other queries on the data in the NUAC's database, you'll have to bone up on your SQL. Then it's up to you to take it from there.

You've converted your webapp to use an SQL database. As your data management needs increase, you can consider alternative *heavy-duty* data management technologies as needed.

This is great work. Your webapp is ready for the big time.

Your Python Toolbox

You've got Chapter 9 under your belt and you've added some key Python tools to your evey expanding Python toolbox.

Python Lingo

• "Database API" – a standardized mechanism for accessing an SQL-based database system from within a Python program.

Database Lingo

• "Database" – a collection of one or more tables.

• "Table" – a collection of one or more rows or data, arranged as one or more columns.

• "SQL" – the "Structured Query Language" is the language of the database world and it lets you work with your data in your database using statements such as CREATE, INSERT, and SELECT.

BULLET POINTS

- The `fieldStorage()` method from the standard library's `cgi` module lets you access data sent to your web server from within your CGI script.

- The standard `os` library includes the `environ` dictionary providing convenient access to your program's environment settings.

- The SQLite database system is included within Python as the `sqlite3` standard library.

- The `connect()` method establishes a connection to your database file.

- The `cursor()` method lets you communicate with your database via an existing connection.

- The `execute()` method lets you send an SQL query to your database via an existing cursor.

- The `commit()` method makes changes to your database **permanent**.

- The `rollback()` method **cancels** any pending changes to your data.

- The `close()` method closes an existing connection to your database.

- The "?" placeholder lets you parameterize SQL statements within your Python code.

CHAPTER 9

10 scaling your webapp

Getting real

It all started with the internal combustion engine, then it was the electric engine, and now there's App Engine. Will this torture never end?

The Web is a great place to host your app...until things get real.

Sooner or later, you'll hit the jackpot and your webapp will be *wildly successful*. When that happens, your webapp goes from a handful of hits a day to thousands, possibly ten of thousands, *or even more*. Will you be ready? Will your web server handle the **load**? How will you know? What will it **cost**? *Who will pay?* Can your data model scale to millions upon millions of data items without *slowing to a crawl*? Getting a webapp up and running is easy with Python and now, thanks to Google App Engine, **scaling** a Python webapp is achievable, too. So...flip the page and find out how.

There are whale sightings everywhere

The Head First Whale Watching Group (HFWWG) coordinates the live cetacean sightings for the entire country. To date, they've provided a PDF form on their website that members of the public can download, fill in, and mail to the HFWWG central office.

The form contains the essential data needed to record the sighting:

Head First Whale Watching Group
Casual Sighting Form

HFWWG.ORG

Name:

Email:

Date:

Time:

Location:

Fin Type:	Falcate	Triangular	Rounded	
Whale Type:	Humpback	Orca	Blue	Killer
	Beluga	Fin	Gray	Sperm
Blow Type:	Tall	Bushy	Dense	
Wave Type:	Flat	Small	Moderate	
	Large	Breaking	High	

After a busy sightings weekend, the central office is swamped with completed forms for **thousands** of sightings…which is a *data-entry nightmare* as all those forms can take an age to process manually. There's nothing worse than being stuck in front of your computer entering data when all you want to do is be out on the water looking for humpbacks…

The HFWWG needs to automate

Suggesting to the HFWWG that they invest in an expensive web hosting solution isn't going to make you any friends. It's way too expensive to buy the capacity they'll need for the busy weekends and a total waste of capacity when sightings are infrequent.

Suggesting that they invest in a large, state-of-the-art web server that can be hosted in the central office is also a nonstarter: there's no one to look after a setup like that, and the broadband link required to handle the anticipated traffic would blow the their budget right out of the water.

Is there another option?

Build your webapp with Google App Engine

Google App Engine (GAE) is a set of technologies that lets you host your webapp on Google's cloud computing infrastructure.

GAE constantly monitors your running webapp and, based on your webapp's current activity, adjusts the resources needed to serve up your webapp's pages. When things are busy, GAE increases the resources available to your webapp, and when things are quiet, GAE reduces the resources until such time as extra activity warrants increasing them again.

On top of this, GAE provides access to Google's *BigTable* technology: a set of database technologies that make storing your webapp's data a breeze. Google also backs up your webapp's data on a regular basis, replicates your webapp over multiple, geographically dispersed web servers, and keeps App Engine running smoothly 24/7.

And the *best part*? GAE can be programmed with Python.

And the *even better part*? You can start running your webapp on GAE *for free*.

That sounds perfect for the HFWWG. What's the catch?

Initially, there isn't one.

Google provides this webapp hosting service at no charge and will continue to do so until your webapp processes five million page views per month. Once it exceeds this threshold, you'll need to pay Google for the extra capacity used. If you never reach the limit, your use of GAE is not charged.

Five million page views? That's a lot of sightings…

Download and install App Engine

When your webapp is ready for deployment, you'll upload it to the Google cloud and run it from there. However, during development, you can run a test version of your webapp locally on your computer. All you need is a copy of the GAE SDK, which is available from here:

http://code.google.com/appengine/

Download the GAE Python SKD for your operating system. Windows, Mac OS X, and Linux are all supported, and installation is straightforward.

After installation, Windows and Mac OS X users will find a nice, graphical front end added to their system.

On Linux, a new folder called "google_appengine" is created after a successful install.

GAE uses Python 2.5

The version of Python built into GAE is a modified version of the Python 2.5 release. As when you worked with Python for Android, the fact that you aren't running Python 3 isn't such a big deal with GAE, although you do need to ensure Python 2.5 is installed on your computer. Open up a terminal window and type:

```
python2.5 -V
```

If this command gives an error, pop on over to the Python website and grab the 2.5 release for your operating system.

---
there are no
Dumb Questions

Q: Aren't things going backward here? First, there was Python 3, then it was Python 2.6 for Android, and now we are dropping down to 2.5 for App Engine? What gives?

A: That's a great question. It's important to remember to always code to the restrictions placed on you. You might think that it sucks that GAE runs on Python 2.5, but you shouldn't. Think of it as just another restriction placed on the code you write—that is, it must target Release 2.5 of Python. As with the Android code you created in the previous chapters, the GAE code you are about to write is not all that different than the Python code for 3. In fact, you will be hard pressed to spot the difference.

Make sure App Engine is working

The environment supported by GAE within the Google cloud supports standard CGI or Python's WSGI. To build a GAE-compatible webapp, you need three things: a **folder** to hold your webapp's files, some **code** to execute, and a **configuration file**.

To test your setup, create a folder called `mygaetest`. Within the folder, create a small CGI you can use to test GAE. Call this CGI `sayhello.py`. Use this code:

```
print('Content-type: text/plain\n')

print('Hello from Head First Python on GAE!')
```

It doesn't get much easier than this...a plain-text message is displayed within your browser whenever this CGI runs.

The configuration file *must* be called `app.yaml` and it, too, must be in your webapp's folder. This file tells the Google cloud a little bit about your webapp's runtime environment. Here's a basic configuration file:

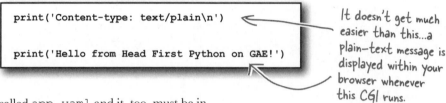

The "application" line identifies your webapp and is the same name as your folder.

"runtime" tells GAE that your webapp is written in and will run on Python.

Think of the "handlers" section of the configuration file as a top-level webapp routing mechanism.

```
application: mygaetest
version: 1
runtime: python
api_version: 1

handlers:
- url: /.*
  script: sayhello.py
```

The "version" line identifies the current version of your webapp (and usually starts at 1).

The "api_version" indicates the release of GAE you are targeting.

This entry tells GAE to route all requests to your webapp to your "sayhello.py" program.

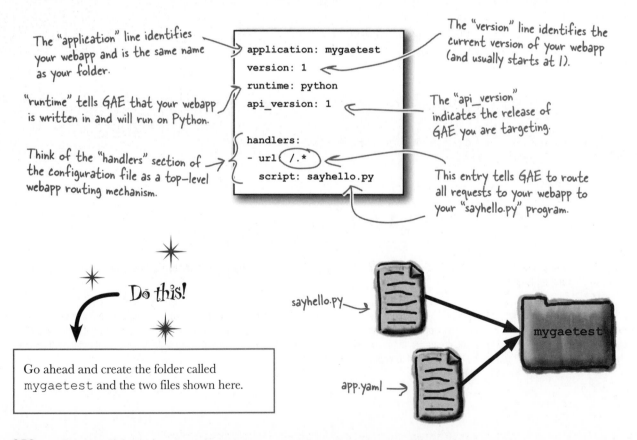

Do this!

Go ahead and create the folder called `mygaetest` and the two files shown here.

sayhello.py →

app.yaml →

mygaetest

TEST DRIVE

The GAE SDK includes a test web server, so let's use it to take your test GAE webapp for a spin. If you are running on Windows or Mac OS X, fire up the Google App Engine Launcher front end. This tool makes it easy to start, stop, and monitor your webapp. On Linux, you'll need to invoke a command to kick things off. If you are using the GAE Launcher, choose File -> Add Existing Application from the menu system to browse and select your webapp's folder. Also: be sure to edit the Launcher's Preferences to select Python 2.5 as your preferred Python Path.

Click this button to start your webapp.

There is no graphical front end for Linux, so start your GAE webapp from the command line.

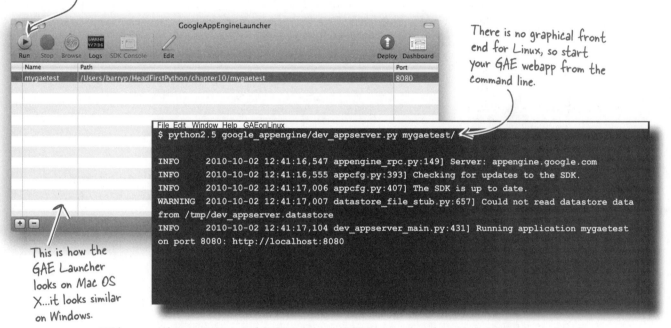

This is how the GAE Launcher looks on Mac OS X...it looks similar on Windows.

With your webapp running and waiting on port 8080, open your favorite web browser and surf on over to the `http://localhost:8080/` web address.

And there it is... the message from your test webapp!

I don't believe it. This is actually more work than plain old CGI...and you're claiming this is better?!?

Yes, it is more work. But that's about to change.

For now, this is more work than you're used to, but remember that this is just a quick test to make sure your GAE test environment is up and running (and it is). When you start to work with some of GAE's web development features, you'll initially see that there's a lot more going on *behind the scenes* than meets the eye.

App Engine uses the MVC pattern

Google has built GAE to conform to the familiar Model-View-Controller (MVC) pattern.

Like your webapp from the previous chapter, the model component of a GAE-enabled webapp uses a back-end data storage facility that's known as the **datastore**. This is based on Google's *BigTable* technology, which provides a "NoSQL" API to your data, as well as a SQL-like API using Google's Query Language (GQL).

GAE's views use templates, but unlike the simple string templates from the previous chapter, GAE uses the **templating system** from the Django Project, which is one of Python's leading web framework technologies. In addition to templates, GAE includes Django's forms-building technology.

And, of course, any controller **code** is written in Python and can use the CGI or WSGI standards. Unfortunately, you can't use your `yate` module with GAE, because it is a Python 3 library (and would need to be extensively rewritten to support Python 2). Not to worry: the facilities provided by GAE "out of the box" are more than enough to build *great* webapps.

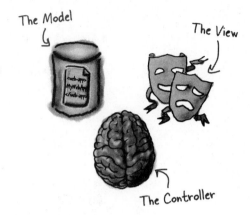

The Model

The View

The Controller

So...like any other webapp that I build, with App Engine I define a **model** for my data, create some **templates** for my view, and then control it all with **code**, right?

Yes, it's the same process as any other webapp.

Google has worked hard to ensure that the move to App Engine is as painless as possible. If you understand MVC (as you now do), you are well on your way to creating with GAE. It's just a matter of working out how GAE implements each of the MVC components.

Model your data with App Engine

App Engine refers to data items stored within its datastore as *properties*, which are defined within your model code.

Think of properties as a way to define the name and types of data within your database schema: each property is like the column type associated piece of data stored in a row, which App Engine refers to as an *entity*.

When you think "row," I think "entity." And when your think "column," I think "property." Get it?

As with traditional SQL-based databases, your GAE datastore properties are of a specific, predeclared type. There are *lots* to choose from, for instance:

- **db.StringProperty**: a string of up to 500 characters

- **db.Blob**: a byte string (binary data)

- **db.DateProperty**: a date

- **db.TimeProperty**: a time,

- **db.IntegerProperty**: a 64-bit integer

- **db.UserProperty**: a Google account

For the full list of property types supported, pop on over to http://code.google.com/appengine/docs/python/datastore/typesandpropertyclasses.html and take a look.

Here's some sample data from the previous chapter.

Store this data as "db.StringProperty".

This data is stored as a "db.IntegerProperty".

This data is stored as a "db.DateProperty".

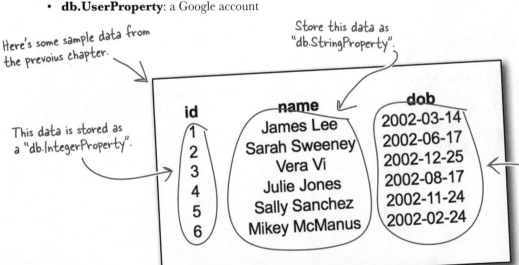

id	name	dob
1	James Lee	2002-03-14
2	Sarah Sweeney	2002-06-17
3	Vera Vi	2002-12-25
4	Julie Jones	2002-08-17
5	Sally Sanchez	2002-11-24
6	Mikey McManus	2002-02-24

Pŏŏl Puzzle

Your **job** is to take the properties from the pool and place them in the correct place in the class code, which is in a file called hfwwgDB.py. Your **goal** is to assign the correct property type to each of the attributes within your Sighting class.

Import the "db" module from the GAE extensions.

```
from google.appengine.ext import db
```

Create a class called "Sighting" that inherits from the GAE "db.Model" class.

```
class Sighting(db.Model):
    name =
    email =
    date =
    time =
    location =
    fin_type =
    whale_type =
    blow_type =
    wave_type =
```

Each property is assigned to a name.

Pool:

```
db.StringProperty()
db.StringProperty()
db.DateProperty()
db.StringProperty()
db.StringProperty()   db.StringProperty()
db.TimeProperty()
db.StringProperty()
db.StringProperty()
```

Pool Puzzle Solution

Your **job** was to take the properties from the pool and place them in the correct place in the class code, which is in a file called hfwwgDB.py. Your **goal** was to assign the correct property type to each of the attributes within your Sighting class.

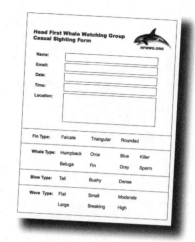

```
from google.appengine.ext import db


class Sighting(db.Model):
    name =          db.StringProperty()
    email =         db.StringProperty()
    date =          db.DateProperty()
    time =          db.TimeProperty()
    location =      db.StringProperty()
    fin_type =      db.StringProperty()
    whale_type =    db.StringProperty()
    blow_type =     db.StringProperty()
    wave_type =     db.StringProperty()
```

Everything is a "StringProperty", except the "date" and "time" fields.

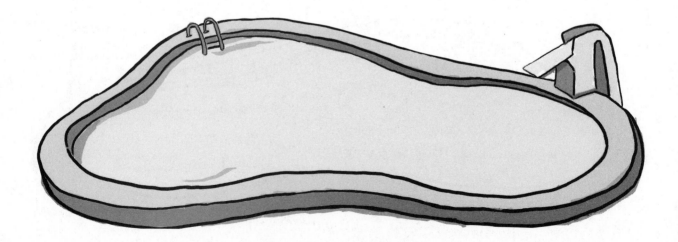

What good is a model without a view?

GAE not only lets you *define* the schema for your data, but it also *creates* the entities in the datastore. The first time you go to **put** your data in the datastore, GAE springs to life and makes room for your data. There's no extra work required by you, other than defining your model in code. It's useful to think of GAE as executing something similar to a SQL CREATE command *on the fly* and *as needed*. But how do you get data into the GAE datastore?

The short answer is that *you put it there*, but you first need to get some data from your webapp's user…and to do that, you need a *view*. And views are easy when you use *templates*.

App Engine templates in an instant

Recall that the templating technology built into GAE is based on technology from the Django Project. Django's templating system is more sophisticated than the simple string-based templates used in the previous chapter. Like your templates, Django's templates can substitute data into HTML, but they can also execute *conditional* and *looping* code.

Here are four templates you'll need for your HTWWG webapp. Two of them should be familiar to you: they are adaptions of those used in the previous chapter. The other two are new. Go ahead and grab them from this book's support website. As you can see, rather that using the $name syntax for variable substitution in the template, Django uses the {{name}} syntax:

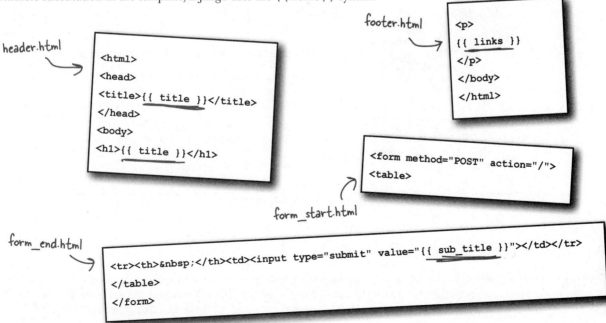

header.html

```
<html>
<head>
<title>{{ title }}</title>
</head>
<body>
<h1>{{ title }}</h1>
```

footer.html

```
<p>
{{ links }}
</p>
</body>
</html>
```

form_start.html

```
<form method="POST" action="/">
<table>
```

form_end.html

```
<tr><th> </th><td><input type="submit" value="{{ sub_title }}"></td></tr>
</table>
</form>
```

Use templates in App Engine

To use a template, import the `template` module from `google.appengine.ext.webapp` and call the `template.render()` function. It is useful to assign the output from `template.render()` to a variable, which is called `html` in this code snippet:

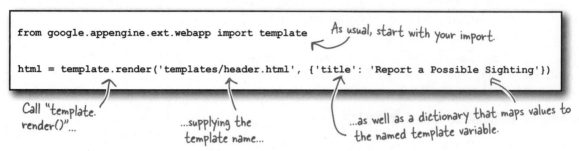

```
from google.appengine.ext.webapp import template
```
As usual, start with your import.

```
html = template.render('templates/header.html', {'title': 'Report a Possible Sighting'})
```

Call "template.render()"...

...supplying the template name...

...as well as a dictionary that maps values to the named template variable.

This is similar to the mechanism your `yate.py` module uses to parameterize the data displayed within your HTML pages.

And I can use a bunch of calls like this to create the view that I need for the HTWWG sightings form, right?

Yes, create your view with templates.

Just like the other webapps that you've built, you can create your view in much the same way using Python code. It's a bummer that you can't use your `yate.py` module, but Django's templates provide most of the functionality you need here.

---
there are no
Dumb Questions

Q: Should I create one big template for my entire web page?

A: You could, if you want. However, if you build up your view from snippets of HTML in templates, you open up the possibility of reusing those HTML snippets in lots of places. For instance, to maintain a consistent look and feel, you can use the same header and footer template on all of your web pages, assuming of course that your header and footer aren't already embedded in an entire web page (which can't be reused).

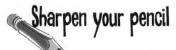

Sharpen your pencil

1 Let's write the rest of the code needed to create a view that displays a data entry form for your HFWWG webapp.

In addition to your web page header code (which already exists and is provided for you), you need to write code that starts a new form, displays the form fields, terminates the form with a submit button, and then finishes off the web page. Make use of the templates you've been given and (here's the rub) do it all in *no more than four additional lines of code*.

This code goes into a new program called "hfwwg.py".

```
from google.appengine.ext.webapp import template

html = template.render('templates/header.html', {'title': 'Report a Possible Sighting'})
```

Extend the contents of "html" with the rest of the HTML you need.

```
html = html +
```
....

Remember: no more than 4 lines of code!

....

....

....

....

....

....

2 Now that you have attempted to write the code required in *no more than four lines of code*, what problem(s) have you encountered. In the space below, note down any issue(s) you are having.

....

....

....

....

Sharpen your pencil
Solution

1 You were to write the rest of the code needed to create a view that displays a data entry form for your HFWWG webapp.

In addition to your webpage header code (which already exists and is provided for you), you were to write code with starts a new form, displays the form fields, terminates the form which a submit button, then finishes off the webpage. You were to make use of the templates you've been given and (here's the rub) you had to do it all in *no more than four more lines of code.*

```
from google.appengine.ext.webapp import template

html = template.render('templates/header.html', {'title': 'Report a Possible Sighting'})
```

The "render()" function always expects two arguments. If you don't need the second one, be sure to pass an empty dictionary.

```
html = html + template.render('templates/form_start.html', {})
```

This is an issue, isn't it?

```
# We need to generate the FORM fields in here...but how?!?
```

```
html = html + template.render('templates/form_end.html', {'sub_title': 'Submit Sighting'})
```
```
html = html + template.render('templates/footer.html', {'links': ''})
```

2 Having attempted to write the code required in *no more than four lines of code*, you were to make a note of any issue(s) you encountered.

This is IMPOSSIBLE to do in just four lines of code, because there's no way to generate the FORM fields that I need. I can't even use the "do_form()" function from "yate.py", because that code is not compatible with Python 2.5... this just sucks!

You may have written something like this...assuming, of course, you haven't thrown your copy of this book out the nearest window in frustration. ☺

Wouldn't it be dreamy if I could avoid hand-coding a <FORM> and generate the HTML markup I need from an existing data model? But I know it's just a fantasy...

Django's form validation framework

Templates aren't the only things that App Engine "borrows" from Django. It also uses its form-generating technology known as the *Form Validation Framework*. Given a data model, GAE can use the framework to generate the HTML needed to display the form's fields within a HTML table. Here's an example GAE model that records a person's essential birth details:

This code is in a file called "birthDB.py".

```
from google.appengine.ext import db


class BirthDetails(db.Model):
    name =           db.StringProperty()
    date_of_birth =  db.DateProperty()
    time_of_birth =  db.TimeProperty()
```

This model is used with Django's framework to generate the HTML markup needed to render the data-entry form. All you need to do is inherit from a GAE-included class called `djangoforms.ModelForm`:

```
from google.appengine.ext.webapp import template
from google.appengine.ext.db import djangoforms
import birthDB


class BirthDetailsForm(djangoforms.ModelForm):
    class Meta:
        model = birthDB.BirthDetails

        ...
    html = template.render('templates/header.html', {'title': 'Provide your birth details'})
    html = html + template.render('templates/form_start.html', {})
    html = html + str(BirthDetailsForm(auto_id=False))
    html = html + template.render('templates/form_end.html', {'sub_title': 'Submit Details'})
    html = html + template.render('templates/footer.html', {'links': ''})
```

Import the forms library in addition to your GAE data model.

Create a new class by inheriting from the "djangoforms.Model" class, and then link your new class to your data model.

Use your new class to generate your form.

There is some code missing from here...but don't worry: you'll get to it in just a moment. For now, just concentrate on understanding the links between the model, the view code, and the Django form validation framework.

Check your form

The framework generates the HTML you need and produces the following output within your browser.

It's not the prettiest web page ever made, but it works.

Use the View Source menu option within your web browser to inspect the HTML markup generated.

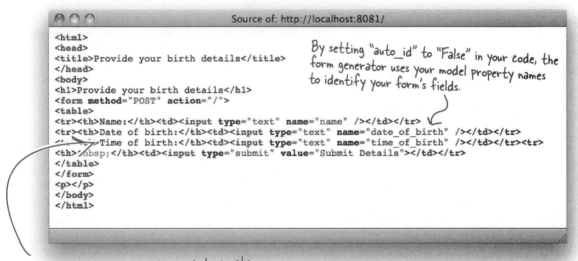

```
<html>
<head>
<title>Provide your birth details</title>
</head>
<body>
<h1>Provide your birth details</h1>
<form method="POST" action="/">
<table>
<tr><th>Name:</th><td><input type="text" name="name" /></td></tr>
<tr><th>Date of birth:</th><td><input type="text" name="date_of_birth" /></td></tr>
<tr><th>Time of birth:</th><td><input type="text" name="time_of_birth" /></td></tr><tr>
<th> </th><td><input type="submit" value="Submit Details"></td></tr>
</table>
</form>
<p></p>
</body>
</html>
```

By setting "auto_id" to "False" in your code, the form generator uses your model property names to identify your form's fields.

The Django framework is smart enough to create sensible labels for each of your input fields (based on the names used in your model).

It's time to tie things all together with your controller code.

Controlling your App Engine webapp

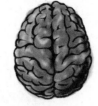

Like your other webapps, it makes sense to arrange your webapp **controller** code within a specific folder structure. Here's one suggestion:

Your top-level folder needs to be named to match the "application" line in your webapp's "app.yaml" file.

hfwwgapp

Put all of your webapp's controller code and configuration files in here.

static

If you have static content, put it in here (at the moment, this folder is empty).

templates

Put your HTML templates in here.

As you've seen, any CGI can run on GAE, but to get the most out of Google's technology, you need to code to the WSGI standard. Here's some *boilerplate* code that every WSGI-compatible GAE webapp starts with:

Import a utility that runs your webapp.

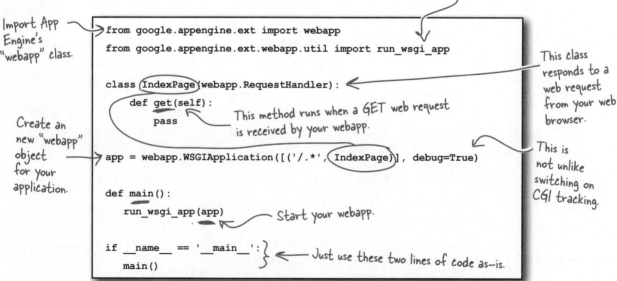

```python
from google.appengine.ext import webapp
from google.appengine.ext.webapp.util import run_wsgi_app

class IndexPage(webapp.RequestHandler):
    def get(self):
        pass

app = webapp.WSGIApplication([('/.*', IndexPage)], debug=True)

def main():
    run_wsgi_app(app)

if __name__ == '__main__':
    main()
```

Import App Engine's "webapp" class.

Create an new "webapp" object for your application.

This method runs when a GET web request is received by your webapp.

This class responds to a web request from your web browser.

This is not unlike switching on CGI tracking.

Start your webapp.

Just use these two lines of code as-is.

App Engine Code Magnets

Let's put everything together. Your model code is already in your `hfwwgDB.py` file. All you need to do is move that file into your webapp's top-level folder. Copy your templates folder in there, too. Your webapp's controller code, in a file called `hfwwg.py`, also needs to exist in your top-level folder. The only problem is that some of the code's all over the floor. Rearrange the magnets to fix things.

```python
from google.appengine.ext import webapp
from google.appengine.ext.webapp.util import run_wsgi_app
from google.appengine.ext import db
from google.appengine.ext.webapp import template
from google.appengine.ext.db import djangoforms
```

> All of the imports have survived...so there's no need to rearrange them.

> Let's test how well you've been paying attention. There's no guiding lines on the fridge door.

What's missing from in here?

```python
        html = template.render('templates/header.html', {'title': 'Report a Possible Sighting'})
        html = html + template.render('templates/form_start.html', {})


        html = html + template.render('templates/form_end.html', {'sub_title': 'Submit Sighting'})
        html = html + template.render('templates/footer.html', {'links': ''})


app = webapp.WSGIApplication([('/.*', SightingInputPage)], debug=True)


def main():
    run_wsgi_app(app)


if __name__ == '__main__':
    main()
```

> There's only one small change from the boilerplate code in that "IndexPage" is not being linked to.

```python
class SightingForm(djangoforms.ModelForm):
```

```python
class SightingInputPage(webapp.RequestHandler):
    def get(self):
```

```python
html = html + str(SightingForm())
```

```python
self.response.out.write(html)
```

```python
model = hfwwgDB.Sighting
```

```python
class Meta:
```

```python
import hfwwgDB
```

App Engine Code Magnets Solution

Let's put everything together. Your model code is already in your `hfwwgDB.py` file. You were to move that file into your webapp's top-level folder, as well as copy your templates folder in there, too. Your webapp's controller code, in a file called `hfwwg.py`, also needs to exist in your top-level folder. The only problem is that some of the code's all over the floor. You were to rearrange the magnets to fix things:

```python
from google.appengine.ext import webapp
from google.appengine.ext.webapp.util import run_wsgi_app
from google.appengine.ext import db
from google.appengine.ext.webapp import template
from google.appengine.ext.db import djangoforms
```

Import your GAE data model code.

```python
import hfwwgDB
```

```python
class SightingForm(djangoforms.ModelForm):
    class Meta:
        model = hfwwgDB.Sighting
```

Use your model to create a sighting form that inherits from the "django.ModelForm" class.

```python
class SightingInputPage(webapp.RequestHandler):
    def get(self):
```

The connected handler class is called "SightingInputPage" and it provides a method called "get" which responds to a GET web request.

```python
        html = template.render('templates/header.html', {'title': 'Report a Possible Sighting'})
        html = html + template.render('templates/form_start.html', {})
```

```python
        html = html + str(SightingForm())
```

Include the generated form in the HTML response.

```python
        html = html + template.render('templates/form_end.html', {'sub_title': 'Submit Sighting'})
        html = html + template.render('templates/footer.html', {'links': ''})
```

```python
        self.response.out.write(html)
```

Did you guess this correctly? You need to send a response back to the waiting web browser and this line of code does just that.

```python
app = webapp.WSGIApplication([('/.*', SightingInputPage)], debug=True)

def main():
    run_wsgi_app(app)

if __name__ == '__main__':
    main()
```

TEST DRIVE

It's been a long time coming, but you are now ready to test the first version of your sightings form. If you haven't done so already, create an `app.yaml` file, too. Set the application line to `hfwwg` and the script line to `hfwwg.py`. One final step is to use the Add Existing Application menu option within the GAE Launcher to select your top-level folder as the location of your webapp.

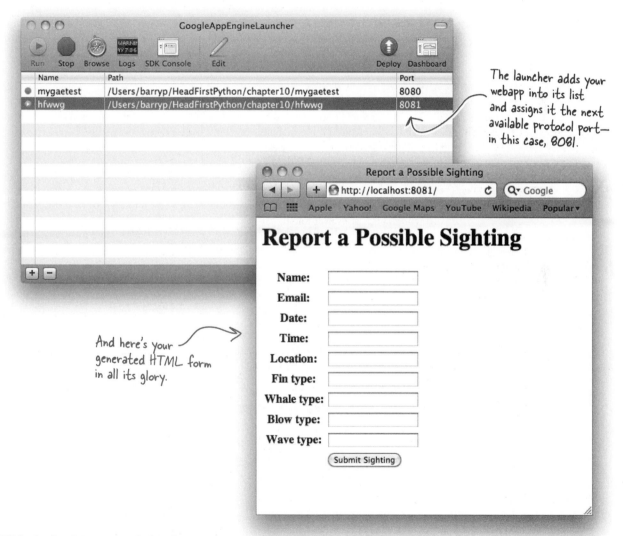

The launcher adds your webapp into its list and assigns it the next available protocol port—in this case, 8081.

And here's your generated HTML form in all its glory.

This is looking good. Let's get a quick opinion from the folks over at the HFWWG.

I know what you're thinking: "With a shirt like *that*, how can this guy possibly know anything about style?"... But let me just say that your form could do with a bit of, well...color, couldn't it? Any chance it could look nicer?

OK, we get it. Web design is not your thing.

Not to worry, you know all about code reuse, right? So, let's reuse *someone else's* **cascading style sheets** (CSS) to help with the "look" of your generated HTML form.

But who can you "borrow" from and not lose sleep feeling guilty over it?

As luck would have it, the authors of *Head First HTML with CSS & XHTML* created a bunch of stylesheets for their web pages and have made them available to you. Grab a slightly amended copy of some of their great stylesheets from this book's support website. When you unzip the archive, a folder called `static` appears: pop this entire folder into your webapp's top-level folder.

There's a file in `static` called `favicon.ico`. Move it into your top-level folder.

Improve the look of your form

To integrate the stylesheets into your webapp, add two `link` tags to your `header.html` template within your `templates` folder. Here's what the tags need to look like:

> Add these two lines to the top of your "header.html" template.

```
<link type="text/css" rel="stylesheet" href="/static/hfwwg.css" />
<link type="text/css" rel="stylesheet" href="/static/styledform.css" />
```

GAE is smart enough to *optimize* the delivery of static content—that is, content that does *not* need to be generated by code. Your CSS files are static and are in your `static` folder. All you need to do is tell GAE about them to enable optimization. Do this by adding the following lines to the `handers` section of your `app.yaml` file:

> Provide the URL location for your static content.

```
- url: /static
  static_dir: static
```

> Switch on the optimization.

TEST DRIVE

With your stylesheets in place and your `app.yaml` file amended, ask your browser to **reload** your form.

Looking good. →

A little style goes a long way...that's looking great!

Restrict input by providing options

At the moment, your form accepts anything in the Fin, Whale, Blow, and
Wave input areas. The paper form restricts the data that can be provided for
each of these values. Your HTML form should, too.

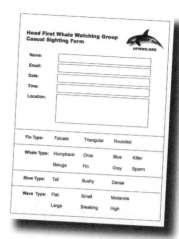

> Anything you can do to cut down on
> input errors is a good thing. As the youngest
> member of the group, I was "volunteered" to
> work on data clean-up duties...

Providing a list of choices restricts what users can input.

Instead of using HTML's `INPUT` tag for all of your form fields, you can use the
`SELECT`/`OPTION` tag pairing to *restrict* what's accepted as valid data for any of the
fields on your form. To do this, you'll need more HTML markup. That's the *bad
news*.

The *good news* is that the form validation framework can generate the HTML
markup you need for you. All you have to provide is the list of data items to use as
an argument called `choices` when defining your property in your model code. You
can also indicate when multiple lines of input are acceptable using the `multiline`
argument to a property.

Apply these changes to your model code in the `hfwwgDB.py` file.

Define your lists of values near the top of your code.

This naming
convention
helps identify
these lists as
containing
constant values.

```
_FINS   = ['Falcate', 'Triangular', 'Rounded']
_WHALES = ['Humpback', 'Orca', 'Blue', 'Killer', 'Beluga', 'Fin', 'Gray', 'Sperm']
_BLOWS  = ['Tall', 'Bushy', 'Dense']
_WAVES  = ['Flat', 'Small', 'Moderate', 'Large', 'Breaking', 'High']
                          . . .
        location   = db.StringProperty(multiline=True)
        fin_type   = db.StringProperty(choices=_FINS)
        whale_type = db.StringProperty(choices=_WHALES)
        blow_type  = db.StringProperty(choices=_BLOWS)
        wave_type  = db.StringProperty(choices=_WAVES)
```

Switch on multiple-line input.

Use your lists of values when defining your properties.

TEST DRIVE

With these changes applied to your model code, refresh your web browser once more.

Your form is not only looking good, but it's more functional, too.

The "location" field is now displayed over multiple lines.

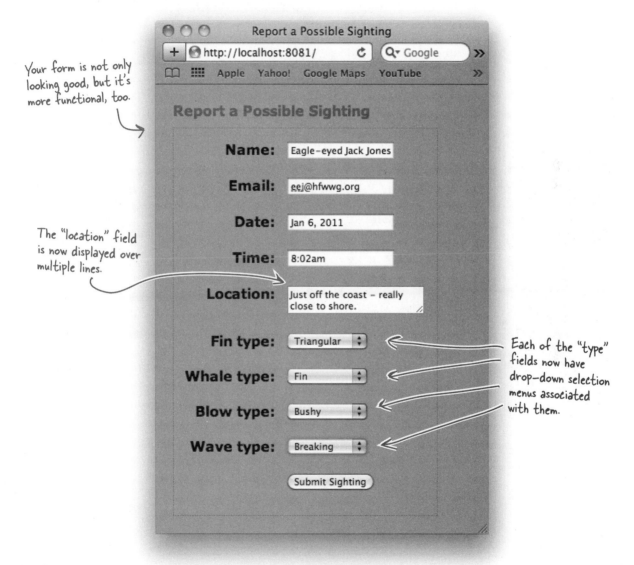

Each of the "type" fields now have drop-down selection menus associated with them.

Your form now looks great! Go ahead and enter some test data, and then press the Submit Sighting button.

What happens?

Meet the "blank screen of death"

Submitting your form's data to the GAE web server produces a *blank screen*.

Whoops...that's not exactly user-friendly.

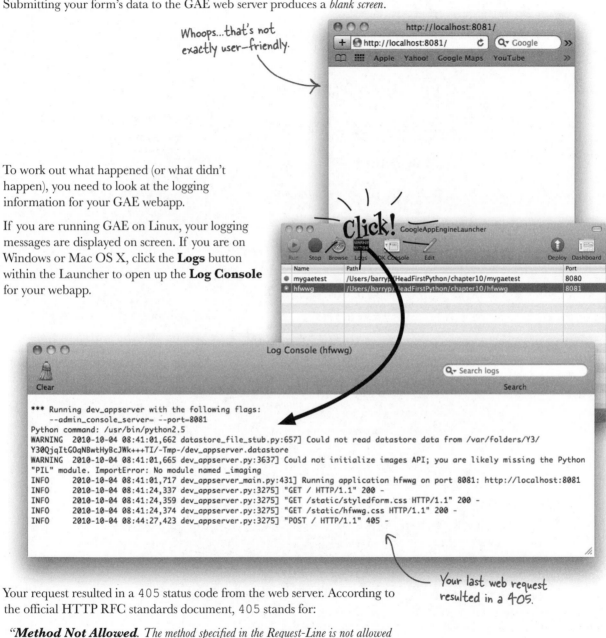

To work out what happened (or what didn't happen), you need to look at the logging information for your GAE webapp.

If you are running GAE on Linux, your logging messages are displayed on screen. If you are on Windows or Mac OS X, click the **Logs** button within the Launcher to open up the **Log Console** for your webapp.

Your last web request resulted in a 405.

Your request resulted in a 405 status code from the web server. According to the official HTTP RFC standards document, 405 stands for:

*"**Method Not Allowed**. The method specified in the Request-Line is not allowed for the resource identified by the Request-URI. The response MUST include an Allow header containing a list of valid methods for the requested resource".*

Ummm...that's as clear as mud, isn't it?

Process the POST within your webapp

What the 405 status code actually tells you is that posted data arrived at your webapp intact, but that your webapp *does not* have any way of processing it. There's a method missing.

Take a quick look back at your code: the only method currently defined is called get(). This method is invoked whenever a GET web request arrives at your webapp and, as you know, it displays your sightings form.

In order to process posted data, you need to define *another* method. Specifically, you need to add a new method called post() to your SightingInputPage class.

Listen, bud, I'll happily process your web requests all day long...just as long as you give me the methods I need!

App Engine Web Server

App Engine handles requests as well as responses

Your get() method produces your HTML form and returns a web response to the waiting web browser using the self.response object and by invoking the out.write() method on it.

In additon to helping you with your web responses, GAE also helps you process your web requests using the self.request object. Here are a few lines of code that displays all of the data posted to your web server:

Define a new method called "post".

Don't forget to use "self" with all your methods.

The "arguments()" method returns a list of the field names used on your form.

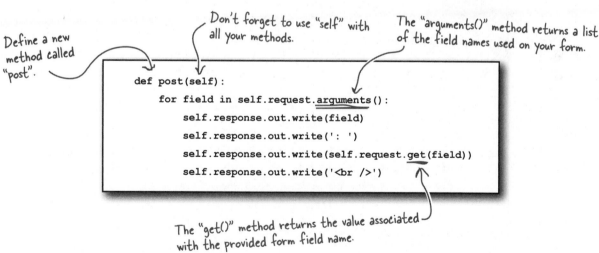

```
def post(self):
    for field in self.request.arguments():
        self.response.out.write(field)
        self.response.out.write(': ')
        self.response.out.write(self.request.get(field))
        self.response.out.write('<br />')
```

The "get()" method returns the value associated with the provided form field name.

So...if you know the *name* of your form field, you can access its value from within your webapp using the self.request.get() method.

But what do you do with the data once you have it?

Put your data in the datastore

Your data is sent to your webapp by GAE and you can use the `self.request.get()` method to access each input field value by name. Recall the `BirthDetails` model from earlier in this chapter:

This code is in a file called "birthDB.py".

```python
from google.appengine.ext import db


class BirthDetails(db.Model):
    name =           db.StringProperty()
    date_of_birth = db.DateProperty()
    time_of_birth = db.TimeProperty()
```

Assume that an HTML form has sent data to your webapp. The data is destined to be stored in the GAE datastore. Here's some code to do the heavy lifting:

```python
def post(self):
    new_birth = birthDB.BirthDetails()          # Create a new "BirthDetails" object to hold your data.

    new_birth.name = self.request.get('name')
    new_birth.date = self.request.get('date_of_birth')    # Get each of the form's data values and assign them to your new object's attributes.
    new_birth.time = self.request.get('time_of_birth'))

    new_birth.put()          # Put (save) your data to the GAE datastore.

    html = template.render('templates/header.html', {'title': 'Thank you!'})     # Generate a HTML response to say "thanks."
    html = html + "<p>Thank you for providing your birth details.</p>"
    html = html + template.render('templates/footer.html',
                          {'links': 'Enter <a href="/">another birth</a>.'})

    self.response.out.write(html)     # Send your response to the waiting web browser.
```

There's nothing to it: **create** a new object from your data model, **get** the data from your HTML form, **assign** it to the object's attributes, and then use the `put()` method to **save** your data in the datastore.

Exercise

Based on what you know about how to put your HTML form's data into the GAE datastore, create the code for the `post()` method that your webapp now needs. Some of the code has been done for you already. You are to provide the rest.

```
def post(self):
```

Put your code here. →

....

....

....

....

....

....

....

....

....

....

....

....

....

....

```
        html = template.render('templates/header.html',
                                    {'title': 'Thank you!'})
        html = html + "<p>Thank you for providing your sighting data.</p>"
        html = html + template.render('templates/footer.html',
                    {'links': 'Enter <a href="/">another sighting</a>.'})

        self.response.out.write(html)
```

Exercise Solution

Based on what you know about how to put your HTML form's data into the GAE datastore, you were to create the code for the `post()` method that your webapp now needs. Some of the code has been done for you already. You were to provide the rest.

Create a new "Sighting" object.

```
def post(self):
    new_sighting = hfwwgDB.Sighting()
```

For each of the data values received from the HTML form, assign them to the attributes of the newly created object.

```
    new_sighting.name = self.request.get('name')
    new_sighting.email = self.request.get('email')
    new_sighting.date = self.request.get('date')
    new_sighting.time = self.request.get('time')
    new_sighting.location = self.request.get('location')
    new_sighting.fin_type = self.request.get('fin_type')
    new_sighting.whale_type = self.request.get('whale_type')
    new_sighting.blow_type =self.request.get('blow_type')
    new_sighting.wave_type = self.request.get('wave_type')
```

Store your populated object in the GAE datastore.

```
    new_sighting.put()

    html = template.render('templates/header.html',
                                {'title': 'Thank you!'})
    html = html + "<p>Thank you for providing your sighting data.</p>"
    html = html + template.render('templates/footer.html',
                {'links': 'Enter <a href="/">another sighting</a>.'})

    self.response.out.write(html)
```

TEST DRIVE

Add your `post()` code to your webapp (within the `hfwwg.py` file) and press the **Back** button on your web browser. Click the Submit Sighting button once more and see what happens this time.

Here's your form with the data waiting to be submitted.

But when you click the button, something bad has happened...your webapp has crashed.

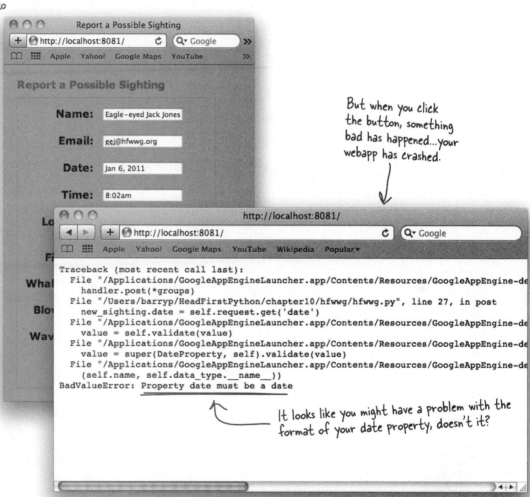

It looks like you might have a problem with the format of your date property, doesn't it?

Phooey...that's disappointing, isn't it?

At the very least, you were expecting the data from the form to make it into the datastore...but something has stopped this from happening. What do you think is the problem?

Don't break the "robustness principle"

The **Robustness Principle** states: *"Be conservative in what you send; be liberal in what you accept."* In other words, don't be too picky when *requesting* data of a certain type from your users, but when *providing* data, give 'em exactly what they need.

If you make it *too hard* for your users to enter data into your system, things will likely things break. For instance, within your model code, consider how date and time are defined:

A date, and NOTHING
but a date will do.

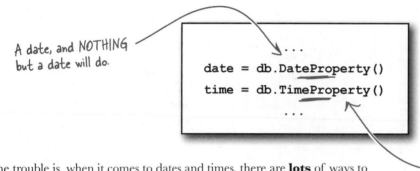

```
. . .
date = db.DateProperty()
time = db.TimeProperty()
. . .
```

You must provide a
valid value for time.
Anything else is simply
UNACCEPTABLE.

The trouble is, when it comes to dates and times, there are **lots** of ways to specify values.

Oh, la, la.. c'est temps
to toot mon flute! It's
14:00hr on 24/04/2011.

Get the low-down on
the hoedown: quarter
after six on 6/17/2011.

I say, old boy, tea is
at noon on the first
of each month.

Accept almost any date and time

If you are going to insist on asking your users to provide a properly formatted date and time, you'll need to do one of two things:

- Specify in detail the **format** in which you expect the data.

- **Convert** the entered data into a format with which you can work.

Both appoaches have *problems*.

For example, if you are too picky in requesting a date in a particular format, you'll slow down your user and might end up picking a date format that is foreign to them, resulting in confusion.

If you try to convert *any* date or time entered into a common format that the datastore understands, you'll be biting off more than you can chew. As an example of the complexity that can occur, how do you know if your user entered a date in mm/dd/yyyy or dd/mm/yyyy format? (You don't.)

There is a third option

If your application doesn't require *exact* dates and times, *don't require them of your user.*

With your sightings webapp, the date and time can be *free-format fields* that accept any value (in any format). What's important is *the recording of the sighting*, not the exact date/time it occurred.

Of course, other webapps might not be as fast and loose with dates and times. When that's the case, you'll need to revert one of the options discussed earlier on this page and do the best you can.

Use "db.StringProperty()" for dates and times

If you relax the datatype restrictions on the date and time fields, not only do you make is easier on your user, but you also make it easier on you.

For the sightings webapp, the solution is to change the property type for date and time within the hfwwgDB.py file from what they currently are to db.StringProperty().

```
    . . .
date = db.StringProperty()
time = db.StringProperty()
    . . .
```

It's a small change, but it'll make all the difference.

Let's see what difference this change makes.

Test Drive

Change the types of `date` and `time` within `htwwgDB.py` to `db.StringProperty()`, being sure to save the file once you've made your edit. Click Back in your web brwoser and submit your sightings data once more.

OK, folks...
let's try
this again.

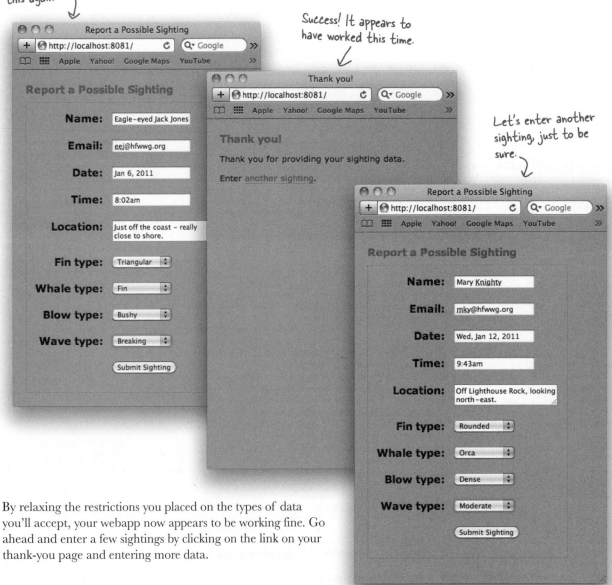

Success! It appears to
have worked this time.

Let's enter another
sighting, just to be
sure.

By relaxing the restrictions you placed on the types of data you'll accept, your webapp now appears to be working fine. Go ahead and enter a few sightings by clicking on the link on your thank-you page and entering more data.

With a few sightings entered, let's use App Engine's included **developer console** to confirm that the sightings are in the datastore.

To access the console, enter `http://localhost:8081/_ah/admin` into your web browser's location bar and click on the **List Entities** button to see your data.

In addition to viewing your existing data in the datastore, you can use the console to enter new test data.

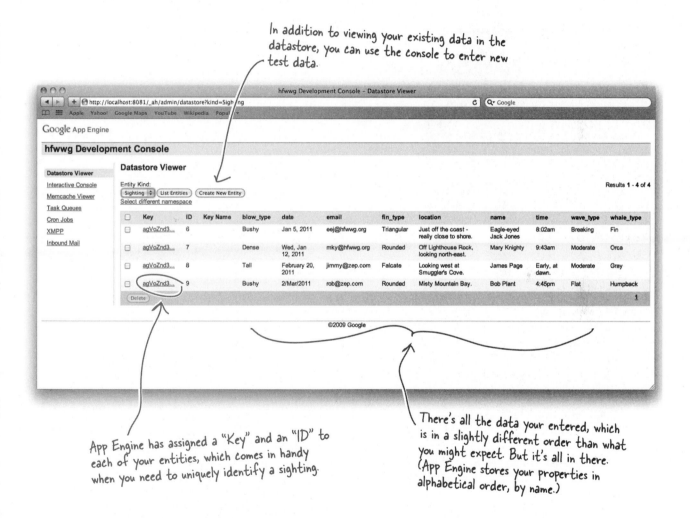

App Engine has assigned a "Key" and an "ID" to each of your entities, which comes in handy when you need to uniquely identify a sighting.

There's all the data your entered, which is in a slightly different order than what you might expect. But it's all in there. (App Engine stores your properties in alphabetical order, by name.)

Your GAE webapp is now ready for prime time.

Before you deploy it to Google's cloud infrastructure, let's run it by the folk at HFWWG to see if they are happy for their webapp to "go live."

It looks like you're not quite done yet

Man, that's looking good! There's just one thing we forgot to tell you... we are worried about spam and need to be sure only registered users can enter a sighting. Is that a big change?

Is this a **big** change?

You would imagine that it would be. You'll have to create an new entity to hold your registered user login information, and you'll also need *another* form to ask users to provide their registration data (which you'll need to store in the datastore). With that in place, you'll need *yet another form* to ask your users to log in, and then you'll have to come up with a mechanism to *restrict* only registered and logged-in users to view your webapp's pages, assuming you can come up with something robust that will work...?

Or...as this is GAE, you could just switch on authorization.

Sometimes, the tiniest change can make all the difference...

The engineers at Google designed App Engine to deploy on Google's cloud infrastructure. As such, they decided to allow webapps running on GAE to access the *Google Accounts* system.

By switching on **authorization**, you can require users of your webapp to log into their Google account *before* they see your webapp's pages. If a user tries to access your webapp and he isn't not logged in, GAE redirects to the Google Accounts login and registration page. Then, after a successful login, GAE returns the user to your waiting webapp. *How cool is that?*

To switch on authorization, make one small change to your app.yaml file:

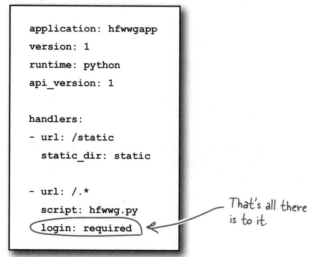

```
application: hfwwgapp
version: 1
runtime: python
api_version: 1

handlers:
- url: /static
  static_dir: static

- url: /.*
  script: hfwwg.py
  login: required
```

That's all there is to it.

Now, when you try to access your webapp, you are asked to log in *before* proceeding.

This is how the login screen looks within the GAE test environment running on your computer.

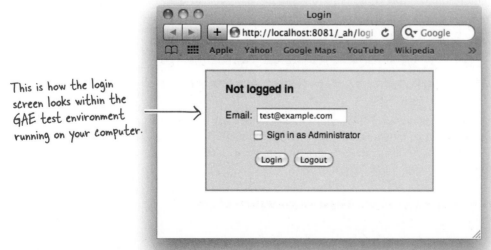

Capture your user's Google ID, too

Now that your webapp requires your users to log in, let's arrange to capture the user login information as part of the sighting.

Start by adding the following property to your entity's list of attributes in your `hfwwgDB.py` file. Add it right after the `wave_type` property.

Create a new attribute in your "Sighting" class...

```
which_user = db.UserProperty()
```

...and set its property type.

Let's ensure that Django's form validation framework *excludes* this new attribute when generating your HTML form. Within your `hfwwg.py` file, change your `SightingForm` class to look like this:

Make sure Django doesn't include the new attribute in your generated form.

```
class SightingForm(djangoforms.ModelForm):
    class Meta:
        model = hfwwgDB.Sighting
        exclude = ['which_user']
```

Staying within your `hfwwg.py` file, add another import statement near the top of your program:

Import GAE's Google Accounts API.

```
from google.appengine.api import users
```

In your `post()` method, right before you **put** your new sighting to the datastore, add this line of code:

```
new_sighting.which_user = users.get_current_user()
```

When you put your data to the datastore, this code includes the Google ID of the currently logged-in user.

Every time a user adds a sighting to the datastore, GAE ensures that the user's Google Account ID is saved, too. This extra identification information allows the HFWWG to track exactly who reported which sighting, and should (hopefully) cut down on the amount of spam your webapp might attract.

All that's left to do is to deploy your webapp to Google's cloud.

Deploy your webapp to Google's cloud

With your webapp developed and tested locally, you are now ready to deploy to the Google cloud. This is a two-step process: *register* and *upload*.

To register your webapp on the Google cloud, click the **Dashboard** button on the GAE Launcher.

The "Dashboard" button opens your web browser and takes you to the GAE "My Applications" page (after you sign in with your Google ID).

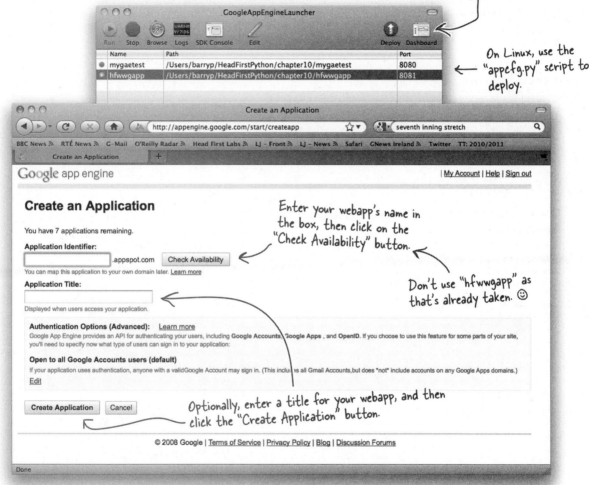

On Linux, use the "appcfg.py" script to deploy.

Enter your webapp's name in the box, then click on the "Check Availability" button.

Don't use "hfwwgapp" as that's already taken. ☺

Optionally, enter a title for your webapp, and then click the "Create Application" button.

Assuming all went according to plan and GAE confirmed that your application has been created, all that's left to do is to *deploy*. Return to the GAE Launcher and click on the **Deploy** button. The console displays a bunch of status message while the deployment progresses. If all is well, you'll be told that "appcfg.py has finished with exit code 0".

Your GAE webapp is now ready to run on Google's cloud.

Test Drive, on Google

Let's take your webapp for a spin on Google's cloud. Open your web browser and surf to a web address that starts with your webapp's name and ends in *.appspot.com*. For the HFWWG webapp, the web address is *http://hfwwgapp.appspot.com*. When you first attempt to go to their webapp, App Engine redirects you to the Google login page.

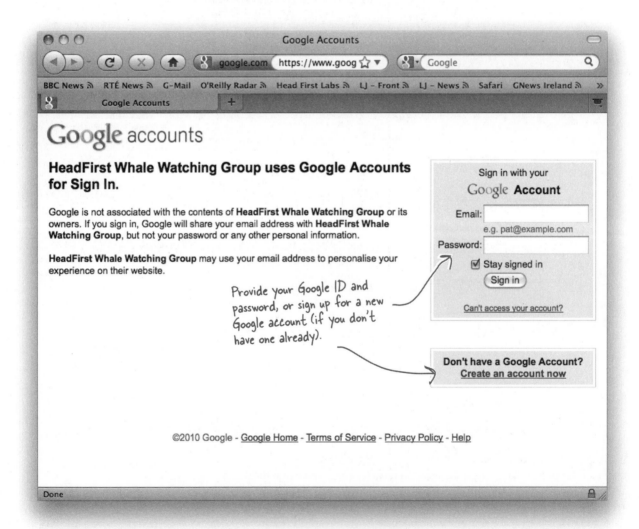

Provide your Google ID and password, or sign up for a new Google account (if you don't have one already).

After a successful login, your sighting form appears. Go ahead and enter some test data:

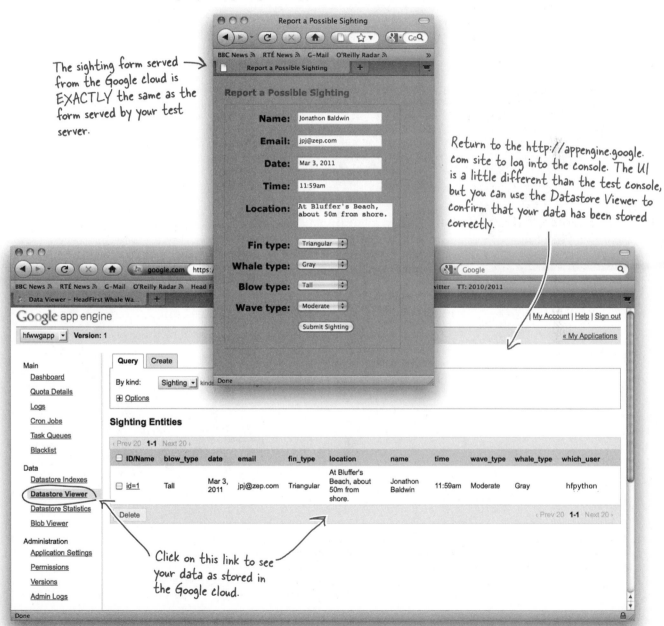

The sighting form served from the Google cloud is EXACTLY the same as the form served by your test server.

Return to the http://appengine.google.com site to log into the console. The UI is a little different than the test console, but you can use the Datastore Viewer to confirm that your data has been stored correctly.

Click on this link to see your data as stored in the Google cloud.

Your HFWWG webapp is deployed!

This is professional work.

You've built a *great data-entry webapp* and *deployed* it on Google's cloud. No matter how busy things get, whether there's a handful of sightings per day or tens of thousands, *your webapp can handle the load*, thanks to Google's App Engine. And, best of all, the cash-strapped HFWWG doesn't pay a penny until their sightings activity reaches the level of *millions* of sightings per month!

← Did you even notice that you wrote all of your code using Python 2.5?

Your Python Toolbox

You've got Chapter 10 under your belt and you've added more great Python technology to your ever-expanding Python toolbox.

App Engine Lingo

• "Datastore" – the data repository used by Google App Engine to permanently store your data.

• "Entity" – the name used for a "row of data".

• "Property" – the name used for a "data value".

- Every App Engine webapp must have a configuration file called `app.yaml`.

- Use the *GAE Launcher* to start, stop, monitor, test, upload, and deploy your webapps.

- App Engine's templating technology is based on the one use in the Django Project.

- App Engine can also use Django's Form Validation Framework.

- Use the `self.response` object to construct a GAE web response.

- Use the `self.request` object to access form data within a GAE webapp.

- When responding to a GET request, implement the required functionality in a `get()` method.

- When responding to a POST request, implement the required functionality in a `post()` method.

- Store data in the App Engine datastore using the `put()` method.

11 dealing with complexity

Data wrangling

Once I build up a head of steam, it's not all that hard to keep on running, and running, and running...

It's great when you can apply Python to a specific domain area.

Whether it's *web development*, *database management*, or *mobile apps*, Python helps you **get the job done** by *not* getting in the way of you coding your solution. And then there's the other types of problems: the ones you can't categorize or attach to a domain. Problems that are in themselves so *unique* you have to look at them in a different, highly specific way. Creating **bespoke** software solutions to these type of problems is an area where Python *excels*. In this, your final chapter, you'll *stretch* your Python skills to the limit and solve problems along the way.

What's a good time goal for the next race?

The *Head First Marathon Club* has spent years collecting and collating data on their distance runners. Over time, this data has helped the club produce a large spreadsheet of *pace data* that helps their runners predict their performance over various distances. The spreadsheet is *huge* and runs to 50 columns of tightly packed data.

Let's take a look at the club's data, as well as the way the runners and their coach use it.

> The runner selects a distance, say 15K, and we time her over the length of her run.

Here's a portion of the Marathon Club's spreadsheet data.

The timed distance is 15km.

The predicted marathon goal.

| File | Edit | View | Insert | Format | Form | Tools | Help |

Formula: V02

	A	B	C	D	E	F	
1	V02	84.8	82.9	81.1	79.3	77.5	75.
2	2mi	8:00	8:10	8:21	8:33	8:44	8:5
3	5k	12:49	13:06	13:24	13:42	14:00	14:
4	5mi	21:1?	21:48	22:17	22:47	23:18	23:
5	10k	26:54	27:30	28:08	28:45	29:24	30:
6	15k	41:31	42:27	43:24	44:23	45:23	46:
7	10mi	44:46	45:46	46:48	47:51		50:
8	20k	56:29	57:45	59:03	1:00:23	1:01:45	1:0
9	13.1mi	59:49	1:01:09	1:02:32	1:03:56	1:05:2?	1:0
10	25k	1:11:43	1:13:20	1:14:59	1:16:40	1:18:2?	1:2
11	30k	1:27:10	1:19:08	1:31:08	1:33:11	1:35:1?	1:3
12	Marathon	2:05:34	2:08:24	2:11:17	2:14:15	2:17:16	2:2
13							

Yes, she's wicked fast!

I run the 15K in 45:01. My coach looks up the closest match for my time along the 15K row.

This benchmark allows me to look up or down the column to select a target time for any other distance, such as a marathon, for example.

This spreadsheet is a little intimidating...but don't worry. You'll sort it out soon.

H	I	J	K	L	M	N	O	
74.2	72.5	70.9	69.4	67.9	66.4	64.9	63.5	6
9:08	9:20	9:33	9:46	9:59	10:13	10:26	10:41	1
14:38	14:58	15:18	15:39	16:00	16:22	16:44	17:06	1
24:22	24:55	25:28	26:03	26:38	27:14	27:51	28:28	2
30:45	31:26	32:09	32:52	33:36	34:22	35:08	35:56	3
47:27	48:31	49:36	50:43	51:52	53:02	54:14	55:27	5
51:09	52:18	53:29	54:41	55:55	57:11	58:28	59:47	
1:04:33	1:06:00	1:07:29	1:09:01	1:10:34	1:12:09	1:13:46	1:15:26	
1:08:21	1:09:53	1:11:28	1:13:04	1:14:43	1:16:24	1:18:07	1:19:52	1
1:21:58	1:23:49	1:25:49	1:27:37	1:29:36	1:31:37	1:33:40	1:35:47	1
1:39:37	1:41:52	1:44:09	1:46:30	1:48:54	1:51:21	1:53:51	1:56:25	1
2:23:31	2:26:44	2:30:02	2:33:25	2:36:52	2:40:24	2:44:00	2:47:42	2

So...what's the problem?

At the moment, we print our data onto multiple sheets of paper, which we carry with us. Most of the time, this works fine. But when it rains or gets really windy, our pages are either soaked through or they end up all over the place.

All these sheets are a pain...especially in the rain.

Not to mention: forgetting the sheets, keeping the sheets up to date, and having to flip back and forth through the sheets looking for a closest match.

Of course, word of your newly acquired Python programming skills is getting around, especially among the running crowd. Ideally, the Marathon Club needs an Android app that can be loaded onto a bunch of phones and carried in each coach's pocket. The app needs to automate the lookup and distance predictions.

Are you up to the challenge? Do you think you can help?

Start with the data

For now, let's not worry about creating the Android app; you'll get to that soon enough. Instead, let's solve the central **data wrangling problem** and then, when you have a working solution, we'll worry about *porting* your solution to Android. We'll begin by getting the data into a format you can easily process with Python.

Most spreadsheet programs can export data to the widely used CSV format. The club has done this for you and created a file called `PaceData.csv`, which includes the data for each of the rows from the original the spreadsheet.

Here's a sample of the raw data from the start of the CSV:

Do this!

Grab a copy of `PaceData.csv` from this book's support website.

The first line of data is the column headings from the spreadsheet. They look like numbers but are actually headings that represent estimated maximal oxygen consumption (or VO2 Max, in ml/kg–min) for the race times in each column. Because the have no affect on the timing data, we'll just treat them as headings.

```
V02,84.8,82.9,81.1,79.3,77.5,75.8,74.2,72.5,70.9,69.4,67.9,66.4,64.9,63.5,62.1,60.7,59.4,58.1,56.8,55.
2mi,8:00,8:10,8:21,8:33,8:44,8:56,9:08,9:20,9:33,9:46,9:59,10:13,10:26,10:41,10:55,11:10,11:25,11:40,1
5k,12:49,13:06,13:24,13:42,14:00,14:19,14:38,14:58,15:18,15:39,16:00,16:22,16:44,17:06,17:30,17:53,18:
```

The first value on each of the rest of the lines is the timed distance or row label.

The rest of each line is a list of recorded run times.

Sharpen your pencil

You somehow have to model the data from the CSV file in your Python program. Can you think of a data structure that might help here? Justify your selection.

....

....

....

....

....

Sharpen your pencil
Solution

You somehow have to model the data from the CSV file in your Python program. You were to think of a data structure that might help here? You were also to justify your selection.

The list of headings can be stored in a LIST.

Ummm... there's lots → The list of times from each row can also be stored in a LIST, but they also need to be associated with the headings in the very first row of data, so maybe a DICTIONARY is what's needed here?

Maybe it's some COMBINATION of the two?!?

Take another look at the data

The first row of data in the CSV file is the **column headings**, with the very first value on the line, the V02 string, being redundant (it won't ever be used in this version of the app). The rest of the first line's data are headings *associated* with the time values in each of the columns.

Of course, the data in the columns is *also* associated with each row, which is identified by a **row label** in the first column, such as 2mi, 5k, and so on.

Let's look at the data in the CSV file again, which has been reformatted to help highlight the associations.

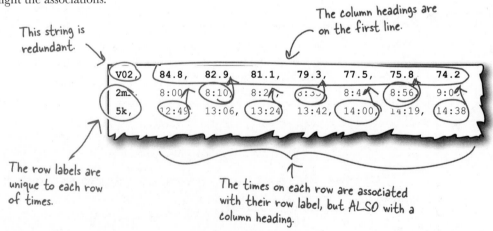

This string is redundant.

The column headings are on the first line.

```
V02,  84.8,  82.9,  81.1,  79.3,  77.5,  75.8,  74.2
2mi,  8:00,  8:10,  8:2?,  8:3?,  8:4?,  8:56,  9:0?
5k,   12:49, 13:06, 13:24, 13:42, 14:00, 14:19, 14:38
```

The row labels are unique to each row of times.

The times on each row are associated with their row label, but ALSO with a column heading.

But can we capture all these associations in code?

Marathon Magnets

Here's some code that reads the raw data from from the CSV data file. The column headings from the first line are loaded into a list called `column_headings`. The rest of the data (all the rows of times) are loaded into a dictionary called `row_data`, with each row of data keyed with the **row label string** from the start of each line. Of course, as luck would have it, someone was cleaning the fridge door, and they've left a bunch of magnets on the floor. See if you can arrange the magnets into their correct order.

What needs to go here? ➤

```
with open('PaceData.csv') as paces:
```

Process the "column_headings" list here. ➜

```
    for each_line in paces:
```

Process "row_data" here. ➜

```
        num_cols = len(column_headings)
        print(num_cols, end=' -> ')
        print(column_headings)

        num_2mi = len(row_data['2mi'])
        print(num_2mi, end=' -> ')
        print(row_data['2mi'])

        num_Marathon = len(row_data['Marathon'])
        print(num_Marathon, end=' -> ')
        print(row_data['Marathon'])
```

With the data loaded, this code lets you check if it's all OK.

```
row = each_line.strip().split(',')
```

```
column_headings =
```

```
row_label = row.pop(0)
```

```
row_data[row_label] = row
```

```
row_data = {}
```

```
paces.readline().strip().split(',')
```

```
column_headings.pop(0)
```

Marathon Magnets Solution

Here's some code that reads the raw data from from the CSV data file. The column headings from the first line are loaded into a list called `column_headings`. The rest of the data (all the rows of times) are loaded into a dictionary called `row_data`, with each row of data keyed with the **row label string** from the start of each line. Of course, as luck would have it, someone was cleaning the fridge door, and they've left a bunch of magnets on the floor. You were to see if you could arrange the magnets into their correct order.

You need to be sure to create an empty dictionary for the row times.

```
row_data = {}
```

```
with open('PaceData.csv') as paces:
```

Create the column headings from the first line of data.

```
column_headings =    paces.readline().strip().split(',')
```

Read a line from the file, strip it of unwanted whitespace, and then split the line on comma.

```
column_headings.pop(0)
```

Delete the first heading, the "VO2" string—you don't need it.

```
for each_line in paces:
```
← Process the rest of the file.

```
row = each_line.strip().split(',')
```

It's the same deal here: take the line, strip it, and then split on comma.

Extract the row label.

```
row_label = row.pop(0)
```

```
row_data[row_label] = row
```

Use the row label together with the rest of the line's data to update the dictionary.

```
num_cols = len(column_headings)
print(num_cols, end=' -> ')
print(column_headings)

num_2mi = len(row_data['2mi'])
print(num_2mi, end=' -> ')
print(row_data['2mi'])

num_Marathon = len(row_data['Marathon'])
print(num_Marathon, end=' -> ')
print(row_data['Marathon'])
```

TEST DRIVE

Load your code into IDLE and, with the CSV in the same folder as your code, run it to see what you get on screen.

Your code in IDLE.

```
marathon.py – /Users/barryp/HeadFirstPython/chapter11/marathon.py

row_data = {}

with open('PaceData.csv') as paces:

    column_headings = paces.readline().strip().split(',')
    column_headings.pop(0)

    for each_line in paces:
        row = each_line.strip().split(',')
        row_label = row.pop(0)
        row_data[row_label] = row

num_cols = len(column_headings)
print(num_cols, end=' -> ')
print(column_headings)

num_2mi = len(row_data['2mi'])
```

The output confirms that each row of data has 50 data items.

The column headings

The "2mi" row of data

The "Marathon" row of data

```
Python Shell

Python 3.1.2 (r312:79360M, Mar 24 2010, 01:33:18)
[GCC 4.0.1 (Apple Inc. build 5493)] on darwin
Type "copyright", "credits" or "license()" for more information.
================================ RESTART ================================
>>>
50 -> ['84.8', '82.9', '81.1', '79.3', '77.5', '75.8', '74.2', '72.5', '70.9', '6
9.4', '67.9', '66.4', '64.9', '63.5', '62.1', '60.7', '59.4', '58.1', '56.8', '55
.5', '54.3', '53.1', '52', '50.8', '49.7', '48.6', '47.5', '46.5', '45.5', '44.5'
, '43.5', '42.5', '41.6', '40.7', '39.8', '38.9', '38', '37.2', '36.4', '35.6', '
34.8', '34', '33.3', '32.6', '31.8', '31.1', '30.5', '29.8', '29.1', '28.5']
50 -> ['8:00', '8:10', '8:21', '8:33', '8:44', '8:56', '9:08', '9:20', '9:33', '9
:46', '9:59', '10:13', '10:26', '10:41', '10:55', '11:10', '11:25', '11:40', '11:
56', '12:12', '12:29', '12:45', '13:03', '13:20', '13:38', '13:57', '14:16', '14:
35', '14:54', '15:15', '15:35', '15:56', '16:18', '16:40', '17:02', '17:25', '17:
49', '18:13', '18:38', '19:03', '19:28', '19:55', '20:22', '20:49', '21:17', '21:
46', '22:15', '22:45', '23:16', '23:48']
50 -> ['2:05:34', '2:08:24', '2:11:17', '2:14:15', '2:17:16', '2:20:21', '2:23:31
', '2:26:44', '2:30:02', '2:33:25', '2:36:52', '2:40:24', '2:44:00', '2:47:42', '
2:51:28', '2:55:20', '2:59:16', '3:03:18', '3:07:26', '3:11:39', '3:15:58', '3:20
:22', '3:24:53', '3:29:29', '3:34:12', '3:39:01', '3:43:57', '3:48:59', '3:54:09'
, '3:59:25', '4:04:48', '4:10:18', '4:15:56', '4:21:42', '4:27:35', '4:33:36', '4
:39:46', '4:46:04', '4:52:30', '4:59:05', '5:05:48', '5:12:41', '5:19:43', '5:26:
55', '5:34:16', '5:41:48', '5:49:29', '5:57:21', '6:05:23', '6:13:37']
>>>

Ln: 9 Col: 4
```

That's a great start: you've managed to read the data from the CSV and put the headings into a list and the data into a dictionary.

What's next?

Did you forget to associate each time on each row with its heading? At the moment, the list and the dictionary are disconnected...

Yes, the two data structures should be linked.

At the moment, the `column_headings` list and the `row_data` dictionary are not linked in any way, and they need to be. What we need is some way to *connect* each of the times in each row with the heading that tops their column of data.

What options do you have here?

When it comes to linking (or associating) two data items with each other, the Python dictionary is the data strucutre of choice, isn't it?

Store each time as a dictionary

Rather than simply storing each time in the `row_data` dictionary as a number, let's store the data as *as a dictionary*, with the *key* set to the time and the *value* set to the column heading. That way, you can quickly and easily determine for any time which column it is associated with, right?

Here's a portion of what the data structure looks like in Python's memory once this association exists:

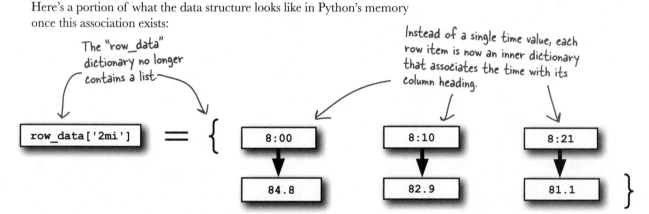

The "row_data" dictionary no longer contains a list.

Instead of a single time value, each row item is now an inner dictionary that associates the time with its column heading.

All you need to do is work out how to populate the inner dictionary with the row data and the associated columns headings…and you'll have all the data you need.

The trick in creating the data structure is to realize that each row, *including the column headings*, are of a **fixed size**: 50 items. Knowing this, it's not much work to create the dictionary you need:

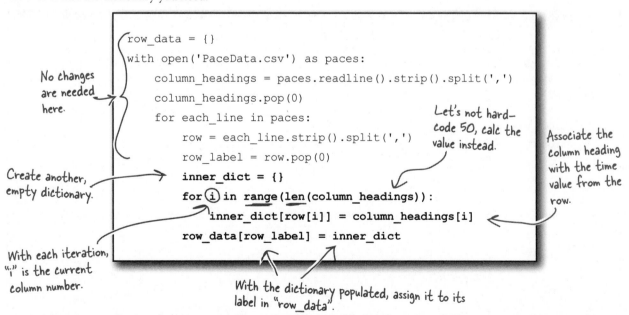

```
row_data = {}
with open('PaceData.csv') as paces:
    column_headings = paces.readline().strip().split(',')
    column_headings.pop(0)
    for each_line in paces:
        row = each_line.strip().split(',')
        row_label = row.pop(0)
        inner_dict = {}
        for i in range(len(column_headings)):
            inner_dict[row[i]] = column_headings[i]
        row_data[row_label] = inner_dict
```

No changes are needed here.

Let's not hard-code 50, calc the value instead.

Associate the column heading with the time value from the row.

Create another, empty dictionary.

With each iteration, "i" is the current column number.

With the dictionary populated, assign it to its label in "row_data".

An IDLE Session

Go ahead and add the extra dictionary populating code to your program. Let's remove all of those `print()` statements from the end of your program, because you'll use the IDLE shell to test your code. Run the code by pressing F5 or by selecting the Run Module option from the Run menu. Use the `dir()` BIF to confirm that your program code executed and that a collection of variables have been created in Python's namespace:

```
>>> dir()
['__builtins__', '__doc__', '__name__', '__package__', 'column_headings', 'each_line', 'i',
'inner_dict', 'paces', 'row', 'row_data', 'row_label']
```

← *All of your code's variables exist.*

VO2	84.8	82.9	81.1	79.3	77.5
2mi	8:00	8:10	8:21	8:33	8:44
5k	12:49	13:06	13:24	13:42	14:00
5mi	21:19	21:48	22:17	22:47	23:18
10k	26:54	27:30	28:08	28:45	29:24
15k	41:31	42:27	43:24	44:23	45:23
10mi	44:46	45:46	46:48	47:51	48:56
20k	56:29	57:45	59:03	1:00:23	1:01:45
13.1mi	59:49	1:01:09	1:02:32	1:03:56	1:05:23
25k	1:11:43	1:13:20	1:14:59	1:16:40	1:18:24
30k	1:27:10	1:29:08	1:31:08	1:33:11	1:35:17
Marathon	2:05:34	2:08:24	2:11:17	2:14:15	2:17:16

Take another look at (part of) the spreadsheet data file above, and let's try and find the column heading associated with the **43:24** time on the **15k** row. Let's then use the column heading to find the predicted time for a **20k** run:

```
>>> column_heading = row_data['15k']['43:24']
>>> column_heading
'81.1'
```
← *The associated column heading is correctly identified as "81.1".*

```
>>> prediction = [k for k in row_data['20k'].keys() if row_data['20k'][k] == column_heading]
>>> prediction
['59:03']
```
← *A time of "59:03" is correctly predicted, too.*

Dissect the prediction code

Let's take a moment to review what just happened at the bottom of the IDLE Session from the last page. This line of code is a *double-dictionary lookup* on the dictionary-of-dictionaries stored in `row_data`:

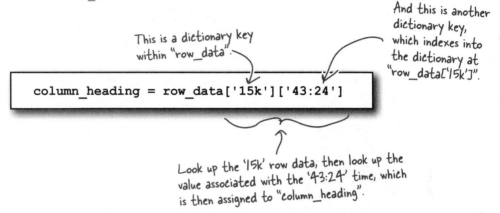

This is a dictionary key within "row_data".

And this is another dictionary key, which indexes into the dictionary at "row_data['15k']".

```
column_heading = row_data['15k']['43:24']
```

Look up the '15k' row data, then look up the value associated with the '43:24' time, which is then assigned to "column_heading".

Working out the predicted time in the **20k** row of data involves **finding the key** in the row's dictionary whose *value* is set to the just-discovered value stored in `column_heading`.

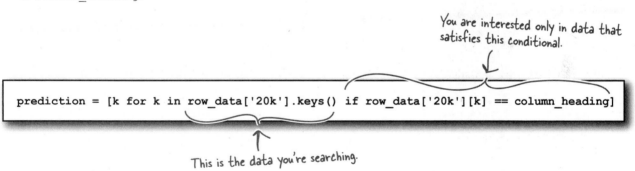

You are interested only in data that satisfies this conditional.

```
prediction = [k for k in row_data['20k'].keys() if row_data['20k'][k] == column_heading]
```

This is the data you're searching.

A *conditional list comprehension* is put to good use here. Recall that the list comprehension syntax is a shorthand notation for a **for** loop. The loop searches through the data in the list of keys associated with the dictionary stored at `row_data['20k']`. If the value associated with the key (in `k`) is the same as `column_heading`, the value of `k` is added to the comprehensions results, which are then assigned to a new list call `predicton`.

There's really an awful lot going on in that comprehension.

Sweet mother of all things Python! What's going on here? I think my brain is going to explode...

Don't let the list comprehension put you off.

Recall that you can always rewrite a list comprehension using an equivalent **for** loop…

Ummm…now there's an idea.

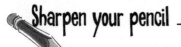
Sharpen your pencil

Rewrite each of the list comprehensions on this page to use a **for** loop.

```
times = [t for t in row_data['Marathon'].keys()]
```

....

....

....

....

....

```
headings = [h for h in sorted(row_data['10mi'].values(), reverse=True)]
```

....

....

....

....

....

....

```
time = [t for t in row_data['20k'].keys() if row_data['20k'][t] == '79.3']
```

....

....

....

....

....

....

....

....

for loop

Sharpen your pencil
Solution

You were to rewrite each of the list comprehensions to use a **for** loop.

```
times = [t for t in row_data['Marathon'].keys()]
```

Start with an empty list. →
```
times = []
for each_t in row_data['Marathon'].keys():
    times.append(each_t)
```

Turn the dictionary's keys into a list.

With each iteration, append the key (which is a time value) onto the "times" list.

```
headings = [h for h in sorted(row_data['10mi'].values(), reverse=True)]
```

Start with an empty list. →
```
headings = []
for each_h in sorted(row_data['10mi'].values(), reverse=True):
    headings.append(each_h)
```

Turn the dictionary's values into a list...

...being sure to sort the values in reverse order (biggest first).

With each iteration, append the value (which is a column heading) onto the "times" list.

```
time = [t for t in row_data['20k'].keys() if row_data['20k'][t] == '79.3']
```

Start with an empty list. →
```
time = []
for each_t in row_data['20k'].keys():
    if row_data['20k'][each_t] == '79.3':
        time.append(each_t)
```

Turn the dictionary's keys into a list.

There's a definite pattern emerging here. ☺

With each iteration, check to see if the column heading (the value part of the dictionary) equals "79.3" and if it does, append the time to the list.

412   Chapter 11

Get input from your user

Now that you have your data within a Python data structure, it's time to ask your user what it is they are looking for.

Specifically, you need to know three things: the *distance* run, the *time* recorded, and the distance a *prediction* is required for.

When you get to move your app onto Android, you can use a nice graphical dialog to ask your user for input, but for now, let's quickly create a text-based user interface, which will allow you to develop and test the rest of the functionality required from your application. When you're done, you'll create the Android app.

> Gimme, gimme, gimme...input() !!!

>>>

Use <u>input()</u> for input

Python has the input() BIF that can help here, which is used to display a prompt on screen, and then accept keyboard input, returning what was entered as a string to your code.

An IDLE Session

Using the input() BIF is best demonstrated with some examples:

```
>>> res = input('What is your favorite programming language: ')
What is your favorite programming language: Python
>>> res
'Python'
```
Provide the prompt to display to your user.

The entered data is assigned to "res" and it's a STRING.

The input() BIF returns a string, which has been stripped of any trailing newline character, which would typically be included at the end of any input string. It is important to note that any input is returned as a string, regardless of what type of data you think you might be entering:

The entered data is assigned to "age" and it's a string, even though you might want to treat it like it's a number.

```
>>> age = input('What is your age: ')
What is your age: 21
>>> age
'21'
>>> int(age)
21
```

[Editor's note: Yeah... dream on, Paul. ☺]

Convert the input to the type you need BEFORE using the data.

Getting input raises an issue...

It's not hard to use `input()` to get the, um, er...input you need. Here's your
code from earlier with three calls to `input()` added to interact with your
user.

```
marathon.py – /Users/barryp/HeadFirstPython/chapter11/marathon.py

row_data = {}

with open('PaceData.csv') as paces:

    column_headings = paces.readline().strip().split(',')
    column_headings.pop(0)

    for each_line in paces:
        row = each_line.strip().split(',')
        row_label = row.pop(0)
        inner_dict = {}
        for i in range(len(column_headings)):
            inner_dict[row[i]] = column_headings[i]
        row_data[row_label] = inner_dict

distance_run = input('Enter the distance attempted: ')
recorded_time = input('Enter the recorded time: ')
predicted_distance = input('Enter the distance you want a prediction for: ')
```

There's nothing to this, as user-interaction with "input()" doesn't get much easier than this..

Ln: 20 Col: 0

When your program runs, your user enters some data, and *look what happens*:

```
Python Shell
>>> ================================ RESTART ================================
>>>
Enter the distance attempted: 20k
Enter the recorded time: 59:59
Enter the distance you want a prediction for: Marathon
>>>
>>>
>>> row_data[distance_run][recorded_time]
Traceback (most recent call last):
  File "<pyshell#76>", line 1, in <module>
    row_data[distance_run][recorded_time]
KeyError: '59:59'
>>>
```

A "KeyError" exception has been raised...but why?

Ln: 205 Col: 4

If it's not in the dictionary, it can't be found.

The data in the `row_data` dictionary originally comes from the spreadsheet and is read into your program from the CSV file.

If the data value entered into the `recorded_time` variable is in the dictionary, things are going to be fine, because there's a *match*. However, if the data entered into the `recorded_time` variable *doesn't* match anything in the dictionary, you'll get a `KeyError`.

But how is this "problem" handled during training?

> If we have a match, great. If not, we look for the closest match and work from there...

The entered time for a 20k run (59:59) falls between these two values on the pace sheet.

10k	26:54	27:30	28:08	28:45	29:24
15k	41:31	42:27	43:24	44:23	45:23
10mi	44:46	45:46	46:48	47:51	48:56
20k	56:29	57:45	59:03	1:00:23	1:01:45
13.1mi	59:49	1:01:09	1:02:32	1:03:56	1:05:23
25k	1:11:43	1:13:20	1:14:59	1:16:40	1:18:24
30k	1:27:10	1:19:08	1:31:08	1:33:11	1:35:17
Marathon	2:05:34	2:08:24	2:11:17	2:14:15	2:17:16

Search for the closest match

All you need to do is search the row of data for the closest match, right?
And guess what? The Head First Code Review Team think they have some
functions that might help here.

There's nothing better
than sharing our code
with our fellow Python
programmers. Check out
our "find_it" module.

This code is in a file called
"find_it.py" and you can
download a copy from this
book's support website.

The "find_closest"
function does a simple
linear search, returning
the value in "target_data"
that most closely matches
the "look_for" argument.

```
○ ○ ○          find_it.py – /Users/barryp/HeadFirstPython/chapter11/find_it.py

def find_closest(look_for, target_data):

    def whats_the_difference(first, second):
        if first == second:
            return(0)
        elif first > second:
            return(first - second)
        else:
            return(second - first)

    max_diff = 9999999
    for each_thing in target_data:
        diff = whats_the_difference(each_thing, look_for)
        if diff == 0:
            found_it = each_thing
            break
        elif diff < max_diff:
            max_diff = diff
            found_it = each_thing
    return(found_it)

                                                             Ln: 22 Col: 0
```

Here's an example of a nested
function, which is allowed
in Python. Given two values,
this function returns the
difference between them.

This may not be the most
efficient search code ever
written, but it works.

An IDLE Session

Let's test the `find_it.py` module to try and determine if it meets the requirements of your application. Load the module into IDLE and then press **F5** or choose Run Module from the Run menu:

```
>>> find_closest(3.3, [1.5, 2.5, 4.5, 5.2, 6])
2.5
>>> find_closest(3, [1, 5, 6])
1
>>> find_closest(3, [1, 3, 4, 6])
3
>>> find_closest(3.6, [1.5, 2.5, 4.5, 5.2, 6])
4.5
>>> find_closest(3, [1, 4, 6])
4
>>> find_closest(2.6, [1.5, 2.5, 4.5, 5.2, 6])
2.5
```

Given a value to look for and some target data, the "find_closest" function seems to be doing the trick.

Let's try it with some of data that more closely resembles your CSV data:

```
>>> find_closest('59:59', ['56:29', '57:45', '59:03', '1:00:23', '1:01:45'])
Traceback (most recent call last):
  File "<pyshell#23>", line 1, in <module>
    find_closest('59:59', ['56:29', '57:45', '59:03', '1:00:23', '1:01:45'])
  File "/Users/barryp/HeadFirstPython/chapter11/find_it.py", line 15, in find_closest
    if diff == 0:
  File "/Users/barryp/HeadFirstPython/chapter11/find_it.py", line 11, in whats_the_difference
TypeError: unsupported operand type(s) for -: 'str' and 'str'
```

Yikes! Something's seriously broken here.

BRAIN POWER

What do you think has gone wrong here? Why does the `find_closest()` function crash when asked to work with data from your CSV file?

The trouble is with time

The data in your CSV file is a *representation* of timing values. Rather than actual numbers, the values in the CSV are **strings**. This is great for you, because *you* understand what the representation means. Python, on the other hand, sees the data only as strings.

When you send your data to the `find_closest()` function, Python *attempts to treat your strings as numbers* and chaos ensues. What might work would be to convert the time-strings into numbers. But how?

When I have to work with times, I always convert my time strings to seconds first...

Yeah, of course! Didn't we write the "tm2secs2tm" module to handle this sort of thing?

The time-to-seconds-to-time module

The Head First Code Review Team's generosity knows no bounds. Sure enough, their rather strangely name tm2secs2tm.py module looks like it might help.

Grab a copy of this code from this book's support website.

Here's the guy's "tm2secs2tm.py" module.

```
○ ○ ○          tm2secs2tm.py – /Users/barryp/HeadFirstPython/chapter11/tm2secs2tm.py

import time

def format_time(time_string):
    tlen = len(time_string)
    if tlen < 3:
        original_format = '%S'
    elif tlen < 6:
        original_format = '%M:%S'
    else:
        original_format = '%H:%M:%S'
    time_string = time.strftime('%H:%M:%S', time.strptime(time_string, original_format))
    return(time_string)

def time2secs(time_string):
    time_string = format_time(time_string)
    (hours, mins, secs) = time_string.split(':')
    seconds = int(secs) + (int(mins)*60) + (int(hours)*60*60)
    return(seconds)

def secs2time(seconds):
    return(time.strftime('%H:%M:%S', time.gmtime(seconds)))

                                                           Ln: 24 Col: 0
```

This function ensures that all times are formatted in "HH:MM:SS" format. This helps keep things simple when doing conversions to seconds.

Given a "time string", convert it to a value in seconds.

Convert a value in seconds to a "time string".

Exercise

Now that you have the tm2secs2tm.py and find_it.py modules, let's create a function that uses the facilities provided by these modules to solve your searching problem. Your new function, called find_nearest_time(), takes two arguments: the time to look for and a list of times to search. The function returns the closest time found as a string:

The code you need has been started for you.

```
from find_it import find_closest
from tm2secs2tm import time2secs, secs2time

def find_nearest_time(look_for, target_data):
```

Unlike in the previous chapter, it is possible to do what you need to do here in only four lines of code.

....

....

....

....

Exercise Solution

Now that you have the `tm2secs2tm.py` and `find_it.py` modules, you were to create a function that uses the facilities provided by these modules to solve your searching problem. Your new function, called `find_nearest_time()`, takes two arguments: the time to look for and a list of times to search. The function returns the closest time found as a string:

Import the team's code. →

```
from find_it import find_closest
from tm2secs2tm import time2secs, secs2time
```

The function takes two arguments, a time string and a list of time strings. ←

```
def find_nearest_time(look_for, target_data):
```

Convert the time string you are looking for into its equivalent value in seconds. →

```
what = time2secs(look_for)
```

```
where = [time2secs(t) for t in target_data]
```
← *Convert the lines of time strings into seconds.*

Call "find_closest()", supplying the converted data. →

```
res = find_closest(what, where)
```

```
return(secs2time(res))
```
← *Return the closest match to the calling code, after converting it back to a time string.*

An IDLE Session

Here's some of your pace data. Let's work with data from the "20k" row.

Let's try out your code at the IDLE shell to see if your time "problems" have been resolved:

10k	26:54	27:30	28:08	28:45	29:24
15k	41:31	42:27	43:24	44:23	45:23
10mi	44:46	45:46	46:48	47:51	48:56
20k	56:29	57:45	59:03	1:00:23	1:01:45
13.1mi	59:49	1:01:09	1:02:32	1:03:56	1:05:23
25k	1:11:43	1:13:20	1:14:59	1:16:40	1:18:24
30k	1:27:10	1:19:08	1:31:08	1:33:11	1:35:17
Marathon	2:05:34	2:08:24	2:11:17	2:14:15	2:17:16

```
>>> find_nearest_time('59:59', ['56:29', '57:45', '59:03', '1:00:23', '1:01:45'])
'01:00:23'
>>> find_nearest_time('1:01:01', ['56:29', '57:45', '59:03', '1:00:23', '1:01:45'])
'01:00:23'
>>> find_nearest_time('1:02:01', ['56:29', '57:45', '59:03', '1:00:23', '1:01:45'])
'01:01:45'
>>> find_nearest_time('57:06', ['56:29', '57:45', '59:03', '1:00:23', '1:01:45'])
'00:56:29'
```

Great! This appears to be working fine.

TEST DRIVE

With all this code available to you, it's an easy exercise to put it all together in your program and produce a complete solution to the Marathon Club's prediction problem. Let's take it for a test run.

```
marathon.py - /Users/barryp/HeadFirstPython/chapter11/marathon.py

from find_it import find_closest
from tm2secs2tm import time2secs, secs2time

def find_nearest_time(look_for, target_data):
    what = time2secs(look_for)
    where = [time2secs(t) for t in target_data]
    res = find_closest(what, where)
    return(secs2time(res))
```
⟵ This code is used "as is".

```
row_data = {}

with open('PaceData.csv') as paces:

    column_headings = paces.readline().strip().split(',')
    column_headings.pop(0)

    for each_line in paces:
        row = each_line.strip().split(',')
        row_label = row.pop(0)
        inner_dict = {}
        for i in range(len(column_headings)):
            inner_dict[row[i]] = column_headings[i]
        row_data[row_label] = inner_dict

distance_run = input('Enter the distance attempted: ')
recorded_time = input('Enter the recorded time: ')
predicted_distance = input('Enter the distance you want a prediction for: ')

closest_time = find_nearest_time(recorded_time, row_data[distance_run])
closest_column_heading = row_data[distance_run][closest_time]

prediction = [k for k in row_data[predicted_distance].keys()
                if row_data[predicted_distance][k] == closest_column_heading]

print('The predicted time running ' + predicted_distance + ' is: ' + prediction[0] + '.')
```

Find the nearest time within the data.

Extract the column heading.

Search for a predicted time at the desired distance and display it on screen.

`Ln: 37 Col: 0`

```
Python Shell

>>> ================================ RESTART ================================
>>>
Enter the distance attempted: 20k          ⟵ Try out your program with the same
Enter the recorded time: 59:59                 data input from earlier.
Enter the distance you want a prediction for: Marathon
Traceback (most recent call last):
  File "/Users/barryp/HeadFirstPython/chapter11/marathon.py", line 31, in <module>
    closest_column_heading = row_data[distance_run][closest_time]
KeyError: '01:00:23'   ⟵ Another "KeyError"...
>>>
```
`Ln: 13 Col: 4`

After all that, you're getting the same error as before. Bummer.

The trouble is still with time...

Or, to be more precise, with how the `tm2secs2tm.py` module formats
time strings. Take another look at the results from the previous IDLE Session.
Do you notice anything strange about the results returned by the call to the
`find_nearest_time()` function?

```
>>> find_nearest_time('59:59', ['56:29', '57:45', '59:03', '1:00:23', '1:01:45'])
'01:00:23'
>>> find_nearest_time('1:01:01', ['56:29', '57:45', '59:03', '1:00:23', '1:01:45'])
'01:00:23'
>>> find_nearest_time('1:02:01', ['56:29', '57:45', '59:03', '1:00:23', '1:01:45'])
'01:01:45'
>>> find_nearest_time('57:06', ['56:29', '57:45', '59:03', '1:00:23', '1:01:45'])
'00:56:29'
```

All the returned times use the "HH:MM:SS" format.

When your code takes one of these returned values and tries to index into
your dictionary, there's no match found, because your dictionary's keys do **not**
confirm to the `HH:MM:SS` format. The solution to this problem is to ensure
that *every time* you use a time-string in your code, make sure it's in `HH:MM:SS`
format:

marathon.py – /Users/barryp/HeadFirstPython/chapter11/marathon.py

```python
from find_it import find_closest
from tm2secs2tm import time2secs, secs2time, format_time

def find_nearest_time(look_for, target_data):
    what = time2secs(look_for)
    where = [time2secs(t) for t in target_data]
    res = find_closest(what, where)
    return(secs2time(res))

row_data = {}

with open('PaceData.csv') as paces:

    column_headings = paces.readline().strip().split(',')
    column_headings.pop(0)

    for each_line in paces:
        row = each_line.strip().split(',')
        row_label = row.pop(0)
        inner_dict = {}
        for i in range(len(column_headings)):
            inner_dict[format_time(row[i])] = column_headings[i]
        row_data[row_label] = inner_dict

distance_run = input('Enter the distance attempted: ')
recorded_time = input('Enter the recorded time: ')
predicted_distance = input('Enter the distance you want a prediction for: ')

closest_time = find_nearest_time(format_time(recorded_time), row_data[distance_run])
closest_column_heading = row_data[distance_run][closest_time]

prediction = [k for k in row_data[predicted_distance].keys()
                    if row_data[predicted_distance][k] == closest_column_heading]

print('The predicted time running ' + predicted_distance + ' is: ' + prediction[0] + '.')
```

Ln: 37 Col: 0

Import the "format_time()"
function from the
"tm2secs2tm.py" module.

Use the function to ensure the times
used internally by your code are
formatted in "HH:MM:SS" format.

Test Drive

Let's try your code one more time. Hopefully, now that all of the time strings within the system conform to `HH:MM:SS` format, your code will behave itself.

```
Python 3.1.2 (r312:79360M, Mar 24 2010, 01:33:18)
[GCC 4.0.1 (Apple Inc. build 5493)] on darwin
Type "copyright", "credits" or "license()" for more information.
>>> ============================= RESTART =============================
>>>
Enter the distance attempted: 20k
Enter the recorded time: 59:59
Enter the distance you want a prediction for: Marathon
Traceback (most recent call last):
  File "/Users/barryp/HeadFirstPython/chapter11/marathon.py", line 31, in <module>
    closest_column_heading = row_data[distance_run][closest_time]
KeyError: '01:00:23'
>>> ============================= RESTART =============================
>>>
Enter the distance attempted: 20k
Enter the recorded time: 59:59
Enter the distance you want a prediction for: Marathon
The predicited time running Marathon is: 02:14:15.
>>> ============================= RESTART =============================
>>>
Enter the distance attempted: 5mi
Enter the recorded time: 23:45
Enter the distance you want a prediction for: 10mi
The predicited time running 10mi is: 00:50:02.
>>> ============================= RESTART =============================
>>>
Enter the distance attempted: 10k
Enter the recorded time: 32:15
Enter the distance you want a prediction for: 25k
The predicited time running 25k is: 01:25:49.
>>>
```

This is the previous test, which crashed with a "KeyError".

This time around, your program behaves itself and works fine.

Another test confirms that things are working well.

And one final test makes sure.

`Ln: 31 Col: 4`

This is working well. You've solved your application's central problem: your program **reads** in the spreadsheet data from the CSV file, **turns** it into a dictionary of dictionaries, and lets you **interact** with your user to **acquire** the recorded time at a particular distance before **predicting** a time for another distance.

Not counting the code provided by the Head First Code Review Team, you've written fewer than 40 lines of code to solve this problem. *That's quite an achievement.* All that's left to do is to port your program to the club's Android's phones.

And porting to Android won't take too long, will it?

Port to Android

Your code is working great. Now it's time to **port** your text-based Python program to Android. Most of your code doesn't need to change, only the parts that interact with your user.

Obviously, you'll want to make things as easy to use as possible for users of your latest Android app, providing an interface not unlike this one.

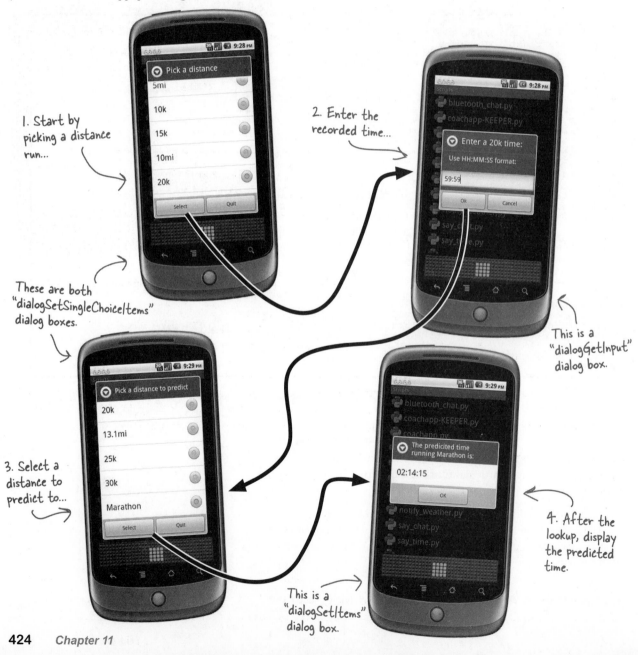

1. Start by picking a distance run...

2. Enter the recorded time...

These are both "dialogSetSingleChoiceItems" dialog boxes.

This is a "dialogGetInput" dialog box.

3. Select a distance to predict to...

This is a "dialogSetItems" dialog box.

4. After the lookup, display the predicted time.

Your Android app is a bunch of dialogs

Your Android app interacts with your users through a series of dialogs. Other than the single dialog that requests data *from* your user, the other three share certain similarities. You can take advantage of these shared features by creating a utility function which abstracts the dialog creation details:

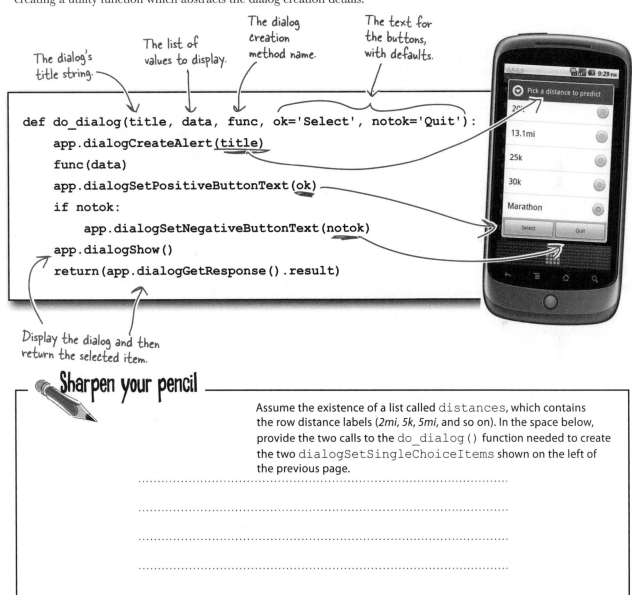

The dialog's title string.

The list of values to display.

The dialog creation method name.

The text for the buttons, with defaults.

```
def do_dialog(title, data, func, ok='Select', notok='Quit'):
    app.dialogCreateAlert(title)
    func(data)
    app.dialogSetPositiveButtonText(ok)
    if notok:
        app.dialogSetNegativeButtonText(notok)
    app.dialogShow()
    return(app.dialogGetResponse().result)
```

Display the dialog and then return the selected item.

Sharpen your pencil

Assume the existence of a list called `distances`, which contains the row distance labels (*2mi*, *5k*, *5mi*, and so on). In the space below, provide the two calls to the `do_dialog()` function needed to create the two `dialogSetSingleChoiceItems` shown on the left of the previous page.

Sharpen your pencil
Solution

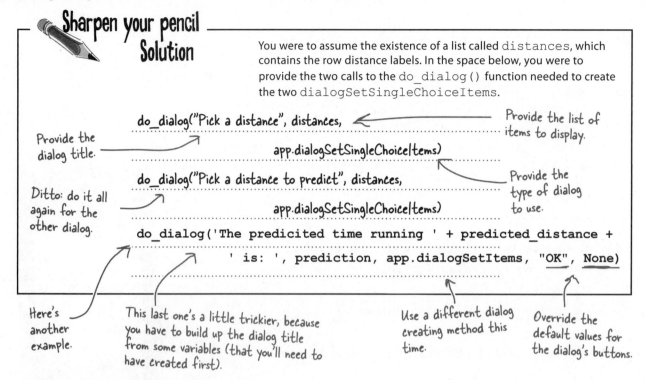

You were to assume the existence of a list called `distances`, which contains the row distance labels. In the space below, you were to provide the two calls to the `do_dialog()` function needed to create the two `dialogSetSingleChoiceItems`.

Provide the dialog title.

```
do_dialog("Pick a distance", distances,
                        app.dialogSetSingleChoiceItems)
```

Provide the list of items to display.

Ditto: do it all again for the other dialog.

```
do_dialog("Pick a distance to predict", distances,
                        app.dialogSetSingleChoiceItems)
```

Provide the type of dialog to use.

```
do_dialog('The predicited time running ' + predicted_distance +
                ' is: ', prediction, app.dialogSetItems, "OK", None)
```

Here's another example.

This last one's a little trickier, because you have to build up the dialog title from some variables (that you'll need to have created first).

Use a different dialog creating method this time.

Override the default values for the dialog's buttons.

Get your Android app code ready

To use your dialog creating code, **import** the necessary libraries, **define** some constants, **create** an Android object, and **reuse** some code from earlier in this book:

```
import time                    Do your imports.
import android

    ...
distances = [ '2mi', '5k', '5mi', '10k', '15k', '10mi', '20k',
                '13.1mi', '25k', '30k', 'Marathon' ]

    ...
hello_msg = "Welcome to the Marathon Club's App"
quit_msg = "Quitting the Marathon Club's App."

    ...
app = android.Android()

def status_update(msg, how_long=2):
    app.makeToast(msg)
    time.sleep(how_long)
```

Create a list of row labels.

Define two friendly messages.

Create an Android app object.

This function is taken "as-is" from earlier in this book.

Andröid Pööl Puzzle

Your **job** is to take the code from the pool and place it into the blank lines in your Android app code.

You can assume that the `row_data` dictionary exists and has been populated. The variables shown at the bottom of the last page have also been created, and the `status_update()` and `do_dialog()` functions are available to you. Your **goal** is to arrange the code so that it implements the UI interactions you need.

```
status_update(hello_msg)
resp = do_dialog("Pick a distance", distances, ...................................................... )

......................................................................
    distance_run = ......................................................
    distance_run = distances[distance_run]
    ..................... = app.dialogGetInput("Enter a " + distance_run + " time:",
                                    "Use HH:MM:SS format:").result
    closest_time = find_nearest_time(format_time( ..................... ), row_data[distance_run])
    closest_column_heading = row_data[distance_run][closest_time]
    resp = do_dialog("Pick a distance to predict", distances, ...................................................... )

    ......................................................................
        predicted_distance = ......................................................
        predicted_distance = distances[predicted_distance]
        prediction = [k for k in row_data[predicted_distance].keys()
                        if row_data[predicted_distance][k] == closest_column_heading]
        do_dialog('The predicted time running ' + predicted_distance + ' is: ',
                        prediction, app.dialogSetItems, "OK", None)
status_update(quit_msg)
```

The dialogGetInput() method displays the input dialog box.

recorded_time

app.dialogGetSelectedItems().result[0]

app.dialogSetSingleChoiceItems

app.dialogSetSingleChoiceItems

if resp['which'] in ('positive'):

if resp['which'] in ('positive'):

recorded_time

app.dialogGetSelectedItems().result[0]

Android Pool Puzzle Solution

Your **job** was to take the code from the pool and place it into the blank lines in your Android app code. You were to assume that the `row_data` dictionary exists and has been populated. The variables you need also have been created, and the `status_update()` and `do_dialog()` functions were available to you. Your **goal** was to arrange the code so that it implements the UI interactions you need.

Ask your user to pick a distance from the list of labels.

```python
status_update(hello_msg)
resp = do_dialog("Pick a distance", distances, app.dialogSetSingleChoiceItems)
if resp['which'] in ('positive'):
    distance_run = app.dialogGetSelectedItems().result[0]
    distance_run = distances[distance_run]
    recorded_time = app.dialogGetInput("Enter a " + distance_run + " time:",
                        "Use HH:MM:SS format:").result
    closest_time = find_nearest_time(format_time(recorded_time), row_data[distance_run])
    closest_column_heading = row_data[distance_run][closest_time]
    resp = do_dialog("Pick a distance to predict", distances, app.dialogSetSingleChoiceItems)
    if resp['which'] in ('positive'):
        predicted_distance = app.dialogGetSelectedItems().result[0]
        predicted_distance = distances[predicted_distance]
        prediction = [k for k in row_data[predicted_distance].keys()
                        if row_data[predicted_distance][k] == closest_column_heading]
        do_dialog('The predicted time running ' + predicted_distance + ' is: ',
                    prediction, app.dialogSetItems, "OK", None)
status_update(quit_msg)
```

Assign the selected distance label to "distance_run".

Ask your user enter the recorded time.

Work out what column heading to use.

Look up the Prediction.

Ask your user to pick a distance from the list of labels to predict to.

Display the predicted time at the selected distance to your user.

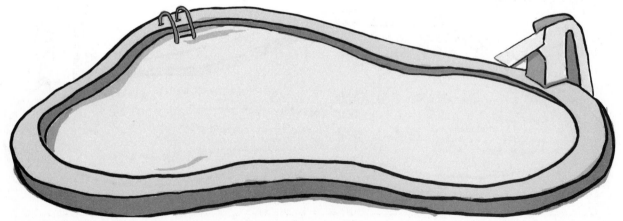

Put your app together...

You now have all the code you need to create your app:

```
○ ○ ○          ·marathonapp.py – /Users/barryp/HeadFirstPython/chapter11/marathonapp.py

import time
import android                    ←── Do your imports.

from find_it import find_closest
from tm2secs2tm import time2secs, secs2time, format_time

def find_nearest_time(look_for, target_data):
    what = time2secs(look_for)
    where = [time2secs(t) for t in target_data]     ←─ Include your "find_nearest()"
    res = find_closest(what, where)                     function.
    return(secs2time(res))

distances = [ '2mi', '5k', '5mi', '10k', '15k', '10mi', '20k', ←─ Declare your constants.
              '13.1mi', '25k', '30k', 'Marathon' ]
hello_msg = "Welcome to the Marathon Club's App"
quit_msg = "Quitting the Marathon Club's App."
                                      NOTE: the location of the data file on the
row_data = {}                         SDCARD is specific to Android.

with open('/sdcard/sl4a/scripts/PaceData.csv') as paces:
    column_headings = paces.readline().strip().split(',')
    column_headings.pop(0)
    for each_line in paces:                           Grab and preprocess your
        row = each_line.strip().split(',')       ←── CSV data.
        row_label = row.pop(0)
        inner_dict = {}
        for i in range(len(column_headings)):
            inner_dict[format_time(row[i])] = column_headings[i]
        row_data[row_label] = inner_dict

app = android.Android()              ←── Create your Android app object and
                                          include your helper functions.
def status_update(msg, how_long=2):
    app.makeToast(msg)
    time.sleep(how_long)

def do_dialog(title, data, func, ok='Select', notok='Quit'):
    app.dialogCreateAlert(title)
    func(data)
    app.dialogSetPositiveButtonText(ok)
    if notok:
        app.dialogSetNegativeButtonText(notok)
    app.dialogShow()                              Display your UI to your user and process
    return(app.dialogGetResponse().result)        the resulting interaction.

status_update(hello_msg)

resp = do_dialog("Pick a distance", distances, app.dialogSetSingleChoiceItems)
if resp['which'] in ('positive'):
    distance_run = app.dialogGetSelectedItems().result[0]
    distance_run = distances[distance_run]
    recorded_time = app.dialogGetInput("Enter a " + distance_run + " time:",
                                        "Use HH:MM:SS format:").result
    closest_time = find_nearest_time(format_time(recorded_time), row_data[distance_run])
    closest_column_heading = row_data[distance_run][closest_time]
    resp = do_dialog("Pick a distance to predict", distances, app.dialogSetSingleChoiceItems)
    if resp['which'] in ('positive'):
        predicted_distance = app.dialogGetSelectedItems().result[0]
        predicted_distance = distances[predicted_distance]
        prediction = [k for k in row_data[predicted_distance].keys()
                        if row_data[predicted_distance][k] == closest_column_heading]
        do_dialog('The predicited time running ' + predicted_distance + ' is: ',
                    prediction, app.dialogSetItems, "OK", None)

status_update(quit_msg)
|                                                                    Ln: 67 Col: 0
```

TEST DRIVE

It's time to test your Android app on the Android Emulator before loading a working application onto a "real" phone. Start your Android emulator and begin by transferring your code and the files it needs onto the emulator's *SDCARD*. Use the `adb` command in the `tools` folder to copy `marathonapp.py`, `find_it.py`, `tm2sec2tm.py` and `PaceData.csv` to the emulator, and then take your app for a spin.

```
File Edit Window Help CopyToEmulator
$ tools/adb push marathonapp.py /mnt/sdcard/sl4a/scripts
43 KB/s (2525 bytes in 0.056s)
$ tools/adb push find_it.py /mnt/sdcard/sl4a/scripts
7 KB/s (555 bytes in 0.069s)
$ tools/adb push tm2secs2tm.py /mnt/sdcard/sl4a/scripts
12 KB/s (628 bytes in 0.050s)
$ tools/adb push PaceData.csv /mnt/sdcard/sl4a/scripts
59 KB/s (4250 bytes in 0.069s)
```

Copy your code and its support files to the emulator with these commands.

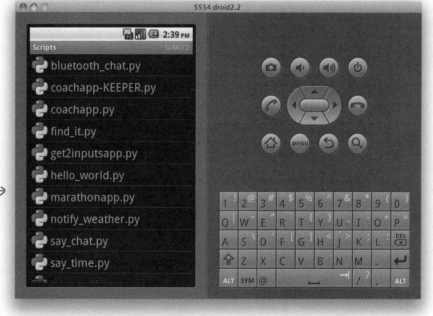

And there it is... waiting for you to test it.

Go on. You know you want to: tap that app!

Your app's a wrap!

All that's left to do is transfer your working Android app to the Marathon Club's phones…and that's easy when you use **AndFTP**. When you show off your latest work, the club's members can't believe their eyes.

> This is fantastic! Now I can work with my coach and the other club members to hit my target times at my chosen distances. There's no stopping me now…

And there's no stopping you!

You've put your Python skills and techniques to great use here.

Whether you're building an app for the smallest handheld device or the biggest web server, your Python skills help you get the job done.

Congratulations!

Your Python Toolbox

You've got Chapter 11 under your belt and you've demonstrated a mastery of your Python toolbox. Congratulations and well done!

BULLET POINTS

- The `input()` BIF lets you prompt and receive input from your users.

- If you find yourself using **Python 2** and in need of the `input()` function, use the `raw_input()` function instead.

- Build complex data structures by combining Python's built-in lists, sets, and dictionaries.

- The `time` module, which is part of the standard library, has a number of functions that make converting between time formats possible.

Python Lingo

- A "conditional" list comprehension is one that includes a trailing "if" statement, allowing you to control which items are added to the new list as the comprehension runs.

- List comprehensions can be rewritten as an equivalent "for" loop.

It's time to go...

It's been a blast having you with us here on Lake Python. Come back soon and often. We love it when you drop by.

This is just the beginning

We're sad to see you leave, but there's nothing like taking what you've learned and putting it to use. You're just beginning your Python journey and you're in the driver's seat. We're dying to hear how things go, so *drop us a line* at the Head First Labs website, ***www.headfirstlabs.com***, and let us know how Python is paying off for **YOU**!

appendix: leftovers

The Top Ten Things (we didn't cover)

I don't know about you, but I think it could do with more spam...

You've come a long way.

But learning about Python is an activity that never stops. The more Python you code, the more you'll need to learn new ways to do certain things. You'll need to master new tools and new techniques, too. There's just not enough room in this book to show you everything you might possibly need to know about Python. So, here's our list of the top ten things we didn't cover that you might want to learn more about next.

#1: Using a "professional" IDE

Throughout this book, you've used Python's **IDLE**, which is great to use when first learning about Python and, although it's a little quirky, can handle most programming tasks. It even comes with a built-in **debugger** (check out the Debug menu), which is surprisingly well equipped. Chances are, however, sooner or later, you'll probably need a more full-featured integrated development environment.

One such tool worth looking into is the **WingWare Python IDE**. This professional-level development tool is specifically geared toward the Python programmer, is written by and maintained by Python programmers, and is *itself* written in Python. **WingWare Python IDE** comes in various licencing flavor: it's free if you're a student or working on an open source project, but you'll need to pay for it if you are working within a for-profit development environment.

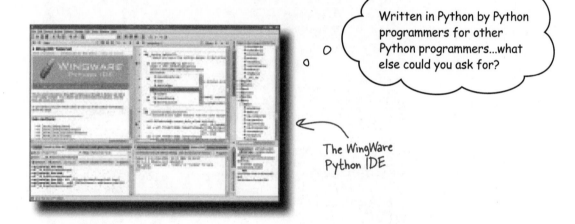

Written in Python by Python programmers for other Python programmers...what else could you ask for?

The WingWare Python IDE

More general tools also exist. If you are running Linux, the **KDevelop IDE** integrates well with Python.

And, of course,there are all those *programmer editors* which are often all you'll ever need. Many Mac OS X programmers swear by the **TextMate** programmer's editor. There's more than a few Python programmers using **emacs** and **vi** (or its more common variant, **vim**). Your author is a huge fan of **vim**, but also spends large portions of his day using **IDLE** and the Python shell.

#2: Coping with scoping

Consider the following short program:

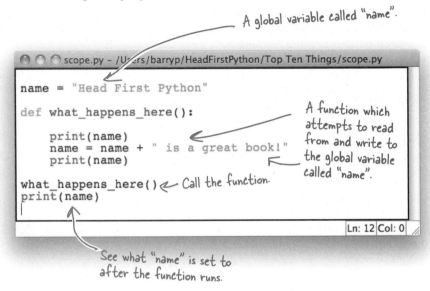

A global variable called "name".

A function which attempts to read from and write to the global variable called "name".

Call the function.

See what "name" is set to after the function runs.

If you try to run this program, Python complains with this error message: *UnboundLocalError: local variable 'name' referenced before assignment*...whatever that means!

When it comes to scope, Python is quite happy to let you access and read the value of a global variable within a function, **but you cannot change it**. When Python sees the assignment, it looks for a local variable called name, doesn't find it, and throws a *hissy fit* and an UnboundLocalError exception. To access *and* change a global variable, you must explicitly declare that's your intention, as follows:

```
name = "Head First Python"

def what_happens_here():

    print(name)
    global name
    name = name + " is a great book!"
    print(name)

what_happens_here()
print(name)
```

Ln: 13 Col: 0

Some programmers find this quite ugly. Others think it's what comes to pass when you watch Monty Python reruns while designing your programming language. No matter what everyone thinks: this is what we're stuck with! ☺

#3: Testing

Writing code is one thing, but **testing** it is quite another. The combination of the Python shell and IDLE is great for testing and experimenting with small snippets of code, but for anything substantial, a testing framework is a must.

Python comes with *two* testing frameworks out of the box.

The first is familiar to programmers coming from another modern language, because it's based on the popular *xUnit* testing framework. Python's `unittest` module (which is part of the standard library) lets you create test code, test data, and a test suite for your modules. These exist in separate files from you code and allow you to exercise your code in various ways. If you already use a similar framework with your current language, rest assured that Python's implementation is essentially the same.

The other testing framework, called `doctest`, is also part of the standard library. This framework allows you to take the output from a Python shell or IDLE session and use it as a test. All you need to do is copy the content from the shell and add it to your modules *documentation strings*. If you add code like this to the end of your modules, they'll be ready for "doctesting":

```
if __name__ == "__main__":
    import doctest
    doctest.testmod()
```

If your code is imported as a module, this code does NOT run. If you run your module from the command line, your tests run.

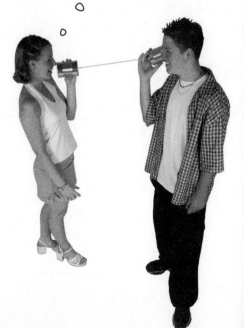

What do you mean: you can't hear me...I guess I should've tested this first, eh?

If you then run your module at your operating systems comand line, your tests run. If all you want to do is import your module's code and not run your tests, the previous `if` statement supports doing just that.

For more on `unittest` and `doctest`, search the online Python documentation on the Web or via IDLE's *Help* menu.

#4: Advanced language features

With a book like this, we knew we'd never get to cover the entire Python language unless we tripled the page count.

And let's face it, no one would thank us for that!

There's a lot more to Python, and as your confidence grows, you can take the time to check out these advanced language features:

Anonymous functions: the lambda expression lets you create small, one-line, non-named functions that can be incredibly useful once you understand what's going on.

Generators: like iterators, generators let you process sequences of data. Unlike iterators, generators, through the use of the yield expression, let you minimize the amount of RAM your program consumes while providing iterator-like functionality on large datasets.

Custom exceptions: create your own exception object based on those provided as standard by Python.

Function decorators: adjust the behavior of a preexisting function by hooking into its start-up and teardown mechanisms.

Metaclasses: custom classes that themselves can create custom classes. These are really only for the truely brave, although you did use a metaclass when you created your Sightings form using the *Django form validation framework* in Chapter 10.

Most (but not all) of these language features are primarily of interest to the Python programmer building tools or language extensions for use by other Python programmers.

You might never need to use some of these language features in your code, but they are all worth knowing about. Take the time to understand *when* and *where* to use them.

See **#10** of this appendix for a list of my favorite Python books (other than this one), which are all great starting points for learning more about these language features.

I know I look complex, but I really am quite useful.

#5: Regular expressions

When it comes to working with textual data, Python is a bit of a natural. The built-in `string` type comes with so many methods that most of the standard string operations such as finding and splitting are covered. However, what if you need to extract a specific part of a string or what if you need to search and replace within a string based on a specific specification? It is possible to use the built-in string methods to implement solutions to these types of problems, but—more times than most people would probably like to admit to—using a **regular expression** works better.

Consider this example, which requires you to extract the area code from the `phone_number` string and which uses the built-in string methods:

```
● ● ●  area_code.py – /Users/barryp/HeadFirstPython/Top Ten Things/area_code.py

phone_number = "Home: (555) 265-2901"

start = phone_number.find('(')       ← Find the opening "(".

start = start+1 ⎤                      Calculate where the area code is
end = start+3   ⎦ ←                    in the string.

area_code = phone_number[start:end]  ← Extract the area code.

print('The area code is: ' + area_code)

                                          Ln: 12  Col: 0
```

Jeff Friedl's regular expression "bible", which is well worth a look if you want to learn more. Look up the "re" module in Python's docs, too.

This code works fine, but it *breaks* when presented with the following value for `phone_number`:

```
phone_number = "Cell (mobile): (555)-918-8271"
```

Why does this phone number cause the program to fail? Try it and see what happens...

When you use a **regular expression**, you can specify *exactly* what it is you are looking for and *improve the robustness* of your code:

```
● ● ●  area_code_re.py – /Users/barryp/HeadFirstPython/Top Ten Things/area_code_re.py

import re

phone_number = "Home: (555) 265-2901"

results = re.search('\((\d{3})\)', phone_number)
area_code = results.group(1)

print('The area code is: ' + area_code)
|
                                          Ln: 10  Col: 0
```

This looks a little strange, but this regular expression is looking for an opening "(" followed by three digits and then a closing ")". This specification is much more likely to find the area code and won't break as quickly as the other version of this program.

#6: More on web frameworks

When it comes to building web applications, CGI works, but it's a little old-fashioned. As you saw in Chapter 10, Google's App Engine technology supports CGI, but also WSGI and a number of web framework technologies. If you aren't deploying to the cloud and prefer to roll your own, you have plenty of choices. What follows is a representative sample. My advice: try a few on for size and see which one works best for you.

Search for the following terms in your favorite search engine: **Django**, **Zope**, **TurboGears**, **Web2py**, and **Pylons**.

The "old timers"...but don't let maturity fool you: these are cracking web frameworks.

The "new kids on the block": leaner, meaner and stuffed full of features.

#7: Object relational mappers and NoSQL

Working with SQL-based databases in Python is well supported, with the inclusion of SQLite in the standard library a huge boon. Of course, the assumption is you are familiar with SQL and happy to use SQL to work with your data.

But what if you aren't? What if you *detest* SQL?

An **object relational mapper** (ORM) is a software technology that lets you use an underlying SQL-based database *without* having to know anything about SQL. Rather than the procedural interface based on the Python database API, ORMs provide an object-oriented interface to your data, exposing it via *method calls* and *attribute lookups* as opposed to columns and rows.

Many programmers find ORMs a much more natural mechanism for working with stored datasets and the Python community creates and supports a number of them.

One of the most interesting is **SQL Alchemy**, which is popular and included in a number of the web framework technologies discussed in **#6**. Despite being hugely popular anyway, **SQL Alchemy** is also interesting because it supports *both* Python 2 and Python 3, which makes it a standout technology (for now).

If you find yourself becoming increasingly frustrated by SQL, check out an ORM. Of course, you have already experienced a similar technology: *Google App Engine's* **datastore** API is very similar in style to those APIs provided by the major Python ORMs.

There's NoSQL, too.

In addition to database technologies that let you avoid working with the underlying SQL-based database, a new breed of technologies have emerged that let you *drop* your SQL database in its entirety. Known collectively as **NoSQL**, these data tools provide an alternative non-SQL API to your data and do not use an SQL-based database management system at all. As these technologies are relatively new, there's been more activity around Python 2 than Python 3, but they are still worth checking out. **CouchDB** and **MongoDB** are the two most closely associated with robust Python implementations. If you like working with your data in a Python dictionary and wished your database technology let you store your data in much the same way, then you need to take a look at **NoSQL**: *it's a perfect fit*.

#8: Programming GUIs

In this book, you've created text-based interfaces, web-based interfaces and interfaces that ran on Android devices. But what if you want to create a desktop application that runs on your or your user's desktop computer? Are you out of luck, or can Python help here, too?

Well…as luck would have it, Python comes preinstalled with a GUI-building toolkit called **tkinter** (shorthand for *Tk Interface*). It's possible to create a usable and useful graphical user interface (GUI) with **tkinter** and deploy it on Mac OS X, Windows, and Linux. With the latest version of **Tk**, your developed app takes on the characteristics of the underlying operating system, so when you run on Windows, your app looks like a Windows desktop app, when it run on Linux, it looks like a Linux desktop app, and so on.

You write your Python and **tkinter** code *once*, then run it anywhere and it just works. There are lots of great resources for learning to program with **tkinter**, with one of the best being the last few chapters of *Head First Programming*, but since plugging *that* book would be totally shameless, I won't mention it again.

Other GUI-building technologies do exist, with the **PyGTK**, **PyKDE**, **wxPython**, and **PyQT** toolkits coming up in conversation more than most. Be warned, however, that most of these toolkits target Python 2, although support for Python 3 is on its way. Search the Web for any of the project names to learn more.

Oh, look: it's one of the GUIs created in "Head First Programming"…and yes, I said I wouldn't mention THAT book again, but isn't this GUI beautiful? ☺

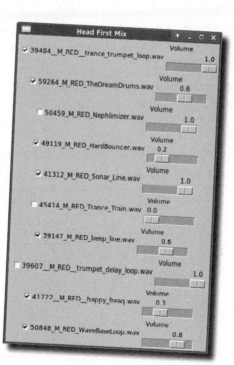

#9: Stuff to avoid

When it comes to stuff to avoid when using Python, there's a very short list. A recent tweet on *Twitter* went something like this:

"There are three types of bugs: your bugs, my bugs... and **threads**."

Threads do indeed exist in Python but should be **avoided** where possible.

This has *nothing* to do with the quality of Python's threading library and *everything* to do with Python's implementation, especially the implementation known as **CPython** (which is more than likely the one you're running now). Python is implemented using a technology known as the **Global Interpreter Lock** (**GIL**), which enforces a restriction that Python can only ever run on a single interpreter process, even in the presence of multiple processors.

What all this means to you is that your beautifully designed and implemented program that uses threads will never run faster on multiple processors even if they exist, because *it can't use them*. Your threaded application will run **serially** and, in many cases, run *considerably slower* than if you had developed the same functionality without resorting to threads.

Main message: **don't use threads** with Python until the GIL restriction is removed…*if it ever is*.

Don't you like my threads...?

#10: Other books

There are lots of great books that cover Python in general, as well as specifically within a particular problem domain. Here is a collection of my favorite Python books, which we have no hestitation in recommending to you.

If you are a sysadmin, then this is the Python book for you.

Includes a great case study involving the porting of a complex Python 2 module to Python 3.

The best desktop reference on the market

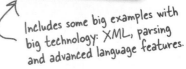

At 1,200 pages, this is the definitive language reference for Python: it's got everything in it!

Includes some big examples with big technology: XML, parsing and advanced language features.

Index

Symbols and Numbers

404 Error, from web server 242

405 Error, from web server 378

>>> (chevron, triple) IDLE prompt 4

: (colon)
   in for loop 16
   in function definition 29
   in if statement 20

, (comma) separating list items 7

{} (curly braces)
   creating dictionaries 180
   creating sets 166

= (equal sign)
   assignment operator 7
   in function argument definition 63

(...) (parentheses)
   enclosing function arguments 29
   enclosing immutable sets 91

+ (plus sign) addition or concatenation operator 138

(pound sign) preceding one-line comments 38

@property decorator 250, 253, 285

? (question mark) parameter placeholder 321, 350

"..." or '...' (quotes) enclosing each list item 7

"""..."""" or '''...''' (quotes, triple) enclosing comments 37

; (semicolon) separating statements on one line 38

[...] (square brackets)
   accessing dictionary items 180, 212
   accessing specific list items 9, 18
   enclosing all list items 7, 18

A

"a" access mode 110

access modes for files 110, 133

addition operator (+) 138

Alt-N keystroke, IDLE 5

Alt-P keystroke, IDLE 5

AndFTP app 288–289

Android apps
   accepting input from 278–282, 295, 304–307
   converting from Python code 424–430
   creating 274–277, 281–282
   data for. *See* JSON data interchange format
   integrating with SQLite 342–348
   running on phone 288–289
   scripting layer for. *See* SL4A
   troubleshooting 277

Android emulator
   installing and configuring 260–262
   running scripts on 264–265, 272–273, 283

Android Market 288

Android Virtual Device. *See* AVD

anonymous functions 439

append() method, lists 10, 14

apps. *See* Android apps; webapps

app.yaml file 356, 395

arguments for functions
   adding 52, 66–68
   optional 63–64, 134

arrays
   associative. *See* dictionaries
   similarity to lists 9–10, 17

as keyword 119, 138

assignment operator (=) 7

associative arrays. *See* dictionaries

attributes, class 190, 194, 212

authorization, user 389–393

AVD (Android Virtual Device) 261, 291

Monty Python 17

multiple inheritance 209

MVC (Model-View-Controller) pattern 221, 232, 253, 359

   Controller 234–238, 244–246, 370–373

   Model 222–225, 360–362

   View 226–233, 363–369

N

NameError exception 44, 118

names. *See* identifiers

namespaces 45–46, 71

next() built-in function 54

NoSQL 359, 442

NotePad editor 35

not in operator 161–162

not keyword 86, 103

numbered lists 54

O

object relational mapper. *See* ORM (object relational mapper)

objects. *See* data objects

open() built-in function 75, 103, 109–110

orange text in IDLE 4

ORM (object relational mapper) 442

os module 76, 300, 350

P

para() function, yate 231, 233

parentheses ((...))

   enclosing function arguments 29

   enclosing immutable lists 91

pass statement 93, 103

persistence 105

   pickle library for 132–137

   reading data from files 222–224

   writing data to files 110–113, 222–224

PickleError exception 133–134

pickle library 132–137, 138

   data modeling using 222–224

   incompatibility with JSON data types 284–285

   transferring data to a database 321–325

plus sign (+) addition or concatenation operator 138

pop() method, lists 10, 175–176

post() method, GAE 379–383, 395

POST web request 379

pound sign (#) preceding one-line comments 38

print() built-in function 10, 32, 124–125

   disabling automatic new-line for 56, 71

   displaying TAB character with 56

   writing to a file 110, 128, 138

Programming in Python 3 (Addison-Wesley Professional) 445

properties, in datastore 360, 395

@property decorator 250, 253, 285

purple text in IDLE 4

put() method, GAE 395

.pyc file extension 42, 49

.py file extension 35

PyPI (Python Package Index) 36

   registering on website 47

   uploading distributions to 48

   uploading modules to 209

Python 2

   compared to Python 3 17

   raw_input() built-in function 432

   running on Android smartphones 258–259, 291

   using with Google App Engine 355

Python 3

   compared to Python 2 17

   documentation for 3, 80, 103

   editors for 35, 436

   installing 3

   interpreter for. *See* IDLE

   learning 445

python3 command

   building a distribution 41

   checking for Python version 3

   installing a distribution 41

   uploading a new distribution 68

U

u_list() function, yate 231, 233

unittest module 438

urlencode() function, urllib 291

urllib2 module 291

urllib module 291

urlopen() function, urllib2 291

user authorization 389–393

user input. *See* forms, HTML; input

UserProperty() type, db 390

V

ValueError exception 78–79, 81–82, 103

values, part of dictionary 178, 180, 212

variables, scope of 437

vi editor 35, 436

View, in MVC pattern 221
  for GAE webapps 359, 363–369
  for webapps 226–233

vim editor 436

W

"w" access mode 110

"w+" access mode 110

"wb" access mode 133

webapps 215–217, 253
  controlling code for 221, 234–238, 244–246
  data modeling for 221, 222–225
  designing with MVC 221
  design requirements for 218–220
  directory structure for 234
  Google App Engine for. *See* GAE
  input data, sending to CGI scripts 300–303
  input forms for. *See* forms, HTML
  SQLite used with 327–341
  view for 221, 226–233

Web-based applications. *See* webapps

web frameworks 441. *See also* CGI; WSGI

web request 216, 253, 395

web response 216–217, 253, 395

web server 216–217, 235

Web Server Gateway Interface (WSGI) 356, 370. *See also* CGI scripts

while loop 16–17, 55

WingIDE editor 35

WingWare Python IDE 436

with statement 120–123, 138

WSGI (Web Server Gateway Interface) 356, 370. *See also* CGI scripts

Y

yate (Yet Another Template Engine) library 226–233

yield expression 439

You can't learn everything from a book.

Now that you're building your knowledge with this book from O'Reilly, why not polish your skills and advance your IT career in the unique interactive learning environment at the O'Reilly School of Technology?

- Work with expert instructors, one-on-one
- Learn at your own pace and set your own deadlines
- Create, compile, and test your programs in a real-world environment
- Earn a professional certificate from the University of Illinois

Our courses won't break your budget, and you can take a test drive with our 7-day refund policy. To find out more, come take a campus tour at **http://oreillyschool.com**.

Certification available through

Get even more for your money.

Join the O'Reilly Community, and register the O'Reilly books you own. It's free, and you'll get:

- 40% upgrade offer on O'Reilly books
- Membership discounts on books and events
- Free lifetime updates to electronic formats of books
- Multiple ebook formats, DRM FREE
- Participation in the O'Reilly community
- Newsletters
- Account management
- 100% Satisfaction Guarantee

Signing up is easy:

1. Go to: oreilly.com/go/register
2. Create an O'Reilly login.
3. Provide your address.
4. Register your books.

Note: English-language books only

To order books online:

oreilly.com/order_new

For questions about products or an order:

orders@oreilly.com

To sign up to get topic-specific email announcements and/or news about upcoming books, conferences, special offers, and new technologies:

elists@oreilly.com

For technical questions about book content:

booktech@oreilly.com

To submit new book proposals to our editors:

proposals@oreilly.com

Many O'Reilly books are available in PDF and several ebook formats. For more information:

oreilly.com/ebooks

O'REILLY®

Spreading the knowledge of innovators   www.oreilly.com

Buy this book and get access to the online edition for 45 days—for free!

Head First Python

By Paul Barry
November 2010, $49.99
ISBN 9781449382674

With Safari Books Online, you can:

Access the contents of thousands of technology and business books

- Quickly search over 7000 books and certification guides
- Download whole books or chapters in PDF format, at no extra cost, to print or read on the go
- Copy and paste code
- Save up to 35% on O'Reilly print books
- **New!** Access mobile-friendly books directly from cell phones and mobile devices

Stay up-to-date on emerging topics before the books are published

- Get on-demand access to evolving manuscripts.
- Interact directly with authors of upcoming books

Explore thousands of hours of video on technology and design topics

- Learn from expert video tutorials
- Watch and replay recorded conference sessions

To try out Safari and the online edition of this book FREE for 45 days,
go to *www.oreilly.com/go/safarienabled* and enter the coupon code OOIZWWA.
To see the complete Safari Library, visit safari.oreilly.com.

Spreading the knowledge of innovators

safari.oreilly.com